HOW TO PLAY

for Sr. Corona,
who also knows
"h˙ ˙ to play;

Love
Gerry

HOW TO PLAY

THE THEATRE OF JAMES REANEY

GERALD D. PARKER

ECW PRESS

CANADIAN CATALOGUING IN PUBLICATION DATA

Parker, Gerald D. (Gerald Douglas), 1936–
How to Play : the theatre of James Reaney

Includes bibliographic references and index.
ISBN 1-55022-119-1

1. Reaney, James, 1926– — Criticism and interpretation.
I. Title.

PS8535.E35Z73 1991 C812'.54 C91-095010-5
PR9199.3.R43Z73 1991

How to Play has been published with the help of a grant from the
Canadian Federation for the Humanities, using funds provided
by the Social Sciences and Humanities Research Council of Canada.
Additional grants have been provided by
The Canada Council and the Ontario Arts Council.

Design and imaging by ECW Type & Art, Oakville, Ontario.
Printed and bound by The Porcupine's Quill, Erin, Ontario.

Distributed by Butterworths Canada,
75 Clegg Road, Markham, Ontario L6G 1A1.

Published by ECW PRESS, 307 Coxwell Avenue, Toronto, Ontario M4L 3B5.

ACKNOWLEDGEMENTS

There are many to whom I owe thanks. I particularly wish to thank Ross Woodman, Richard Stingle, Stan Dragland, Don Gutteridge, Keith Turnbull, Allan Gedalof, and Jerry Franken with all of whom I have had many discussions regarding the theatre and drama of James Reaney, and from some of whom I have received helpful suggestions regarding parts of the manuscript that eventually became this book. Portions of the book originally appeared in *Mosaic* and *Canadian Drama/l'art dramatique canadien.* I am grateful to the editors of these journals for permission to reprint. My thanks, as well, to the Department of English and the Faculty of Arts at the University of Western Ontario for financial assistance over the years and to Launa Fuller who typed the manuscript at various stages of its preparation. My thanks, too, to James Reaney who allowed me to rummage through some of his "play-boxes" of clippings, letters, and pictures, to Robert Lecker for his assistance in the publication of this work, to Ellen Quigley and Jack David of ECW PRESS, and to my daughter Suzanne who managed to make less unfriendly my word-processor with the addition of a "HelpDad" command.

TABLE OF CONTENTS

INTRODUCTION

Well, if you are going to ask questions of a playwright, I think the best place to close is to get him talking about actual theatres he's been in. If they've had any power over him, it just might be that what he is trying to do is help build a society where this fact keeps repeating itself over and over again until our whole nation loses its stiffness and becomes itself a sort of theatre. Not the sort of theatre it is now where Technology (descended from experiments with organ pipes and mechanical clocks and fountains, evidently) creates ever more horrifying and sinister spectacles; no, but a place where we ourselves, with just our bodies and the simplest of props (albeit in abundance) available to everyone, create a civilization where it finally seems true that to be wise is to know how to play. ("James Reaney" 160)

An examination of the plays of James Reaney will disclose one central fact: as a playwright, he is an indefatigable experimenter with form and voice, and his work draws upon and reflects many of the competing and complementary forms and voices to which the modern theatre has become habituated. Among these are some of the gaudier and vigorous features of plot, characterization, and language originally derived from gothic romance and popular nineteenth-century melodrama. Apart from their strictly technical and formal influences, these features present a world generally commensurate with Reaney's own, a world of heightened, often hyperbolic action in which character and narrative are informed by an underlying moral Manicheism, and in which the surface of the ordinary world, as a verifiable and "documented" given, is shown to bear highly potent signs of a hidden, mythic world of the "moral occult" (Brooks 5). Another is modern folk drama, particularly as represented by such playwrights as Gabriel Garcia Lorca, Georg Büchner, and John Millington Synge in whose plays we find the fusion of naïvity and literary sophistication, as well as a tragic understanding of the land

9

as a force that shapes human destiny. Reaney's folkloric imagination and repertory also reflects, on another level, something of the spirit of André Obey, Thornton Wilder, J.M. Barrie, and, in modern painting, Marc Chagall, Paul Klee, and Joan Miró among others in its fusion of celebratory, playful, and ironic approaches to the deceptive realm of the ordinary. We also find, in the range of his drama, echoes of some of the prodigious array of theatrical languages that have become familiar to the modern theatre by way of W.B. Yeats, T.S. Eliot, Thornton Wilder, Jean Cocteau (whose concept of the *poésie de théâtre* is especially pertinent), Joan Littlewood, and Joseph Chaikin, whose "image plays" at the Open Theatre from 1963 to 1973 added immeasurably to the spatial and auditory vocabulary of contemporary performance. Other voices and forms would include the Peking National Opera, to which Reaney pays tribute in his Production Notes to *Listen to the Wind*; the popular Medicine and Minstrel shows, which, for Reaney, recall in their turn the "agility of early Italian opera just after Monteverdi" ("Letter from James Reaney" 3); Elizabethan and Jacobean drama with its extraordinary "verbal invention" demanding of the audience "quick ears" ("James Reaney" 145); Old Comedy; Romantic Opera; films (". . . they get at your dream life in a way no other artform save music quite does" ["James Reaney" 151]); shadow plays (used to particular effect in *Handcuffs: The Donnellys, Part III*); mime and puppetry (in the Donnelly trilogy, *Colours in the Dark*, *Baldoon*); magic lantern shows; the circus, which Reaney acknowledges as the source of the "multiple focus effect" ("Letter from James Reaney" 2), which is reminiscent of the annular stage of Guillaume Apollinaire, who in 1917 expressed his tribute to

> the full unfolding of our modern art
> Often connecting in unseen ways as in life
> Sounds gestures colours cries tumults
> Music dancing acrobatics poetry painting
> Choruses actions and multiple sets! (Apollinaire 66)[1]

In many of Reaney's plays since the mid-seventies (*The Dismissal: or Twisted Beards & Tangled Whiskers*, *Traps*, *Gyroscope*) and at times in such earlier works as *The Easter Egg* and *Colours in the Dark*, we are reminded of the "alchemical" theatre of French surrealism, and the creative tension in performance and theory between André Breton's *l'alchimie du verbe*, and Antoinin Artaud's *l'alchimie du corps* — between verbal and purely corporeal modes of expression. Reaney also shares at times, in theory and practice, something of the surrealist enthusiasm for *bricolage*, a "do-it-yourselfery" (Hughes 227), which favours the relatively untutored *naif* "artist" challenging the established cultural community with a more direct sense of "play." The surrealist aesthetic is also frequently echoed in Reaney's apparent acquiesence to the role of chance in artistic creation. *Le merveilleux* was often evoked in surrealism, as, earlier in drama, it had been by August Strindberg, through chance associations. "Our memories," Strindberg wrote, and the analogy with Reaney's *One-Man Masque, Colours in the Dark,* and *Gyroscope* is striking, "lie in confusion, unformed and undefined, like pictures in a kaleidoscope. But when we turn the wheel, they merge together and form pictures, sometimes significant, sometimes not, depending" (*Son* 29).[2]

These, and other plays by Reaney — and parts of plays, especially parts of the Donnelly trilogy — also seem to embody some of the features of what Northrop Frye calls the "archetypal masque," which he identifies as "the prevailing form of most twentieth-century high-brow drama, at least in continental Europe, as well as of many experimental operas and unpopular movies." The action of such drama, Frye comments, "takes place in a world of human types, which at its most concentrated becomes the interior of the human mind. This is explicit even in the old moralities, like *Mankynd* and *The Castle of Perseveraunce,* and at least implicit in a good deal of Maeterlinck, Pirandello, Andreyev, and Strindberg." Of particular interest, because Reaney's plays often display a similar structural propensity and, in such plays as *One-Man Masque, Baldoon,* and *Gyroscope,* a substantive one as well, is Frye's account of some of Maeterlinck's earlier plays in which ". . . the constant undermining of the distinction between illusion and reality, as mental projections become physical bodies and vice versa, splits the action up into a kaleidoscopic chaos of reflecting mirrors." Frye concludes his brief look at such drama by suggesting that ". . . the further the archetypal masque gets from the ideal masque, the more clearly it reveals itself as the emancipated antimasque, a revel of satyrs who have got out of control" (*Anatomy* 291). Such a tendency is observable in those plays of Reaney that directly exhibit his strong caricatural bias, informed by a miscreant, or what Frye called his "puckish humour" (*Bush Garden* 90). When such a spirit is accorded a darker, sometimes sinister hue, then Reaney's plays are most reminiscent of the satiric-grotesque sensibility of such playwrights as Bertolt Brecht, Friedrich Durrenmatt, Max Frisch, and Ödon von Horvath, in many of whose plays the dominant image is that of an impregnable social order that operates as a murderer, exhibiting what R.B. Heilman calls "retaliatory malice" against individuals, races, or classes in which dissent is apparent or suspected (47). The montage and narrative techniques associated with some kinds of documentary theatre become increasingly important to Reaney's presentation of such a vision, just as in his earlier plays the dramatic verse techniques of Yeats, Eliot, and others appear to have provided *verbal* models for a vision somewhat less determined by a menacing social milieu.

In short, as with a number of modern playwrights and artists (the almost boundless eclecticism of Paul Klee and, say, Jean Cocteau comes to mind) Reaney assimilates in varying degrees a generous profusion of modern experiments and directions in theatre. Andrew K. Kennedy has observed that ". . . much of contemporary theatricality amounts to parodistic montage — not necessarily satirical or 'debunking' — but critically conscious" (35). It is probable, he writes, "that there are only a limited number of dramatic languages, and that we have heard most of them before." Not only have we heard them before, but we often hear them now speaking *together* in a single dramatic work, in what Kennedy calls "dramatic collage-languages." New and unexpected kinds of "stylistic tension arise in the work of the dramatist," he says, "who refuses to accept the language of imitation as *the* style, who becomes aware of an extended spectrum of possible dramatic language" (8).

A creative, sometimes confusing, pluralism permeates the dramatic work of many writers, especially those, like Reaney, who are *critically* conscious of the succession and simultaneity of "avant-garde" movements which, as Jacques Barzun wryly observed, "form a jungle in which all but Mowgli and Tarzan lose their way" (130). However, what appears to be a problematical aesthetic kaleidoscope in the drama of Reaney converges in two very important ways. First of all, Reaney is what Jay Macpherson called "a poet of the learned kind" (66), and, as is the case with much of his equally eclectic poetry (the extraordinary range of English metrical form in *A Suit of Nettles* is an obvious case in point) in which references to many forms and voices of classical and English poetic tradition abound, Reaney's classic literacy requires us to try to identify and to appreciate the formal and substantive *coherence* of diverse dramatic, theatrical, and literary voices. Such a mythopoeic-synthesizing perspective is what attracted Reaney to such figures as Blake and Frye. What their "structuralism does," he wrote, "is send you up in an airplane to show you not only the field patterns, but the buried fort, the remains of the chieftain's barrow — all things you might miss for years in the myopic approach" ("Identifier Effect" 28). This is a literacy, as George Steiner (lamenting its absence in our world) described it, "of that minimal gamut of shared recognitions and designative codes without which there can be neither a coherent society nor a continuation however attenuated, however transitional, of a 'lived' culture" (*Bluebeard* 78). It is also a literacy, as we shall observe later, which has often left Reaney susceptible to the charge of being "too literary" — often (not always, however) as misplaced a criticism as is the diametrically opposite charge that he is "too regional."

Important aesthetic convergence of Reaney's pluralism also occurs when we are brought more closely into touch with the *art-act* itself. The "resonances" and "reverberations" of significant poetic imagery, Gaston Bachelard remarked, awaken creativity within us. Through its novelty, he writes, ". . . a poetic image sets in motion the entire linguistic mechanism. The poetic image places us at the origin of the speaking being. . . . we feel a poetic power rising naively within us. . . . The image offered us by reading the poem now becomes really our own. It takes root in us. It has been given us by another, but we begin to have the impression that we could have created it, that we should have created it. It becomes a new being in our language, expressing us by making us what it expresses; in other words, it is at once a becoming of expression, and a becoming of our being. Here expression creates being" (*Poetics of Space* xix). Just such an ontological understanding of creativity, of poetry itself as an exegesis of creation, lies within Reaney's notion of the art-act. Again and again, Reaney challenges us with intricately related verbal and scenic images so dense in meaning, and so theatrically disciplined, that we feel entirely free of the cacophonous artistic echoes, and, instead, at the centre of the *act* of creation. One example would be the episode at the close of Act I of *Colours in the Dark* where, within a yellow hue, the actors form a family tree pyramid, reciting the poem "It Takes / The Remembering / Of Four Seasons . . . / To make one soul," which then *"reverses so it is an arrow pointing at a child standing on the trestles."* This child turns his face, the stage directions tell us: "He is masked and dressed as Adolf Hitler." The singing of a Nazi children's song, and the sound of a Nuremberg rally complete the image (*Colours* 47). Others include the use of the cat's-cradle image for the surveying of Biddulph ("fates with string entangling people's lives") in *Sticks & Stones: The Donnellys, Part 1* (47); the bird-shadow image in *Handcuffs* (81) with its evocative range of both scenic and verbal meaning; the concluding scenic image of *The Dismissal* when the actors, as "farmerish shapes," fan out in the formation of a book (54), scenically encapsulating the play's central thesis concerning the "integral versus the fractional" (39), the former signified in the portrayal of Professor Dale, the farmer at the Weston stockyards with the copy of Livy's *History of Rome*.

   In each of these, and of course in many others, Reaney attempts to place the spectator/auditor at the *centre* of the art act from which vantage point he can hear, most immediately, something of his own voice, and something of the speech of the place. Reaney's spectator is urged to move towards a recognition of creative accord with the playwright and the actors. The multitudinous theatre languages and signs are meant to act in performance as creative vehicles through whose vital energy the spectator renders less hidden, less circum-scribed, his *own* creativity with which he can learn "how to play." The work of art becomes the quintessential deed, and its *process* and magic are to be shared by author, actor, and spectator. Reaney has tried, for his own purposes, as Wallace Stevens says, to

> . . . construct a new stage. It has to be on that stage
> And, like an insatiable actor, slowly and
> With meditation, speak words that in the ear,
> In the delicatest ear of the mind, repeat,
> Exactly, that which it wants to hear, at the sound
> Of which, an invisible audience listens,
> Not to the play, but to itself . . . ("Of Modern Poetry" 240)

However, like many playwrights in Canada, and elsewhere, Reaney recognized that there could be no truly vital theatre with such ontological reverberations as Bachelard celebrated in his study of poetic imagery, no theatre that can maintain a sure hold on our sensibility, until ". . . the man in the audience echoed in his heart and with his heart the same words spoken by the man on the stage" (Copeau, qtd. in Ghéon 15).

   In the following chapters, Reaney's plays will, in part, be examined within the context of the diverse tendencies in modern theatre and art I have sketched here. Through the identification of these, the several "languages" of his drama become explicable. The internationalization of art, the "aesthetic Faustianism" (Poggioli 15) of formal, pluralistic experimentation unbounded by time and place, was recognized as a fundamental feature of the "new art" as long ago as 1891 when the Belgian poet Emile Verhaeren wrote, "There is no longer any single school, there are scarcely any groups, and those few are constantly splitting. All these tendencies make me think of moving and kaleidoscopic geometric patterns, which clash at one moment only to unite at another, which now fuse and then separate and fly apart a little later, but which all nevertheless revolve within the same circle, that of the new art" (qtd. in Rewald 7). Such a view of modern art is familiar to us through numerous accounts of the "heroic epoque" of Montparnasse before the first World War and of the Paris of the twenties and thirties to which many a "gentil folke" journeyed. It was in this setting, Harold Rosenberg writes, that ". . . necessary blendings could be made and mellowed, where it was possible to shake up such 'modern' doses as Viennese psychology, African sculpture, American detective stories, Russian music, neo-Catholicism, German technique, Italian desperation." What happened here, Rosenberg concludes, "demonstrated clearly and for all time that such a thing as international culture could exist . . . that a whole epoch in the history of art had come into being without regard to national values." However, and most importantly, "because Paris was the opposite of the national in art, the art of every nation increased through Paris. No folk lost its integrity there; on the contrary, artists of every region renewed by this magnanimous milieu discovered in the depths of themselves what was most alive in the communities from which they had come" (*Tradition* 210–11).

An aesthetic, and an artistic program, which thus combines nationalist and internationalist ("modernist") principles is not at all uncommon in our time. It is, one concludes, precisely what Reaney encountered in his own "heroic epoque" at the University of Toronto in the 1940s as an undergraduate and the later 1950s as a doctoral student. Aspects of these years crucial to his development as a writer are recounted in Reaney's article "The Identifier Effect," where his readings in Blake, Spenser, Milton, Yeats, and others (the "history of thought" for instance) are described. He also, most importantly, recalls the impact upon him of Frye's study of Blake, and his *Anatomy of Criticism: Four Essays*: "Once I absorbed both Frye and Blake on 'Poetry is allegory addressed to the intellectual powers' what happened was that I was finally able to stand in the house of literature and close the door on philosophy, theology and history until I needed them. In short, you can explain literature in terms of itself, something that is so obvious in mathematics and music, but seemed so difficult in my first years at Toronto" (28). Some of the other things Reaney was reading and doing during his first years at university are briefly alluded to by Richard Stingle in his account of the relationship between Reaney and Frye. Reaney, Stingle writes, "was preoccupied with contemporary writers and composers. He gave papers on Edith Sitwell and Evelyn Waugh to our Literary Club and he often played Satie and Debussy on the piano on more informal occasions. 'Golliwog's Cake Walk' and Reaney's own little composition 'Penny Arcade' still establish the rhythm of those days for me" (34).

The movement in Reaney's artistic and critical life suggested here is of some significance and analogous to that of such writers as Synge, Yeats, Samuel Beckett, and W.H. Auden. Auden expressed something of it when he wrote in his "New Year Letter,"

> . . . set in order sense
> And feeling and intelligence,
> And from its ideal order grew
> Our local understanding too. (162)

Reaney moves away from the view of literature as concerned primarily with the minute and temporal particularities of philosophy, religion, and history, towards a view of literature as something in itself, an "ideal order," informed, like music (and, we might add, much in modern painting) by transhistorical values, a *lingua franca* of artistic impulses and designs. Yet, in his drama, especially after *Listen to the Wind*, Reaney returns, like Rosenberg's ideal artist, renewed by the "magnanimous milieu" of modernism, to explore those very particularities of temporal and spatial identity in his own community. Frye wrote during Canada's Centennial year that "Complete immersion in the international style is a primary cultural requirement, especially for countries whose cultural traditions have been formed since 1867, like ours. Anything distinctive that develops within the Canadian environment can only grow out of participation in this style" (*Modern* 57). A similar observation was made by the New York art critic Hilton Kramer in an issue of *Artscanada* devoted to the relationship between art and nationalism. "It is only by abandoning nationalist criteria," he wrote, "that the objectives of the nationalist ambition can ever be truly realized" ("Reflections"

22). Such sentiments have tended to prevail in music, painting, and drama for some considerable time as our century's accelerated global aesthetic interchange has captivated and informed the work of numerous artists and performers. The journey back towards the particularities of individual communities, however, is not always taken. When it is not, the global artistic vocabulary (whether musical, pictorial, and, in the case of drama, physical as well) is frequently in danger of becoming and remaining essentially decorative, part of an autonomous aesthetic vehicle that promotes more estrangement than it does truly ontological creativity.[3]

Some of the problems that seem to derive from this divided loyalty to art and to region, especially as they concern dramatic speech, will be examined in the third chapter, " 'the magic tongue.' " In Reaney's theatre, through his own awareness of what resources the modern theatre offers and through the receptive and generous sensibilities of many in the theatre with whom he has worked (John Hirsch, John Beckwith, Bill Glassco, Keith Turnbull, Jerry Franken, among others) immersion in the "international style" was apparent from the beginning. As a non-dramatic poet, Reaney fully recognized such an artistic obligation when he wrote, "There's no doubt at all that if a Canadian poet wants to be terrific he has to assimilate what Yeats, Rilke, Eliot and all have done, or else. Whether you have to expatriate or not in order to do this is part of the poet's predicament here; we have as few ruins and ancient cathedrals as Idaho or New York and dozens of Americans — James, Pound, and Eliot — show you the way" ("Canadian Poet's Predicament" 292–93). His critically conscious immersion in the most prominent currents in the modern theatre is less easily traced. Certainly, it was not primarily (if at all) the result of "trendy" reading in the Established Voices of the *avant garde*. He once expressed dismay over such an approach when he wrote that "most Canuck playwrights reach for the *Village Voice* clichés when they try the urban vision" (*14 Barrels* 162). A similar invitation to look beyond the more obvious contemporary sources of style and vision was issued when he rebuked a reviewer of a Calgary production of *The St Nicholas Hotel: The Donnellys, Part II*: ". . . I just would like to say that I don't think the real explanation of our style is: the one time I saw O'Horgan's *Tom Paine* in San Francisco. Some day we'll do a tour where the critics will have done such an unheard of thing as read up on the back issues of *Alphabet: A Semiannual Devoted to the Iconography of the Imagination*, the little magazine I used to publish before theatre hit me" (*14 Barrels*

92). Nor is there substantial evidence of aesthetically fastidious theatre going, or of easy and direct contact with the "international" shapers of a contemporary theatrical idiom. Reaney's complex idiom resulted, rather, from the "universal" perspectives of a classic literacy; from some aspects of a particular honours system at the University of Toronto (which, as Stingle notes, was finally abolished to the regret of Reaney and Frye [35–36][4]); from highly sympathetic contact with the structuralist principles formulated and taught by Frye; from his interest in the writings, paintings and music of such figures as Erik Satie, Gertrude Stein, Edith Sitwell, Jean Cocteau, Paul Klee, and many others; from his personal quest as a poet for unifying symbols and structures; from films; and, very importantly, from his enthusiasm for and knowledge of the *lingua franca* of children — play. There are many instances of a close connection between modern theatre aesthetics and children's play, which have been explored by many writers. The ontological implications of such play, and the apparent extra-national spatial, auditory, and corporeal structures implicit in children's games and improvised storytelling have always been of central concern to Reaney, and his theatre is heavily indebted to them.

This study is divided into three parts. In the first, " 'this native land business,' " I examine Reaney's drama in terms of its relationship to some "ideas" of the theatre (for example in Wagner, Cocteau, Yeats, Peter Brook, Artaud, and others) and in terms of its Nationalist principles rooted in Reaney's desire to disclose what was "most alive" in the community from which he had come. In this section, Reaney's almost gluttonous archival impulses to depict the "essence of country life in Ontario" (Woodman, *Reaney* 21) are outlined, and some of the ways in which a fidelity to documentary material informed and shaped his theatre are examined. In addition to the plays, Reaney's critical writings in *Alphabet*, in various journals, as well as his important *Halloween letters*, are examined as these shed light upon his evolving theatre aesthetic and his particular political, social, and "mythopoeic" concerns. In the second chapter, " 'making up patterns (scribbling with your body/bodies),' " I examine the scenic patterning of Reaney's plays. Reaney's propensity for what Rudolf Arnheim calls "visual thinking" is evident in his poetry and his drama and has important analogies in the theory and art of two distinct but related modernist movements. One of these includes Klee, Wassily Kandinsky, and Miró; the other, Vsevolod Meyerhold, Edward Gordon Craig, Jacques Copeau, and, more recently, Joseph

Chaikin, Peter Brook, Richard Schechner, and many others, who experimented widely with the distinctive languages of the theatre through a variety of disruptive challenges to actors and spectators to become more fully alive to the corporeal and spatial dynamics of performance. In the third chapter, " 'the magic tongue,' " I discuss the ways in which Reaney uses language in the theatre. In this context, Reaney's relationship to other modern verse dramatists is briefly examined; in addition, his increasing skill with a wide range of purely theatrical "languages" — seen especially in his work following *Listen to the Wind* — is explored. As Reaney's dramaturgical experiments led him towards the writing of verbally and scenically more complicated plays, dramatic collage, including verbal collage, became the formal *donnée* within which, and with the techniques of which, the array of voices was to be assembled. Collage, among other things, is a form of play. As such, it subsumes whatever it finds available. What Reaney found available were all imaginable forms of public and personal utterance, including the dramatic and non-dramatic literature of the past. The increasingly complex intertextual nature of Reaney's drama necessitated the exploitation and "playing" of different languages, creating a linguistic pastiche in which all voices were accorded theatrical life.

HOW TO PLAY

"THIS NATIVE LAND BUSINESS"

There is something to this native land business. After all, any-body is as their land and air is. Anybody is as the sky is low or high. Anybody is as there is wind or no wind there. That is what makes a people, makes their kind of looks, their kind of think-ing, their subtlety and their stupidity, and their eating and their drinking and their language. (Stein 258)

Sometimes this is called plight; situation is too mild a word, but I have plight, situation and predicament in mind when I think of the poet or indeed any artist in Canada. . . . Another thing I rather worry about is whether it's any use talking about the poet's predicament in national terms. It's sensible if you think living in a certain kind of nation has any shaping effect whatso-ever upon that country's imagination. I happen to think that Canada is a very peculiar and different country; whether its national colour and shape have anything to do with the colour and shape of its poetry is a question that you might as well say yes to, again — just to see what happens. ("Canadian Poet's Predicament" 284)

An enquiry into the Canadian poet's national tradition is, according to Reaney, an obvious obligation of an educated Canadian reader or practicing poet. "Of course, first find your native poetic tradition," he writes: "The native tradition . . . is something that repays inquiry, repays it as I've tried to indicate not only with the acquisition of interesting heirlooms but with imaginative life that can still beget more imaginative life, with some passages even that can change your life" ("Canadian Poet's Predicament" 292). In this essay Reaney traces some of the more prominent poetic forms and voices of the Canadian sensibility, from the Native lyrics, through Isabella Valency Crawford, Sir Charles G.D. Roberts, E.J. Pratt, to Margaret Avison and others. Throughout this account, Reaney unapologetically indulges in free-flowing nationalist boosterism, enthusiastically and somewhat uncritically, endorsing a wide range of Canadian writers. With what enthusiasm, and with what results, would a similar enquiry into the national tradition in drama be undertaken? A comment by Merrill Denison in 1928, or an equally witty variation, has often been used to set the mood of such an enquiry — at least of one which might have been undertaken as late as the 1950s. "Writing about the Canadian theatre or drama," Denison remarked, is "depressingly like discussing the art of dinghy sailing among the bedouins" (74). In "James Reaney," an interview, Reaney once provided a lengthy list of plays he had read, and some he had seen, while growing up and while studying at the University of Toronto. Among these were the plays of Shakespeare, Jonson's *Volpone* and *Epicoene*, such Jacobean plays as Webster's *The Duchess of Malfi*, Wilder's *Our Town* and *Skin of Our Teeth*, Eliot's *The Family Reunion*, Beckett's *Waiting for Godot*. Unsurprisingly, he mentions no Canadian plays — although elsewhere he alludes to the discovery in 1954 of Hilda Mary Hooke's volume of *One-Act Plays from Canadian History* in a Goodwill shop in Winnipeg: "Mrs. Hooke I admire no end because she was skillful enough and committed sufficiently to her region to get something ready for the hungry generations that might follow her" ("Topless Nightmares" 4).

Mrs. Hooke's anthology notwithstanding, Reaney's education in theatre and drama was typically Canadian. In an essay on the development of a Canadian theatre, Ross Stuart wrote that "a basic reading list for theatre people in England would contain plays by Shakespeare, Jonson, Sheridan, Wilde and Shaw." Who, he asks, "would be on a similar list in Canada? . . . few, if any, plays from our past are still good enough by current standards to provide our contemporary professional theatre with an alternative to new plays and the best from other lands. As far as most of our theatres are concerned, Canadian playwriting began with James Reaney or George Ryga" (6–8). "We look in the mirror," Mavor Moore wrote in 1957, and "there is nothing there. Some sceptics have even suggested we have no mirror — that is, none or few of the arts reflective of our character, as these arts have reflected the character of other nations past and present. We own the world's most famous blank face" ("A Theatre" 1). A few years earlier, Robertson Davies offered a similarly depressing picture in a special study for the Royal Commission on National Development in The Arts, Letters and Sciences, 1951:

Is not the theatre of the civilized world interested in plays by and about Russians, Norwegians, Frenchmen, Swedes, Hungarians, Italians, Belgians and even — God bless us! — Irishmen and Scotchmen? Are Canadians so cut off from the charity of God and the indulgence of mankind that they alone are of no interest to their fellow-beings? . . . I will confess to you that the agent who hawks my plays in England keeps mum about the fact that I am a Canadian. He says that it would work against him. Nobody thinks that there is anything odd about an Englishman or an American writing a play, but apparently it is still considered unpropitious for a play to come from Canada. Still, I think that the prejudice will be overcome and that we shall see Canadian plays performed abroad when we have the playwrights capable of bringing that about. (33)

"The tendency in the society in which I lived," Reaney wrote, was "to see drama as, first, something somebody else wrote thousands of miles away" ("Ten Years" 55). George Ryga responded angrily to a similar situation and to the development of what he called the "dinosaurs like the Stratford Festival and the self-indulgent thing at Niagara," which offered no satisfactory solution to the Canadian dramatist's predicament. "I did not know of Canadian Theatre when I began writing drama," Ryga wrote, and

Fifteen years later, I still know nothing of a Canadian theatre. There is a collection of theatre literature — of which a company here and there periodically produces an item — but there is no Canadian theatre I know of . . . a national theatre, a full-bodied, dynamic theatre of people for people is not going to happen in English-speaking Canada until we clear our heads and move forcefully beyond the outer limits of restriction imposed by the funding agencies through the proliferation of theatrical charlatans and economically-vested boards of directors. We have been trapped 40 years behind actual history. A viable national theatre must strive for nothing less than a vanguard position in expression of national ideals and international humanism. (29)

In his brief response to the Appelbaum-Hébert Report of the Federal Cultural Policy Review Committee, Reaney voiced similar disappointment:

Failures first: (a) — Theatre. Everyone expected that the National Arts Centre would do what Joe Papp did for Public Theatre in New York — reach out dynamically into the country and forge us a genuine national theatre with our own plays midwifed out of the story of our people (after all, even the Australians have managed this) as well as a dynamic response to the classics. This hasn't happened. . . . ("Sizing Up" 7)

Considering the near homogeneity of their complaints, it is somehow fitting that Reaney first saw his two main players for the Donnelly trilogy performing in Ryga's *The Ecstasy of Rita Joe* at Theatre London. Patricia Ludwick and Jerry Franken were in Ryga's play, and to Reaney "They looked like Mr and Mrs Donnelly" (*14 Barrels* 10).

The critical enquiry to "find your native poetic tradition," then, insofar as dramatic writing was concerned, was filled with obstacles. It was certainly possible to "rediscover" such dramatic figures from our past as Merrill Denison, Herman Voaden, or even Hilda Mary Hooke and remark upon their isolated attempts to create a national theatre. It remains true, however, that, as Ross Stuart observed, most "artistic directors are undoubtedly not aware of Canadian plays written in the past. Large numbers of these plays have never been published or are long out of print. Yet even if these situations were remedied, performances of plays written prior to 1953 would probably remain rare in our regional and alternative theatres" (6). Margaret Atwood's familiar characterization of the Canadian artist who "came to maturity" before the sixties is one with which Reaney identified.

He looked around and found himself in a place where people read, it's true, and looked at pictures, but most of the books they read were imported from England and the States and most of the pictures they looked at were either old Group of Seven or travelling exhibitions from abroad. Usually he found that his own work would be dismissed by sophisticated Canadian critics as "second-rate," "provincial," or "regional," simply for having been produced here; by the unsophisticated it might well have been denounced as immoral. In some decades he might have been mindlessly praised for being "Canadian," in other decades just as mindlessly denounced for the same reason. The situation in either case was impossible. (*Survival* 181–82)

Reaney's first major statement on the situation of the aspiring playwright in Canada was made in an *Alphabet* editorial of 1962. In it, the "impossibility" of his situation is suggested. "I seem to hear voices at this point," he wrote,

> mocking voices saying, "What do we need a native drama for? Why all this absurd nationalism?" Because I don't believe you can really be world, or unprovincial or whatever until you've sunk your claws into a very locally coloured tree trunk and scratched your way through to universality.
>
> We do not really know if we understand the plays from abroad that are our dramatic fare until we have "stood" works equivalent from our own environment. If Eliot's verse plays had been premiered incognito in Ontario in the forties one wonders what audiences would have done. Would they have stood for it at all? Given the proper clues (Anglican poet, English sounding) and the same audience laps up libation scenes and birthday candle rituals it would never take from a local poet. What a maddening situation for the artist! Always this feeling of circumference for the native artist, centre for everybody else. (3)

The truth, of course, was that audiences here or abroad did not exactly "lap up" Eliot's "libation scenes and birthday candle rituals" either, that the kind of verse drama practiced and critically advocated by Eliot (and for a time generally emulated by Reaney) was engaged in what was to become a losing battle with quite a different kind of *poésie de théâtre*. Nonetheless, the circumferential situation of the Canadian dramatist remained obvious, although this was soon to change.

Many writers have traced different aspects of the radical change in the Canadian theatre, for Canadian playwrights, directors, and performers, during the later 1960s and throughout the 1970s.[1] Towards the close of Reaney's second decade as a playwright he could speak of this:

> I would like to see Canadian colonialism finally disappear. . . . If only there'd be a bit more push all down the line by the community: everything is latent. After being scoffed at in the sixties for nationalism and writing plays at all, it is almost bewildering to see the influx of new plays and national seasons. Such organizations as Tarragon and Playwrights Co-op and the

rest of the theatre movement in Toronto (Dupont Street, Holy Trinity and Duke Street) have finally got writers and ideas moving. More intensity? Yes, no one can make enough demands on their time. ("James Reaney" 158)

During these years, Reaney's voice was one among many urging the development of a theatre better able to reflect and to explore what Atwood called the "unknown territory" of Canada (*Survival* 17–18). In 1967, Len Peterson wrote of the need for "theatres working exclusively on indigenous works. . . . Include wide reading, research in Canadiana, extensive exposure and involvement in the place where we live, till it becomes our bedrock" (19). Two years earlier, in an editorial for the newly established *Stage in Canada*, Tom Hendry wrote: "It is time we began to emulate another characteristic [of Max Reinhardt's] theatre practice, the use of original material to form a significant percentage of repertoire. We have been checking our nationality along with our overcoat, when attending theatres in Canada, for far too long" (1).[2] By the mid-seventies, all of the theatres mentioned by Reaney, and many more in Toronto and throughout Canada, were actively promoting new Canadian playwrights and performers. Paul Thompson's Theatre Passe Muraille, founded in 1968 at Rochdale College (under James Garrard) had in its Trinity Square facilities produced more than sixty new plays, and the company's work in exploring aspects of Canadian history had by this time achieved national recognition. "The kind of work he's doing in cultivating local traditions," Reaney wrote, "is exactly what needs to be done right soon before it's too late" (*14 Barrels* 95). Ken Gass's Factory Lab Theatre, founded in 1971, had likewise introduced many new playwrights. George Luscombe's Toronto Workshop Productions was nearly fifteen years old by 1975 and had contributed to a variety of writing and performing styles. John Juliani's "Savage God" experiments had been influential, by this time, within the training programs of professional and amateur groups in Vancouver, Montreal, Toronto, and Ottawa, as had his PACET (a "Pilot Alternative Complement to Existing Theatre"). In Edmonton and Calgary, new works by Rudy Wiebe, Sharon Pollock, Rod Langley, and others were being performed. Bill Glassco's Tarragon Theatre in Toronto, founded in 1971, had produced many new works by such playwrights as Carol Bolt, David French, Michel Tremblay, Erika Ritter, and, of course, Reaney, whose Donnelly trilogy was given a highly successful run there. Glassco's manifesto stated, in part: "To produce plays of one's own culture and to be a part of their inception through the act of collaboration with the playwright. . . . To nurture Canadian playwriting talent is Tarragon's primary aim. Canada and its theatres *need* their *own* plays" (23). At the Tarragon, and elsewhere, an important step was taken in helping to provide the playwright greater access to the means and the process of actual production, a problem being faced by playwrights everywhere.[3] Also, by the mid-seventies, the Lennoxville Festival had completed its first years of producing only Canadian plays; by 1974, plays by George Ryga, Mavor Moore, Ann Henry, David Freeman, and others had been staged. William New, with obvious good cause, was able to remark in his Introduction to *Dramatists in Canada: Selected Essays* on the "recent vitality of playwriting in Canada" (9). About this time Don Rubin examined one major tendency of such writing in a *Canadian Theatre Review* editorial:

> Of late, there have been positive indications that we are at last beginning to show some curiosity about our past. No longer is it unusual to find a major new play dealing with events from Canadian history. One thinks immediately of Toronto's Theatre Passe Muraille which is making an entire docu-dramatic repertoire from such things as the farmer's revolt of 1837; of James Reaney's trilogy of the notorious Donnelly family being produced at the Tarragon; of Tom Hendry's anatomisation of Canadian participation in the Dieppe raid; of Sharon Pollock's *Walsh* (produced at both Theatre Calgary and Stratford) and Rod Langley's *Bethune* (produced by both Regina's Globe Theatre and Montreal's Centaur Theatre). There have been other plays, of course, which have looked back, but it is probably safe to say that never in our theatrical history has history itself become quite so popular on our stage. ("Aside" 4)

To a large extent, this "body of consciousness-raising, myth-making plays dealing with historical subjects" (Rubin, "Celebrating" 21) reflected a considerable effort on the part of the Canadian playwright to locate and define the "landmarks and bearings" of the Canadian space. That is, a strictly nationalist impulse informed such drama. On the other hand, insofar as a number of these plays dealt with political issues — certainly, as in Langley's *Bethune*, Theatre Passe Muraille's *1837: The Farmer's Revolt*, and Reaney's Donnelly trilogy, with political ways of informing and interpreting personal and collective experience — then the

Canadian drama of the seventies shared the political-historical consciousness of playwriting nearly everywhere. In England, such writers as Edward Bond, Peter Barnes, Robert Bolt, Steve Gooch, Roger Howard, David Edgar, Bruce Birchall, and many others dealt almost exclusively with present or past historical events and issues of primarily *national* importance through a variety of political perspectives. In the United States, the sixties especially had seen the ascendency of such a politicized theatrical activity in the work of the Living Theatre, Richard Schechner, Herbert Blau, Joseph Papp, and others. In Germany, there was the work of Rolf Hochhuth, Peter Weiss, and of such theatre collectives as *Rote Rube*. In France, a strongly political-historical theatre had been attracting serious attention since the sixties when Armand Gatti, André Benedetto, and others experimented with the techniques of *écriture collective* designed to involve the spectators — especially young spectators in schools — in the process of dramatic creation. During the seventies, such work was continued by the Théâtre Action de Grenoble, Théâtre Populaire de Lorraine, Théâtre du Soleil, and by Roger Planchon's municipal theatre of Villeurbanne near Lyon. Many of Planchon's techniques, and his vision of a politically motivated populist theatre, were transplanted and further developed in Canada by Thompson, who had acted as Technical Director of the London, Ontario, Summer Theatre Season of 1965 and, in 1966, was producer for *Names and Nicknames*.

The "influx of new plays and national seasons" applauded by Reaney in the late seventies, then, reflected obvious national aspirations and achievements. To a considerable degree, historical consciousness became the bedrock of the regional and national *idea* of the theatre. As Steiner remarked, "The echoes by which a society seeks to determine the reach, the logic and authority of its own voice, come from the rear" (*Bluebeard* 13). Such echoes, however, were being sought throughout the serious drama of many countries at the same time, and that of Canada inevitably shared in the *political* focus and "international style" of such work.

I I

By the summer of 1965, when the Campus Players of the University of Western Ontario mounted a season of plays in a converted London, Ontario, nightclub called The Oasis and included in the season *The Sun and the Moon* (written earlier but still unperformed), Reaney's dramatic work included *The Killdeer* (first produced in 1960 and soon to be produced abroad at the Glasgow Citizen's Theatre as part of a Commonwealth Arts Festival); *One-Man Masque* and the libretto for *Night-Blooming Cereus* (both produced at Hart House, University of Toronto in 1962); and *Names and Nicknames* (first produced under John Hirsch's direction at the Manitoba Theatre Centre in 1963). Keith Turnbull describes the time thus:

> I was putting together a season. People at that time always did things from everywhere else, as a deeply defended principle (laugh). And I found out that there was this guy in town who had written some plays, and that they'd been published. People tried to persuade me away from going to the library to get a copy of the plays. "No, no, you wouldn't like them, no." I went and got the plays, and I really liked *The Sun and the Moon*. I just went "Wow, this is wonderful." And I thought the idea of actually working with a real live author, someone who is really right there instead of dead or in New York would be really exciting. So I went to meet him, and we co-directed it. (McKay 151)

In the following year, Reaney joined with Turnbull in the mounting of an entire season of Canadian plays. In his "Report on Summer Theatre," Turnbull wrote:

> The last few months have been very busy for members of our company, and when our regular season opens at Althouse College of Education on July 5th we will be providing London and all of Canada with a type of theatre long overdue in this country. For years the chilly reception given Canadian play-wrights by our theatres has forced many of them to leave Canada or to let their talents lie dormant . . . it is our belief that the icy reactions of Canadian theatres to Canadian plays is completely unwarranted. In view of this, an entirely Canadian bill will be presented and the authors will in almost all cases be working with us to the advantage of the author and our company. This adventure will be the first of its kind in Canada. (1)

Much later, in 1980, Reaney looked back on this season:

My recent plays are part of a playwrights' manifesto and movement which are rooted in Summer Theatre '65, '66, '67 at
Western here; rooted also in the militant regionalism of painters
Greg Curnoe and Jack Chambers. Just by inches we missed
founding an alternative theatre here devoted to the above named
principle, but the idea has spread across the country and *King
Whistle* is one late expression of it. ("Story" 50)

Diane Bessai has justifiably observed with regard to this statement
that the "implication that the late 1960s dramatic activity in London,
Ontario, was the initiating influence in all that followed elsewhere is
questionable" ("Documentary Drama" 195). Nonetheless, the 1966
summer season of Canadian plays, when *Listen to the Wind* had its
first production, was, in fact, the "first of its kind in Canada."
Considering some of the people associated with this and subsequent
development (Tim Bond, Martin Kinch, Alan Stratton, Paul Thompson) and the interest (including some acrimonious debate) aroused
in London and elsewhere by various manifestations of regionally
inspired and rooted artistic endeavours, these years of Canadian
summer theatre were certainly of importance. In 1967, the final year
of the all-Canadian season, called Festival of Canadian Theatre,
Anne Brodzky arranged a show at the London Art Museum entitled
"Cultural Heritage of This Region." Ross Woodman gave this
account of the closing night of the exhibition:

> . . . a group of London artists gathered to read from their own
> works. Taking up positions within the beam frames of the
> various exhibits superbly assembled from all over southern
> Ontario, they looked as much a part of the "cultural heritage"
> as the objects themselves. There they sat — James Reaney,
> Colleen Thibaudeau, Jack Chambers, Greg Curnoe, George
> Bowering, Ron Bates — like craven images, and when they rose
> to read their voices sounded at once contemporary and ances-
> tral. And their words, it seemed, were as regionally rooted as
> the objects. ["London (Ont.)"]

The plays produced that summer were Reaney's *The Easter Egg*
(directed by Pamela Terry), John Coulter's *Oblomov* (an adaptation
of Ivan Goncharov's novel), John Reeves's *A Beach of Strangers*, and
Mavor Moore's *Sunshine Town*, a musical adaptation of Stephen
Leacock's *Sunshine Sketches of a Little Town*.

When the 1966 season aroused predictably churlish criticism in London ("It's tragic to prefer Canadian plays to good plays." "What I do object to is a doctrinaire acceptance of plays, good or bad, for performance on the basis that they are Canadian; I cannot believe that some of the work put on last summer was read before it was accepted" [Rans]). Reaney responded that the season might not "have accomplished total lack of boredom, but . . . it was brave in a way that a well-balanced season of Pinter, Weiss, Ionesco, Kopit, etc. is dully not. . . . If we always produce Pinter, Genet and Ionesco we may end up giving young writers the feeling that original work is done only in London and Paris." Thus the season, he continued,

dull plays, dull parts of plays and all, at least got playwrights' attention, began to build their audience, focused all eyes on the need for more plays. Surely one group is to be allowed to do that now and again. Put on 3 native plays and 2 West Enders — a Royal Courters — and you lose impact. . . . No, the idea must be single and extreme and carried out to the hilt. . . . And I mean the sort of idea that makes drama provide a rooted soul for a community — the way Emily General's Forest Theatre does at Oshwekan near Brantford, or Abbey Theatre did for Dublin or Joan Littlewood.

One of the aims we must have is to find our own style of writing and acting. In my programme notes to *Listen to the Wind* I speculated on the development I could see — out of John Hirsch — and out of Jean Gascon. I feel also that a theatre could be built up around the ideas of Norrie Frye and Marshall McLuhan. Then after we've got out our own style and some sort of collection of good workable plays — then we can turn to classics and good contemporaries — and put them on with a point of view — instead of letting them put us on. We're not true to Ionesco or Weiss' creativity by giving them those uncertain college productions with sweet, virtuous people imitating nasty, vicious. The real way to put on Ionesco is to put yourself in his position if he lived in our society — and write a play from that viewpoint. ("Reaney Replies")[4]

Years later, in *14 Barrels from Sea to Sea*, Reaney related some "theatre horror stories" concerning the Stratford Festival, the National Theatre School, and the Chalmers Theatre Awards in Toronto, from which he draws a moral similar to his viewpoint in 1966:

Take ninety percent of the content of these yarns away and you still have evidence of just how twisted and hilarious and sterile our attempts at dramatic development can be. Somewhere along the line — and it goes back to the turn of the century when the Governor-General, I gather, had to *start* a drama Festival — alienation leaked in and is not going to disappear until young men and women arise, get themselves in the right slots and suddenly one day fifty years from hence? the theatres do express ourselves naturally in the classics, the moderns and the patriotics — not with this twisted, transplanted, letter-first, spirit-third feeling which the horror story waxworks is, in the end, a reflection of. (*14 Barrels* 68)

Informing Reaney's passionate, almost messianic, concern for a genuinely vital national theatre, expressed in these and other statements I will be examining shortly, are certain main principles. (1) Such a theatre must possess a distinctive voice and vision to which a Canadian audience can respond *directly*, so that, to a significant degree, it listens, as Stevens says, "Not to the play, but to itself." Such a national theatre must, in its mimetic reach into the country's "landmarks" and "bearings," possess truly ontological assertiveness. (2) Playwrights, along with directors and actors, should demonstrate a strong pedagogical bias in their assertions of what Hamlet called "the purpose of playing." Stan Dragland has mentioned some of the "good" and "bad" teachers who play major roles in many of Reaney's plays and rightly points out that

It hardly needs the push of Reaney's comment to Jean McKay ["Well, officially, I'm really a teacher" (McKay 146)] to focus the realization that Reaney is always a teacher, whatever he's doing, whether lecturing, writing essays, poetry or plays, or conducting drama workshops. . . . Reaney not only teaches with and in his own work, he also reflects on the value of the traditional discipline of education, and his aim is to reach as wide a student body as possible, child and adult, across the country. (226)

At times, this pedagogical bias assumes a less secular focus when Reaney associates the creative purpose and process with more privileged shamanistic impulses. Such an association was not uncommon among many of the surrealists earlier in the century who stressed the material and spiritual liberties to be enjoyed through the saving power of art, insofar as such power disclosed *le merveilleux*. To cite but one such instance in Reaney's writing, referring to a study of the mask in Eskimo society by D.J. Baker, he wrote,

> Through the mask this society joined subject and object and implemented the very poetic belief . . . that Baker sums up in: "Not me in the world, but the world in me." There was one difficulty though; suppose you couldn't make a good enough mask, and so the shaman *did also* make a mask whose subject was itself, or rather the art of mask-making: look it up — the larger mask for the shaman's face has a smaller mask attached to it and I guess there was a dance with this mask on to ensure successful mask-making. My theatre is after this Mask that controls all other masks, and I happen to think that it's the idea of PURE STORY. ("Letter from James Reaney" 5)

(3) Theatrical activity should be rooted, as much as possible, in the peculiarities and pressures of the community, with the fullest possible participation by the community. At times the ready, almost formulaic evocation of the Community in discussions of artistic purpose by Reaney, Thompson, and many of their European counterparts in *écriture collective* such as Planchon, appear to echo revolutionary evocations of the People in discussions of political purpose and destination. And, as with the latter, considerable disillusionment can result from too close a contact. (Keith Turnbull's many such contacts with communities led, once, to an exclamation that "I think finally after *Antler River* we made very clear, we're not having any more to do with those god damn community god damn workshops. They're wonderful training, actually, for a director, they're superb training. From that point of view, I never regret them. But creatively, it's just — uhhh" [Turnbull, "Interview" 159].) Reaney's enthusiasm, however, even though tempered by some realistic and ironic perspectives gained from actual involvements (as accounts of different communities throughout *14 Barrels* amply demonstrate) continues to be central to his idea of theatre. Perhaps the most definitive statement on this was made in "James Reaney," an interview:

> Plays demand co-operation from a community of the most eager and energetic sort; not until I started going down to the Listeners' Workshops at Halifax nor till these got started here

at home did I feel this necessary community; but the demands
on sticking power are enormous. (153)

My ideal is an Eskimo solstice celebration I once read about in
which in one big underground igloo the whole community
gathered and put on their annual us-against-winter play; masks,
chanting women all sitting on a bench, but swaying and miming;
men being crows, animal marionettes entering by invisible
means, and total audience enjoyment. That's a style I'd like to
reach up to. (156)

Such an ideal "reach," however, does not always fit comfortably
with Reaney's other, equally fervent, less heroic perspective on his
own and other communities. Reaney's idealism, as we shall see, is
seldom completely free of his "Punch's stick" (*Poems* 146). What I
called earlier his caricatural bias results in the depiction of communities whose "tribal signals" (for instance those of Edna and the
ladies of the Millbank Women's Institute in *The Sun and the Moon*,
or those of Stratford as depicted in *King Whistle!*) are not exactly of
the same creative and possibly noble order as those of the chanting,
swaying, and miming women in the big underground igloo (4). The
theatre should demonstrate and promote the idea of sustained
creativity, in which the playwright, the actors, and the audience are
together involved in a complex process of both seeing and form-
making. Once again, in the light of his various assertions of ontological creativity (and certainly in the light of his pedagogical impulses)
Reaney's creative affinities with Klee seem particularly apt.[5] Harold
Rosenberg has shown how in Klee's theory and art there seems to be,
neither in nature nor in the self, any fully identifiable "point of
completion." In Klee's world, he observes, ". . . all forms, past and
present, float together in a sea of potentiality." This meant that
beyond the whole critical question of "inherited styles," influences,
and the like, there "exists the art act as the irreducible essence of art
and of man, whether performed in ancient Babylon, in the jungle, in
the kindergarten, or in the test tube." In all art-acts, "Artist and
spectator alike passed from discovery to discovery, from possibility
to possibility" (*Artworks* 48–49). In Klee's own words, the artist
comes "more and more to see that the essential image of creation is
genesis." And the crucial thing about genesis is that, as a process, it
is never finished. Thus the artist, Klee says, "hazards the bold
thought that the process of creation can scarcely be over and done

with as yet, and so he extends the universal creative process both backward and forward, thus conferring duration upon genesis" ("On Modern Art" 51).

Such principles are asserted throughout Reaney's art and critical writings and, appropriately, coalesce in his statement regarding *Colours in the Dark* (in which he also acknowledges some affinity between the form of this play and Klee's painting *Magic Squares*) when he says "That's the kind of art I'd like to create out of where I was born — something that's never finished" ("Colours" essay 144). In the workshops and seminars that attended the national tour of the Donnelly trilogy, Reaney wrote, ". . . since our own plays came from a poet improvising with actors and children we had determined to show how this worked on the tour which was not to be just another road show, but an exploration of just how much we could cultivate young and old's taste for the creative process behind the trilogy" (*14 Barrels* 35). Perhaps the most extreme statement regarding the value of such a process of *form-making* creativity as an end in itself, is Reaney's observation that "I'd far rather do something that could never be done again. You know, just a thing the community does and that's it" (McKay 148). Such a position, dependent in part, as we shall see later, upon a particularly keen apprehension of the disharmonious and incoherent existence "tyrannized over by the mechanical geometry of 'go-aheadism' and 'enlightenment' " (*Myths* 262), speaks directly to what Frank Lentricchia called the "myth of radical creativity which has tempted many since Coleridge." The "alienated postromantic artist," he wrote, "becomes an exemplary figure of courage and health who teaches us that our making of gardens, baskets, rooms, and the like are acts similar to his (though, of course, less exalted), acts which may purchase some sanity for us. In a world bereft of form, form-making becomes the ultimate value, and artistic types necessarily an intellectual elite" (55). Reaney's sensibility aspires to the various spiritual and material assurances of form and form-making for the self and the "community." It also celebrates the ontologically affirmative values of art. However, such a sensibility frequently wars with an equally insistent ironic perspective, and the dialectical relationship between the two extreme positions (suggesting the *co-existence* of the "ideal" masque and the antimasque) provides both the near-messianic urgency of his radical creativity and the simultaneous disclosure of destructive "local mythologies" (Stevens, "Noble Rider" 17) with particular dramatic power. However, the juxtaposition of such competing voices, particularly in the plays since the Donnelly trilogy, can also result in an indiscriminate and uncertain dramatic tone.

In his critical observations on other Canadian writers and artists, Reaney seeks out degrees of the regionally inspired and rooted voice and radical creativity outlined in these principles. Reaney, as artist-teacher, is concerned with identifying and advancing certain "artistic types" whose achievements he finds especially beneficial and revelatory to an *emerging* community of readers, listeners, and watchers who, in time, should also become adept and willing players. An important example, especially in the earlier years of his work as a playwright and theorist-teacher, was the London painter Greg Curnoe. Curnoe, like Reaney, was busy during the sixties assembling a catalogue of images that would express different layers of local feeling and consciousness. He also, like Reaney, produced an art whose regional essence was contained within the readily identifiable idiom of a thoroughly modernist (international) aesthetic. "You want to encourage art in this town, eh?" wrote Reaney, then "I think Greg Curnoe's approach is so right — he edits Region, he loves bus transfers, he incorporates old verandah posts into his paintings. He takes a sign right off the Spittal Straw Hat Warehouse. You feel he likes reflecting where he lives. . . . You want to put on plays that express the character of this place. You look at the faces on Dundas Street — grotesque, comic, strange. Or the fantastic drifters in Wellington Square on Saturday afternoon. Or the old Negro who smokes a bediamonded hookah near the Court House. Or Jessie who wanders about on her bike" ("Broughdale"). In this appeal, and in many more yet to come proddingly, cajolingly at numbers of students, actors, writers, and directors, we hear yet again Apollinaire's enthusiastic invocation in *Zone* to the muse of a popular, thus commonplace, *and* emblematic modernity:

> You read the handbills the catalogues the singing posters
> So much for poetry this morning and the prose is in the papers
> Special editions full of crimes (9)
> . . . .
> The inscriptions on walls and signs
> The notices and plates squawk parrot-wise. (11)

or of Cocteau's impressions of the "little American girl" he created for *Parade*: "The Titanic — 'Nearer My God to Thee' — elevators . . . submarine cables . . . dynamos . . . the sheriff's daughter — Walt

Whitman ... Negroes picking maize ... the declarations of President Wilson ... the tango ... ice-cream parlors ... posters ... the list of the victims of the Lusitania ..." (qtd. in Brown, *An Impersonation* 128–29).

In his account of London, Ontario, regionalist activity in the sixties, Woodman suggests that Curnoe, especially, strove "with an almost religious devotion to keep the Second Commandment." Employing a viewpoint advanced by Rosenberg, Woodman continues:

> ... if a person lives in what he believes to be a sacred world, he *finds* rather than *makes* his art, and that the Old Testament banned graven images because the natural objects of its landscape belonged to a world of miracle and could at any moment 'start to glisten with meaning and become memorable.' The same is true, according to Rosenberg, of Walt Whitman: 'instead of constructing images, he catalogues objects of the American scene, the idea being that art is anything that appears in the aura of the wonderful.' ["London (Ont.)"]

Reaney has continued to practice such an activity, which, in an essay recounting his initial exploration of Winnipeg, he called providing "an imagery count of the environment" ("Manitoba" 96). In his graduate course on Ontario Literature and Culture, he recommends several authoritative guides to the physiographical as well as cultural landmarks and bearings. These include everything from John Kenneth Galbraith's *The Scotch* to Father Joseph François Lafitau's *Customs of the American Indians Compared with the Customs of Primitive Tribes*, from Tim Bucke's *Cosmic Consciousness* to *The Ontario Leaf Album*, which was "useful to enable students to take time to look around themselves at leaves and bark; there's a great deal of mooning about forested landscapes but precise knowledge shows real love and breeds the same quality. Tree worship is to be encouraged" ("ABC" 2). In Reaney's vision and aesthetic, such imagery-counts reflect both the "aura of the wonderful," and something of that literacy which discloses, as Steiner describes it, "a personal, unforced intimacy with the names and shapes of the natural world, with flower and tree, with the measure of the seasons and the rising and setting of the stars." The principal energies of our literature, he asserts, "draw constantly on this set of recognitions. But to our housed, metallic sensibilities, they have become largely artificial and decorative. Do not, today, enquire of the reader next to you whether he can identify, from personal encounter, even a part of the flora, of the astronomy, which served Ovid and Shakespeare, Spenser and Goethe, as a current alphabet" (*Bluebeard* 84–85). The artist-teacher in Reaney, then, celebrates the "aura of the wonderful," as it exists in itself and as it encourages in a separate, closely related activity, a rich degree of environmental enquiry that teaches us to see where we are. We are also taught to read much more sensitively and profoundly into the recorded testimony of an artistic élite who, presumably, scratched their several ways through to universality on their own locally coloured tree trunks. Many years after endorsing Curnoe's collage technique, and even more years after expressing a similar bias in such an early poem as "The Antiquary," with its "jars and casks" of wildly assorted gleanings from a purely literary environment ("Wordsworth's vegetables," "the coughs of Emily Brontë," the "urine of Dr. John Donne") (*Poems* 7), Reaney was still urging playwrights, as a creative exercise, to make collage character dolls "based on the humanity of their area . . . the dolls to be made of local materials: e.g., cedar twigs from Lake Simcoe, Pre-Cambrian pebbles from Bancroft, street car transfers from Queen Street West and pages of the Sarnia *Lambton-Observer*" ("Coathanger" 17).

Viewing the local controversy surrounding Reaney's season of Canadian plays in 1966, Curnoe wrote,

> It looks as if we are going to see a public dialogue between the local view point and the international view point, or between the manufacturer and consumer or between the amateur and the professional but it becomes obvious that no dialogue is possible because Reaney doesn't stand still. His identity and what it stands for is developing rapidly and in a revolutionary direction. He may actually have found an answer to the stigma of "the theatre" and all of its class implications. . . . It is obvious that plays, inventions, songs, etc. are created from points of view, that a person's environment is central to what he does, that a knowledge and sympathy for Reaney's background and environment (rural Souwesto Canadian University) is necessary for an understanding of his work.
>
> It is also interesting to consider that John Cage has compared himself to the camera manufacturer (which is the position that Reaney has put himself in) and that the other notable (and for

me valid) use of amateurs that comes to mind is "the happenings" and some of them (notably James Dine's) are autobiographical. They are also very regional. Finally consider that parents can and probably will go to see their children be in Jamie's plays in the same way that they go to see them play in a pee wee hockey game.

Around this time in London, Curnoe designed the set and costumes for a production of Reaney's marionette play, *Red Riding Hood*, in which Granny was a yellow tin teapot — an *"objet trouvé* — and when she spoke her lid wagged; children shrieked with joy at this." Their parents, Reaney recalled, "deep sunk in what Blake calls the Pit of Ulro, usually walked out in a huff" ("Letter from James Reaney" 4).

Reaney first encountered Curnoe and other London artists in Selwyn Dewdney's house. It was here, he wrote in a personal tribute, a "farewell portrait of Selwyn Dewdney," that "I saw my first Jack Chambers painting . . . here also I first heard the name of Greg Curnoe and heard tales of the high school and community satirized in *Wind Without Rain.*" One of Dewdney's paintings, Reaney observed, particularly impressed him:

> . . . it was of a tree whose root taps deeply through rock the waters of an underground stream. A great deal of the political and creative traditions in our city here do the same, and not only for our region, for, when you realize that not only Jack Chambers and Greg Curnoe, but Norval Morrissay were visitors at this house you can then trace a far-reaching influence that is never going to stop. . . . Like the buried stream of his painting, Selwyn Dewdney lies at the root of a great many freeing personalities and artistic achievements in our society. He was one of our identifiers; for example, our local river is called the Thames, but it was in this man's house that I first heard that its correct name is Askunesippi — Antler River. ("Farewell Portrait" 80)[6]

Within a short time of his encounter with the circle of artists associated with Dewdney, Reaney had established his Alpha Centre where the Listeners' Theatre Workshop "group of people" tried "to write a play history of their London, Ontario called *Antler River*, the Indian name for the Thames River" (Editorial, *Alphabet* 13:2). Implied throughout Reaney's assessment of Curnoe's techniques as an artist, his suggestions of how to "put on plays that express the character of this place," his course in Ontario Literature and Culture, and his sympathy with Dewdney's role as an "identifier," is an increasing predilection for documentary material. In Margaret Atwood's review of several years of Reaney's *Alphabet*, she says "The documentarist's (and *Alphabet*'s) stance towards such raw material, and thus towards everyday life, is that it is intrinsically meaningful but the meaning is hidden; it will only manifest itself if the observer makes the effort to connect." In *Alphabet*, "He merely gathered pieces of writing, both 'literary' and 'non-literary,' and other subjects . . . and let the echoes speak for themselves." For Atwood, Reaney's journal was indicative of a "Canadian habit of mind" that "for whatever reason — perhaps a history and a social geography which both seem to lack coherent shape — is synthetic. 'Taste' and 'technique' are both of less concern . . . than is the ever-failing but ever-renewed attempt to pull all the pieces together, to discover the whole of which one can only trust one is a part" ("Eleven Years" 62–63). Reaney's critical assent for a wide range of Canadian writing, painting, and music is first disclosed in *Alphabet*, where what he much later called the "Identifier Effect" was practised. Looking back on the years of *Alphabet*, he wrote,

> In the end, what does all this produce socially? I think it might be called the Identifier Effect. For example, another student of Frye, Jay Macpherson, read an article on the Narcissus myth at the Graduate Club in 1958; another student afterwards said how much the mirror imagery reminded her, a twin, of being a girl in a mirror; this gave me the idea for a magazine called *Alphabet* in which you started off with a myth — Narcissus, and also presented its most extreme displacement — a document on being a twin; in between these poles you magnetized the other things little magazines published. For nineteen issues, a new myth each time, we kept identifying the cities, gardens, and wastelands around us in a way that would not have been possible without the drive to clarify started by this teacher [Frye]. ("Identifier Effect" 30)

In an editorial tribute to Pratt in *Alphabet* 8, Reaney commented upon the "imaginative force which sees ways of making more meaning out of the world, finding the clue that joins up the different maze like levels of our inner and outer worlds." Pratt, Reaney asserts, was a supreme story-teller in this "muskeg of indifference spotted with colonies of inherited, somehow stale, tradition. What our poets should be doing," he concludes, "is to show us how to *identify* our society out of this situation" (5). As Woodman has observed, the "publication of *Alphabet* launched a new phase in Reaney's career, one in which he became more actively involved in the development of a Canadian identity" (*Reaney* 25). Among the many whose efforts to "identify" Reaney critically endorses in *Alphabet* were Wilfred Watson, R.K. Webb, Margaret Atwood, John Beckwith, Jack Chambers, John Hirsch, Gwendolyn MacEwen, bpNichol, George Bowering, and Alden Nowlan.

A sort of updating of such a list, and a much more personal appreciation of their several achievements as identifiers, is provided in *14 Barrels*. While in Halifax during the tour of the Donnelly trilogy that *14 Barrels* records, Reaney tells us that he recollected something from E.H. Gombrich's *Art and Illusion* "which I read when last at home — 'schema and correction' — our imagination projects a schema into the reality chaos around us; we keep projecting and re-projecting until we mysteriously get it right." Just as the Donnelly cycle itself was such a projected, re-projected schema into the "Bottomless" well of "old newspapers, registry office records, criminal records for Middlesex and Huron Counties" (139), which held the story of the Donnellys, the journal account in *14 Barrels* is a projected schema into, first of all, the "reality chaos" of a theatre tour; secondly, into the nature and spirit of Canada; and, finally, into the imaginative-creative process itself.

Throughout the book, Reaney asks us to see the land, buildings, and people, through the multitudinous windows of other artists — painters, writers, musicians — whose names seem to come to his mind as naturally, as inevitably, as do the names of cities and streets. Here we find Lemoine Fitzgerald, whose *Doc Snider's House* is "the essential painting if you want to understand Winnipeg in the winter." The possibility of such a work welcoming visitors to the Winnipeg airport, Reaney remarks, was spoiled when "the artists from Chicago came up and took over the Manitoba School of Fine Arts. . . . " What serves as the airport mural instead is "a big structuralist thing (by Eli Bornstein) that suggests a reconstituted airplane, carefully taken apart and then carefully stacked like pick-up sticks here and there and Piet Mondrian knows where — over there" (32). Just outside of Winnipeg, into St. Boniface with its "Franco-Manitoban hinterland" (34), we find the territory whose identity has been established by

Gabrielle Roy, whose "powerful technique," Reaney wrote in a much earlier account, "puts the so-called real world of life here into the much more real world of art" ("Writing"). In *14 Barrels*, there is Réal Berard with his "Giant animaux, chateaux de glace, petite esquimaudes, oiseaux, objects divers — at last a decent, professional showman or rather showwoman for the carnival; such a relief after the Playboy Bunnies in front of the frat houses in Ontario" (34). Others include W.O. Mitchell, Chester Duncan, David Milne, Emily Carr ("who celebrated D'Sonoqua, the Indian goddess of birth and death" [57]), Murray Schafer (whose circle "is extremely interested in sounds and the trilogy just happens to be a complex web of little and big sounds" [65]), Sheila Watson (whose "great novel *Double Hook* started so much going for anyone interested in metaphor" [82]), John Hirsch (who, in Ottawa for an interview "sails by in a blue suit" [110] — a sartorial observation somewhat less vivid than Hirsch's description of Reaney first arriving in Winnipeg "in a blue suit made by a blind tailor" [41]), Charles G.D. Roberts ("misunderstood artist . . . you feel he is the forests and the rivers . . . maybe he should have married a she-bear out of the woods he naturalized in as a boy" [132]), Ernest Buckler ("the Maritime Hesiod"), Alden Nowlan, Alex Colville (the colours, "green and blue in the interiors we frequented," at Mount Allison University, "seemed to be from an Alex Colville painting, and you felt happy right away" [146]), Michael Ondaatje, and bpNichol ("glad bp showed up because concrete choruses in *Handcuffs* were influenced by poems of his I set up in *Alphabet*" [172]). Reviewing such a list only adds more fuel to Reaney's exasperated cry "Why do fellow Canucks keep asking what their identity is? Jesus Christ, Isabella Crawford, Ned Pratt, Stephen Leacock, Emily Carr . . . long ago spent their creative energy in breeding works of art which describe what our soul is like in letters 9 miles high" ("Letter from James Reaney" 7). Such a nearly evangelical advocacy of the more recent story-tellers, painters, musicians, and poets — mythmakers and "documentarists" alike — throughout Reaney's critical writing is a central aspect of his *idea* of a Canadian theatre. He believes that our theatre can profit from such *diverse* signs of regional and national expression, that it can, and must, draw upon such material for its own stories, characters, images, and the like: in short, theatre must not be creatively isolated from everything else that is happening. He also believes that a critical *discourse*, in which such artists' achievements help to direct and inform thought, feeling, and memory, to provide those creative "echoes" that, as Atwood observed, "speak for themselves," is essential if our theatre is, in fact, to be ours, providing in its own way the Identifier Effect.

In his advocacy of the all-Canadian season of plays in 1966, Reaney insisted upon the development of "our own style of writing and acting . . . then we can turn to the classics and good contemporaries — and put them on with a point of view — instead of letting them put us on." Such a development, he was to argue some years later, is impossible without a wider educational base: "We can't have a theatre with any depth to it until we get some sort of literary and historical programme going" ("Identifier Effect" 8). To help promote such a program, in which the theatre is recognized as a central vehicle in the articulation of regional and national consciousness, Reaney began writing a series of "Occasional Theatre Letters." He called this series *Halloween*

because that festival is the one theatrical event put on in this country which doesn't seem to need directors brought in from foreign lands; it is put on by thousands who are really into their parts and are not just worrying as the actors do at the St Lawrence Centre in Toronto about the dread possibility that the director might let the rehearsal go on past the time for a coffee break; the audience for Halloween numbers in the millions, understands the script thoroughly even when it involves the most esoteric and ancient matter of Light's yearly fight with Darkness; no character or situation is beyond the technical range of the participants — I have seen them dressed up as everything from TV sets to tramps to demons to Adolf Hitler and all without Canada Council support, yet fed so well that the participants can sometimes barely struggle home from the take. So everything that Halloween stands for — direct, sentimental, sensational primitive theatre is one thing this series of letters is going to be about. ("Letter from James Reaney" 2)

Halloween is Reaney's "rough theatre," imbued with the directness of an unembarrassed hyperbolism; it is sensational, popular, effortlessly accessible, and yet revelatory of universal Manichean divisions. Like many others in our time, working in different media, Reaney objects to much of what Eric Bentley called the "thin-lipped, thin-blooded . . . prestige of dry irony" (198) by according special value to some of those "unsophisticated" sources of art that have had to disencumber themselves of critical disregard and misunderstanding. As Peter Brook observed in his celebration of the "rough theatre,"

> every attempt to revitalize the theatre has gone back to the popular source. Meyerhold had the highest aims, he sought to present all of life on the stage, his revered master was Stanislavsky, his friend was Chekhov; but in fact it was to the circus and the music hall that he turned. Brecht was rooted in the cabaret: Joan Littlewood longs for a fun-fair: Cocteau, Artaud, Vakhtangov, the most improbable bedfellows, all these highbrows return to the people. (*Empty* 68)

A similar point is made by Peter Brooks in his examination of modern fiction's "renewal" through the use of popular forms, and of what Claude Levi-Strauss called "mythemes" (x). Later, in an examination of Reaney's plays, especially beginning with *Listen to the Wind*, we shall see more clearly the degree to which such popular forms are directly assimilated into the verbal and scenic structures and such "mythemes" used to inform different levels of story and style. The "coarse vigour" (Brook, *Empty* 76) of Reaney's *Halloween* carries with it much of what a theatre of immediate accessibility requires and what many playwrights, directors, and theorists of the sixties especially emphasized: a spontaneous, unselfconscious communitarian flow of energy, shared languages, and illusions. That such an impulse in Reaney as in many others (for example in some of the works of Luscombe, Juliani, Brook, Artaud, Schechner, Judith Malina and Julian Beck at the Living Theatre), is co-existent with far less accessible symbolism, historical and literary allusion, and private reverie is one of the paradoxes that renders the creative embrace of popular sources problematical.

Reaney's *Halloween* letters, along with many passages in *14 Barrels*, provide the best evidence of his artistic and critical interest in the sources, forms, and aims of theatrical activity, of the creative continuum within which both the dramatic *text* and the *performance* exist. Like so many other poet-playwrights of our century — among them especially Yeats,[7] Cocteau, Eliot, Auden, and Bertolt Brecht — Reaney mourns the loss of a single, authoritative idea of what the theatre should do or be. Yet the impulse to restore such an *idea* remains unbroken — as indeed it has since the seminal rumblings over the *Gesamtkunstwerk* in the writings of Wagner in 1850. As Francis Fergusson has observed,

We cannot understand the arts and the visions of particular playwrights, nor the limited perfection of minor dramatic genres, without some more catholic conception of the art in general. Thus the prior effort to appreciate contemporary playwrights leads behind them and beyond them. It leads, I think, to the dramatic art of Shakespeare and the dramatic art of Sophocles, both of which were developed in theatres which focused, at the centre of the life of the community, the complementary insights of the whole culture. We do not have such a theatre, nor do we see how to get it. But we need the "Idea of a Theatre," both to understand the masterpieces of drama at its best, and to get our own bearings in our own time. (15)

For Reaney, one of the possible models for such a theatre lay in the Indian Forest Theatre at Oshweken in the Grand River Valley in Ontario, "our native Bayreuth in a far truer sense than the Stratford Festival" (*14 Barrels* 60–61). This theatre, established at the Six Nations Indian Reserve, has annually mounted a series of plays by William Smith and others dealing with the history and folklore of the Indian community from the founding of the Iroquois Confederacy, through to the involvement of Joseph Brant and Cornflower in the American Revolution, to the migration of the Iroquois from New York State to Ontario, to more recent history, involving accounts of E. Pauline Johnson, and the activities of the Grand River Indians in the wars of our century.[8] In *14 Barrels*, Reaney describes a scene from *The Life of Pauline Johnson* where ". . . she comes to Ottawa and meets Duncan Campbell and Archibald Lampman in evening dress at a poetry recital. In front of the outdoor stage winds a small creek for actors' canoes to come up; and all around stretch the forests and farms of the Six Nations country. That's theatre!" (61). The pageantry — both natural and manufactured — the active communitarianism evidenced in the acting, directing, costuming, and designing of the productions and the rich mythic-documentary sources and reach of the plays themselves are of obvious appeal to Reaney's ideas of what the theatre should be and do. On another, less personal level, we find a suggestion of what has sometimes been evident in this century's periodic interest in *al fresco* drama, from, say, Louis H. Parker's *Warwickshire Pageant* in 1905, through to various outdoor festivals in the American south and southwest, to Paul Green's "symphonic drama" *The Lost Colony* (see Free and Lower), to such outdoor productions as *Tecumseh* in Chillocothe,

Ohio (Aronson 3). "In these days when the world is talking vaguely of another great renaissance of the art of the theatre," Sheldon Cheney writes, "and is waiting expectantly for the new artists who will express their age as characteristically as the Greeks have expressed theirs and Shakespeare his, one may read a new meaning into the recent revival of interest in the *al fresco* drama" (*Open-Air* 1–2).

In his first *Halloween* letter, Reaney impatiently poses the question: "Why do drama critics look blank in this country when you mention the Indian Forest Theatre at Oshweken, Ontario? Does a theatre devoted to husbanding the traditions of the Six Nation tribes mean nothing in an era when we're all wondering how we can do this with our own shattered cultural patterns?" ("Letter from James Reaney" 6). The cultural mission of theatre, then, is clear. It is to help sort out, shape, and shore up the fragments of personal and collective, present and past experience that, like the historical and mythical interweaving of the Iroquois plays, will identify our selves and our place, providing as well, one would hope, what Yeats called "new images to the dreams of youth" (*Essays* 242). Reaney's first *Halloween* letter exudes such a dream of youth in its unqualified reaction to existing cultural institutions at Stratford, Toronto, and Niagara-on-the-Lake. The anti-intellectualism of these theatres, their absence of serious ideological and creative discourse, their resistance to innovation, and their ignorance of a possibly supportive literary and artistic milieu already strengthening its hold on young readers, listeners, and lookers is depicted by Reaney as a grievous betrayal of creative energy and money.

Reaney's attack, like that of Ryga noted earlier, is hyperbolically calculated to unsettle various artistic and financial vested interests and to alert existing and potential critics to the *real* needs of a theatre that purports to articulate "the complementary insights of a whole community." Peter Brook's account of the "Deadly Theatre," and the responsibility of theatre critics towards it, is similar to Reaney's irritation over critics who "look blank" at or fail "to pick up the trail" ("Letter from James Reaney" 6) of centrally innovative experiments and achievements. Brook remarks that

> Our relations with critics may be strained in a superficial sense: but in a deeper one the relationship is absolutely necessary: like the fish in the ocean, we need one another's devouring talents to perpetuate the sea bed's existence. However, this devouring

is not nearly enough: we need to share the endeavour to rise to the surface. This is what is hard for all of us. The critic is part of the whole and whether he writes his notices fast or slow, short or long, is not really important. Has he an image of how a theatre could be in his community and is he revising this image around each experience he receives? How many critics see their job this way? (*Empty* 32)

Reaney's response would be not very many. The *Halloween* letters and, especially, *14 Barrels* (which reprints most of the newspaper reviews the trilogy received during the tour — as a sort of critical exhibit) contain many indictments of critical inertia, ignorance, and indifference. The fullest statement is, perhaps, this from *14 Barrels*:

> Like the London Drama Bench, the Toronto Drama Bench profess interest in original plays but were silent about our presence in Toronto; the one exception was the John Fraser review of *St Nick*. Advance notices; yes, but it is reactions to the drama itself that are needed. Yes, we were penniless and could not afford any ads, but . . . how often does a critic get a chance to see a whole trilogy in one week and then in one day? If our culture were properly alive you'd have the critics out in front, not lagging behind. As an artist I don't want praise, I want understanding and dialogue from reviewers and critics. The imagery of their articles (if they cannot produce any theories) should provide audience and writer alike with a vision of what *kind* of theatre we might have and should have. There's a whole range of critical activity that should be taking place which is notoriously absent and an organization called a Drama Bench you would think would have the root of the matter somewhere in its collective bowels; perhaps it may, at any rate, here are some things it would be nice then to have: reviews of Stratford productions that use Frye's Shakespearean criticism. A book on the European productions that influence Stratford productions of the classics; articles and books on the provenance of the formulas the so-called 'new' Toronto theatres are using; articles and books on what playwrights should be up to next in this country: we need more of this sort of informed and native cultural leadership. Otherwise, the cultural bell-wether is always New York (Clive Barnes — "Miss Redgrave always reminds me of a startled fawn") or Wroclaw or Stratford on Avon. (170)

On another occasion during the tour, in Hamilton, Reaney reflected upon a similar assortment of social, aesthetic, and national obligations for serious criticism:

> It is the meeting of human experience with, and the translation of human community back and forth into, myth, rituals & ceremony, that keeps me focused on this kind of criticism. . . . One of the dreams often discussed in bars on the tour has been the idea of somewhere a theatre we can call home where we would take poetics, take the verbal universe and translate them into the community of a theatre; this is what the regional theatres (and the National Arts Centre) should be doing . . . as the company's work with students and kids proves, the community deserves to be trusted; you can't feed them muddled avant-garde and *Camelot* pap forever; what our critics should be boosting and our audiences should be demanding is a theatre that is a Globe, takes in the universe, the heights and depths of the soul, like the Frances Yates Memory Theatre. . . . (*14 Barrels* 160–61)

In his first *Halloween* letter, Yates is also recalled as Reaney answers his own question, ". . . what would you do if you were to be given a theatre?" "My answer," he says, is

> somebody give it to us and find out. To my mind a theatre might be a small one, but not a disused factory, perhaps one freshly built along some such a scheme as the Globe Theatre (see Frances Yates' *Theatre of the World*) even perhaps with the cosmology of Robertson Davies' recent remarkable trilogy in mind . . . well at any rate this building would house the actors (there should be a farm for them to grow their food on and their drink and also to let them get rid of their nerve troubles by wielding hoes) who would join themselves to the community they lived in by writing the story of the place they were the intellectual centre of. . . . I'd like to have a large room in this theatre where all the children of the city would come in regularly to play at the great game of theatre. ("Letter from James Reaney" 8)

Somewhere in here lurks another version of Reaney's "farmer . . . with the copy of Livy's History of Rome" celebrated in *The Dismissal*

(154): a whole acting company in creative physical and intellectual accord with various theatrical crafts and arts, with a surrounding community with its particular history and stories, with the demands of serious, informed, highly literate discourse about the possible *ideas* of a theatre, and with hoes. It is, indeed, the "dream of youth," but one (fortunately) tempered on occasion, especially throughout *14 Barrels*, by Reaney's never-forsaken irony as he witnesses various members of the touring company on and off stage in a manner more reminiscent of Vincent Crummles in the provinces than fully initiated inhabitants of the imaginatively reconstituted Garden. But the meddling, modifying irony, playing the same role within the Culture-Counter-Culture dialectic as it did within that of the ideal masque and antimasque, does not challenge the underlying seriousness of Reaney's advocacy of generously open critical discourse. The search for an *idea* of the theatre that will articulate verbally and spatially (in part the problem is architectural) the private, communal, and national "purpose of playing," is never abandoned in the *Halloween* letters and *14 Barrels*.

In these essays, the various expressions of a resolutely global theatrical destination, behind which we find, among other models, the Greek theatre, the Elizabethan theatre of the world, and the messianic Shavianism of the preface to *Back to Methuselah*,[9] are frequently counterbalanced by a far more particularized advocacy of what regional and national stories need to be told in Canada. In *The Struggle of the Modern*, Stephen Spender wrote of the penchant for "exploiting the historic past as contemporary dream, fortress and granary of stored impressions, which are accessible to a modern, just as he uses childhood for the same purpose" (80). Such an acute historical consciousness, ontologically revelational, dictates some of the subjects suggested by Reaney for theatrical expression:

We have all sorts of stories that are never told: here are some of them — Tecumseh, the Horsburgh Affair, Wacousta (our first prose romance and obsessed with our great national problem of borders), the Baldoon Mystery . . . the attempt to take over our culture by the Yankees in the sixties, Professor Dale and the young Mackenzie King at University College in the nineties when the students struck for free speech after Dale's dismissal; the Crowe Case — in short, the sort of thing Russian theatre is right into right now with plays about Lermontov and Pushkin, not just these figures but the eras around them.

He elaborates on some of these subjects, and suggests others, throughout *14 Barrels*. Meeting the daughter of William Dale (who became the central figure in *The Dismissal*) "set him thinking of a new play. . . ." In Dale's journals, he says,

> . . . he speaks of the way the people of Ontario are 'estranged' from their University by the practice of hiring staff from abroad. As an early 'nativist' he is denounced by such join-the-Statesers as Goldwin Smith and fired by such intellectual leaders as Sir William Mulock. In his journals he also wonders if some day we will have not only a country as opposed to a colony, but also such fruits of a secure civilization as sculpture, painting, theatre. . . . (17)

The Reverend Horsbourgh story, he tells us, was treated first by Theatre Passe Muraille ("got ahead of me on this one" [17–18]). Reaney says ". . . if ever the Calvinist heart of Souwesto revealed itself, it did so in the fifties persecution at Chatham of this United Church minister" (17). A possible puppet play is considered while in Winnipeg, "the idea of which is supposed to be — better, more humane streets while its colour design is to be based on the David Milne painting, 'Billboards' " (40). In Vancouver, there is another example of "whole university departments Americanized overnight" (69).

"Strange," he writes,

> after all these years of Canadians being students of philosophy and sociology, that the country still cannot provide any of the breed, not only for philosophy departments and sociology departments, but even self-employed home-staying ones who might come to a student lecture series. There's a play here and in discussing the story-line with friends in History they tell me that the trick is this: in the final climatic scene when the Premier of the Province is brought in and the Yanks are being forced to take out citizenship at long last, see that the wives also take it out. No, I couldn't write that; that would be xenophobic, cruel, malicious, etc. etc. On the other hand, would it be cruel, malicious and adelphophobic to say some time dramatically that Canucks are too wambly, shy and quite unable to prevent themselves from being culturally raped over and over again? (70)

In Edmonton, he writes, ". . . we did an improvisation about rats in an experiment; one of the tragic stories heard on tour was of a man who had for years experimented in sensory deprivation, no doubt doing some of the things the actors and the students thought of acting out in the rat-mazes; when he learned that the CIA was using his published papers to train torturers in Uruguay, he jumped into the river" (82). This story was to become the basis of Reaney's mime-play *Traps*, first produced in 1980. In Medicine Hat, ". . . something hasn't happened here that's happened everywhere else we've been — some late little devastating twist from the media has failed to virus here and you could work up something in community drama that might be very pure and kind. I wonder if in the next ten years our group will produce other groups that seed off from places we're caught in to places they're free to grow in as long as they like" (95). The legends of the Ottawa valley, he suggests, having met Robin Mathews's "young actor-scholars" called "The Great Canadian Theatre Company," are a "rich source" for theatrical treatment, ". . . the only problems are how to do lumber rafts on stage and how to focus on just one or two legends so you can see your way through the motif-tangle." Also, in Ottawa, Reaney suggested film projects based upon the poems of Archibald Lampman and Duncan Campbell Scott, "where everybody chalks these men's poems continuously on as many streets of the town as possible" (107). In Fredericton, Reaney wonders, "if, I've or I'm passing the window where that American professor holed up for three months and wouldn't come out because he was protesting the identification photos on the new library cards." This professor, Reaney learns,

is presently married to a bishop's niece and with fifty cats lives in the wilds somewhere across the river. . . . It's typical of our country, I reflect, that Joyce Carol Oates was the first to fiction-alize this fantastic story — she being an Amerk at Windsor: I'm itching to handle it somehow — you'd have this basic box set — his office with the waste paper baskets as latrines and police, student rioters, enemies, no one, deans knocking at the door and trying to come in the window. The parents were rich psychia-trists in New York or New Jersey and it must be our fate to attract such thunderbolts because I know I've talked to people who fled McGill because of "those dreadful pseudo-Maoists from the Bronx." (128–29)

Still other topics were suggested by Reaney's interest in Canadian critical thought. In his defence of the 1966 summer session of Canadian plays, he suggested that a "... theatre could be built up around the ideas of Norrie Frye and Marshall McLuhan" ("Reaney Replies"). Ten years later, in the first *Halloween* letter, he expanded upon the idea:

> ... you could make some really total theatrical experiences out of (a) a satirical revue based on McLuhan's *Gutenburg Galaxy* — can't you see those nasty printers and Ramists drying up brains and causing Gonerils and Regans to sprout up all over Europe with assembly line techniques; well, perhaps you can't, but there's something there that would be fun to try. Similarly with Frye and Bucke I find both *Fearful* and *Anatomy* to be great sources for stage experiences; in the case of Anatomy I feel that you could found the theatre's acting school on the discussion of eiron and bomolachos alone — a new commedia de l'arte as a matter of fact. Bucke's *Cosmic Consciousness* would probably shape up as a play about the London Lunatic Asylum called "Mad Song" with two great trees in the set — one evil and dead, one alive and blossoming. Ballets begin to spring to mind and if Rudolph would only leave us alone maybe we could do something else than *Swan Lake* over and over and over again. I think one of my biggest problems is that I'm not an existentialist, but really probably an essentialist so that my ideas of play and doing mental dances with metaphors may seem rather unfashionable in an age so dominated by Angst. We have to work out *our* own way through and given my roots I can only say that the above is what grows out of me. . . . I do believe with Blake that you can transform this world we live in, and the theatre I'm after represents the sort of mad marriage I've just described. ("Letter from James Reaney" 8–9)

In a workshop session at Mount Allison University conducted in this same year, Reaney explained to his actors and directors that the structures of thought and feeling underlying his basic plot owed much "not only to *Seven Samurai* but also to the levels and modes of Frye's Anatomy and the states in William Blake's system" ("Cycle" 77).[10] Jay Macpherson has examined some of the images and props in *One-Man Masque* in terms of their relationship to "the most basic Fryekit do-it-yourself can-opener" (70); Richard Stingle explores many facets of the connection between Frye and Reaney in his discussion of *Gyroscope*, as does Ross Woodman in his study of the poems and plays up to *Colours in the Dark*. Needless to say, the Letters, as well as *14 Barrels* encourage such a critical discourse. But they do so in a fairly typical Reaneyesque fashion. Reaney's tone throughout these occasional ruminations on theatre and art shifts constantly, challenging the reader to sort through the cacophony of idealism, combativeness, fierce nationalism, satire, defensiveness, mischief, practicality, silliness, hyperbolic posturing, genuinely held convictions, and *reductio ad absurdum* asides and throwaways.

It is clear that his advocacy of a theatre with genuine roots in a regional and national consciousness and style is based upon much more than a narrow and parochial concept of regionalism or nationalism (despite the churlish interjections "she being an Amerk at Windsor" and so on), that it is informed by a particular reading of human history, experience, and value — a reading to which the Bible, Blake, Frye, Marshall McLuhan, and others have made their contributions. It is such a reading that underlies his uneasiness with the cultural imperialism to which Canada has so often been subjected, whether in the attempts to perform Peter Weiss and Eugène Ionesco in those "uncertain college productions with sweet virtuous people imitating nasty," or in the sudden arrival in his home county of the Stratford Theatre Festival in 1953. This unease was expressed in a review of the opening of the Festival Theatre in which the Stratford, Ontario, setting is portrayed as a fantasy of Old World place names that "may have appeared to some natives as being rather embarrassing." Not, however, to "a very clever publicist, Mr. Tom Patterson." One wishes, Reaney writes,

there were something a bit more heroic behind the Festival than this: a sturdy native stage tradition of great hoards of cultured citizens reading Shakespeare to each other for years back, but such is not the case. Besides bearing up under the name and providing a very pretty setting, the town has not really deserved its good luck; buying it with wit money is not deserving it. Stratford is part of that doctor-dominated civilization of lawns under which Western Ontario has long lain asleep. When the doctors are Sir Thomas Browne and Faustuses, this sort of civilization is all right, but everyone knows they are not. ("Stratford Festival" 112–13)

Copeau's man in the audience who can murmur "in his heart and with his heart the same words spoken by the man on the stage" (qtd. in Ghéon 15), is not, in brief, the one tending the lawns. No adequate literary and historical program has evolved which would begin to bridge the cultural and creative gulf between spectator and actor, between the surrounding life and the play, and enhance the Identifier Effect of such a theatre. To a degree, the arrival of Sir Tyrone Guthrie, Tanya Moiseiwitsch, Alec Guinness, and the sound of the 8:15 p.m. canon, "heard far out in the country" as the "usual crowd walked along beneath the trees behind the Normal School and turned to its right into a tent theatre whose interior, with its blue drooping ceiling, resembled that of a pavilion in old romance," was exhilarating to Reaney ("Stratford Festival" 113). But at the same time, there is a note throughout Reaney's first, and subsequent, impressions of this theatre of seeing it from the circumference, or from some place in the still "unknown territory." It was to the exploring of this territory as a "space you inhabit not just with your body but with your head" that Reaney turned as a writer of verse and of drama. All of the plays are given to the representation of such landmarks and bearings as the physical landscape, the social environment (religious, political, educational), and what Frye calls the "cultural" as well as the "historical" past. Our culture, Frye argues, is "our real and repressed social past, not the past of historical record but the great dream of the arts, which keep recurring to haunt us with a sense of how little we know of the real dimensions of our experience" (*Creation* 13). Altogether, Reaney's many plays resemble a giant canvas on which the landscapes and the multilevel exposition of social, cultural, and historical documents and narratives exist in a complex relationship to both real and imagined space and time. The accumulation and presentation of such detailed observations is, finally, informed by Reaney's essentialist's predilection for myth, metaphor, and pattern through which the ordinary becomes monumental.

I I I

We have the country itself; I never fail to find books on the physiography of the country exciting, particularly ones about my native province. The moment you start thinking about the history of the land's shape you start to think of a poem. . . . ("Canadian Poet's Predicament" 284)

Throughout *14 Barrels*, Reaney presents vivid accounts of the landscape as an essential Identifier. George Woodcock has observed that "It is in regions that landscape combines with history to create traditions. . . . the growing regionalist consciousness of Canadian artists and poets is of obvious importance to our vision of the future of this country as well as to the history of its arts. . . . if there is anything to which modern man seeks to place himself in totemic relationship, it is the land" (37). The ideal of such a totemic relationship lies at the heart of the Donnelly tragedy itself. As Mr. Donnelly proclaims in *Sticks & Stones*,

> Because I loved my land so and stuck to it
> I killed and in turn you broke my bones, burnt my home
> Harvested me and my sons like sheaves and stood
> Us to die upon our ground
> Where now nothing will ever grow.
> And this earth in my hand, the earth of my farm
> That I fought for and was smashed and burnt for
>
> .   .   .   .
>
> Now my body belongs to its dust
> Which dust once belonged to me. (71)

And it is there in Reaney's work from the beginning, in the poet's frequently reiterated close relationship to the land in such poems as "The Birth of Venus" (1947), "Winter's Tales" (1949), "The Plum Tree" (1949), "The Upper Canadian" (1949), "The Great Lakes Suite" (1949), and "The Morning Dew" (1958). A totemic vision inspires, especially, the speaker's relationship to the land throughout all stages of "The Young Traveller," where, as George Bowering observed of Reaney's Middlesex County generally, nature "is inhabited by the human imagination and social memory" (4), as it does the careful, precise observations that inform "The Great Lakes Suite," "In This Round Place," and many other poems.

After leaving the "flat, level fields of West Nissouri Township," where "people's lives seemed to be cut out into more magnetic designs than anywhere else in the country," on the beginning of the national tour of the Donnelly trilogy, Reaney flew over northern Ontario:

> Outside the porthole, the fur of the planet strokes the glass;
> beneath us, the black, unending forest of Northern Ontario rolls

along; pictographs, Bearwalkers and big stone nests made by shamans to have eagle-dreams in are down there somewhere as well as our two trucks filled with the props and the fourteen barrels all moving towards the same place I'm going, but in a different capsule that's not quite so superhuman. (*14 Barrels* 31)

This elegant and moving stroke of the planet's fur, however, is soon enough roughened by "grim fantasies." These are the very forests which produce *Time*, the Chicago papers, the *New York Times* and *Portnoy's Complaint*: "the reason I stopped subscribing to Partisan Review — I can see the bleeding stumps." Then the Manitoba farms "start unrolling with river, silver pocket of lower Lake Winnipeg" (*14 Barrels* 32), and, in St. Boniface, the elms and oaks which suggest "however fleetingly — Quebec, Paris, Martinique, Pondicherry — strained through veils and scrims of prairie dust and flatness and railways and stockyards" (*14 Barrels* 34). Countless memory-shadows: images of the land which situate themselves in the centre of reverie and consciousness, dichotomous images juxtaposing the idyllic with the grotesque, unaccommodated and unaccommodating nature with the bleeding stumps, Bearwalker with Southern Ontario junk mail, Martinique with the stockyards — Reaney's shifting perspective keeps working the landscape into stories of different hue and meaning.

He recalls studying about the Selkirk Settlement, while staying near the Assiniboine River where it meets the Red,

> and being appalled at the idea of flat, treeless prairie. I think that my teacher then pointed out that it wouldn't be so bad right where the rivers met — there'd just have to be some trees there, and they are there . . . elms and oaks gently letting their leaves go for you to walk on in the dim twilight made by the street lamps mixed with the Indian Summer night. (*14 Barrels* 32)

After Manitoba, he is floating above the "fearsome mountains":

> looking not high, but like a really big unpleasant and endless doormat it would not be nice to fall face down on. Whereas before Northern Ontario had old Bearwalker waiting to grab us, here it was crunch and Sasquatch and maybe even D'Sonoqua, that Indian goddess of birth and death Emily Carr is fond of describing. (*14 Barrels* 57)

Many years earlier, Reaney recorded in an editorial to *Alphabet* 9 similar cross-country impressions,

> which proved enlightening with regard to the magic space of Canada. There was tightly woven detail from Dorchester to Burlington — cows duck-ponds and herons. Next Metro — a new kind of wilderness. Next Northern Ontario — a day and a night across, lonely, white birched and mysteriously rocked; the odd glimpse of Mishepeschoo foaming down towards the culvert our train was hollowly announcing. . . . Vancouver Island . . . oaks with long scraggly arms eyelashing the horizons of low mountains. (3)

Now, again on the ground in British Columbia, at Simon Fraser University, "on top of a mountain and looks like Lhasa. . . . Everything is built along a huge Aztec stairway that leads to the clouds and the very top of the mountain . . . many of the open spaces are straight out of Nurenberg rally time" (*14 Barrels* 63). Here there is a lecture on land tenure — "surveying, farmlots, fences, fenceviewers, pioneer wills that subdivide property and stories about boundary litigation." Once the students begin to speak, Reaney writes,

> . . . it came out that British Columbia doesn't seem to have submitted to the grid system that the Donnellys were caught in and as a matter of fact it's hard to think of Simon Fraser being on a rectangular lot. Then we got into rundale and conacre. Irish land systems which show up ever so shadowily in nineteenth century Biddulph. The actors chalked down lists of settlers on the boards, or showed off some catscradle tricks as an illustration of how geography and land tenure become stage images. (*14 Barrels* 69)

And, he might have added, how the reverberations of such stage images reach through to nearly all facets of the Donnelly story — personal, social, political, religious, and economic: "fates with string entangling people's lives" (*Sticks* 47). From the coast back over the mountains to Edmonton, and "bluffs of golden aspens like islands in huge heaths of brown-streaked stubble seas — a landscape like the back of a sleeping pheasant" (*14 Barrels* 79). On to Saskatchewan, "no bugles or neon or huge gardens and motels to tell us that we were entering the most socially advanced community on the continent, and the best governed, slowly inching towards an historic potash confrontation with the American behemoth" (*14 Barrels* 95). After a variety of city-scapes, the land once again, in the Maritimes. In New Brunswick, "a square shape that reminds one of some European country. . . . a square of wild forest . . . lined with pastorales, a great river veining the middle of it, so it's possible to get around it without doing the air trick, or suffering agoraphobia" (*14 Barrels* 123). Then, "on the edge of the Tantramar Marshes, at a turning point — a ledge in our country that hinges your life. You're between two provinces, or almost between them and their spirits are sufficiently different to make an interesting cross-current in your memory" (*14 Barrels* 148).

The truly central landscapes, however, are those of the home county in Ontario. From L.J. Chapman and D.F. Putnam's *The Physiography of Southern Ontario* Reaney learned "how you talked about the landscape around my birthplace other than to mumble such imprecise words as 'kind of flattish' or 'gravel ridge' or 'swamp.' 'Till plain' and 'kame' and 'aquifer' are much better and enable you, since we have a rather thin 200 B.C., to think about mile-high glaciers breeding landscapes in their bottoms" ("ABC" 2). On three occasions, during the tour of the Donnelly trilogy, the deep, enriching roots of his mother's farm near Stratford provide other, more human images of Reaney's "place." After Ottawa,

> Out at my mother's farm. I take up a row of turnips and store them in the pit for the winter. Then my stepfather helps me make the cold frame I've brought a secondhand storm window for. . . . I plant seeds — lettuce, radishes — and the idea is that in the winter I'll be able to look down through snow falling on the planes of the stormwindow and see green. (*14 Barrels* 112)

The image here of the restorative window on the farm plays an important part in *The Dismissal*, written shortly after *14 Barrels*, when Professor Dale returns home to his father's farm after being dismissed from the University of Toronto and breaks the ice for the thirsting cattle: "dark brown on the hill running down over the snow to the window I've made" (39). In a *Globe and Mail* interview, Reaney recalls that Frances Dale, William Dale's daughter, first told him of her father's fate at the University of Toronto. She told him "that her dad had gone back to farming after being dismissed from university. Why was he dismissed? I asked her. 'Oh for a letter he wrote to the *Globe & Mail* about the student strike.' What were they striking about? 'Oh, the same things as today — foreign professors, freedom of speech.'" "What grabbed me about Dale," Reaney continues, "was the same theme as the Donnellys, this kind of tenacious integrity. There's a sense of triumph in Dale, the ruined academic, going back to the farm — he wasn't afraid to work with his hands — and to write a history of Rome out there" (Interview with James Reaney 35).

There are two more references to the home county in *14 Barrels* worth noting here. After the visit to Hamilton, on Highway 8,

> through frames of bare branches, back past my mother's farm and up to the place Mrs. Donnelly walks to in the play over all those ladders — Goderich on another blue lake. Down this same road my ancestors from Scotland had first come to their new homes in Perth County. (*14 Barrels* 164)

Through such images of place and ancestry, Reaney's landscape becomes ontologically effective. It is, to him, a comprehensively *known* place, and, as Bowering remarks, it is *knowable* (4) — or, as Reaney the dramatist-teacher would insist, it must be rendered knowable to an audience both as fact and as myth. Landscape itself, particularly one so settled into "magnetic designs" that *visually* project a social and, in Biddulph, a racial narrative, becomes more than the literal space so matter-of-factly represented in the numerous maps that Reaney uses as scenic devices in the plays following *Listen to the Wind*. It is also communicative at a deeper level as a repository of mythopoeic resources. The final image of his mother's farm signifies the end of the tour:

> ... one end-of-the-year dark night in front of my mother's house where the truck arrived to store the props etc. in my stepfather's strawshed. . . . all saying farewell to each other, crying, and hugging each other at the end of the lane — the wind beginning to bring snowflakes more and more thickly. (*14 Barrels* 173)

Many years before, soon after arriving in Winnipeg in 1949 to teach at the University of Manitoba, Reaney describes how this image of his home county, "the feeling of place, of home [as] a power within us" was creatively restorative and, finally, not "necessarily dependent on Perth County." His poetry changed, he remarks:

I finished *A Suit of Nettles* in the Winnipeg Public Library, a formal poem solving all sorts of . . . technical and attitude problems. In the very "cool" environment of Manitoba it was possible to tackle the problem of expression through a convention. By the end of 1959 I had started *Killdeer*, completed *One-Man Masque*. ("Manitoba" 96)

Before writing these plays, Reaney had written *The Rules of Joy* (later revised as *The Sun and the Moon*) for a *Globe and Mail* Stratford Festival Contest. In the Note to this he declared his intention to present "the essence of country life in Ontario as I know it," and in the Prologue the speaker summons up his "father's kingdom. . . . the realm of love where people learnt the rules of joy. I can see that summer in my father's house. Summer in the village, in the church, in the fields, those roads, the people . . ." (qtd. in Woodman, *Reaney* 21).

In *A Suit of Nettles*, lines by Dorcas disclose something of the inaudible "unknown territory" of Reaney's home county:

> But the people living here are yet much
> Like us: brick upon brick — they are new born,
> They grow up, earn a living, learn prudence,
> Depress a bed, beget a blockhead; mourn —
> For the next brick seals them down, down, down, down.
> And so this farmhouse stands upon the heels
> Of forty-three large fields, their knot and crown.
> Within, an ancient voice the silence steals:
> Their heart beat, skull-hum, when it cries, are scarcely heard:
> 'Take us back to our beginning, white sail shipbird,
>
> Uncut this forest old and our old countries green. (*Poems* 151)

In an earlier poem, "The Upper Canadian," this place, for Reaney, was a

> . . .   round pond
> Where the geese white as pillows float
> In continual circles
> And never get out.
>
> Sometimes I wish that I
> Hadn't been born in this dull township

Where fashion, thought and wit
Never penetrate. . . . (*Poems* 56)

In his essay, "Literary Form and Social Hallucination," Harold Rosenberg quotes what James Baldwin calls "the most intense problem of American literature today." "Nothing," Baldwin writes,

> is more difficult than deciphering what the citizens of this time and place actually feel and think. They do not know themselves; when they talk, they talk to the psychiatrist; on the theory, presumably, that the truth about them is ultimately unspeakable. . . . The writer trapped among a speechless people is in danger of becoming speechless himself. For then he has no mirror, no corroborations of his essential reality; and this means that he has no grasp of the reality of the people around him. (*Discovering* 13)

Such is obviously part, and has always been a part, of the Canadian poet's predicament — of Reaney's predicament in reaching through to the "ancient voice," or *any* voice, of his "dull township." Finding a corroborative mirror is always difficult for a writer. For the dramatist, certainly for Reaney, a partial solution lay in both community workshops and in a continuing discourse with critics, participants, and spectators. The solution was also, as Reaney discovered in Winnipeg, aesthetic in nature, one which involved an essentially formalist reorganization and representation of what Auden called "our local understanding." Reaney says that, after writing *A Suit of Nettles* and starting to "think about what I should be writing about and researching next, I realized that I simply had to get back to my roots. I was homesick for the Souwesto landscape . . . to live again near such things as red-caned dogwood and yellow branched willows against the snow; Georgian farmhouses with Gothic Revival gables, such buildings as the Dutch Renaissance (!) City Hall at Stratford, such people as say 'the saf' for 'this afternoon' and 'gool' for 'goal' . . . and a whole host of human and near-human beings and things that I had always loved and been curious about" ("Souwesto Theatre" 14). Interwoven throughout the earlier poems, these statements of intention, as well as those concerning his home county in *14 Barrels* and elsewhere, and, of course, in the many plays which were to follow *A Suit of Nettles*, are several strands of emotion and vision. There is the evident nostalgia, the "homesickness" for roots, blending frequently into recollections of childhood; the careful, knowledgeable recording of empirical observation; the burdensome sense of an inarticulate, "dull township" that thwarts ontological creativity; and the recognition of the real and potential mythic dimensions of ordinary life.

I V

In Reaney's earliest plays, *Night-Blooming Cereus, The Killdeer, The Sun and the Moon, The Easter Egg,* the sense of place is outlined in general, broad terms simply as the rural, pastoral village world and with detailed images of a specific landscape, containing a specific society. Louis Dudek commented once that ". . . in studying Reaney we must . . . be aware that we are pursuing private imaginative locales, of his childhood and youth, as poetic touchstones, rather than objective dramatic contexts" (24). Yet for all of the ways in which these plays evoke the symbolic arrangements of personal and collective experience, a direct apprehension of *specific* time and place remains unbroken. As Ernst Cassirer observed,

> The mythical form of conception is not something super-added to certain definite *elements* of empirical existence; instead, the primary "experience" itself is steeped in the imagery of myth and saturated with its atmosphere. Man lives with *objects* only in so far as he lives with these *forms*; he reveals reality to himself, and himself to reality, in that he lets himself and the environment enter into this plastic medium, in which the two do not merely make contact, but fuse with each other. . . . (73)

It is just such a fusion of directly perceived *"objects"* and the "mythical form of conception," for instance, that we find in Yeats's setting for the symbolic play *The Only Jealousy of Emer* when at the beginning his Musician calls

> . . . before the eyes a roof
> With cross-beams darkened by smoke;
> A fisher's net hangs from a beam,
> A long oar lies against the wall.
> I call up a poor fisher's house . . . (*Selected Plays* 122)

We can also see this in Joan Miró's painting *The Farm* (1921–22), in its fusion of a precisely rendered assortment of living and working structures, ladders, trees, kitchen and farm implements, animals, paths, and natural colouring — the rich browns, greens, and blues — with a highly sophisticated aesthetic and symbolic arrangement. There is a sure sense in this painting that Miró and the environment do "fuse with each other" and that the boundary between the primary experience and mythical form is, finally, non-existent. As Miró explained later regarding the image of the ladder, "In the first years it was a plastic form frequently appearing because it was close to me — a familiar shape in *The Farm*. In later years, particularly during the war, while I was on Majorca, it came to symbolize 'escape,' an essentially plastic form at first — it became poetic later. Or plastic, first; then nostalgic at the time of painting *The Farm*; finally symbolic" (432). The abundance, even crowding, of strictly rural details in the painting — evidence of Miró's own "imagery count of the environment" — fused with its more cosmopolitan signs (in its overall composition, in the representation of a carefully placed copy of the avant-garde artistic magazine *L'Intransigeant* beneath the watering can), its obvious interleaving of *common* folk (thus shared), more rarefied *modernist* "aesthetic," and entirely *private* experience, is analogous in many respects to the way(s) Reaney chose to approach the places, events, history, and people of Southwestern Ontario. The details observed by Yeats and by Miró are like the carefully catalogued items of Mrs. Brown's house in *Night-Blooming Cereus*, of Mrs. Gardner's cottage in *The Killdeer*, or of the multitudinous props used in *One-Man Masque*, *Listen to the Wind*, and the Donnelly trilogy: they are important aspects of the primary experience, and, on another level, they are inseparable from those "mental dances with metaphor" that Reaney identified as an activity fundamental to the essentialist.

In one of the first of Reaney's works for the theatre, the libretto for the opera *Night-Blooming Cereus*, the action takes place "in front of a painted curtain which represents the village of Shakespeare, Ontario. Although it is late March the fields and roofs and yards are still covered with white snow. The houses grouped about the red-brick tower of the First Presbyterian Church are either red, brown, blue or yellow. They have the look of trees and the large trees feel like houses" (*Night-Blooming* 197). The central images and events of this opera, Reaney explained years later, were derived from newspaper accounts that ". . . last night in the village of Blankville neighbours gathered to watch Mrs. So & So's Night Blooming

Cereus come out, which only blooms once a century and then only after midnight." He then asks us to imagine

> the kind of world in which the blooming of a flower is important enough to get into the newspaper. So what I was really present-ing to the composer was a pastoral village in which people sing hymns while they're washing dishes, hear Sam Slick Connecticut clocks strike the hour, listen for the train whistling as it goes down to Toronto and from time to time rock rhythmically in rocking-chairs. ("Evening with Babble and Doodle" 38)

Later in the opera, this train's noise fuses with that of the clock striking midnight creating a particularly effective theatrical coales-cence of visual and auditory values. This is described by Reaney in a lengthy stage direction in which the less idyllic, less pastoral world of the village presents its grimace:

> . . . the train is right upon Mrs. Brown's cottage shaking every-thing, drowning everything — then not so upon as the passenger cars rattle by — travellers intent on Kitchener or Guelph or Georgetown or Limehouse or Weston or Toronto. Dirty mouthed train-men in their dark blue uniforms discussing some girl who was laid by some impossible number of men before she married somebody who hadn't — cuspidors, mere reproductive machines, all the personality of tickets rattling on, slaves of the whirring clock until just a receding red light blurred in snow blurs, black branches. For a moment the houses of the villages that had windows, and Mrs. Brown's was one of them, felt like trains too — why not? with our square headlights through the snow but the trees held them back and the houses settled back and some of the windows went out. (*Night-Blooming* 221)

The train, as Jay Macpherson observes, acts as "the principle of chaos and disorder opposed to the dream of innocence" (69). It permits us (at least in the *reading* of the published libretto, since only here do we learn of the "dirty mouthed trainmen") to discover the double aspect of Reaney's rural world as it presents alternately, and sometimes simultaneously, its idyllic, innocent, pastoral self and its grimace, one particular quality of which R.B. Parker calls its "stifling provincialism" dominated by time (280).

The settings of these early plays are all well established in small-town Canada. The houses, rooms, gardens, paths, streets, woodlots, churches, stores and the surrounding swamps, farms, and country lanes to which there are direct scenic and verbal references are intended to portray a highly cohesive social identity. They function, ultimately, as topographical signs of external and, insofar as the setting informs the action, of interior life. As images of being, they evoke a wide variety of response — smug contentment, exempt from the unsettling effects of "fashion, thought and wit;" a life-denying resignation to boredom and vacuity; rebellion; and, in the case of the imaginatively and spiritually gifted few, a richer understanding of sources, "the nest below where I was born," as Harry puts it in *The Killdeer* (38).

The Sun and the Moon is placed for us in the fictional village of Millbank, with a road running beside the Manse with its "great elm, and its green lawns" (192). *The Killdeer* is partly permeated by the atmosphere of Mrs. Gardner's rural cottage and by the surrounding landscape (one to which Reaney appealed in totemic terms in his earlier poems) into which Rebecca proposes to "drive / The old blind horse out of town down the road / Into the country until the marsh gets closer and / Closer" (21–22). *The Easter Egg* is set in "The parlour of a large old house somewhere in the English part of Canada" (3). In a 1971 preface to *Masks of Childhood*, a collection that includes this play, Reaney remarked that "Bethel and her setting were suggested by stories told at an academic party in Kingston; stories about the past on a campus somewhat farther east" (v). Although less specific in geographical location[11] and, unlike *The Sun and the Moon* and *The Killdeer*, restricted to one setting, there are clear evocations throughout *The Easter Egg* of the small village, with its gardens, fences, lawns, and its Big Pond to which as a child Kenneth "ran naked, / Through the sleeping village, the meadow, / Naked through the forest — just for fun" (16). In these plays we find a lyrical representation of the village as an entirely generalized locale — much as rural England is represented in the verse-plays of John Masefield, Christopher Fry, Ronald Duncan, Charles Williams, or the Andalusian world is evoked by Lorca, or Grovers Corners by Wilder in *Our Town*, to which Millbank is particularly similar — theatrically represented "simply . . . by a piano on one side of the stage and a roadside boulder with a signpost beside it on the other side of the stage" (92).

There is also, however, a more precise rendering of place in these three plays as Reaney injects more of his environmental "imagery count." In *The Sun and the Moon*, such a count includes the hut by the swamp where Andrew and Susan once played and watched "the herons nesting or looked for a scarlet tanager feather" (103–04) and where a weasel now has its nest; the village "late afternoon sounds — a cow mooing, a crow cawing;" the sound of the "wild song sparrow" (103); the prize pickles at the Stratford Fall Fair; the half bottle of "Niagara Harmony Table Wine" (112); the China Factory, putting handles on the teacups in a mimed assembly line activity. Then there are numerous references to Toronto with its "fallen girls" (110), its old house on the edge of the slums, its King George Hotel with working toilets. In *The Killdeer*, we hear of Mr. Lorimer in London (Ontario) "Taking his bed apart and putting it together again" (17), of Mr. Coons "the Royal Bank of Canada's this branch's / Manager" (13) who lives on Waterloo Crescent, and who thinks the universities "breed — communists" (26), of the village park with its swans and cannons, of the surrounding fields of "nightshade and bladder campion" (41), of those "vultures / At Osgoode Hall" in Toronto (36). In *The Easter Egg*, there are specific references to "some pawnshop in Montreal" (54), Woolworth's, Birk's Jewellery Store, the Traveller's Motel and a restaurant in Regentsville, to Cole's Book Market, to the Bishop of Montreal's bigotry.

The society of *The Sun and the Moon*, *The Killdeer*, and *The Easter Egg* is also presented in both generalized and more specific, regionalist terms. On one level, these plays evoke a highly charged world in which polar forces of darkness and light, evil and good, sterility and imagination co-exist and for which the individual (usually a child) functions as the point of intersection. As with the depiction of place, then, the characterization is to a certain degree determined by allegorical and symbolic predilections that accord such figures as Madame Fay, Mrs. Gardner, Bethel, Kenneth, Polly, Mrs. Shade, Clifford, and Rebecca set roles in Reaney's psychomachia. Seen in this perspective, there is little to identify these characters as especially rooted in Southwestern Ontario — even if they do say "the saf," "gool," and, presumably, live in or near Georgian farmhouses with Gothic Revival gables. Like the various figures of his poem *The Dance of Death at London, Ontario* —

Executive Esquire & Grocery Boy
Man, Woman, Doctor, Child, Bishop
The Scavenger & the Rich Young Lady
Painter & Poet & Cop (*Poems* 235)

— those of the early plays possess such strong typological definition necessary to their prearranged status in the social and spiritual narrative. However, just as Eliot's allegorical characters Agatha, Amy, Reilly, and Celia have a *primary* location in the English manor houses and Mayfair flats, and, say, Obey's *Noah* draws upon a readily observable society of rural France, Reaney's characters are born, bred, and shaped in the "round pond" of "The Upper Canadian" (*Poems* 56), where the local bank, the church, the china factory, croquet and lemonade, the Women's Institute on Saturday, the odd bottle of Clergyman's delight, and the "Two little boys on chamber / Pots" (*Killdeer* 12) together create an "environmental bubble" ("Myths" 253), sustained, as Reaney was to remark later, by the newspapers and journals.

Clara Thomas has observed of Reaney's region that when he "grew up there in the 1940s it was still overpoweringly conservative in its dominant social traditions, a long distance in time from the exigencies of the frontier; and the facades of its citizens and institutions alike still presented a formidable, well-nigh impenetrable hedge of thorns to the questing writer" (10). A major component of this hedge was the newspaper, which was gradually to play an important role in Reaney's writing. "Protests are insignificant," he wrote, "in the face of what seems a silent mass acceptance of the newspaper as a producer of knowledge and power: to be civilized is to read the newspaper . . ." ("Myths" 254). ". . . printed rhetoric . . . was just beginning to wrap itself around Canadian life with the ideals of a technological 'go-aheadism' that is eventually destructive of not only man, but of the newspaper itself" ("Myths" 257).

In Eliot's *The Family Reunion*, Harry describes people

> To whom nothing has happened, at most a continual impact
> Of external events. You have gone through life in sleep,
> Never woken to the nightmare. I tell you,
>   life would be unendurable
> If you were wide awake.

As embodiments of such a leaden, abandoned world, Eliot's chorus, composed of his versions of the contemporary performers in the dance of death, exclaims,

> We all of us make the pretension
> To be the uncommon exception

To the universal bondage.
We like to appear in the newspapers
So long as we are in the right column.
We know about the railway accident
We know about the sudden thrombosis
And the slowly hardening artery.
We like to be thought well of by others
So that we may think well of ourselves.
And any explanation will satisfy:
We only ask to be reassured
About the noises in the cellar
And the window that should not have been open.
Why do we all behave as if the door might suddenly open,
    the curtains be drawn,
The cellar make some dreadful disclosure, the roof disappear,
And we should cease to be sure of what is real or unreal?
Hold tight, hold tight, we must insist that the world is
    what we have always taken it to be. (*Complete* 242–43)

Within a like rhythm of gossip ("Do you know what we're like,"
Mrs. Budge asks in *The Killdeer*, "Two old crows / Gliding over the
spring fields trying to pry out / Where that delicious decaying smell
is from" [17]), indifference, guilt, and fear ("You, Eli, / Are the hawk
— a falcon — afraid to build / The tower of air and cast the field of
fear" [66]), the society of Reaney's early plays is formulated and
entrapped. And, with a large measure of retaliatory malice, this
society attempts to entrap others who seek something different.

In the course of Reaney's plays from *The Killdeer* through to the
Donnelly trilogy, his relatively mild, almost good-natured description of the "doctor-dominated civilization of lawns under which
Western Ontario has long lain asleep" ("Stratford Festival" 112), is
replaced by a far less charitable view of a generally hostile, sometimes
threatening, social milieu. The homesickness for the "Souwesto
landscape" experienced in Winnipeg does not easily translate into an
equally longing feeling towards the people of the place. The strong
creative urge to Identify his region, to establish a communally rooted
theatre, is based, not upon any real hope for the existing, established
society there, but upon the possibility of creating a brand *new* social
order in which the artist-teacher, reaching through to disclose and
release the latent radical creativity of the child, will "create a
civilization" that fully understands the why and the how of playing.

In these plays, Reaney's sympathies for the child, for creative, sometimes visionary eccentrics, for the imaginative, and for the victims of society are well defined, are in fact entirely unmistakable — as authorial sympathies always are in melodramatic vision and structure. In his expression of such sympathy, Reaney departs significantly from other folk-dramatists, for instance, Lorca, Obey, Wilder, because the *secular* as well as the spiritual Manicheism that so strongly informs his drama precludes the wider, warmer, more tolerant (even at times more *tragic*) sympathy for both the place and the *people*. The more comprehensive, vitally celebratory impulse, which on one level inspired a return to his "Souwesto" roots (felt, for example, in his manifesto for the summer season of Canadian plays in 1965 and evoked on occasion in his *Halloween* letters), is counterbalanced, often overtaken, by a more critical and satirical impulse that finds any real charity towards the self-congratulatory philistinism and " 'go-aheadism' " of his region impossible.

As the purely allegorical, symbolic values in the early plays give way to, or are better informed by, a more detailed, regionally precise representation of place, people, and event, then the social milieu in Reaney's plays is seen differently and made to function differently. This milieu becomes increasingly menacing as it ceases, in Arnold Hauser's words, "to be simply the background and external framework and now takes an active part in the shaping of human destiny." Human action, as a consequence, appears informed by "something that does not originate in the subject and which makes man seem the product of a mindless and soulless reality" (409). The "environmental bubble" is, essentially, one dimensional. Reaney uses a quotation from Marshall McLuhan's *War and Peace in the Global Village* as an epigraph to his article "Myths in Some Nineteenth-Century Ontario Newspapers" that contains this term: "One thing about which fish know exactly nothing is water, since they have no anti-environment which would enable them to perceive the element they live in" (253). In Reaney's plays, the milieu, perceived in such a light, is increasingly accountable for the unique shape that gifted, imaginative individuals, and, in the case of the Donnellys, social outsiders, give their lives. Reaney, like McLuhan and Frye, relates the pervasive strength and structure of this "bubble" to various forms of communication. Frye writes of the "extent to which this almost one-dimensional country has been preoccupied with communications of all kinds, from the most physical to the most ethereal." Disclosing and explaining such a preoccupation, he says, are such figures as Harold Innis and his "disciple" Marshall McLuhan, who are "interested in the totality of communication, and the essential unity of its activity, whether it is building railways or sending messages." Innis, in particular, studied the ways in which "the control of communication media by a certain class or group in society conditions that society." Frye draws from this an important lesson, which, of course, was Reaney's lesson as well. "A similar sense of the unity of communication has affected me," Frye writes, "and has had a good deal to do with what I have called my evangelical attitude to the teaching of literature" (*Spiritus* 24).

As Reaney tends towards increasing use of choric utterance (different voices fusing as one in the manner, for instance, of Eliot's foursome in *The Family Reunion*) and towards a greater and more direct use of documentary material in his plays — especially material from the newspapers — the surrounding social milieu acquires the major determining function described by Hauser. The powerful "environmental bubble," with its known and *secret* sources of control becomes, to an ever more prominent degree, both the meaning and the form of the drama. This will be best seen in the Donnelly trilogy where Reaney, in his guise as folk-historian, allows the documents to speak in their own voice, permitting them to be seen and felt in the surrounding *mise en scène*, with its pictorial depiction and evocation of a particular, regionally fixed world. Geographical surveys, landgrant maps, public and private letters, legal documents, posters, ecclesiastical papers, newspaper head-lines and stories, trial transcripts, and, sometimes, simply dozens of place-names chalked on the walls of the playing *and* watching spaces — all such archival material in the trilogy provides both foreground and background, both protagonists and chorus alike, with a shape and a voice.

In the earlier plays, however, such a use of documents is not yet evident. Instead, place, character, and event remain largely generic-poetic as opposed to documentary constructions. *Listen to the Wind* was originally conceived as a play about the Brontë children. Such an idea for a play, Reaney says, was prompted in part by John Hirsch after his production in Winnipeg of *Names and Nicknames*. The format, however, was changed, although a "Brontë version" of *Listen to the Wind* was written and remains in manuscript form. Reaney changed the locale and the central characters from the Brontë children to those of his own childhood, with whom he used to put on plays. *Listen to the Wind*, then, occurs in a Perth County farmhouse during the thirties, yet, as in the case of *The Sun and the Moon*, *The Killdeer*, and *The Easter Egg*, there are only a few images — both verbal and scenic — to render such a location more than a generic space suitable for the representation of complex correspondences between the actual and the imaginative lives of the four children. "Sometimes," Owen says to the other children, "I feel I don't really live or die here in Ontario, but I lived a century ago in an old manorhouse in England. . . . With the rain beating down on the window. . . . And the wind whistling around the eaves" (16). Except for a few references to Ontario place-names (for instance, the Northwest Wind comes down from "Temiskaming, / Algoma, Patricia, / Down from the North over the wilderness" [17]) and the poetic evocation of the sort of rural landscape already seen in the earlier plays, there is little to precisely establish the Southwestern Ontario milieu. Although this play does mark a very significant change in Reaney's dramaturgy, in its assimilation of a denser *theatricalist* vocabulary and in its linguistic structure.

Colours in the Dark is the first play verbally and scenically to assimilate and represent a whole host of documentary material related to the places, events, history, and people of Southwestern Ontario. This material, in the course of the play, becomes as much actor as it is background. The play narrates several intricately related stories for which collage techniques were developed in the theatrical realization. To a degree unknown in the earlier plays, although first seen in *Listen to the Wind*, *Colours in the Dark* utilizes what will become customary in all of Reaney's subsequent plays: an extraordinary plasticity in which visual and physical configurations are held as equal partners to verbal language, permitting different levels of meaning to pass from the verbal to the visual image and back again. In his account of the preparation for the play's first Stratford Festival production in 1967, Reaney recalls that

John Hirsch had mentioned wanting to try magic lantern effects, trick effects — dishes floating through the air as in Czech illusion theatre and big marionettes as in *America Hurrah*, perhaps even movie screens. Having sequences tied to colours in the rainbow was one result of this, and episodes tended to develop around the mood or idea of a colour. . . . At the time of writing I had no idea what the slides would be like. Neither John Hirsch nor I saw *Labyrinth* at Expo until after the opening. In a five-squared cruciform the projections gave a giant feeling not unlike some of the effects in Roman Kroiter's project. One ingredient in *Colours in the Dark* — the fact that the play not only runs through a life, through Ontario's story since the last glacier, but also through the whole Bible — meant there'd practically have to be back projections and huge screens, just to take up the slack. ("Colours" essay 142)

The designer Eoin Sprott was sent into the surrounding country-side to take photographs of forests (used to reinforce the sequence following the last retreat of the ice when, as Reaney writes in *Colours*, "dreadful fights . . . took place between the trees," physically represented in a staged battle between "fir branch bearers and maple branch bearers" [19]) and of Perth County roads ("White gravel roads running by fences, woodlots, villages" for the Walkers sequence [40]). Other slides depict Stratford's main street, Sharon Temple, Yonge Street in Toronto, a Perth County General Store in 1910, primitive sculptures by Laithwaite in Goderich, Ontario, University College, Toronto, scenes of Winnipeg, especially of Winnipeg's winter as the mimed train goes from Toronto through Northern Ontario, whose names, like those earlier in the train sequence from Stratford to Toronto, are chanted. These specifically regional images alternate with others of a more general, often abstract nature, intended to evoke and represent moods usually associated with colours: "Dance of Death for purple, Orange parade for orange, Angry Schoolmaster for red," and so on. Yet others depict children's drawings (for instance, "a kid's drawing of Indian Camp" to represent the battle of Moraviantown in 1813 [33]), artistic-religious analogues (Heronimous Bosch's "demons attacking St. Anthony" [15], Alfred Durer's *Adam and Eve*), historical events and personages (boats with immigrants on board "waiting for the new country" [34], thirties radio figures and advertising material, the "kind of lettering they use in the New York Automat" [39], a Swastika, reinforced by the Child masked as Hitler; portraits of Frye, McLuhan, and other teachers at the University of Toronto). All such regional, national, and extra-national images are intended to reinforce the various strands of the action wherein the personal story (from a child in Southwestern Ontario, to a student at the University of Toronto, to a teacher in Winnipeg) is joined, at different levels, with central events in the interlocking stories of Canada's natural, social, and historical life. "Dimly we realize that not only are we going through the hero's life and stories he heard as a child, but we are going through Canada's story — glacier and forest, also the world's story" (*Colours* 21).

As was common in performance theory and practice during much of the sixties, many of these documentary, *projected* images are also corporeally rendered by the actors. There is, for instance, the miming of the Laithwaite sculptures and the formation of the Ontario Coat of Arms, with Gramp as "Dexter — an Indian habited proper" and Gram as "Sinister Britannia helmed and cuirassed." Other documents used by Reaney are verbally evoked. He tells us, for example (although we would have no way of realizing this during performance), that the accusations levelled at Pa, while the screen initially depicts the Bosch demons attacking St. Anthony, are taken from the Criminal Records for the Huron and Bruce District, 1850:

Have you committed —

Robbing orchards
Refusing to give half the road
Driving a Sleigh Without Bells
Travelling on Sunday with a
loaded wagon of whiskey.
Trespass, vagrancy. . . . (16)

For the visit of the Royal Train, an actual letter is recited relating the mishap as the train "whizzed by the school children at 10 miles an hour (it was only supposed to go 3 miles an hour) . . . by 17,000 disappointed school children" (36). For the "Fable of the Babysitter and the Baby," a reading of the actual newspaper advertisement: "Wanted: one capable babysitter, college student preferred. No references. Ap. 22B, 1224 College St., Thornview Apartments" (83); for the "Ode on the Mammoth Cheese," a reading of the original poem by James McIntyre (44). On other occasions, familiar poems, hymns, and the like are used, each carrying particular and identifiable political, social, religious, and, of course, personal associations. Michael Tait observed that Reaney "does not discover the secret of Canadian identity on platforms of any kind. He investigates instead the archives of rural newspapers, repositories of the 'small history' of the land. His special knack is to seize upon some inert record mired in oblivion, a petty crime or a sale of crinolines, and to make it blossom into an epiphany" ("Everything" 140–41). As we can see, this is partly true; yet the presentation of this "small history" in

Colours in the Dark is nearly always associated, by means of verbal and scenic juxtapositioning, with other, generally larger, more readily recognized signs of our times. In short, Reaney does not neglect the less personal, universally significant communicative platforms of education, politics, religion, art-history, advertising (Apollinaire's "morning poetry"), and geography to which the small history is intricately related.

Diane Bessai has examined the particular shape and scope of Canadian documentary theatre and has shown how Reaney's plays, especially the Donnelly trilogy, shared in the development of a variety of "presentational styles as a way to investigate actuality in the theatre." Of particular note, Bessai writes, was the extent to which the "investigatory process itself became a major part of the dramatic design" ("Documentary" 191). The modern documentary theatre is, on one level, a theatre of straight reportage, which takes authentic material and puts it on the stage. It is also, as Peter Weiss has observed, "a reflection of life as we witness it through the mass media" (41). The "environmental bubble" is created by the mass media, and, Reaney notes, ". . . the minds of the editors, journalists, and advertisers . . . hoped to shape the mind of their community" ("Myths" 253). The collage techniques necessary to the theatrical presentation of this world — as both background and foreground — proved to be central to Reaney's development as a dramatist following *Listen to the Wind*. They also proved crucial to the resolution in theatrical terms of the two main principles he advocated as essential to a national theatre: the direct apprehension and depiction of the "landmarks and bearings" of our respective regions and the nation and, secondly, the idea of radical creativity — which ultimately meant the sharing by the playwright, actor, and audience in the essential art act itself.

Since it was first seriously developed as a visual language in the earlier phase of cubist art, collage has proved to be the most adaptable and suitable style for the goals of an intellectual and aesthetic vision that seeks to find, as Reaney said in his review of Pratt, "the clue that joins up the different maze like levels of our inner and outer worlds." What is most noteworthy in Reaney's vision, as it was with the cubists as well, is that this maze of inner and outer pressures, forms, feelings, impulses, and insights is not static, and neither is the one (the poet) in the maze looking for clues. In Reaney's world the poet is most likely to be riding a version of the Heraclitian horse at the merry-go-round at Mome Fair in *A Suit of Nettles*, "a fiery steed! it goes up and down like nothing but and its whole form keeps flowy-changing; as a matter of fact you can't seem to sit in the same saddle twice on it it seems" (*Poems* 174).

Collage was never intended to articulate visually fixed forms or relationships. It speaks, instead, to and from an inherently pluralistic bias that seeks endless, multiple meanings and values and that prizes process above product, becoming above being. Its visual establishment of a plane of shifting perspectives and formal relationships is intended to embrace within its own unfinished art-act the artist *and* the on-looker. An aesthetic was emerging very early in our century in which the values of simultaneity, change, and inclusiveness were paramount and in which the spectator was asked to share in the creation of the work.

What was needed, wrote Robert Delevoy, "was to integrate into a social order, which itself was cast into the melting-pot, a new order of art, an art that took full account of the values of mobility, tension, energy, and co-ordination and, by the same token, of the forces activating the science, philosophy and the great politico-social movements of the day. Thus only could the parameters of becoming replace the rigid configurations of the perspectival system. The effects of this bold innovation made themselves felt, successively, in the techniques of the cinema, of collage, and photomontage, and also reacted on the structure of the picture" (*Dimensions* 169–70). A classic affirmation of such an aesthetic was, of course, Sergei Eisenstein's description of montage in films. "The strength of montage," he wrote,

> resides in this, that it includes in the creative process the emotions and mind of the spectator. The spectator is compelled to proceed along that selfsame creative road that the author travelled in creating the image. The spectator not only sees the represented elements of the finished work, but also experiences the dynamic process of the emergence and assembly of the image just as it was experienced by the author. . . . The image planned by the author has become flesh of the flesh of the spectator's risen image. . . . Within me, as a spectator, this image is born and grown. Not only the author has created, but I also — the creating spectator — have participated. (34–35)

This is an affirmation of the ontological creativity Bachelard spoke of in his account of the poetic image and Reaney in his various statements regarding the value of play. By joining the artist in the act of creating an image (and, as Bessai says, this means in part a *sharing* in the whole investigatory process), the action of identifying, of exercising the imaginative and intellectual impulses to render *knowable* a wide range of external "documented" reality is also, simultaneously, turned inward towards the greater ambiguity but still potentially knowable world of the inner maze. The spectator/reader is ideally engaged in the double activity of identifying existing form and in form-making. Such activity is at the root of Reaney's aesthetic humanism, and the various presentational techniques of dramatic collage, especially as these inform contemporary documentary theatre, once fully seized upon by Reaney in the writing and producing of *Colours in the Dark,* proved to be most suitable.

The theatre workshops to which Reaney devoted so much of his time during the late sixties were, of course, the laboratory within which the collages took shape. In these workshops, explorations into the primary acts of looking and listening nourished the important dramaturgical development towards a greater artistic polylingualism. Writing in 1930, and representing one very prominent tendency towards a highly synaesthetic theatricalism that reaches back to Wagner's *Gesamtkunstwerk*, Jean-Ricard Bloch wrote,

> Like music, the theatre can no longer survive on a simple stage in a limited hall. The problem of simultaneity and ubiquity arises at this juncture; and music will join hands with the cinema. The theatre implies seeing and hearing; and the cinema and music together may be able to point the way towards salvation and resurrection. (qtd. in Moussinac 19)

Reaney's avowed artistic aim, expressed in his editorial in the first issue of *Alphabet,* to "rouse the faculties" (1), discovered, in the collage techniques of *Colours in the Dark,* new musical and cinematic vocabularies with which to represent the increasing density and shifting planes (both objective and subjective, external and internal) of verbal, auditory, and visual experience. Like Eisenstein's cinematic montage, his theatricalist aesthetic strives more and more to "force the audience to work out richness" ("James Reaney" 146), compelling it to be more creatively susceptible to the multiple visual, verbal, and auditory statements and patterns, to be, as he said, "folded in to the goings on" ("Ten Years" 58).

The sources for such vision and technique are, however, not only to be found in cubist art, cinematic montage, and musical form. They reside as well in the verbal copiousness, the multi-dimensional narrative sweep and technical fluidity of the Elizabethan drama. Jay Macpherson recalls a talk by Reaney in which he explained why "reading or watching Shakespeare was a so much more satisfying experience than most other writers could give. It was all those inner consistencies and interlocking details — 'it's a sort of filigree, you aren't expected to notice it, but if it weren't there you'd certainly feel the difference' " (65). Peter Brook was equally enthraled by Shake-speare's "marvellously free technique," in which texts in perform-ance "continually change gears." If one could "extract the mental impression made by the Shakespearean strategy of images," he wrote, "you would get a piece of pop collage" ("Finding Shakespeare on Film" 118). Brook, like many modern directors and writers, sees a play in performance as a "series of impressions; little dabs, one after another, fragments of information or feeling in a sequence which stirs the audience's perceptions. A good play sends many such messages, often several at a time, often crowding, jostling, over lapping one another. The intelligence, the feelings, the memory, the imagination are all stirred" (Introduction v). Looking in the same direction, Reaney said that good plays should "dance with the audience; make each person use parts of his soul he hasn't been using for some time and make him use various parts of his soul in succession during the evening" ("James Reaney" 143). The almost limitless flexibility of the collage form became, during the sixties especially, as appropriate a formal response to the omnipresence of the milieu (as Hauser and others described it) as realism had been for an earlier generation of writers. Collage entailed the freeing of dramatic and theatrical structure from the conventions and restric-tions of a linear framework, and yet it accommodated various forms and levels of narrative, as well as the complex interlacing of referen-tially public and private experience.

In much of Reaney's poetry, in the editorial aims, selections, and design of *Alphabet*, in the constantly shifting gears of *14 Barrels* and the *Halloween* letters, in his early endorsement of Greg Curnoe's collages, and increasingly in the plays beginning with *Colours in the Dark*, Reaney engages in what Levi-Straus called "intellectual tinker-ing," which, he noted, was one characteristic of the mythopoetic perspective (qtd. in Delevoy, *Dimensions* 119). The invitation to the play becomes an invitation to play, to do one's own tinkering, as an active spectator, with the miscellaneous data assembled by Reaney.

Much of this data originated in what Bachelard called the "intimate space" of the wardrobe and chest, where, paradoxically, there "exists a centre of order that protects the entire house against uncurbed disorder. Here again reigns, or rather, this is the reign of order. Order is not merely geometrical; it can also remember the family history" (*Poetics of Space* 79). Reaney's intimate space from which *Colours in the Dark* received its creative ordering and from which centre the various less intimate stories moved into an ever-widening circumference of shared experience, was his play box.

In his preface to the play, Reaney describes how such a repository of intimacy reaches outwardly into the multilevelled milieu, and inwardly into the processes of creativity:

> I happen to have a play box and it's filled with not only toys and school relics, but also deedboxes, ancestral coffin plates, in short a whole life. When you sort through the play box you eventually see your whole life — as well as all of life — things like Sunday School albums which show Elijah being fed by ravens, St. Stephen being stoned. The theatrical experience in front of you now is designed to give you that mosaic-all-things-happening-at-the-same-time-galaxy-higgledy-piggledy feeling that rummaging through a play box can give you. But underneath the juxtaposition of coffin plate with baby rattle with Royal Family Scrapbook with Big Little Book with pictures of King Billy and Hitler — there is the back-bone of a person growing up, leaving home, going to big cities, getting rather mixed up and then not coming home again but making home and identity come to him wherever he is. The kids at the very end of the play manage to get their lightning rod up and attract the thunder that alone can wake the dead. Or on the other six hands, as Buddha says, there are any number of other interpretations that fit the mosaic we're (director, writer, actors, kids, designers, composer) giving you. (*Colours* 5)

Learning how to play, and then actively playing, the aroused spectator is "folded in to the goings on," in to the mosaic of familiar and unfamiliar things in our personal, regional, and national stories and, most importantly, in to the creative act itself with its own verbal, physical, and scenic choices and possibilities. Throughout the play Reaney invites us to be folded in to the interlocking experiences of the child as he matures; of the land as it becomes inhabited (we re-create the battle of Maple and Fir after the glacier's retreat; we arrive with the assorted immigrants); of our times as these have been informed by newspapers, advertising, war, teachers, visiting royalty, silly poems, hymns, music, geography, politics, artists, and by Dr. Button, who cannot see that several secret and marvellous affinities, myths, and patterns lie waiting to be unveiled beneath the crust of merely external events — "A flower is like a star" (*Colours* 67). The regional world of the play is meticulously presented through the documentary material assembled by Reaney as he abandons the more generic landscapes that informed his earlier plays. We know very precisely where we are and what large and small landmarks in Southwestern Ontario Reaney wants us to notice. But such a strictly regional bias and representational plane is not what folds us in to the theatrical event: it is, rather, the creative *act* and the shaping and ordering possibilities of art *form* that engage us. Frye's poet is in place here, the one whose primary "quest is for form, not content. The poet who tries to make content the informing principle of his poetry," he observes, "can write only versified rhetoric, and versified rhetoric has a moral but not an imaginative significance: its place is on the social periphery of poetry, not in its articulate centre." Form springs from the shaping power of metaphor, and metaphor, "in its radical of form, is a statement of identity: that is that, A is B" (*Bush Garden* 176–77). Reaney's consciousness of loyalty towards the order of art itself and to the ontological explicitness of metaphor give his plays from *Colours in the Dark* on a somewhat uncertain, at times only tangential, association with the regional expressions of Joanna Glass, Michel Tremblay, John Cook, John Murrell, and others, and the documentary approaches of the Canadian and foreign "collectives" of the sixties and seventies. As Bessai has noted, Reaney cares little for what he considers "the gray shape behind a great many soggy historical documentaries" ("Letter from James Reaney" 4). In the scenically and verbally metaphorical configurations of his plays he goes beyond "the presentational element as an end in itself, compiled at most into loose episodic structures" which, Bessai says, tends to characterize the work of the collectives ("Documentary" 190).

But Reaney did share fully in the often enthusiastic investigatory *process* that the documentarists and the collectives endorsed and which turned the region and the nation into a "play box." In one of his *Halloween* letters, "The Story Behind *King Whistle!*", Reaney describes in considerable detail the personal and collective action of Identifying and playing that led up to the 1980 production in Stratford, Ontario, of his play about the 1933 strike in his home town. He, his actors, and, as much as possible, the community became engaged in the accumulation of archival material, personal reminiscences, diaries, letters, and so on in order to re-inhabit collectively the social, political, religious, and, above all, economic milieu of the 1930s. Adhering to the general aims of collective playwriting, which try "to convey the particularities of the specific milieu they are portraying — the local voice as well as the local subject" (Bessai, "Documentary" 187), armies of school-children/actors/teachers compiled records of that time and that place: ". . . if you're going to write a play about a community, particularly a Stratford which in 1933 came out on the streets and shouted what it wanted, then you have to persuade the students and teachers to do likewise, to explore the roots of the community in every way possible" ("Story" 50).

Such an investigatory process had been employed earlier, though with much less community involvement, in the writing of the Donnelly trilogy. In seeking out the speech of the place where the Donnelly family lived, farmed, drove, fought, and died, Reaney immersed himself in the multitudinous Donnelly documents that have served, in their musty and intoxicating complexity, as the inspiration for a large number of authors and historians. He recounts his initial encounter with this story in the early poem "Winter's Tales":

> Then the farmer told them stories
> That his father had told him
> Of the massacre at Lucan
> Where the neighbours killed all the McKilligans dead
> Except one little boy who crawled under a bed. (*Poems* 36)

The history of the Donnelly family, he later wrote,

> was so rivetting to me that it led me like a Jack-o-Lantern through an enormous, 8 year swamp of legal MSS, newspaper microfilm, archival vigils and the like without one solitary regret; as Catherine Roddy, a specialist in old graveyards, once said to me in Western's Regional Archives, "My idea of Heaven is to spend it in an Archive," and I agree. ("Letter from James Reaney" 4)

The poem's evocation of a winter's tale that can make the imagination of the child "move in far dances round its fire" (36) fuses with

THIS NATIVE LAND BUSINESS

the equally engaging spell of records and documents. In the fusion of the two, the inner and outer directions of the poetic-historical investigatory process are evident. "That's how poetry works," Reaney writes in the first issue of *Alphabet*, ". . . it weaves street scenes and twins around stars in legendary pools. Let us make a form out of this: documentary on one side and myth on the other: Life & Art. In this form we can put anything and the magnet we have set up will arrange it for us" (Editorial 1). The past is reclaimed by way of memory, story, myth, and by visiting the library. "What was it like in the past?" Reaney asks in the "Seventh Letter" of *Twelve Letters to a Small Town*:

> Find out in the archives of the Public Library. In a small cellar room, there they keep the tea coloured files of the town's newspapers. A shaky fading paper rope into the darkness of the past some more than a century long. You open the door with a skeleton key — the door, has it a white china doorknob? And there in the dark little room, the summer sunlight smothered by a frayed yellow drawn down window blind — there is the past.
> (*Poems* 218)

Reaney's immersion in all that the "shaky fading paper rope" took him into had significant consequences for his development as a playwright. First of all, it led him further into a variety of views on the Donnelly family and massacre as these were reflected in the press, in songs, in books, medicine shows, in the letters, trials, and so on. Secondly, it led him towards a view of the "environmental bubble" created by the newspapers. As he wrote later,

> During the last four or five years I have been reading the nineteenth-century files of such newspapers as *The St. Marys Journal-Argus*, the *Stratford Beacon-Herald*, and the *London Free Press*. With the last named I have read some decades continuously day after day, week after week so that I might possibly share, if not the minds of all those long-dead readers, at least the minds of the editors, journalists, and advertisers who hoped to shape the mind of their community. . . . As I invite the reader to step back and regard the environmental bubble the *Free Press*, in particular, must once have formed, I am hoping to show that the newspaper kept expressing certain popular myths, certain cliches or accepted ideas which editors and

readers alike may never have examined objectively, from the outside. (*Myths* 253)

Thirdly, the experience influenced in very direct ways Reaney's dramaturgical development in that the spell of such an archival muse reinforced the collage techniques he had used in *Colours in the Dark*, making of the archives a wider, less personal, more communally referential play-box. Lastly, the "paper rope" also led Reaney into a wider verbal range that would include the various forms of discourse displayed in the sources.

The Donnelly trilogy uses the dense archival material throughout to provide foreground and background, protagonist and chorus, visual and verbal articulation. To a degree only hinted at in *Colours in the Dark*, the signs of archival research are often left to envelope scenically the play and the spectator. The physical presence of so many props (the 14 barrels' worth of props), maps, signs, documents, and artefacts fosters the feeling of being in close contact not only with Reaney's indefatigable investigatory process, but with the primary art act itself, in which one shares something of the initial, and *continuing*, wrestling with the tensions and choices within the creative triad of facts, story, and style. Both the acts of playing and the objects of play, then, participating fully in the pluralistic bias of collage, fold the aroused spectator in to a world, and in to the ambiguous and shifting perspectives available within this world.

"When you immerse yourself in this play," Reaney writes in his Foreword to *Sticks & Stones*, "you may find that your experience matches my own when I immersed myself some eight years ago in documents which had lain for years and years in the attics of two local courthouses: after a while I couldn't stop thinking about them" (7). In his Introduction to *14 Barrels*, he tells us how he set about to answer the questions of some actors who were involved in early workshops on this story in Stratford. *Why*, some wanted to know, were the Donnellys killed. His years of archival research in "old newspapers, registry office records, criminal records for Middlesex and Huron Counties — the sort of material that you find in the attics of old courthouses and in the minds of ninety year olds" (*14 Barrels* 10), provided the answers. These documents, pertaining to the central event of the Donnelly massacre, 4 February 1880, as well as to the multitudinous voices of the surrounding milieu and to the roots of local terror in the ancient Tipperary feud, provided Reaney with the most fruitful avenue into the speech of the place he was determined to delineate in dramatic terms after *A Suit of Nettles*. Without abandoning the "mythical form of conception" that informs the earlier plays, he employed these documents to provide a solid grounding in the minute particulars of nineteenth-century Southwestern Ontario. At this time, the essential cross-beams of a variety of commercial, religious, and political powers were fixed in place. These separate, but closely intertwined powers, along with their most obvious material manifestations (roads, railways, factories, towns, churches, banks, stores, taverns, stage-coaches) constitute a world that Reaney had characterized as "tyrannized over by the mechanical geometry of 'go-aheadism' and 'enlightenment.' "

Among the events that helped to shape this society, and which find varying degrees of representation in the trilogy, are the establishment in 1830 of the Wilberforce Settlement near what became the town of Lucan, Ontario, by refugee Negro slaves; the arrival of Irish settlers, and the surveying of Biddulph township, which results in the near eradication of the Wilberforce community; the arrival of more settlers during the 1844 famine in Ireland; the first major census of Canada West in 1848; the growth of various commercial and manufacturing interests in Southwestern Ontario; the election of 1857 in which the Liberal Holmes defeated the Conservative Cayley in the Biddulph riding; the firm establishment of Protestant and Roman Catholic spheres of educational and political influence; the establishment of Canada as a Dominion in 1867; the growth of rival stage coach lines in the early 1870s; the Federal General Election of 1878 in which Sir John A. Macdonald is victorious; the Provincial election in the North Middlesex riding in 1879; the shift from a stage coach to a railway economy during the 1870s and 1880s, and the establishment of the Canada Southern Railway. Into the half century of such rapid social, political, religious, and economic growth and change the private story of the Donnelly family, their feuds, commercial and agricultural exploits, their real or rumoured involvement in a variety of "good" and "bad" activities is carefully woven, so that it is very rarely possible to see the family existing separately from the surrounding milieu. J.-K. Huysmans' "era of mercantilism and haste" (qtd. in Delevoy, *Symbolists* 11) is as much in the centre of Reaney's vision as is the fascination of the Donnelly massacre. The world evoked by such events and developments is a world preoccupied by taxes, pricing policies, land values, mortgages, banking powers, salesmen, trainmen, commercial competition, increasing industrialization, newspapers, toll gates, road-building, legal obligations, political and religious machinations. In the trilogy, *all* of the characters outside of the Donnelly family are associated in one way or another with this world. Their dramatic characters are founded almost entirely upon their occupational pursuits and roles. As such they resemble the figures who make up the societies of such plays as Brecht's *St. Joan of the Stockyards*, Frisch's *Andorra*, Dürrenmatt's *The Visit*, Henrik Ibsen's *Enemy of the People*, Büchner's *Woyzeck* — not to mention the large typologically defined casts of nineteenth-century melodrama. At times, they come to resemble and share the dangerously sterile perspectives and social power of the speaker in Reaney's poem "The Man Hunter," his heart and brain assembled by society, walking through the "arranged spaces" of the city (*Poems* 131). Apart from their primary roles within the social milieu of the plays, they exist simply as supporters or enemies of the Donnellys.

It is ultimately *their* world that attracts, consumes, judges, and punishes the weak or the rebellious. It also rewards those whose investment in the laws of their "mechanical geometry" is sufficient, and of the right order, to allow them to belong, and to kneel.

Donnelly turns to us for the first time. He is a small square chunk of will.

MRS DONNELLY.   He opened the door and came out.

OTHERS.   Oh Jim Donnelly. Jim, the Whitefeet hear that you let one of your mares stand to Johnson's stallion last Monday coming home from the fair.

MRS DONNELLY.   To which your father replied *he comes towards us and them with affability.*

MR DONNELLY.   It was love at first sight. Shure Johnson's stallion was mounting my one mare before I could stop him. Would you have me break up a pair of true lovers? Would you? And I had my back turned for the merest minute getting the other mare's tail out of a thornbush.

OTHERS.   Did you not know, Jim Donnelly, that no Whitefoot is to have any dealings with the Protestant and the heretic Johnson?

MR DONNELLY.   Yes, but it was. *They extend two lighted candles to him.*

OTHERS.   ·Kneel, Donnelly. Get down on your knees. *But he stands. The barrel is rolled back and forth in front of him.* Swear *striking a book* by the holy evangelists that you will always be joined to this society known as the Whitefeet and

86

that you will forever and forever obey —
MR DONNELLY. But you see I won't kneel. And I won't, I will
not swear that. (41–42)

In this passage from *Sticks & Stones*, and in a later one from
Handcuffs where kneeling is even more a sign of obedience to very
particular social, political, and religious expectations, we can see the
work in Reaney's own terms as a "play about a man who refused to
kneel" (Letter to Keith Turnbull). In *Handcuffs*, the Bishop hears
from Father Girard about the troubles in Biddulph: "Father Girard,
what is going on in your parish? I see from my tower the twinkling
lights of burning barns, I see crops rotting in the field, I hear a constant
gnashing of teeth, and of one family I hear — I see in the daily press
constant reference" (48). The election of 1879 is underway, and the
Bishop wants to change the voting pattern of Girard's parish: ". . .
up here — you see we are hoping for a Catholic Conservative member
of Parliament. So the Donnellys must change their voting pattern. . . .
it is unfortunate for them that this riding cannot be won unless a
party takes a majority of the votes, the Catholic votes in the ward,
and the Conservative party shall take a majority of those votes. They
must kneel with the rest of the parish" (48–49).
    In these two passages, we witness the interlocking of the ancient
Tipperary feud and the act of kneeling which, in the passage from
Sticks & Stones, is accompanied by a private, secret society ritual
with candles, while in *Handcuffs* its context is more institutionalized
through the Bishop's reference to a parish mass. That is, the terms of
the feud have broadened to encompass the increasingly fixed values
of a particular ecclesiastical, social, political, commercial, and legal
world to which the Bishop, along with the other major representatives of society, is fully committed. Kneeling is no longer merely the
command of one belligerent faction to another. The action has also
become a sign of belonging to an established society, confident in its
mores, determined to maintain its outward manifestations of order
and its instruments of control. The victimization of the Donnellys
thus shifts from an essentially private context to a broader social one
in which political power is invested with sectarian religious sanction-
ing, in which predetermined, socially authorized roles (Black, Irish,
merchant, farmer, land-owner, priest, politician, Orangeman, and so
on) supersede individual aspirations, particularly those which derive
from spiritual and natural impulses. Such a society, Raymond
Williams observed, was "an impersonal process, a machine with

built-in properties." Furthermore, the cynicism and the structures of exploitation inherent in such a society "are paid for not only in social and political coin; they teach ways of feeling, and in turn are taught by them, which tend to find their way into the most personal experience" (71) and, into the structure and uses of language, into a sterile grammar of polarization, "just beginning to wrap itself around Canadian life."

The Donnellys operate within this world; they pay taxes, acquire and work the land, engage in various commercial dealings, use its judicial processes, vote in its elections, attend its churches, adapt to its economic " 'go-aheadism.' " They are also, however, associated with natural and spiritual values that struggle to remain vitally independent of the immediate obligations of such a world. Part of this struggle between what Mrs. Donnelly called "the spiritual mark called a character which lasts forever" (*Sticks* 37), and the secular forces that threaten such a sense of character, is concretely drama-tized in the way in which Reaney uses the "shaky fading paper rope" to his region's past. The density and complexity of the archival material that verbally and scenically permeates the trilogy is, of course, understood as the prime source of the central characters and events. The Donnellys — Farl, Keefe, Stud, Cassleigh, Carroll, and the others — are, in a sense, released from their archival existence by means of their documentary definition; the available documents, which tell us what they said and did, illuminate and define the circumference of their being just as, for instance, the central figures of Lorca's *Blood Wedding* were initially defined by lurid newspaper accounts of murderous family feuding. In Lorca's play, however, these documents never surface directly. They never have to compete in theatrical terms with the concentrated lyricism that gives mytho-logical significance to the victimized young couple of the play. In the trilogy, the documents are inextricably fused with the characters, their story, and the story-style to which collage is central. This fusion approaches a tragic dimension as the spectator hears and sees the documentary definition become, to a degree, a documentary entrap-ment. Like the passionate and haunted figures of Pirandello's *Six Characters in Search of an Author*, or, more recently, Sharon Pollock's *Blood Relations*, Reaney's Donnellys strive to understand and to escape their strictly documentary role and, to a degree, their "story." They strive to achieve a more human face within the "maze of truth and life that rests unresolved."

An example of this is remarked upon by Reaney in a teaching kit distributed to schools during the National Tour of the trilogy. Referring to the use of shadow plays in *Handcuffs*, he writes: "As an image of the play I think that shadow versus reality was one of the persistent possibilities; the Donnelly Tragedy involves so much investigation of shadows; then one draws the curtain and discovers quite something else behind there. They are caught in a world of shadows; we all drag behind us — as Mrs. Donnelly finds out in her confessional scene with Father Connolly — a shadow part of which is us, part of which is made by somebody else and their manipulation of our image" (NDWT). On the other hand, their passion for justice, for a legal clarity unequivocally detached from the corrosive pressures of prejudice, rumour, and a particular social contract, necessitates — as it generally does, incidentally, in melodrama — an almost obsessive attachment to documents of all sorts. Documents, then, release and imprison, create and destroy, in a seemingly endless round that finally engages us all — playwright, actor, and spectator — not simply in mounds of archival material, but in a totally captivating milieu in which the implications of a deepening participation in the events alerts us to the underlying tragic structuring of these events. The documents, in their multitude, their complexity, and ambiguity, function doubly as Muse and as Fate, and the action of the trilogy moves, as in the plays of Pirandello, with certain epistemological as well as ontological reverberations. Reaney's "fading paper rope" extends its reach far beyond the mere re-creation of historical personages and events. It extends into what Bowering called the "secret alphabet . . . of the region's translucent bonds" (6). The search for the alphabet is the search for those significant points where the speech of the place and that of the emerging creative self intersect, and the documented region is internalized. The prime *locus* of archival research becomes the Self.

In the plays immediately following the Donnelly trilogy, Reaney's insistent archival muse continued to lead him into a number of events and stories which inform at different levels "this native land business." *Baldoon, Wacousta!, The Canadian Brothers, The Dismissal,* and *King Whistle!* deal, altogether, with events in Canadian history from the siege of Fort Detroit in 1763 to a strike in Stratford in 1933. In his theatrical representations of Pontiac's uprising, the mysterious happenings near Wallaceburg in 1829, the students' strike at the University of Toronto in 1895, and the social and political confrontations in small town Stratford in 1933, there persists, as firmly as ever, the dichotomous impulses of Reaney's art: "documentary on one side and myth on the other." Equally firm in these plays are the several theatre languages with which Reaney had been assembling and presenting his vision of Canadian life since *Colours in the Dark*.

In the *Halloween* letters "Topless Nightmares" and "The Story Behind *King Whistle!*" Reaney recounts (in increasingly combative tones, we might add) something of the "nativist kick" ("Topless Nightmares" 2) that informs the plays. Following the national tour of the Donnelly trilogy he "decided that it might be less wearing for the NDWT company if they concentrated on a provincial tour with a local legend. They had no idea what to do next; in an unguarded moment I opened my big mouth and said 'I know next to nothing about the Southern Border area of Ontario, Windsor etc. Why not beat the bounds of Southwestern Ontario by putting on plays about stories from down there and let us have the premieres in the places the stories occurred in?'" ("Story" 50). This was an area, he asserted, "that not only is filled with traditions from our deepest past, but is also filled with millions of Canadians who, until just lately, went over to shop at Hudson's in Detroit — this last named town and store having for them the magnetic pull of the black stone at Mecca" ("Topless Nightmares" 2).

Baldoon was written collaboratively with the Windsor poet, play-wright, and editor Marty Gervais, whose mother's account of pol-tergeists at Pointe-aux-Roches initially articulated for him some of the powerful cross-currents of the natural and the supernatural that lie at the centre of the play. "It was my mother's face of horror," Gervais wrote, "that blossomed into the writings of *Baldoon*" (*Baldoon* 116–17). Reaney saw in the story signs of a world "where the laws of atheism, progress and materialism suddenly break down" (*Baldoon* 119). The *Baldoon* mysteries represented for him another instance of a more highly prized playing field for emotion and metaphor than that provided by the commercial and rationalist silt of modern life. The strictly nationalist and regionalist impetus to "beat the bounds and show the flag," is fused with, indeed generally superseded by, the more important and engaging poetic task of exploring the mythic cross-beams whose forms and secrets respond more assuredly to the ontological prospects of Reaney's artistic program. In the end, we do not necessarily feel sympathetically responsive to the especially *regional* claims to our attention. These are but a conduit, as such highly generalized regional claims were in *The Sun and the Moon*, *The Killdeer*, and *Listen to the Wind*, for another kind of knowledge related to an inner, rather than an outer, geographical space. "Each one of us," writes Bachelard, "should speak of his roads, his cross-roads, his roadside benches; each one of us should make a surveyor's map of his lost fields and meadows. . . . Thus we cover the universe with drawings we have lived. These drawings need not be exact. They need only to be tonalized on the mode of our inner space" (*Poetics of Space* 11).

The mode of Reaney's inner space is suggested by his preoccupation with the "folklore phenomenon of both oral and literary dimensions" ("Topless Nightmares" 4) that the Baldoon mysteries disclose. The opening scenic image of *Baldoon* appropriately encompasses this folkloric dimension as well as the more specifically regionalist and archival plane. The play opens with a bare stage with

> a large back curtain that is an old map of the very southern part of Upper Canada; this may show the shoreline and hinterland from Walpole Island sweeping over to Long Point. I have a feeling that it could be upside down because behind it are going to be shadows through serim . . . of McTavish and McDorman journeying through the fens and wilds on their eighty mile trek from Baldoon to Long Point; this is easier to suggest if they seem to be wading through a lower band of dark material; the land masses on the map could be made of bulrushes. . . . This map places us in a locale and now its legends enact themselves in front of us. (1)

Other scenic and sonic images and effects are designated to represent the lake, the Syne River, the general absence of topographical highlights ("There's very little for a shooter to hide behind . . . for miles around. No trees. Just grass, and the river" [26]) and particularized atmospheric qualities (a "drowsy, summer humming heat sound in the air and the cries of lake gulls" [9]). There are also copious verbal references to specifically Windsor-area names and events: Sombra township where rye straw is gathered; tourists arriving on a steam boat from Detroit and Chatham; the pillory of the market square of Sandwich; the Corcas Methodist Orphan asylum in Chatham. Most of the important scenes of the play occur inside the houses of Dr. Troyer and McTavish and in the church, represented both as a model (based in part upon architectural features outlined in *Hallowed Walls* by Marion MacRae and Anthony Adamson [*Baldoon* 61]) and as an acting space with a pulpit.

Dr. Troyer's house is established near the beginning of the play. It is here that the two travellers from Baldoon, McTavish and McDorman, are heading, pursued by witches "cackling and playing with hats" (9). Dr. Troyer, somewhat like a softer more charitable version of George Bernard Shaw's Captain Shotover, looms powerfully as the spiritual ambassador of another time and place. His chief antagonist, the Reverend McGillicuddy, on the other hand, serves up in large sweeping measures the spiritually drear, guilt-ridden, joyless, but economically secure cross-beams of Scotch Presbyterianism. These cross-beams, in time, helped to formulate the "brick upon brick" oppressiveness of Reaney's own township, which he delineated in *A Suit of Nettles*, his earliest plays, and was to yet again in *King Whistle!*. Dr. Troyer champions a "happiness filled with frankincense and citrons and dancing and music and love" (*Baldoon* 73) and a world, as Reaney puts it, in which he "did have magic beneficent powers and could with his scrying stone see a great deal farther into the levels of existence above and below our modern, natural one than TV aerials even manage" (118). Much of the play focuses upon this opposition between Dr. Troyer's life-force and Presbyterian gloominess. There is, as well, the historically antecedent opposition between the Natives and the white settlers, one of whom, John McTavish, "bought" his land "for a bottle of whiskey" (48–49). The archival, documentary treatment of these oppositions is evident in the very precise selection of hymns, the recreation of an early Presbyterian service, the use of near-by Native names Re-nah-sewa and Par-tar-sung, and, of course, the theatricalization of many of the mysterious happenings described in the vast variety of sources consulted by Reaney and Gervais. These include an actual trial for witchcraft conducted 14 April 1830 at Sandwich, which was stopped when the Provincial Secretary reminded the court that the "Act Against Witchcraft, Pretensions to" was repealed "in all his Majesty's dominions, even Essex and Kent County of Upper Canada two years ago" (46). The precision with which Reaney also approached and attempted to re-create the variety of dialects represented by the different religious and social sectors of the Windsor area in the early nineteenth century further discloses the purely archival instincts that underlie the poetic.

These poetic instincts are privileged throughout *Baldoon*. Reaney is clear on this. The more he experienced the area surrounding Windsor, he writes, with its "Indian traditions, its great marshes and a rich folklore lode that runs from Lake St. Clair right over to Long Point where Dr. Troyer lived on Lake Erie, I have the feeling that it's a place rather like Circe's island, Aiaia, an isle of the dead where you go to be reborn. Marshy country breeds fen-ghosts and jack o' lanterns? *Baldoon* gives us the chance to write and think about other worlds" ("Topless Nightmares" 4). The image of this area then, as an ontological catalyst, as another example of a "surveyor's map of . . . lost fields and meadows," is similar to the generalized locales of Reaney's earliest plays — especially *The Killdeer*, where a dominant image is that of a swamp with its "damp sweet darkness" wherein discoveries are made and personal identities established (22).

The locales of Reaney's next two plays, *Wacousta!* and *The Canadian Brothers*, are similarly generalized and, perhaps, even less evocative of regional cross-roads and drawings of any kind. This is due, in part, to the same preoccupation with myth that underlies *Baldoon* and to the particular literary, as opposed to experiential, sources from which the stories of Wacousta, de Haldimar, Pontiac, and the events around Fort Detroit in the late eighteenth century were taken. The investigatory process that informed the workshops for these two plays was not, like that for *Colours in the Dark*, or the Donnelly trilogy, and later for *The Dismissal* and *King Whistle!*, regionally and archivally inspired; it was, rather, focused upon how to play — upon story and story-style.

There are very few theatrically important images accompanying that of the "giant dream figure" ("Topless Nightmares" 3) Reaney found in John Richardson's account of Wacousta that serve to locate geographically the actions of heroism, betrayal, and revenge, which constitute the primary concerns of these plays. Those we do find are, in the end, as minimally indicative of specific place as are the emblematic signatures of the Elizabethan theatre — Arbour, Cave, Castle, Mountain, and so on. The sense of a particular place, and of a unique social milieu informing character and action, is not evident here.

This emblematic quality of *Wacousta!* is evident in the opening scenic arrangement:

The action takes place in forts Detroit and Michilimackinac in the fall of 1763. A backcloth shows the Detroit River banks as if seen by an English water colourist whose profession is that of a military surveyor. In front of that a raked stage with two pictures painted on its floor: stage right an heraldic lion; stage left a shaman pictograph. Scaffolding up right. A tall flagpole dominates with its imperial symbol. (10)

Character and action throughout *Wacousta!* embody the bifurcation of experience implied by these iconic representations of the lion and the shaman pictograph. On a space simply identified verbally as the "green island of Belle Isle" (22), Charlotte and Le Subtil gesture towards the icons which inform their separate worlds. Le Subtil touches the shaman pictograph on the floor, then catches a floating dandelion seed. Charlotte identifies this seed for him:

> It is known as the dent-du-lion — the dandelion or the lion's tooth. Why here it is growing even here, and, Le Subtil, if you don't watch out, his teeth *as she touches the heraldic lion on floor* will grow over the ground your forests root in, the farms and the cities underneath which our people will lie buried. (22)

In the next scene, Charlotte's father, de Haldimar, reminds her of the racial and cultural divisions residing at the core of their personal and historical stories:

> Look, girl, get over your romantic thinking you can be his *pointing at the shaman pictograph* You cannot be anything other than your type which is that *points at lion* and which, like a real name, lies hidden beneath all our personalities' dust and dirt. When living amid savage scenes and unexplored countries, this lesson must be particularly taken to heart by all of us. . . . (25)

Implied in these passages, and elsewhere, is what Reaney refers to as a disastrous process of desacralization. For "thousands of years," he writes, "shamans have been drawing magic circles over the land of North America and making it holy with incantations over the dead; come pioneer time and presto! Wallaceburg plunks itself down on top of the local Indian cemetery and a sewage farm in Stratford is established at the salt lick where Indians waited for deer" ("Topless Nightmares" 5–6). In *Baldoon*, John McTavish's house was built upon Native lands, and the "hidden ones" must be confronted in the deeper stages of McTavish's self-examination. At one point in the play, "a masked shaman drums with a black dog dancing in front of him or running in circles endlessly. We hear the word 'Mama-gwase-gwug' — the Indian name for the fairies underneath McTavish's house" (87). In *Wacousta!*, in an exchange between Pontiac and de Haldimar, the opposition between shaman and lion results in an image of an ultimately desacralized Detroit: "Toy friction cars swarm over the stage. In effect, a giant Pontiac stands exactly where the

Renaissance Building stands now in Detroit with modern traffic swirling about his feet" (61).

The depth and the irreparability of the shaman-lion division is further explored in *The Canadian Brothers*. In this play, a significant aspect of the "native land business" is essentially expatiatory, focusing, as it often did in *Baldoon* and *Wacousta!*, upon the guilt of civilization. "There must be some arrangement in the world for the wronged," exclaims the enraged Matilda as she holds a snake above her head, "no matter how weak, to revenge themselves on the strong. How else may the stony heart ever learn mercy and justice?" (*Canadian Brothers* 684). The representation of events in the War of 1812 as "document" is intended to provide an historical framework for the mythic and ontologically compelling substance Reaney locates in the complicated story of the de Haldimar family and the effects of Wacousta's curse. Despite the numerous verbal and scenic evocations of actual places, times, and events (the battles of Queenston Heights and Fort Meigs, the occupation of Sandwich in Upper Canada by the Americans, the capture of Fort Detroit by the British, the naval engagements around Bois Blanc Island and Grosse Island) and the representation of historical figures (General William Hull, Major Montgomerie, Tecumseh, Commodore Barclay, General Brock), the broad regional references are translated into even broader imaginative and mythic ones. Reaney's account of Wacousta is strongly reminiscent of Yeats's representation of daemonic powers in such a figure as Cuchulain:

> I find this giant figure haunting and he is, I think our reply to the Americans' Captain Ahab, only most Canadians don't know about him. This white man who's gone over to the Indians and somehow procured a costume for himself that would drive most hippies mad with envy is charismatic enough to invite comparisons with Lord Byron, Satan, Heathcliff, Thoreau, Achilles, Hamlet, a whole nation of souls protesting the way so-called civilization irons out individuality, fantasy and the passions. . . . What is Wacousta thinking about? Whatever it is it is something that as the story develops the reader sees as having himself lost too: a girl, an Eden, a unity that used to be. ("Topless Nightmares" 3)

A world characterized by complex and intersecting political, military, religious, and commercial powers encloses and entraps the Canadian brothers Gerald and Henry de Haldimar, just as one did the Donnelly family. Reaney's dramatization of this world, however, is not particularized in such a way as to draw attention deliberately to a rich archival foundation. Instead, we are drawn towards the heightened structures and emotions of Romance. Gerald and Henry are victims of "other people . . . like gods set over us" (678), people, we're told, like Napoleon, President Madison, Governor Harrison of Indiana, Tecumseh, General Brock. But, more significantly, their fate is sealed by a curse, the story of a curse, and by the unexpiated layers of personal, social, racial, and existential guilt:

> GERALD. Trapped by a border river in the centre of a continent.
> HENRY. Where can we go?
> GERALD. And the gods answer:
> HENRY. Nowhere.
> BOTH. And those who cursed us say:
> ELLEN AND WACOUSTA. Your ancestors still in your blood started this.
> HENRY. For one moment I felt I was a character in a romance and the paper sky above me cleared so that through the ink I glimpsed the author about to hack off my arms in a battle scene and I cried:
> BOTH. Change the story. (679)

Although the theatrical scale is immensely different and far more complicated in *The Canadian Brothers*, the intermingling of a melo-dramatic story and personal identity reiterates the situation of *Listen to the Wind*, and, as with the earlier play, specifically regional explorations remain of secondary importance.

A sense of a specific milieu, however, is strongly evoked in Reaney's next two plays, *The Dismissal* and *King Whistle!* — occasional plays originally commissioned, respectively, by the University of Toronto and by Reaney's high school, Stratford Central Collegiate. In both plays, the primary experience is investigatorial. Both plays deal with particular values of the "very locally coloured tree trunk" in the larger context of educational, political, and economic interests and tendencies.

In *The Dismissal*, Professor William Dale exclaims to the University's Executive Council,

> . . . we still invite our young people to be culturally raped by teachers who couldn't get a job in Britain or the States. Take my

own case. I was a farmboy from Blanshard Township who almost became a full professor at the university, but. . . . All the young people in my native township and its capital — St. Mary's — they began to see this university as theirs because I was here. But when they came down — down to Toronto they found that I was the exception. For the big, important appointments are made to foreigners from Oxford, Glasgow, Edinburgh, New York — men with accents and manners that sometimes would freeze the blood. Look, if my family had stayed in Yorkshire, I would have just now taken over my father's forge — a black-smith. He came to Ontario and at first it seemed a different society — but, oh no, a new hierarchy forms, new ways are thought up to alienate the people from their birthright and so I wrote that letter to show you that when you appointed me in 1885 to the tutorship in Latin, you didn't appoint my soul or is it lying around here perhaps in one of your filing cabinets, well I claim it back not with money or power or influence, but the effluence of the same ink bottle I've marked thousands of your children's themes with, ink, pen words — I claim my soul with the only thing that matters — its language — a letter, letters. (38)

This current of xenophobia, here somewhat stretched to consider-ations of a Latin professor's soul, informs Reaney's "nativist kick" from time to time. It was, for instance, evident on several occasions during the tour of the Donnelly trilogy when ideas for *The Dismissal* were being gathered. In Winnipeg, Reaney observed, ". . . artists from Chicago came up and took over the Manitoba School of Fine Arts" (*14 Barrels* 32), thus increasing the aesthetic authority of abstract expressionism. Also in Winnipeg, there was no invitation to perform in the Warehouse Theatre, part of the Manitoba Theatre Centre: "Rumour has it that the director sent the Reaney scripts to New York, whither he'd recently come himself, for information as to these scripts' quality; by the time we arrived, permission from New York had still not arrived" (*14 Barrels* 34). Later, in Vancouver, British poetic imperialism is the fear: ". . . like everything else in Canada, the Poetry League is always being threatened with takeovers and you have to keep fighting. Over our porridge, Colleen was being congratulated at her skill in helping table the English lady's motion to join us to some iambic guild in Britain that would have flooded us with freeloading larks at our own expense (or some such scheme)" (*14 Barrels* 61). At Simon Fraser, ". . . the theatre director . . . was seen scuttling down a corridor, never to appear again, even to scuttle. The rumour was that they were all American and that they were honour-bound to see us fail." Finally, however, "Canucks rallied round" (*14 Barrels* 64). Still in Vancouver, over "pappadums and steamed rice the following collage emerged: Summer Theatres always do *The Fantasticks*. At first they cast the part with a Canuck girl, but when the new New York director comes in, since we up here don't know how to do this complex play as yet, he always re-casts the girl's part with an American girl" (*14 Barrels* 67). Soon afterwards, Reaney talks with a student at the Faculty Club of the University of British Columbia; he, we're told, "hadn't watched a nation's roots being sold, he'd watched our minds being sold in the sixties when whole university departments Americanized overnight." As Reaney reflects on the possibility of a play about this phenomenon, he asks whether it would be "cruel, malicious and adelphophobic to say some time dramatically that Canucks are too wambly, shy and quite unable to prevent themselves from being culturally raped over and over again?" (*14 Barrels* 70).

Willie King was not particularly shy, but, in Reaney's view, he was wambly enough to equivocate for obvious personal and political reasons during the course of the student strike at the University of Toronto in 1895. This strike eventually led to the establishment of a Royal Commission on Discipline at the university. The causes of the crisis were many and included serious jurisdictional disputes between the university and the Provincial government; questions concerning freedom of speech (specifically focused upon the attempt to have the "ex-Quaker and communist" Phillips Thompson speak to a student assembly); the qualifications and national origin of teachers and administrators; personality clashes of all sorts — particularly one between the Vice Chancellor and the Chancellor and President. As Peter Razgaitis states in his "Synopsis of Events Surrounding the Student Strike of 1895,"

The students wanted to expose the "hidden" dimensions of the University — dimensions which were negative influences over their own education, over the faculty, and over the administration's ability to proceed to make improvements to the physical facilities and quality of university instruction; they resented the seemingly excessive control that the administration attempted to exert over the expressions and functions of their activities and in 1895 they took steps to publicly disrupt the apparent routine of University life in order to draw attention to their grievances. (56–57)

These several inter-woven political, educational, and personal situations are treated in *The Dismissal* in four major actions: (1) the strike itself, complete with speeches, ambiguous motions, mass meetings, and the like; (2) William Dale's dismissal and questions regarding Canadian and foreign teachers; (3) the expulsion of James Tucker; (4) the political and moral machinations of the young William Lyon Mackenzie King. As a crowded backdrop/framework to these central actions, Reaney attempts to create "the feeling of the place" through an assortment of period songs and hymns and through a sequence of scenes arranged to depict the college life of the class of 1895 from the time of its arrival on campus through to graduation. Here we have Reaney's Heraclitian horse at full speed as examinations, lectures, convocation, initiation rites, study sessions (mountains of books), Halloween antics (especially the tearing down of an old shed on campus by King and others, an episode honoured by a Glee Club song), dining-room confusion (mountains of buns), council meetings, athletic events, and, of course, all the commotion associated with the strike compete for stage space and time, expressing directly in complex scenic images and kinetic patterning the excruciatingly frenetic dash of life called undergraduate education.

The various confrontations in *The Dismissal* — between Dale and the Council; between Tucker and the University Administration; between Tucker and King — are particularized, often rooted in their respective documentary sources (including King's diaries). However, they are also assimilated into an overriding confrontation, the terms of which Reaney draws from one of the entries in Dale's journal: "integral versus fractional life" (39). Following his dismissal, Dale retired to his father's farm where his boyhood vision of being "independent of the literal for life" is rediscovered and reinforced (38). Dale acquires his emancipation and clarification partly through language and metaphor. The image of Dale's world (similar to Reaney's own — his mother's farm near Stratford, evoked on several occasions in *14 Barrels*) is in sharp contrast to the world of Sir Daniel Wilson, George Squair, President Fury, and King, who recall the "caesars, kaisers, mutes and jackasses" Reaney delineated in "The Dead Rainbow" (1948) and some of the pedagogical figures satirized in such works as *A Suit of Nettles*, *Twelve Letters to a Small Town*, *The Sun and the Moon*, *One-Man Masque*, *Three Desks*, and

Colours in the Dark. In the former reside the restorative powers derived from the active interpenetration of life and thought, life and labour, reason and imagination, inner and outer experience. In the latter we become mired in a menacing, meaningless "fractional life" born of the proliferation of "things."

The dual claims of a documented primary experience (the strike and the particular educational and political issues of 1895) and of mythical form (intuited through language and the metaphorical dimensions of Dale's private world) result in the play's double life as a college review and an exploration of the Canadian psyche. Such a double life is seen, for instance, when Reaney presents a typically chaotic university eating sequence (during which King, in a mad rush for a seat "dives under the table and emerges in a seat on the other side" [16]) is followed by a lecture on ancient Rome by Dale during which a fundamental distinction is drawn between King and Tucker:

> DALE. How many of you believe that a she-wolf suckled Romulus and Remus? *Tucker's hand goes up.* And how many of you believe the other story that it was not a lupa who suckled them but a common prostitute named Lupa? *King and the others put up their hands.* We must remember that what the Romans themselves believed no matter how unbelievable to us is a very important part of their history. It may be a part of our history one day, the history of Ontario, that we believed only those things that could so obviously have really happened. (17)

Such a narrowing of imaginative life was described earlier by Reaney in his essay on Ontario's newspapers:

> The power geology gives to find oil in Lambton County and iron at Marmora will soon seem much more important than the imaginative power the first chapter of Genesis can produce in a society which used to see the week, particularly the first week of time, as having a pattern that shaped life, shaped it in a human-divine relationship quite unlike the ratract time of the busy printer inventing machines which will put him out of work or of a factory operative whose goods must be consumed by a society madly producing too many such goods already. Not far away waits a world in which the idea that the County Court House is modelled on Solomon's Temple will seem very strange; the *Free Press* cannot see that its very prose, its very type

perhaps, builds up the destruction of the world picture it sup-
posedly favours. ("Myths" 261)

The relationship between the educated imagination and the external
social and economic order, between the separate mappings of inner
and outer experience, is central to Reaney's evangelical urge to create
a better society. The "fractional" world of unrelated things depicted
in *The Dismissal*, like the mechanical " 'go-aheadism' " celebrated
by the Ontario newspapers, infers the stultifying, ultimately
imprisoning reification that reduces reality to a particular disposition
of objects and economic *données*. In Reaney's next play, the character and actions of the hero are defined in terms of his place within,
and reaction to, such an economic *donnée*. In his account of *King
Whistle!*, Reaney situates Ollie Kay, "a Sunday School Superinten-
dent who was also foreman of the first floor in the Stratford Chair
Company," within the company of such figures as Wacousta, Dr.
Troyer, the Canadian brothers, and William Dale, the principal
figures in his plays since the Donnelly trilogy. Reaney describes the
general movement as one from legend to history, from myth to event.
Dale and Kay belong to a world endangered by visible and powerful
deputies of fractionalism. They are not attacked by the "demonic
revengers," witches or poltergeists, that informed the worlds of
Wacousta!, *The Canadian Brothers*, and *Baldoon*. Instead, Dale
must contend with "a bunch of academic stuffed shirts involved in
power games about money and tenure," and Kay with the " 'Uptown
Bunch,' the usual 1/2 dozen vested interests you get in any smallish
Souwesto City. . . ." Thus, Reaney writes, ". . . after six years, I am
writing a play about almost contemporary life; about factories,
about economic problems, about Marxism and Capitalism"
("Story" 50). He was also writing a play in which most of the
characters are exteriorized into Relief Lady, Girl, Reporter, Hockey
Boy, Wagon Boy, Farmer's Wife, Single Man, Policeman, President,
and so on. These are typologically representative figures that suit
both the thirties musical comedy format of the work (everyone-in-
the-community-can-participate), and the informing ideological
perspective that necessarily provides a plethora of predetermined
economic, political, religious, and social roles. A central component
of this perspective was, Reaney notes, Christianity:

One thing the research taught me was not to underestimate the
effectiveness for social justice of the Christian Church as it

existed in Stratford in 1933. A great many of the strike leaders belonged to churches — usually Baptist or United Church; their ministers supported them to the hilt, and the kind of society these people find possible is neither Marxist nor Capitalist, but what I would call pragmatic — Christian. In other words, religion not politics is the final way of controlling money — which even today seems like an uncontrollable demon in our society. In William Blake such a force is known as the Spectre of Urthona, the personification of our will to control the environment, which often gets away from us and starts controlling us. ("Story" 50–51)

The conflation here of Blake and what Reaney elsewhere called the "new sects of the Protestant Left" ("Canadian Poet's Predicament" 294) reinforces the inseparability in Reaney's thought and art of the imagination and social reform. Woodman has described how Reaney's "mature vision reveals the influence of an evangelical conception of the world in the clutches of Satan awaiting the inevitable Judgement." Though the vision, he writes, "is essentially secularized-imagination replacing grace — Reaney himself emerges in his work as a member of a defined poetic Elect whose task it is imaginatively to redeem the times" (*Reaney* 10). Satan in *King Whistle!* is represented by the figure of money who, reminiscent of the child as AntiChrist in *Colours in the Dark* dreaming of "especially inverted, upside-down churches" (50), is described as a "young, elegantly dressed child, divinely sure of himself and insolent beyond belief." Kay, on the other hand, is described as a "slender tough intellectual: farm, church, books." The opposition between the two is established at the beginning of the play:

KAY.   Money isn't everything, you imp.
MONEY.   If it isn't . . . why are you working so hard for it then?
KAY.   Jesus Christ didn't need you.
MONEY.   Yeah, he let Judas carry me for him and boy, did I ever get the two of them in a cleft stick . . . well you'll never do without me and you'll never control me and all of you will never have enough of me to get off the treadmill. . . . (7)

Money is present in person, or spirit, throughout the play. In "almost every scene in the play, we should sense his presence" (18). In a Sunday School episode he teaches some children to play craps;

at a meeting of the Stratford Town Council, he plays the part of a Clerk as the Mayor and representatives of the "usual 1/2 dozen vested interests" vote down Kay's motion concerning a relief voucher system. His presence is felt when the President of the factory, Jamieson, confronts Kay on the question of minimum wages and part time workers:

> PRESIDENT. Kay . . . There's no law says that I have to give minimum wage to part time workers.
> KAY. Who've been kept part time workers for ten, fifteen years — no, oh no Mr. Jamieson, there is a moral law.
> PRESIDENT. Go into the ministry then you madman a factory's not a church.
> KAY. Well it is. Can you be a man and look down there at that house across the road where you fired the father and hired his son and not see the immorality of it? (19–20)

The immorality of unfettered capitalism, of a " 'go-aheadism' " impervious to collective welfare in conflict with a "pragmatic Christianity," is presented by Reaney in terms of characters whose individual impulses (for money, justice, work, profit) merge with historical processes. In a sense, the Manicheism that informed the vision and dramatic structure of such plays as *The Killdeer* and *The Sun and the Moon* is transferred to the almost entirely secular realm of a play "about factories, about economic problems, about Marxism and Capitalism." Reaney's reading of history and economics finds itself compatible with an obvious dualism of values (rich and poor, management and labour, city and farm) from which an equally obvious melodramatic perspective arises. In the presence of such clear, unequivocal choices, as Wylie Sypher has observed, the imagination is "pressed away from the neutrality of the world towards overstatement" (432).

However, the several components of this larger perspective on contemporary life, while informing the structure, characters, and language of *King Whistle!*, do not by any means displace the prime locus of Reaney's imaginative recreation of industrial unrest in his native city during the thirties. *King Whistle!*, fully as much as any play since *Colours in the Dark*, appears to luxuriate in an accumulation of what Bessai calls "concrete localisms" ("Documentary" 198). As Reaney made clear in his account of the play, the investigatorial process was almost unrestrained as a community "paper rope" was constructed through interviews, books, letters, newspapers, mountains of legal and industrial documents in order to locate a Stratford, Ontario, that, "in 1933 came out on the streets and shouted what it wanted to be" ("Story" 50).

Reaney had, as a child of seven, heard this shout and had "seen the strikers parading down Ontario Street with a Union Jack at their head." Fortunately a home movie was located that recorded the Mayor reading the Riot Act to a large assembly in the Market Square, the soldiers forming in order, as Reaney put it, to "quell the revolution," and the strikers on parade with "their Big Bertha, an old garbage can satirizing the army's machine guns, with their hand-made signs asking after all for just a living wage" ("Story" 51). All of this, of course, is represented in the play. Act 1 concludes with a miscellany of scenic and sonic effects intended to convey the exaggerated confrontational tones of the event: a radio voice reporting on the riot (". . . it was the worse I'll ever see, for it was an all night affair started by the girls in the plucking department aided by 1,000 sympathizers going on all night with property damage and sabotage of the power system"); images of soldiers assembling; the sound of marching music and military commands; the Mayor reading the Riot Act; a manufacturer *"Borne on two men's shoulders"* shouting the intention of the plant owners to replace the striking workers; the sound of the whistles blowing, and the workers defiantly singing of their resolution:

> But we have left in our control
> Our individual selves and souls
> Our wills to work, whom to obey
> We have the right ourselves to be.
> Men and Women. (28)

This song reiterates the ideal of an individual birthright which Dale had asserted in his speech before the University Council; it also, of course, embodies the Spectre of Urthona operating against an economic system that appeared to diminish the significance of the self.

The "concrete localisms" of *King Whistle!* also include such choric lists of names and places as helped to provide the documentary detail of *Colours in the Dark*. In a sequence entitled the "industrial history of Stratford," for instance, we are taken from the "sluggish town" of 1871 with its "eighty-three cows and forty-three sheep, / Five thousand people all dead asleep," through the arrival of steam trains, railway shops, chair factories "In which there hums the god machine / Fed by Niagara's electric stream" (19), to the establishment of such firms as Imperial Rattan Grosch Felt Shoe, Farquharson-Gifford, Faultless Castor Company, Avon Knit, Swift's and Stratford Chair. A number of songs in the play resonate with names of streets and personalities ("Summer's here & Tony Cryan's / Trumpets, trombones, sax and drums" [13]). We are constantly reminded of the very specific life and times of Stratford as it dealt with industrial growth and with the complex labour and political issues that affected most Canadian towns during the thirties.

The strike in Stratford created as deeply felt divisions in the community as the Donnelly massacre had in the Lucan and London areas. For a time, the Stratford that Reaney had described as part of a "doctor-dominated civilization of lawns" became known as "Red Town" ("Story" 51). The image of a tranquil, untroubled town becoming so completely unsettled, so confusedly engaged in an array of historical currents alien to the quieter affairs of Southwestern Ontario, captivated the young and the older Reaney. His miscreant, caricatural bias seems to have enjoyed the upheaval in the same way as the children in *Listen to the Wind* enjoyed the fantasies of a "terribly melodramatic" story capable of releasing them momentarily from debilitating reticence and parental authority (16). The play works through the events of the strike in two dominant keys. The mixture of messianic and caricatural impulses in Reaney results in the differing voices expressive, on the one hand, of the socioeconomic world infused with Marxist, Protestant, and Blakean categories, and, on the other, of the childlike relish taken in the disruption of well-tended lawns.

Another voice, that of the countless newspapers, letters, and interviews investigated and edited by Reaney and his theatre workers, served the more direct purposes of Reaney's "nativist kick," bringing into light the very particular ways in which his "sluggish" Stratford found itself with tanks facing workers singing the Internationale. At the end of the play, ". . . after the conflicting tunes have erased each other," we return to an Interior scene to encounter the newly elected Mayor, Ollie Kay, who rounds off his association with President Jamieson with the exclamation ". . . as mayor of this town with a labour council at my back it's not going to be for the few anymore; it's going to be for all the citizens of Stratford." The chorus then reiterates the ideal of what, in *The Dismissal*, was called the "integral." This is a power derived from qualities Reaney had discovered in the model for Ollie Kay, Oliver J. Kerr, "the first working class mayor of Stratford after the strike was over." He was interviewed by Reaney and his director Jerry Franken in Peterborough:

I was amazed at what Ontario had given me for the hero of my play out of farm, bank, Bible, church (Presbyterian), Sunday School, the sanding machine he invented, the pragmatism which in the end used both Marx and Capitalism in a determined attempt to get one very simple end — more money for the little man. ("Story" 51)

In his study of literary ideas in modern society, Gerald Graff observed that the "visionary view is . . . a kind of formalism on the offensive, projecting the autonomous imagination and its categories outward onto the practical world, elevating the imagination into the status of a universal legislator. In the visionary view, the real world does not disappear so much as become a kind of malleable raw material, to be shaped, transformed, and 'ordered' by consciousness" (14). As we have observed, a "visionary view" informs Reaney's representation of both Dale and Kay and their reactions to their respective academic and economic situations. Both men project outwardly upon the myriad signs of temporally rooted "fractionalism" the claim of the ideal. Both men believe in the possibility of a Blakean transformation of inner and outer life. In Reaney's next play, the visionary view is equally "on the offensive," however its target is less the practical world of academic, political, and economic concerns than it is the "malleable raw material" of consciousness itself. The self-referentiality of consciousness in this play has the obvious effect of displacing the central characters, of removing them from the kinds of identifiable historical contexts within which Dale and Kay, but also Wacousta, the Canadian brothers Gerald and Henry, and most of the figures of *Baldoon*, existed. *Gyroscope*, at times in the manner of the late plays of Strindberg, represents, first of all, Reaney's confrontation with, as he put it, "images of personalities spinning into other personalities" (Introd., *Gyroscope*) and, secondly, as Stingle has commented, "an exploration of the nature of poetry as Frye's 'building of worlds out of words'" (45).

The "native land business" of *Gyroscope* is not derived from an essentially archival muse that had directed so much of the investigatorial process informing the plays since the Donnelly trilogy.

Instead, the play provides the sort of perspective Reaney ascribed to the structuralism of Blake and Frye. The "concrete localisms" in this play are entirely imaginative constructs. They are fields of play for the poetic instinct as it explores both existing and possible worlds. As an answer to some who might think the personality and verbal puzzles of *Gyroscope* too "wild and extreme," Reaney explained,

> Not so, if you can see that my play may be like one of those scientific models or experiments in which nature is sped up in the interest of discovering a universal law. As yet, no one has been around long enough to see the complete wobble our spinning earth makes — an event which takes twenty thousand years to complete and which is called the precession of the equinoxes. But in two minutes a toy called a gyroscope will show you, can show you exactly how it works and what it looks like. Likewise, I hope that my play provides a model for a great many of the loose threads, empty caves, war memorials, Brazils, Canadas, trap doors, roof gardens, dreams, confrontations that living with other people mysteriously and troublingly involves. (Introd., *Gyroscope*)

In this play, Reaney has reasserted the primacy of what he calls the "secret alphabet or iconography or language of symbols and myths" that informs a society that has learned "how to play." In *Gyroscope*, the fragmented, fractionalized world against which such figures as Dale and Kay struggle is interiorized. The secret alphabet sought is, ultimately, one that will revolutionize the self. Such an interiorization means that the play's true story lies beyond what, in the plays from the Donnelly trilogy through to *King Whistle!*, Reaney presents as the world of social, historical, economic events. This story of spinning personalities, words, sounds, dreams, and ontological creativity is, as Richard Gilman observed of Strindberg's equally interiorized drama, "larger, less explicit, and more permanent than the physical life chosen for its exhibition." However, as he comments further, the "invisible has always to be made known through the visible but is never coterminous with it, and the resulting gap between idea and incarnation is the theatre's perennial problem" (93–94).

There is a visible and superficially, at least, knowable world within which the five characters of *Gyroscope* pursue their respective words, sounds, sexual identities, gyroscopic balances and imbalances. There is a world of the Restaurant Cafe operated by Henry, who will "change into the mycologist named Nicholas who will then change into the astounding Professor Puzzle," just as the Cafe itself will "elasticize" into an apartment, then "balloon into a crowded lab cafeteria," then into a YWCA cafeteria and a used clothing and second-hand bookstore. In the manner of Strindberg's *A Dream Play*, in which as Strindberg said the "characters are split, double and multiply . . . evaporate, crystallize, scatter and converge" (*Six Plays* 193), Reaney's characters and places "are forever spinning out of one phase into another" (*Gyroscope* i). A vaguely identifiable London, Ontario, world is evoked through passing references to such things as Hilda's hearing "the aeroplane to Cleveland" (6), to "Scarborough, / Toronna . . ." (29) in one of Hilda's poems, to the "war memorial soldier across the street with that cigarette in your mouth" (42), which, as Stingle explains, is a "reference to a memorial statue of a soldier in Manor Park, London, Ontario. Vandals periodically knock off its head" (62), to the parking lot at Simpson's, the Embassy Tavern, to the names of some Canadian poetry journals — *Fiddlehead, Matrix, Unicorn*. There is Reaney's parodic representation of a poetry guild, of a PhD candidate, a "Mother Courage of the archival steppes" (ii), pulling about a small wagon that holds an old-fashioned tape-recorder. Such references in the collage are, in some measure, similar to the numerous "imagery counts of the environment" with which Reaney characterized the many cities visited during the Donnelly tour and described throughout *14 Barrels*. These and other remnants extracted from "today's poetry" are like the highly personal collage boxes of Joseph Cornell, or Greg Curnoe's assemblage-paintings. They come to represent, as Rosenberg said of Cornell's "symbolic accretions," a means of "participating in the common life while holding himself strictly apart from it." Cornell, he writes, "becomes a member of the crowd by making anonymous use of its games" (*Artworks* 78).

Reaney's often very private coding of his imagery results in a similar feeling of his participation in and estrangement from his community. He locates myriad identifiers, establishing a generally familiar, regional outline. These images of place, person, and time, however, are in a sense relocated through the poetic spinning of the play's central image, the gyroscope, which, like Strindberg's kaleidoscope, shifts them on to other planes of meaning. These other planes, having to do with consciousness itself, with ways of poetically re-creating the "malleable raw material" of the so-called real world, with the discovery of what seems to be secret connections between personal (including sexual) identity and language, situate *Gyroscope* beyond the archivally inspired regional explorations that have been so central to Reaney's artistic program since *Colours in the Dark*.

Reaney thought Curnoe's approach to art was "so right" because ". . . he likes reflecting where he lives" ("Broughdale"). There is, however, always the question of dual citizenship for the poet, especially for one whose instincts are visionary. Such a poet "lives" inwardly as well as outwardly. The whole idea of the "native land business," in this case, involves what Reaney asserted in his essay on "The Canadian Poet's Predicament." Exploring the "native tradition," he said, "repays inquiry . . . not only with the acquisition of interesting heirlooms but with imaginative life that can still beget more imaginative life, with some passages even that can change your life" (14). *Gyroscope*, as a play by a poet about the begetting of imaginative life, asserts the constitutive power of "playing" to help us, as Canadians, "to work out our own way through" and "transform this world we live in" ("Letter from James Reaney" 9).

"MAKING UP PATTERNS
[SCRIBBLING WITH YOUR BODY/BODIES]"

The last play of the Donnelly trilogy, *Handcuffs*, concludes with the burial service of the murdered Donnellys during which the coffins are carried into the graveyard while the chorus sings,

> May the angels take you into paradise
> in tuo adventu suscipiant te Martyres
> And lead you into the holy city of Jerusalem
> Chorus angelorum te suscipiat

Then the pall bearers, the company of actors, who in the course of the trilogy have played the various members of the Donnelly family as well as the farmers, merchants, priests, bankers, and politicians of Biddulph, abandon all personal and social identity and return to the stage to mime the "growth of a wheatfield," evoking the seasonal design that, like the structure of the Mass, finally informs and encloses the story of the Donnellys:

> March! the snow has gone
> The green field John & Tom sowed
> Still there green
> April! growing again growing again
> May! taller and longer with longer
> Days until
> June and July
> July! until ready for harvest
> August
> Shivering and rippling
> cloud shadows summer wind
> cloud shadows

At this point, the stage directions tell us, a "golden light sweeps the stage. We should feel that around the Donnelly farmyard lies a big field of wheat ready for harvest" (157). This image echoes in purely scenic terms Mrs. Donnelly's admonition to Cassleigh's mob in *Sticks & Stones* during the Raising Bee at Callagher's: "There's fields of grain to garner with bread for you all and you'd rather be thorns to each other" (131). Further definition is accorded the image as the remaining Donnellys — Pat, Robert, William, and Jennie — each place a stone at the four corners of the "house / home" (157). This image also reverberates with the visual echoes of the pile of stones at the very opening of the trilogy, that Jane, a small girl, has made playing house with four small stones on the ground (*Sticks* 122) and of two earlier scenes in *Handcuffs*, one depicting a coffin containing four stones (38), the other curious sightseers snatching souvenirs from the ruined Donnelly house represented by the four stones (138). During a performance at the final stop of the National Tour of the trilogy, the Bathurst United Church in Toronto, Reaney became aware of another dimension:

> One very new, exciting thing was that the ramp leading out of the audience onto the stage allowed Mrs. Donnelly and Tom to whirl up in their buggy as if out of a memory shadow and, as the last scenes came on in *Handcuffs*, because of the church's shape — Methodist rounded, focusing all on the Word; as they climbed up to the stage, the actors seemed to be blades of wheat growing out of the darkness. (*14 Barrels* 172)

Multiple meanings result from the intricate interweaving of verbal, aural, and visual values in this scene. In its sheer theatrical density it calls to mind Peter Brook's description of Weiss's *Marat/Sade* as a "hall of mirrors or a corridor of echoes . . . one must keep looking front and back all the time to reach the author's sense" (Introd. vi), and it plainly manifests Reaney's account of his "story style" as directed towards the "making of a statement on several levels at once" ("Letter from James Reaney" 3). In the fuguelike arrangement of this scene, Reaney brings together several patterns, themes, and images that have shaped the Donnelly story and its theatrical expression: the Mass, the seasons, the home, the theatre itself. The theatre is self-consciously evoked through multiple role-playing and through the "memory-shadow" cast by the particular architectural features of the playing space. Bachelard writes of the sort of space that "is unwilling to remain permanently enclosed," which "deploys and appears to move elsewhere without difficulty; into other times, and on different planes of dream and memory" (*Poetics of Space* 53). In *14 Barrels*, Reaney calls our attention to the especially creative reciprocity between space and idea, between architecture and theatre vision. In Ottawa, for instance, he visited an empty Romanesque church where "I kept thinking of the mediaeval cycles you could do here — the space itself, a copy of some faraway Ravenna model, had the most powerful effect on me; you felt the secret numbers of its architectural organization forcing you to gesture, to kneel, to lift up your head" (*14 Barrels* 110).

Reaney frequently reiterated the idea of a theatre "that is a Globe, takes in a universe, the heights and depths of the soul, like Frances Yates's Memory Theatre. . . ." His dramaturgical convictions regarding the primacy of the "verbal universe" and the symbiotic relationship between architecture, the community, religion, and theatre do, in fact, recall Frances Yates's account of Shakespeare's theatre wherein, she writes,

> The arrangement of the stage wall is of basic importance for staging and action. And, through this interpretation the stage is organically linked with the theatre as a whole. The entries and exits of the characters take place within a Theatre of the World, cosmic in its ground plan, religious in its meaning. . . . The Globe Theatre was a magical theatre, designed to give fullest support to the voices and gestures of the players as they enacted the drama of the life of man within the Theatre of the World. (*Theatre* 188–89)

Such a theatre was assumed by Hamlet in his speech to the players, in which, as Francis Fergusson has observed, he

> was referring to the drama he knew, and to the theatre in which it had its life. He assumed the symbolic stage of the Elizabethans and, behind it, the traditional scene of human life which the stage itself represented; the starry firmament above, the stage-house facade which could indicate various versions of the human City — market-place or court or castle; and the platform for the players, from which the trap-door opened down into Hell or the cellar. If he could ask the players to hold the mirror up to nature, it was because the Elizabethan theatre was itself a

mirror which had been formed at the centre of the life and awareness of the community. (14)

The presumed absence of such a theatre today, one which can undertake a central role in the structure and meaning of personal and collective experience, is of special concern to many poet-playwrights. Throughout Reaney's resolute pleading on its behalf, we can detect many of the tones and moods (visionary-messianic hope alternating with a realistic apprehension of the drowsy, entropic direction of most cultural institutions) that pervade the writings of Yeats, Eliot, Maeterlinck, Paul Claudel, Edward Gordon Craig, and others who were equally committed to the idea of a theatre that is cosmic and symbolic. Such an ontologically complete theatre is present in Thomas Heywood's poem prefixed to the *Apology for Actors* (1612) and cited by Yates in her account of the Elizabethan-Jacobean theatre as "moral emblem":

> Then our play's begun
> When we are borne, and to the world first enter,
> And all finde exits when their parts are done.
> If then the world a theater present,
> As by the roundnesse it appears most fit,
> Built with starre galleries of hye ascent,
> In which Jehove doth as spectator sit,
> And chiefe determiner to applaud the best,
> And their indevours crowne with more then merit;
> But by their evill actions doomes the rest
> To end discrac't, whilst others praise inherit;
> He that denyes then theatres should be,
> He may as well deny a world to me. (164–65)

We have become somewhat habituated in our time not to the easy certainty that "Jehove doth as spectator sit," but to the cruel ambiguity informing Beckett's Estragon in *Waiting for Godot* as he "does the tree, staggers." "Do you think God sees me?" he asks (149–50), evoking one of the many instances in Beckett's drama of that contemporary theatre-consciousness, which, like Eliot's "Sweet Thames, run softly, till I end my song" (*Collected Poems* 42), casts its own *ironic* memory-shadow.

The act of the remaining Donnellys in squaring the scenically rendered "big field of wheat ready for harvest" with the four stones within the architectural organization afforded by the Methodist structure, accompanied as the act is by song, verse, and mimic gesture, provides an ideal for Reaney in which there is no apparent dissociation of word, gesture, meaning, and space. In *The Art of Memory*, Yates accounts for the important role of memory in the formation of imagery (112). The magical moment for Reaney occurs when the church/theatre space seems itself to release a "memory shadow" that both inspires, and, later, helps to explain the conjunction of an inner and an outer drama. If we see the miming of the field of wheat, and the "rounded" Methodist structure as signifying, spatially, a circle, then the act of squaring this space assumes further meaning in the light of the memory shadow. In the theatre memory system of Robert Fludd, a major consideration in Yates's study, there is a clear distinction drawn between "round art [*ars rotunda*]" and "square art [*ars quadrata*]." The former represent ideas "which are forms separated from corporeal things, such as spirits, shadows, souls and so on;" the latter deals mainly with corporeal things, representing the human world and the existence of physical structures. The "round art" is considered, Yates writes, " 'natural' using 'natural' places and is naturally adapted to the microcosm. Whereas the square art is 'artificial' using artificially made up places and images" (315–16).

Two separate but closely intertwined worlds of the Donnelly trilogy are manifested in this final scene. One encompasses both nature and the spirit, evoked by the representation of the wheat field, by the seasonal pattern addressed in the choric song, and by the informing spirituality of the mass with its own choric expression of death and resurrection and mystery. The other is that of humanity, both alone and in society, attempting to impose order and contending with the world of nature and spirit, with his or her own corporeal demands and creations. In a story of the early settlement and development of the land, such an imposition has particularly creative properties and contains a sacred reference as well if one considers the "precious stones" in *Revelation* that define New Jerusalem as a squared space. The Donnelly house, here signified by the squaring of the space, embodies this second world. In performance, the scenic conjunction of the two — the circle and the square — in these final images of *Handcuffs* reinforces the tragic resolution of the Donnelly trilogy in which the opposing claims of spirit and matter, nature and society, are embodied in the single figure of Mrs. Donnelly. Mrs. Donnelly, we are reminded, could see "straight ahead past this stupid life and death;" but, as a tragic figure, she also saw and experienced the inward "moments of dread" (*Sticks* 119) and the vital, inescapable outward connections of the self with the surrounding milieu. Bachelard writes that "In the dynamic rivalry between house and universe, we are far removed from any reference to simple geometrical forms. A house that has been experienced is not an inert box. Inhabited space transcends geometrical space" (*Poetics of Space* 47). This is quite obviously the case as we attempt to read the complex, jostling, over-lapping messages that this scene presents. Yet — and this is of the utmost importance in the *physical* structuring of the theatrical performance, in which the relationship between architecture and mnemonic kinaesthesis is a crucial element (Kaplan 105–16) — the confident understanding and utilization of the physical and symbolic properties of geometrical space can lead directly to the more resolutely substantive experience that "takes in a universe, the heights and depths of the soul."

Such large claims on behalf of the *art of the theatre* itself, and such deliberate attempts to use every element of production — space, language, sound, gesture, music, setting — as agents of form and vision, make clear yet again Reaney's close relationship to the aims and techniques of modern symbolist theatre since Wagner's Hellenic dream of the rebirth of a mythic-mimetic community:

> With the Greeks the perfect work of art, the drama, was the abstract and epitome of all that was expressible in the Grecian nature. It was the nation itself — in intimate connection with its own history — that stood mirrored in its artwork, that communed with itself and, within the span of a few hours, feasted its eyes with its own noblest essence. (Wagner 63)

In the last chapter, Reaney's almost gluttonous archival impulses to depict the "essence of country life in Ontario as I know it," were outlined, and some of the ways in which a fidelity to documentary material shaped his theatre were examined. In this chapter, we will be chiefly attracted to the vision and pattern that, in Reaney's theatre, lie outside the realm of disorder and disconnection and yet can be so intuited by the perceptive imagination as to enter reality and thus transform it. Indispensable to the desire to transform reality is what Frye called the "informative" creative act through which the world in which "we feel lonely and frightened and unwanted" is changed into a home (*Educated* 16).

Space and language are the primary concerns of Reaney's symbolic theatre. Through these elements, "ordinary" experience is accorded symbolic, mythopoeic re-ordering and is thus transformed into "artistic" experience. Such artistic experience is what ultimately creates the desired "civilization where it finally seems true that to be wise is to know how to play." As Reaney stated in his editorial to the first issue of *Alphabet*,

> The most exciting thing about this century is the number of poems that cannot be understood unless the reason quite reorganizes his way of looking at things or 'rouses his faculties' as Blake would say. *Finnegans Wake* and Dylan Thomas' "Altarwise by owl-light" sonnet sequence are good examples here. These works cannot be enjoyed to anywhere near their fullest unless one rouses one's heart, belly and mind to grasp their secret alphabet or iconography or language of symbols and myths. A grasping such as is involved here leads to a more powerful inner life, or Blake's "Jerusalem's wall." It seems quite natural, then, in this century and particularly in this country, which could stand some more Jerusalem's wall, that there should be a journal of some sort devoted to iconography. After all Ernest Cassirer defines man as a symbol-making animal. . . . Let us make a form out of this: documentary on one side and myth on the other: Life & Art. In this form we can put anything and the magnet we have set up will arrange it for us. (2)

Yeats was excited by a similar poetic-symbolic task, and his theatre, like that of Reaney, was devoted to revolutionary ends. In his study of Spenser and Yeats, Reaney vehemently defended the privileges and the radical ends of such artistic endeavour:

> The mythopoeic tradition [in this Reaney includes Spenser, Milton, Blake, Shelley, Keats, and Yeats] as we have seen in our earlier discussion of Spenser's symbolic language and as we see in Yeats when he implies that poetry *has the right* to consider all things as symbolic, that is put the universe inside one's head, is a tradition that sees poetry and the human imagination as the way back to Paradise. ("Influence" 225)

II

In his tribute to Frye, "Some Critics Are Music Teachers," Reaney discussed the problem of architectural space and the idea of a theatre:

I should now like to say more about how a critic or 'music teacher' can influence the production of a play to such an extent that an audience member might say, 'This must be a new idea of what theatre is all about.' First of all, let's go to your local regional theatre and see plays by Chekhov, Ibsen, James and Shaw. But, before the curtain even rises, we perhaps inspect the shape of the theatre we have just entered. What relationship does it bear to the play produced tonight? Such a critic as Frances Yates in *The Art of Memory* shows how the symbolism of the Globe Theatre's architecture echoes the order of the Shakespearean universe. At Stratford, Ontario, the Festival Theatre there does have such overtones. A theatre in the round with a hierarchy of playing areas that go from trap-door to balcony and even higher, it works well with the Shakespeare productions and creates such feelings about the Chekhov and Ibsen produced on its boards that one longs for more variety and adventurousness in other theatres visited, most of whose architects seem to have been content with the usual picture stage. Now the 'music teacher' critic in me keeps saying that the physical theatre itself makes a big difference with regard to effective production of all plays and that certain playwrights might definitely profit from having their works produced in a theatre that echoes their world-picture. With regard to Shaw, for example, what would a theatre look like whose architect knew of this dramatist's desire, as he says in *Back to Methuselah*, to provide an iconography for creative evolution? The curtain goes up; we must be thankful that we are in a theatre at all, but one cannot help thinking of how wonderful a real union between literature and architecture might some day be. (299–300)

One might argue that the stage form adopted by Ibsen and Chekhov does, in fact, embody the "diminished scene of rationalism" (Fergusson 159) from which the realist vision developed, and that the spatial arrangements of the nineteenth-century box set are to some degree eminently suited to the depiction of the surly and static provinciality from which a wider symbolic-mythic world has so injuriously been excluded. And one can argue that the aesthetic pluralism of the modern theatre renders especially problematical, if not impossible, the desired union between literature and architecture in the sense of any *single* shape having the authority to articulate fully every possible voice from Ibsen to Yeats to Pirandello to Beckett to Weiss. Nonetheless, the urge to discover crucial links between space and idea, to incorporate spatial elements into the form and vision of theatrical production, is clearly stated by Reaney and invites a scrutiny of his own theatre in the light of such a perspective.

One of the many mediaeval and renaissance texts cited by Yates in her *The Art of Memory* is Jacobus Publicius's *Ars memorativa* (1482) from which the following is taken: "Simple and spiritual intentions slip easily from the memory unless joined to a corporeal similitude" (93). Just such an acquisition by thought and feeling of a plastic consciousness is fundamental to what we understand as the histrionic sensibility. In our century, one of the most radical expressions of what Tom Driver has called the "pursuit of the corporeal" (253) is to be found in the writings of Artaud, who never ceased seeking the concrete incarnation of thought. "Words, forms of phrases," he wrote; "I am in constant pursuit of my intellectual being. So, when I am able to seize upon a form, however imperfect it may be, I fix it, in the fear of losing all my thought" (qtd. in Driver 353). As Driver observes, the "paradoxical drive to incarnate that which has no existence (or even subsistence) if it is *not* embodied, this drive of the spirit downward into specific, concrete, and finite form, is, it can be seen, an ultimate predication of a positive theatricalism" (360). Artaud's stage language of animated hieroglyphs required, of course, a reorganization of theatre space. In one of his comments on such space, he advocated something akin to the "magical theatre" described by Yates and the sacred space discovered by Reaney in the empty Romanesque church in Ottawa. "Abandoning the architecture of present-day theatres," he writes, "we shall take some hangar or barn, which we shall have reconstructed according to processes which have culminated in the architecture of certain churches or holy places, and of certain temples in Tibet" (96).

This "positive theatricalism," frequently expressed in less absolutist terms than we find in Artaud, is what unites in common purpose and achievement those playwrights, directors, designers, and architects who are involved in the artistic exploration of what Richard Schechner calls the "endless ways space can be transformed, articulated, animated" (*Environmental* 1). Reaney's essay, "Search for an

Undiscovered Alphabet," written in 1965, thus almost contemporaneous with the exploration and articulation of three-dimensional space that he undertook in the theatre workshops of the mid to late sixties, offers some clues to his own "positive theatricalism," to the spatial scoring of scenes, and of plays as a whole.

"An interest in symbolism," Reaney writes in this essay, "leads sooner or later to a fascination with the diagram. The diagram lies behind any image that can be seen. Things seen occupy space, or appear to, and so can be simplified into a diagram of some sort or other." He then proceeds to disclose the spatial diagrams that permit a hieroglyphic reading of such works as Donne's "Valediction: Forbidding Mourning," Virginia Woolf's *To the Lighthouse*, and Carol Reed's *Odd Man Out*. In Donne and Woolf, he observes, "intricate and profound trains of insight are eventually summed up in the simplest of diagrams. Love that is present in absence is a triangle and a circle." In Reed's film, ". . . the camera contrasts static vertical scenes with scenes that flow sideways across the screen. Every moment of the film is absorbed into the resultant cross shape." Apart from seeking out the irreducible visual signs (triangle, square, circle, cross, and so on), which function as "devices for communication and structure" (38), Reaney asks whether "there is a possible key to the way they can directly express reality?" The search for such a key is prompted in part by Frye's commentary on the Job engravings of Blake, in which, he writes, ". . . we are getting down to the very bed-rock of imaginative communication, a series of images which are at once pictures and hieroglyphs, rather like what the characters of Chinese writings must originally have been, in which the common basis of writing and drawing, that is of poetry and drawing, has been re-established. . . . Blake's pictographs are to be interpreted in terms of their sequential relationship to one another, as a progression of signs, which like the alphabet, spell out not a word but the units of all words." In the light of such a possibility, Reaney writes,

What we want is an alphabet of diagrams; 'alphabet' suggests that we discover the first letter and the most important letter if we can. What I have tried to show the reader so far is that there appear in various literary forms fascinating hieroglyphs which resemble letters from an as yet undiscovered alphabet. Works of art flow past in which triangles, circles and crosses, circles, with dots in the centre of them and so on, appear. Can the circle shape be assigned a meaning that is not intuitively grasped but logically deducted and grammatically applied? I eventually discovered that the first letter in an alphabet of diagrams would have to be a simplification of the human eye — that is, a circle with a central dot.

Various kinds of circles from a wide range of art are examined. First of all there is the circle as a symbol of perfection, "a final reality . . . a piece of Paradise within us," found in the *Timaeus*, in Spenser, and Yeats. Then there is the circle "that stands for the imprisoning environment of Life or the Terrestrial Condition," which "is not just a plain circle, like the circle of Eternity, but a circle with a dot in the centre of it" (39). In a discussion of Walt Whitman's *Song of Myself* and Emily Dickinson's "I saw no way — the heavens were stitched," Reaney observes how the dual properties of the circle image — as perfection, involving, generally, a centrifugal movement, and as imprisoning, involving a centripetal movement — co-exist, informing one another in a variety of ways, directly testifying to humanity's dual nature within and without history: "man in the centre of an imprisoning universe, an island of joy washed by seas of dread." In Dickenson's poem, he writes, ". . . the centrifugal escape is final because it is an escape through death. The environmental circle crushes man so completely that it over-reaches itself and produces a man who first fills it, then overfills it as the soul spills over into Eternity" (40). To return briefly to the spatial imagery of the concluding scenes of *Handcuffs*, we can now suggest further readings. Both circles are present here: the surrounding milieu as an imprisoning environmental circle, which crushes the Donnellys ("I hate the fact," Mrs. Donnelly says in *Sticks & Stones*, "that there's moments each like a bridge of dread and why does there have to be an earth that goes round and round" [119]), and the larger, centrifugal circle of a "final reality" as the souls of the Donnellys spill over into an eternity characterized by both seasonal regeneration in the "big field of wheat ready for harvest," and spiritual life in the choric evocation of the "holy city of Jerusalem."

Reaney concludes his discussion of the circle image in a manner that echoes, on another level, something of the ontological value of the theatre-as-globe image:

> Have we not seen . . . that the image of the eye includes "all substances" since it contains the essential diagram of man's first

condition and this diagram looks as if it will evolve smoothly
into diagrams of all other states? What could be more basic or
essential than a circle with a dot in the centre of it? Why it is the
pupil of a human eye! In the perceived world our eye is literally
the *first* thing and what an eye sees when it gazes at man's
situation is also itself. Therefore, when Henry James, Virginia
Woolf, John Donne, Carol Reed and Antony Tudor use diagrams as a means of organizing their works, perhaps they are
using the letters of an as yet undiscovered alphabet. If the iris
and the pupil of the human eye are indeed the first letter of this
alphabet we perhaps have an explanation for the peculiar effectiveness of designs and diagrams. We like to see things with our
own eyes. (41)

"Eye am the I of the World," Reaney's Painter asserts in *The Dance
of Death at London, Ontario* (*Poetry* 248). Bachelard cites Claudel's
description of the eye as a "sort of scaled down, portable sun, and
therefore, a proto-type of the ability to establish a radius (*rayon*)
from it to any point on the circumference." Thus the eye, Bachelard
remarks, "is the centre of a world, the sun of a world" (*Poetics of
Reverie* 184). We find other apt analogies in Giorgio de Chirico's
"Zeus the Explorer," where he describes the large painted eye motif
in Cretian art: "Even the fetus of a man, a fish, a chicken, a snake in
its first stage is exactly an eye," he writes; "One must discover the
eye in every thing" (qtd. in Delevoy, *Symbolists* 447); in Odilon
Redon's lithographs of the separated eye as a global image in *Vision*
(from the series *Dans le Reve*, 1879) and *The Eye, Like a Strange
Balloon, Travels Towards Infinity* (1882); in Goethe's observation
that the eye is the "organ of totality" (qtd. in Delevoy, *Symbolists*
63). Frank Lentricchia, in his commentary on Frye's symbolic structures (which, because of their "closed, coherent, and self-contained"
qualities, he finds "unremittingly spatial") describes the sort of
ontological comprehensiveness and wholeness that characterizes
Reaney's account of the eye. "As a special unarbitrary mode of
language," he writes, "symbol not only permits us a vision of
ultimate being . . . but, because it 'partakes' of being . . . symbol
permits *us*, as well, to partake of being as it closes the distance
between our consciousness and the ultimate origin of things" (6).
The global, "magical theatre," then, understanding and utilizing
such a view of itself as ontologically symbolic, acts upon the active,
alert spectator in the same demanding way as did the collage

technique in the assembling and presentation of documentary fragments of observation and experience. Ultimately, such a spectator is
"folded in to the goings on," and thus he partakes of being, as, and
because, he partakes of creativity: "playing" and symbol-making/
reading become synonymous activities.

Reaney's propensity for what Arnheim called "visual thinking" in
which "perceptual and pictorial shapes are not only translations of
thought processes but the very flesh and blood of thinking itself," is
evident in his poetry and his drama and has important analogies in
the theory and art of two distinct, but related, movements. One of
these includes Klee, Kandinsky, and Miró; the other Meyerhold,
Edward Gordon Craig, Alexander Tairov, Jacques Copeau, and,
more recently, Antonin Artaud, Joseph Chaikin, Peter Brook, Richard Schechner. Many such figures have experimented widely with
the distinctive languages of the theatre through a variety of disruptive
challenges to actors and spectators to become more fully alive to the
corporeal and spatial dynamics of performance, which include, of
course, the architectonic dimensions of the actor-spectator relationship. In the art of Klee, Kandinsky, and Miró, as Robert Delevoy has
observed, ordinary, generally uninspiring elements in the environment "could change the artist's way of seeing, react on his sensibility,
and lead him to counterbalance the processes of mechanic automatism by interventions of the active psyche" (*Dimensions* 116). These
elements, chosen from the same assortment of common "things"
(posters, bus transfers, advertisements, traffic signs, machines) from
which Curnoe and Reaney had constructed their regional collages,
include many items associated with a mechanized way of life, items
ultimately reducible to such forms as circles, triangles, spirals,
arrows, numbers, letters, and so on. In the careful codification of
such elementary forms in the Bauhaus lectures of Klee and
Kandinsky, we discover the creation of a new symbolic language
through which, as Klee remarked, we can reach into "the world
beyond the world" (qtd. in Delevoy, *Dimensions* 116). In this way,
some of the oppressive aspects of the "environmental bubble"
informed by the "mechanical geometry" are themselves transformed
into sources of creativity with special ontological value. In addition
to witnessing the transformation of ordinary into artistic experience,
we also see signs of a creative reconciliation between science and art,
the mechanical and the vital, matter and spirit. Through such
mimetic means, the feared, distrusted, alienating power of the industrial environment — in the face of which we feel "lonely, frightened

and unwanted" as Frye observed — is rendered more accommodating to the artist. By learning and utilizing the language of the mechanical geometry itself, the artist transcends it, escaping its imprisoning grasp. In Klee's account of a journey — strikingly similar in its utilization of primary geometrical forms to Reaney's readings of Donne and Woolf — we find a good example of such an accommodation. "Breaking away from the dead center (point)," Klee writes,

. . . we make our first move (line). After a while comes a pause to draw breath (broken or, after several pauses, articulated lines). A backward glance to see how far we have come (countermovement). Weigh the pros and cons of paths in several directions (cluster of lines). A river lies in the way, so we take a boat (wave movement). Upstream there may have been a bridge (series of arches). On the other side we meet a like-minded traveller, also bound for the land of deeper understanding. At first we are joyfully united (convergence), then gradually differences arise (divergence). We cut across a plowed field (planes crisscrossed by lines), then through dense woods. . . . Later it gets sultry and night comes on (spatial element). A flash of lightning on the horizon (zigzag line), though the stars are still twinkling overhead (scattered points). . . . Even so short a journey is very eventful. Lines of all kinds, dabs, dots. Smooth surfaces, hatched and dotted surfaces. Wave movement, delayed and articulated movement, counter-movement. Crisscrossing, interweaving. Walls scaling away. Monody, polyphony. Lines dying out or gathering strength (dynamics). (qtd. in Delevoy, *Dimensions* 117)

Implicit in such a verbal-visual narrative are two competing modes of articulation: the linear-discursive and the simultaneous. As Susanne Langer writes, "Visual forms — lines, colors, proportions, etc. — are just as capable of *articulation*, i.e., of complex combination, as words. But the laws that govern this sort of articulation are altogether different from the laws of syntax that govern language. The most radical difference is that *visual forms are not discursive*. They do not present their constituents successively, but simultaneously, so that relations determining a visual structure are grasped in one act of vision" (*Philosophy* 86). The theatrical equivalent of such a language of dots, lines, and surfaces is what Reaney has sought since the Listeners' Workshops of the 1960s. This is a theatrical language in which the elementary forms, the *lingua franca* of spatial signs, can first of all release creativity in the participant and, secondly, be formally articulated as agents of mimetic and symbolic meaning. He has also sought, primarily through the language of collage, the theatrical terms whereby both discursive and simultaneous modes of articulation can be interwoven so that, as Mitchell writes of Blake's composite art, "Neither the graphic nor the poetic aspect . . . assumes consistent predominance: their relationship is more like an energetic rivalry, a dialogue or dialectic between vigorously independent modes of expression" (4).

In his first *Halloween* letter, Reaney alludes to the special properties of children's art (to which as we have noted Klee was similarly indebted) as sources of visual scoring in performance:

> Would like to examine Rhoda Kellogg's books on Children's Art as a possible source for stage movement and drama convention since she says that the child artist's hand after going through a 22 scribble pattern spiral ends up dancing a Mandala. ("Letter from James Reaney" 6)

Earlier, in "Ten Years at Play," he describes one of the early workshops in which a freer collage of the verbal and the visual was sought:

> One wild idea I had, for example, was to drop the script, get everybody together and run through the whole story in mime and improvising it as if we were making it up among ourselves. This idea was pooh-poohed by a really good actor in the cast, who just was not used to thinking in that way; no, there had to be a script and you followed it word for word. What I wanted, of course, was for them and me to get a physical feeling of the design of the play, the sort of thing you do get when you think about *Macbeth* after having seen it, or watch a ballet version of *Hamlet*. I have a feeling that *Twelfth Night* started with thinking about a clown with a little drum: and that's the way I would direct it. Gather the cast around, listen to the drum, improvise along the main lines of the Shakespeare plot and then start adding the text.

Towards the close of this essay, published in 1969, Reaney comments upon how this physical sense for the shaping of event and emotion was assisting him in his next major work:

In the sabbatical year I am now enjoying, I've been working on *Donnelly*, or *The Biddulph Tragedy*, an attempt to apply what techniques I've collected to a story in the past with all its longhand archival detail. When I started this play about an Ontario family who were massacred by their neighbours on the night of February 3, 1880, I could tell that a lot had changed since the English Department office at Acadia. I kept seeing all the Donnelly events in terms of two viewpoints that cross — *some tell it this way/some tell it this way*: the Donnellys were at heart decent people who were persecuted/the Donnellys were mad dogs who *had* to be destroyed. This resulted in stage movement, scene settings, speeches that form St. Patrick's X/s. *Listen* and *Colours* also had patterns behind them. I wonder if this sense of design I didn't have 11 years ago comes from the intervening workshop experiments. There I've got used to eliciting flows as they come out of people playing with other people the game of mimicking reality. This is the way Hirsch and Terry direct and this is what I want my plays to be wrapped around — the delight of listening to words, the delight of making up patterns (scribbling with your body/bodies) of movement for fun and in play. ("Ten Years" 61)

Workshop activities directed towards the development of such physical consciousness and formal articulation were by no means unique to Reaney, nor were they especially novel, either in Canada or elsewhere, in the 1960s. Meyerhold's concept of "plasticity," for example, through which both physical and spiritual levels of being could be explored and which was expressed through gestures, poses, glances, and through a pattern of movement, had inspired large numbers of directors and actors since the 1920s. His "Sixteen Etudes" (the third of which was an étude of the mad scene from *Hamlet*) and pantomimes were developed to train actors in the principles of scenic movement, some of which concentrated upon the representation of the elementary signs of the circle, the square, and the triangle (Gordon). Meyerhold also joined with others of his generation, and earlier, to explore the spatial dimensions of the theatre itself. Edward Gordon Craig, Jacques Copeau, Alexander Tairov, Louis Jouvet, Erwin Piscator, Max Reinhardt, and many others had examined the artistic, and for some the spiritual, potential in the reorganization of theatrical space, creating wholly new spatial structures, which, like much of the painting of the period, demanded new ways of seeing and understanding.

These new spatial structures in theatre/scenic design and move-ment, as in painting (most notably in the work of Klee, Kandinsky, Kassimir Malevich, El Lissitzky, and Fernand Léger) were meant to challenge the static forms of the perspectival system (fundamental, of course, to theatrical realism) and led to the new optical experi-ences of collage, photomontage, and the cinema. Piscator speaks for many such innovators in spatial articulation when he enthusiastically endorses the limitless possibilities of montage. "Montage of action," he writes, "of thought, of conflict — a montage of drama. It is a blending of things, people and events. What a succession of images, to illustrate the association of ideas, clear as headlines! What a release from petrified painting! It is not accidental that the spiritual metamorphosis in the arts comes at the same time as the technical transformation of its tools. It is the same in the theatre" (qtd. in Ley-Piscator 54–55). These technical transformations led to the development of new structural arrangements of *phenomenal* space, in which, as Delevoy states, the "existential condition of contempo-rary man" might be disclosed without "resorting to any method of re-presentation" (*Dimensions* 170). In the art, including the theatri-cal designs of Piet Mondrian, Kassimir Malevich, and El Lissitzky, primary geometrical forms and colours were considered to be expres-sive of the underlying principles of existence. What Beckett called the "savage economy of hieroglyphics" (119) became a means of bypass-ing ordinary, largely perspectival visual experience. Delevoy cites Maurice Merleau-Ponty's statement regarding man's need for "an absolute in the relative, for a space that does not glide over appear-ances, is not 'given' with them, in the realist manner, and can outlast their disintegration." This basic need, Delevoy says further,

> explains why the classical conception of space as a locus of relations between things is replaced by the notion of space as a phenomenon — 'phenomenal space' — an imaginary ambiance in which tectonic values, tensions, articulations and groupings of forms disclose 'certain equilibria basic to the scheme of things, to both the natural and the spiritual world' (Moulod). Thus the spatial potentialities of color are associated with the tectonic organization of the picture and the montage of the signs — lines, squares, triangles, circles — which, repelling or attracting each other, combine to build up plastic forms at once translucent and unlimited in scope. (*Dimensions* 172)

The workshop reading of a play's story through mime and improvisation, in order to get a "physical feeling for the design of the play," is a creative reading of a montage of signs and, as Reaney remarks elsewhere, a projection of certain "geometrical obsessions" ("Kids" 30). Such readings are also a way to begin experiencing phenomenal space, which offers the actor-participants and spectators a release from given, predictable spatial relationships and appearances, drawing them closer to what Frye saw in the pictographs of Blake. Klee made a similar claim when he advocated an art-act that did not simply attempt to "re-present" the world, but, rather, to "present" it. Klee, like Kandinsky and others, sought an altogether different order of mimesis in which art "goes beyond the object" and "imitates the forces which created and are still creating the world" (qtd. in Delevoy, *Dimensions* 118). The experiencing of phenomenal space, which involves the recognition of its translucent and *unlimited* properties, is one very important way in Klee's art, in Meyerhold's bio-mechanics, and in Reaney's theatre, in which the spectator's "faculties are aroused" and drawn in towards the *act* of creation itself. Employing Roland Barthes's crucial observation regarding the *participatory* as well as the communicative value of symbolism, Delevoy explains the extent to which in the art of Klee and others the distinction between the "significant (the image) and the signified (what the image represents) is disappearing." The "nexus 'signifying-signified,'" he concludes, requires the use of a "lorgnette — direct, undeviated observation. Only yesterday the picture still presupposed a drama with three characters: painter, subject and spectator. Now it invites a dialogue between maker and spectator, is comprehended in virtue of a give-and-take between two personalities, and takes full effect only when there is active emotive co-operation by the person whom it bids 'complete' it with his gaze" (*Dimensions* 118). Recalling Reaney's strong advocacy of an *informed* critical discourse, we can suggest how perilously the work of art exists when "active emotive co-operation" is absent. Mark Rothko speaks on behalf of the artist's predicament when he writes that a picture "lives by companionship, expanding and quickening in the eyes of the sensitive beholder. It dies by the same token. It is therefore a risky act to send it out into the world. How often it must be impaired by the eyes of the unfeeling and the cruelty of the impotent who would extend their affliction universally" (qtd. in Waldman 62–63). Despite such an obvious and common risk, Reaney's advocacy of a theatrical experience that will "force the audience to work out richness," compelling it to be more creatively susceptible to multiple visual and auditory patterns and statements, to be, in some sense, almost as artistically polylingual as the creator of the work, is evidence of the enhanced creative dialogue *expected* in Reaney's theatre between "maker and spectator."

The spatial dimensions of this dialogue have been of primary importance in many critical and practical theatrical investigations throughout the course of this century. Schechner, in discussing the combination of live performers and technology in the Polyvision and Diapolyecran rooms of the Czech Pavilion at Expo 67, remarked that to "achieve this mix of technical and live performers nothing less than the whole space is needed. There can be no further bifurcation of space, in which one territory is meted out to the audience and the other to the performers. The final exchange between performers and the audience is an exchange of space, the use of audience as scene-makers as well as scene-watchers" ("6 Axioms" 48). In Reaney's theatre, the dialogue between maker and spectator, and between performer and spectator, assimilates a similarly central spatial vocabulary based at times upon the exchange of space, and upon the phenomenal experiencing of space, of "scribbling with your body/ bodies" and of "reading" such scribbles as an alphabet of signs. Ideally, this dialogue involves centrifugal as well as centripetal movement — as did Reaney's image of the eye and Yates's account of the Globe theatre. Centrifugally, it awakens us to the idea of perfection (the "piece of Paradise within us"). Centripetally, it awakens us to the ambiguous, sometimes oppressive qualities of the "environmental" circle and, most importantly, to the realization that this environment can be *changed*, that "the forces which created and are still creating the world" can be invoked and utilized for the purposes of spiritual and social redemption. Of considerable importance here is the reminder that the art and theory of Mondrian, Klee, Meyerhold, Kandinsky, and others shares with that of Reaney and some of his theatre contemporaries a significant *political* afterimage in its promise of a restructured spiritual and social existence. Mondrian's close associate Theo van Doesburg articulates this aspect in his account of Neo-Plasticism, "Toward Collective Construction" (1923), in which he comments upon those who were building the new life, using the grammar of spatial signs (the "undiscovered alphabet") as agents of utopian vision.[1]

Lee Simonson calls them the "Theatre's Theologians," artists whose theorizing was often informed by a "sense of sin and a hunger for salvation." "Original sin," he writes,

> has been successively paint and the scene-painter, the actor and
> the spoken word, realism of any sort, decoration in any form.
> And the prototype of salvation has been discovered in every
> golden or gilded past; the baroque ball-room of the Hofburg
> Palace in Vienna hung with tapestries and lighted with crystal
> chandeliers, the platforms of Elizabethan inn-yards, the naves
> of cathedrals, the ritual dances of Asia and Africa, and the
> amphitheatres of Greece. (19)

Almost all such means of deliverance are spatial in nature. The
evangelical voice with which so many of them were, and still are
advanced, is not at all uncommon among those, since the 1890s, who
have been inspired to one degree or another by Wagner's concept of
the *Gesamtkunstwerk*, with its promise of "aesthetic will-freed
contemplation," through which we apprehend the "immediate consciousness of the oneness of our inner essence with that of the outer
world" (183). Among the great many who articulated in their
theatres and their writings such idealistic "theology" were Paul Fort
at his Théâtre d'Art, Paul Larochelle at the Théâtre de la Rive
Gauche, Lugné-Poë at the Théâtre de l'Œuvre (where, as in Jacques
Rouches's Théâtre des Arts, attempts were made to make staging
correspond to the artistic visions of contemporary painters), and
Jacques Copeau's Théâtre de Vieux Colombier. In a brief examination of Copeau's work Henri Ghéon observed that ". . . the theatre
demands a *different concept of space*, not enclosed within four walls,
a different concept of time, not measured by our watches, *a language
of signs*" (68). Others include Alexander Tairov at the Moscow
Kamerny Theatre, who was strongly influenced by Craig, Adolf
Appia, and the evolving cubist aesthetic in his exploration of spatial
values. "The voice of the actor," he writes, "must sound like music,
his movements must give rhythm to the play, his technique must be
the external form of the internal. The stage that serves these expressions must have different rhythmic levels and the scenery height,
width and moving surfaces" (qtd. in Fuerst and Hume 61). Appia
had written earlier that the "arbitrary conventions of our auditori-
ums and stages placed face to face still control us! Let us leave our
theatres to their dying past and let us construct elementary buildings
designed merely to cover the space in which we work" (qtd. in
Roose-Evans 41). Erwin Piscator, seizing upon the spatially expressive potential of new technology, sought means through which the

theatre could "learn to use the physical world of the stage as freely as a painter uses his palette." Film and television, he wrote, "hold tremendous possibilities for the theatre. Also the use of music and sound effects can lead to contrasts within the dialogue — such as the spoken and the subconscious thought. Only in this way will the director really come into his own and help to create a theatre that will be of our modern age." Perhaps Piscator's most comprehensive statement regarding the ontologically expressive claims of theatre space is the following:

> An audience will shake off its inertia when it experiences the surprise effects of space transformed. By shifting the scene of action during the performance from one stage position to another and by using a system of spotlights and film projectors, transforming walls and ceilings into moving-picture scenes, the whole house would be animated by three-dimensional means instead of 'flat' picture effects of the conventional stage. . . . Thus the playhouse itself, made to dissolve into the shifting, illusionary space of the imagination, would become the scene of action itself. Such a theatre would stimulate the conception of playwright and stage director alike; for while it is true that the mind can transform the world, it is equally true that structure can transform the mind. (qtd. in Ley-Piscator 188)

Throughout the major theatre centres of Europe such claims on behalf of what Alexander Bakshy called "The Theatre Unbound" were promoted, and the plastic values of the stage's three-dimensionality, and of the overall theatre structure itself, were explored for symbolic and expressive purposes. Lydia Popova constructed her machine for acting; Terence Gray created a Constructivist stage for *Antigone* at the Cambridge Festival Theatre; Max Reinhardt staged a series of productions for which new spatial (including architectonic) arrangements were devised according to a variety of historical models — Greek, Mediaeval, Elizabethan, and so on; El Lissitzky planned his elaborate "Electro-mechanical Peepshow," *Victory Over the Sun*: "We are constructing a stage on a square," he writes, "which is open and accessible on all sides; that is the machinery of the show. This stage offers the 'bodies in play' all the possibilities of movement" (qtd. in Hamand 104). Bakshy revelled in a theatre freed from all "illusionism," in which "Performance, now so unrecognizable in its ponderous representational garb, will appear in its divine nakedness. No longer will it be a picture of events as these are shaped in some real or imaginary world. It will be an event, but an event in the life of the theatre, a happening in that real world which is a gathering of actors and spectators come together the first to practice and the second to watch the act of undisguised and glorying make-believe." And, of the stage itself, Bakshy asks,

> Will it remain mutilated and distorted by painted or built up scenery purporting to give pictures of everything that human imagination can conceive of, save one thing — the stage itself? No, out of its present degradation it will be restored to the dignity it possessed in the ancient days. It will be a stage and nothing but a stage, a part of the theatre building serving as a pedestal on which the plastic structure of the dramatic show is raised by the actors. And in doing this it will be playing a distinct and tremendously important part in the general scheme of the dramatic spectacle. Made vocal, proclaiming its identity in every phase of the action as it is being developed, it will become a live and potent thing. The yoke of the proscenium arch destroyed, the unsightly tatters which it has been forced to wear, cast mercilessly away, and itself being given the shape worthy of its part, the stage will once again appear resplendent in its natural beauty. (18–19)

The appearance of such manifestos as this in *Theatre Arts*, with its vivid foreshadowing of more recent "performance" theory and activity, signified an American attempt to move its own theatre within reach of the most advanced aesthetic principles of the European theatre. This journal was founded in 1916 and edited by Sheldon Cheney, whose *The New Movement in the Theatre* had appeared two years earlier. Following Craig, Appia, Reinhardt, and others, Cheney sought what he called the "re-theatricalizing" of the drama: "an attempt to bring all the arts of the theatre into more perfect relation with the limitations of the playhouse; and to invent a stagecraft that will serve to mount beautifully the plays of either the aesthetic or psychologic type" (*New Movement* 16). Another contributor to *Theatre Arts* was Kenneth Macgowan, in whose two books, *The Theatre of Tomorrow* (1921) and *Continental Stagecraft* (1922), we find an equally fervent advocacy of significant theatrical form in which the re-arrangement of spatial components was a critical consideration. Such expressions of a "positive theatricalism," carrying, some of them, a "theological" importance, were current in many theatre circles and schools when Herman Voaden studied at Yale in the early 1930s. In 1929, Voaden's article "What Is Wrong with the Canadian Theatre" demonstrated that a sensitive reading of what was happening elsewhere in theatre could only throw the uninspiring Canadian performance into a dismal light. The failure of the Canadian amateur theatre to "achieve anything noteworthy — its lack of imagination and originality," he wrote — "is in no way so clearly exemplified as in its neglect of the principles and practice of the modern Art Theatre." The remedy seemed clear:

> If our stage is to save itself, it must be no longer the scene for the actor and producer in the narrow sense of the term. It must enlarge its vision and scope to embrace the playwright, the student, the thinker, the poet, the musician, the designer and the artist. More Canadian artists are especially needed. In Europe the greatest achievements in the theatre have been made by artist-directors, like Pitoëff, who represents Craig's idea of the master director, or through the close co-operation of artists and directors like Reinhardt and Stern, Jessner and Pirchan in Berlin, and Weichert and Sievert in Frankfurt. Surely the remarkable native work being done by many Canadian painters should lead to the establishment of a new philosophy and technique of stage design in Canada. (qtd. in Evans 37)

In 1931, Voaden established a theatre workshop in Toronto in which the principles of what he called "Symphonic Expressionism" were developed (Sherrill). The voices of Wagner, Appia, Craig, Piscator, and others are unmistakable in his account of this program:

> The expressionist artist has reached out to enhance other artistic media, to draw them into the theatre. Music, light and design are no longer incidental to the production; they are woven into its very movement and being. They become positive, equal in importance to the words and 'business.' In the emotion, movement and rhythm of the play, a new voice speaks from out of the theatre; the arts are welded into a composite art; the theatre at last gains its utter freedom in a new and independent medium. (qtd. in Evans 41)

In commenting upon his first play, *Rocks*, Voaden outlines the spatial expressiveness that he sought in the reorganization and articulation of the playing space:

The North is viewed as a participant in the action, an unseen actor. To present this theme effectively, every means has been utilized. The lighting constantly varies in intensity as the moods of the characters change. The whole stage has been rigorously divided into areas, each of which has a separate emotional or mood tone. Through these, the characters move as their emotions change. To secure clarity, the movements have been stylized and completely simplified. The areas have been arranged geometrically and in balance, with only formal screens framing the proscenium to localize the action. The cyclorama lighting, which is also a constant variant in both intensity and colour, expresses the North.

Simple melodies on violin and cello introduce the emotional themes developed in the actor's lines. Rhythmic drum-beats are symbols of gathering emotional intensity and the progression of the fate-motif.

Two groups of dancers are employed to provide the rhythmical counterpart of and complement to the speeches. . . Fluid light, body rhythms, lyrical speech, the drum beat and musical themes, together with the formal setting, have been considered supplementary elements, none of which is emphasized so as to subordinate the others. (qtd. in Evans 41–42)

The fragmentation and arrangement of scenic volumes, the musically inspired and regulated ensemble of colour, lighting, and movement, testify directly to the scenic language of Georges Pitoëff, Leopold Jessner, and others. In their designs, as in Voaden's, a variety of scenic abbreviations — specially designated playing areas, screens, panels, colour tones, set-pieces supplying the slightest suggestions of place (a house-frame, tree, window-pane) — function to provide visual reinforcement to language, character, narrative, and mood.

I I I

This is the very *language of the theatre* that Reaney was to learn as he came, in Frye's terms, to see "more intensely by means of his medium" (*Creation* 10). In Voaden's separated stage-areas, stylization, musical motifs, "fluid light," and so on, we see the scenic and spatial premises of many of Reaney's plays, especially since *Listen to the Wind*. We also see, in these plays, the influence of what, following

Voaden, was the only significant attempt in Canadian theatre to reflect in major architectonic terms the vision of "The Theatre Unbound." Tyrone Guthrie had written to Dora Mavor Moore that he was intensely interested to "produce Shakespeare on a stage which might reproduce the actor/audience relation for which he wrote — viz: the audience closely packed *round* the actors" (qtd. in Forsyth 221). Reaney's comments on what eventually was constructed from Tanya Moiseiwitsch's model, which Guthrie carried around with him in a shoe box, were included in a review of the first Stratford season in 1953:

> The new theatre in which these plays were produced was itself one of the festival's stars. It provided a high, deep, many sided stage-frame in which all the inventive spectacle with which these productions were filled, awakened and touched the audience in the most powerful way. The theatre gave one the rare feeling of looking into the globular beehive of the outside world itself; one or two moments achieved in it had the quality of circus moments; the simple but magnificent effect of Richmond's forces, brilliantly clothed, charging straight into the audience all the way from the deep back of the stage. People left this very simple, sensible theatre with their imaginations stimulated, sometimes exhausted; sometimes by Shakespeare, sometimes as the lines blurred and important speeches whizzed by, by something else. ("Plays" 135)

In 1958, Reaney wrote the play "The Rules of Joy" specifically "with the Festival Theatre in mind," and, therefore, he observed, the play "uses the poetic symbolism and pageantry that theatre's shape demands" (qtd. in Woodman, *Reaney* 21). The play was originally submitted to the *Globe and Mail* Stratford Festival Contest, won no prize, and was not produced. In his note to the play Reaney expresses a very direct understanding of *symbolic space*, which, in all of the many plays to follow — including the revision of "The Rules of Joy" as *The Sun and the Moon* — he attempts to assimilate into the structure of dramatic action.

However, in the earlier plays — with, as we shall see, the important exception of *One-Man Masque* — this articulation of symbolic space is achieved through essentially conventional means. In *The Killdeer*, *The Sun and the Moon*, *Night-Blooming Cereus*, *The Easter Egg*, and *Three Desks*, the proscenium stage is employed along with many of its perspectival and audience/spectacle assumptions. Space in these plays is not as fully inhabited or dramatized as it is in the works beginning with *Listen to the Wind*. Nor is the entire space, including that of the audience, the watching, potential "scene-makers," available for play. It is not yet itself, as Piscator said, the "scene of action," including the possible mental play with memory shadows that the physical structure itself can provide. The spatial volumes *within* the proscenium framework, however, are generally fluid and predicated upon a fusion of realistic and non-realistic poetic principles. The realistic representations of assorted "minute particulars" in the interiors of various village rooms (Mrs. Gardner's in *The Killdeer*, Reverend Kingbird's in *The Sun and the Moon*, Mrs. Brown's in *Night-Blooming Cereus*, and Bethel's in *The Easter Egg*) are counterpoised by anti-illusionist effects in lighting and, in some instances, by particular details of scenic design intended to reinforce the poetic levels of action.

In the first version of *The Killdeer*, for example, the oppressive environmental entrapment that Mrs. Gardner's room, Rebecca's cell, and the courtroom represent, and which is to some degree scenically evident, is challenged when special lighting is employed to establish a suggestion of symbolic space and time (in the moonlight effects in Rebecca's cell, for instance, which scenically reinforce the movement from a "constructed to a dreamed world" (Bachelard, *Poetics of Space* 23), or the flashback-lighting effects in Act III in the recalled encounter between Eli and Clifford). In *The Sun and the Moon*, the "real" presence of Kingbird's room is scenically realigned from the beginning of the play by the theatricalist premise evident in Reaney's opening stage direction: "Scene: THE MANSE, both inside and outside, at Millbank, Ontario. A road runs past the Manse, its great elm, and its green lawns. This can be simply presented by a piano on one side of the stage and a roadside boulder with a signpost beside it on the other side of the stage" (92). Such a spatial arrangement of inner and outer physical volumes establishes an important loosening of strictly perspectival controls, as similar arrangements did in the symbolist drama of Strindberg and others. Concomitantly, there is a movement towards symbolic space, which, in this play again as in symbolist drama, is intended to reveal the interaction of ordinary and mythic experience. *Night-Blooming Cereus* commences with a similarly theatricalist scenic statement: a painted drop curtain (designed, for the first production in 1960, by Louis de Niverville) depicting the village of Shakespeare, Ontario. The first scene of the opera occurs in front of this curtain and culminates in a tableau that Reaney describes thus: "They stand tableau still as if time had quietly and suddenly stopped while in the gray sky above the village appears a vision of the Night-blooming Cereus opening in slow beach crashing swarming splendour and glory, a blossom larger than airplanes or zeppelins, four times really the size of the village, three times the size of Toronto, twice the size of Bethlehem and once the size of Eden. Then it fades as times comes back" (202). For a theatre audience, the image (reminiscent of the growing castle and opening chrysanthemum in Strindberg's *A Dream Play*) possesses filmic qualities, adding still another visual dimension to the juxtaposition of live actors and painted backdrop. The transition from this scene to the next in Mrs. Brown's house is also envisaged by Reaney in primarily filmic terms:

> The two girls EMMY and MARY disappear. ALICE turns and steps into the village scene. She walks away from us until her figure gets smaller and smaller until actually it gets larger and larger since in the twilight the dark tree trunks and the darkening air flow into her figure. The four street lamps might have been about to come out but, instead, the snow descends.
>
> .   .   .   .
>
> The sky, the trees and houses of the village and snowy ground float up, disappear, to reveal the interior of Mrs. Brown's house, a very crowded place, but in a two-room cottage everything gets mixed in together — kitchen, parlour and bedroom. (203–04)

Here, and at the close of the opera when the flower opens once more, Reaney uses an arrangement of physical objects (among them a harmonium, a clock, table, house-plants, door, and rocking chair) and scenic projections within the conventional proscenium frame to re-direct the spectator's sense of time and space so that the mythic ("operatic") dimensions of the small world of Mrs. Brown are disclosed.

The Easter Egg is, on one level, perhaps, the most realistic of the earlier plays in terms of its general economy of scale, its single set, few characters, and sense of time. As Reaney observes in a note to the play, "Stage time is continuous even through audience intermissions, and stage time is real time: the whole action of the play takes place during the time it takes to perform the play, except for some of KENNETH's speeches in Act III which are flashfronts and should be specially lit and emphasized" (3). These lighting effects scenically assist in expressing the temporal dimensions of Kenneth's emerging sense of self and momentarily disrupt the linearity of the play's narrative. On the whole, however, the play's strictly spatial language is dependent upon a fairly conventional perspectival arrangement of figures and objects, of men and women within a recognizable, "real" room. For this reason, the play is less complicated in *theatrical* terms than the previous ones — a fact also acknowledged by Reaney in his preface to the play.

The same is true of *Three Desks*, a play about university professors sharing an office who kept rearranging each other's desks. In this work, there are very few important spatial features other than those created through the movement of the three desks. "No set-changes, please," Reaney commented; "The whole story should flow around a few permanent things — three desks, a bare stage, a small platform" (Preface, *Masks* viii). The theatre space is intended to represent the "interior of a small liberal arts college somewhere in Canada." Within such a generalized locale we find the office with its desks and several doors. Another scenic, and obviously sonic, feature of the set is a "great clock so mechanized as to ring a bell that signals the ends and beginnings of lectures. That bell rings continually and continuously night or day, full or empty, vacation or term" ("Author's Notes," *Masks* 95).

One-Man Masque differs from these plays in its handling of space. In this work, theatrical space is phenomenally and symbolically realized to a much greater degree, and the creative co-existence of discursive and simultaneous modes of articulation is more experientially explored. Reaney describes the work as a masque "in the sense of a series of tableaux and spectacles, or stage images" ("Evening with Babble and Doodle" 41). The series of poems that, in a sense like many of Blake's, were to be accorded pictorial restatement and reinforcement, suggested to Reaney a "stage picture that started out with a candle, proceeded through chair, table, bed, rocking-chair to coffin, turned back again through the purgatorial world with rain barrel, hall tree, dresser and mirror, tree branch, ladder and cardboard box." The poems themselves "moved in a circle through Life, into the world of Death and so into Life again" ("Evening with Babble and Doodle" 42). Jay Macpherson suggests that the "circle of twelve props, not yet become sixteen, looks like so to speak, a Zodiac, or comprehensive cyclic scheme of the kind that governs, say, *The Faerie Queene*, Blake's The Mental Traveller, Yeats's *A Vision*, or Reaney's *A Suit of Nettles* — or the smaller scheme of the

'Four Living Creatures of Ezekiel's vision' claimed to be present at the blooming of the Cereus" (66). As a spatial phenomenon, the complete cyclical scheme is, of course, evident to the spectator in "one act of vision." We see the collection of objects in a circle at the centre of which are "two mannequins sitting on false chairs, a man and a woman" (175). Several possible readings, in addition to that of the Zodiac, present themselves in this simple configuration: the circle with the dot in the centre, the "pupil of the human eye;" the circle as the "imprisoning environment of Life" and as "a final reality . . . a piece of Paradise within us;" the circle as a "global" theatre ("As by the roundnesse it appears most fit") that casts particular memory shadows — towards the mediaeval theatre, for instance, with its precisely symbolic arrangement of sacred/theatrical space and its juxtaposition of discursive and simultaneous modes of articulation. There is also the sense of space simply as a place to "play" — where the actor/narrator "skips round the circle of objects" (176), "raises the small chair to indicate growth" (179), mimes a telephone conversation and a series of characters in different life and death experiences. The actor's body plays out its own language, reading and articulating in its own terms the spatial relationships and values of the several objects (barrel, ladder, cradle, coffin, megaphone, rocking chair, and so on) and, of course, of itself as it expresses its own delight in "making up patterns (scribbling with your body/ bodies) of movement for fun and in play."

As Macpherson reminds us, the verse, some of the objects in this masque, and some of the gestures and movements of the speaker "compress a remarkable range of sources into incisive images — or rather, perhaps, kernels of vision drawn around themselves chunks of handy reference" (66). In and through the primary, richly metaphorical circle, the ladders, the spinning wheel, the bodily scribbled "bird with wings 'vast and outstretched' moving over the waters," the *spatial* suggestions of depth and height, darkness and light, Reaney's "positive theatricalism" brings matter and spirit, a linear narrative and a completed pattern, into the even more elementary field of pure "play." What appears more evident in *One-Man Masque* than it does in the other of Reaney's earliest plays is that the sophisticated, learned reach of his work — a classic literacy which reverberates with numerous theatrical as well as literary sources and echoes — is thoroughly grounded in the *naif* artist's preference for and obvious fun with *bricolage*. The space, the odd collection of ordinary objects, and the "body-scribbling" of *One-Man Masque* appear well within the domain of a do-it-yourself creativity. Just such a tone informs Reaney's editorial on the situation of the Canadian theatre in *Alphabet* 4 written shortly after these first four works:

> How can those interested in making life better in this country help our drama? There should be a club that does nothing but seasons of plays by Canadians. It should do them in a bare, long room up above a store, probably infested by Odd Fellows or Orangemen on easily avoidable nights. Nobody should have any truck with that grand Bugaboo-Lighting. Five two hundred Mazda watters always turned on will do for any play that lights its own way, as a play should. (3)

Later, recalling these early years, Reaney added: "Whatever the style is called that blasts the box-set-with-lighting concept apart is the style for me. After watching producers struggle so disastrously with the change of set that divides the central act of *Killdeer* I determined never again; so anti-illusionist from now on" ("James Reaney" 156).

In "Ten Years at Play," Reaney describes something of the experiences that led to the establishment of the Listeners' Workshop in the loft of an old Legion Hall, where the joys of *bricolage* were encountered and shaped into the radically different theatrical language of a series of plays beginning with *Listen to the Wind*. "I wanted a society," he wrote, "where directing a play is not equated with stage managing, where the lighting, costumes, all that money can buy disappear and what we have instead is so much group skill and sense of fun in imagining out things that richness re-appears all over the place for nothing" (55). It was in these workshops that Reaney seized the opportunity to develop further the theatrical premises of *One-Man Masque*, one of which was the creation and employment of space for ideational as well as "playing" purposes. It was here, on the floor of the loft, that a spatial language — a grammar of spatial signs — was fashioned. This language was intended, on one level, to visually articulate a complex set of readings and patterns. On another level, it was to be directly expressive of phenomenal space wherein an inherent sense of play, of spontaneous scribbling, is realized:

> On the floor . . . are strips of coloured tape put there for organizational purposes; also a drummer, a pianist, and a prop table filled with the things you need to put on Genesis with. For

example, mailing tubes for the angels to beat Adam and Eve out of Eden with; a long strip of cheesecloth to hold in front of the Eden scenes to give that effect of dream. Cardboard boxes to build the Tower of Babel with, and a green garden hose for the serpent. Anything else we need can be suggested with the human voice or body, and in my Listeners' Workshop at London, Ontario, I usually had 25 of these ranging in height from two feet to six, and in age from three to sixty. Every Saturday morning at ten. . . . ("Ten Years" 53)

One morning in June, 1968, I watched the Listeners' Workshop do Genesis before an invited audience. There had been no dress rehearsal, we were not worried about forgetting, there were lots of people in the group who were directing from inside the mass of actors. And it unfolded, like some homemade thing out of brown paper with all sorts of fascinating rough edges and accidental effects. In the Babel sequence the ingredients of the tower engulfed anything moveable in the room the audience wasn't sitting on. I think there were some participants who had just arrived that morning, but it made no difference — they were folded in to the going on. ("Ten Years" 58)

"Let the other marvels vanish, and, for the new works, leave us with a bare stage!" (Copeau, qtd. in Bablet 65). Jacques Copeau's *petit tréteau nu* has had its special appeal to playwrights and directors since he established his Vieux Colombier in 1913. With it, space was to become the white blank sheet of paper, the plain empty canvas within which new experiences could be shaped with words, objects, lights, and what Herbert Blau has called the "inscriptions of the actor's body, coded, genetic, generative, the ghostlier demarcations" (40). Such an exploration of *physical* as well as verbal and psychological truths and patterns marked the theatrical activity of an entire generation of playwrights and directors during the sixties. Reaney's *Listen to the Wind* was his first major work after *One-Man Masque* to exhibit a visceral and ideational space sense with which the ontological aims of his theatre could be advanced. As his account of *Genesis* suggests, in his Listeners' Workshops, playing space was expected to overflow into watching space so that the act of watching itself became, for the "aroused" spectator, an act of playing.

Some of the most important sources of the radical change in dramatic style that this play represents would include the Peking

National Opera performance of *At the Fairy Mountain Bridge*, which Reaney had seen a few years earlier. He observed, the "orchestra sat on stage. Gestures and mime took the place of props and sets. I remember a fabulous boat just made by two actors pretending. Art is made by subtracting from reality and letting the viewer imagine or 'dream it out' (as Owen is told to in the play)." Another source, also acknowledged by Reaney in his notes to the published text of *Listen to the Wind*, was the work of John Hirsch when he directed *Names and Nicknames* at the Manitoba Theatre Centre in 1963:

> Four years ago, John Hirsch directed one of my children's plays, *Names and Nicknames*, at the Manitoba Theatre Centre. With a dozen children, six young actors (among them Martha Henry and Heath Lambert), and words taken from my father's old *Practical Speller*, John Hirsch created a magic hour that has remained with me ever since. The simpler art is — the richer it is. Words, gestures, a few rhythm band instruments create a world that turns Cinerama around and makes you the movie projector. (117)

Later, in his interview in *Stage Voices: Twelve Canadian Playwrights*, Reaney recalled some of the other plays and theatre experiences that seem to have informed his decision to "try writing a different kind of play altogether." These include some of the Shakespearean productions mounted in the earlier years of the Stratford Festival. One of his favourite plays was *Pericles*, "with its wonderful leaping back and forth in reality; years erased by just a word from the bearded old storyteller" (143). "You may remember," he wrote in his first *Halloween* letter, "that there is a Narrator, Gower, who comes right out on stage and changes scene, time and tone with his narration; all the rest of the actors in the play are really in his mind, a mental landscape that like the Mediterranean itself with its dreamlike shifting swimmers can assume any shape it pleases" ("Letter from James Reaney" 3). Other plays cited by Reaney were the Punch and Judy shows with their "demonic sudden killings;" Greek plays "constructed like jewel weed pods" ("James Reaney" 143); Thornton Wilder's *Our Town* and *Skin of Our Teeth*, the latter

> beautifully produced by Peter Dearing some years ago at the Grand Theatre here in London, Ontario, interested me with its putting everything in; at the end of the evening the cycle behind

all the shifting scenes actually appeared — clouds (magic-lantern projections) and visions of godlike figures *in a circle.* On the superb proscenium stage of this Ambrose Small theatre as one looked around at an enthralled audience — you felt this is the globe of life, this is the ultimate audience. ("James Reaney" 144)

Other ideas came from Old Comedy, a "rich mine of ideas that look new if you steal them straightforwardly enough; I like direct address by the author to the audience (parabasis), the ghost of the marriage ceremony at the end, food thrown to the audience, rather like the Christmas Concert where Santa Claus appears at the end with food" ("James Reaney" 149). Then there was the influence of films that "get at your dream life in a way no other artforms save music quite does; and of the cinemas I've known . . . all great temples where, in their prime, in religious darkness, one drank in silver visions that engraved themselves more deeply when they were not in colour" ("James Reaney" 151). Finally, he cites the example of Carl Orff whose experiments in the acoustical juxtaposition of percussion and melody, and in the expressive range of voice effects, he had seen in the choric work of Tyrone Guthrie at Stratford, to which he compares the "failures at chorus acting in productions of Eliot" ("James Reaney" 148).

What we see throughout all of these statements and experiences is Reaney's growing sense of theatricality itself as a powerful and poetic language. As James Stewart Reaney points out in his detailed analysis of *Listen to the Wind*, Reaney's sense of theatre, in this play, appears to approach the self-consciousness of Barthes's "cybernetic machine" with its complex systems of significations (73). That space is to be established and experienced phenomenally both by actors and audience is evident from the outset when Reaney presents us with a nearly bare stage that contains four chairs, a ladder, and a prop table. To one side are the musicians and chorus. The conventional spatial authority of the proscenium is very simply overturned as we become "dimly aware that there are three girls in the aisle playing with a ball that passes over our heads, back and forth. They are walking down the lane to a farmhouse to stay for the summer. As they step up onto the stage, the boy rises to greet them. The ball is thrown into the chorus, one of whom retrieves it" (*Listen* 11). Through the simplest of means we are invited to share real and imagined space with the performers; the theatre itself is to become *our* "West Room" where, like Owen and the three girls, by being "folded in," we too are "putting on plays." These props — weather-vane, window frame, branches, flags — join with many others as scenic abbreviations through which a series of actions can produce their own spaces. The scenic language of the theatre is released from subservience to the verbal text and permitted to function autono-mously and fluidly in the articulation of inner and outer space. The play moves rapidly from Owen's house to Caresfoot Court ("These four chairs can be the house" [18]) with its old tree (a step-ladder), to an avenue of trees (the four chairs again) leading up to Hawkscliffe Hall, to the edge of the forest (". . . one of the chorus runs across the stage with a pair of antlers" [25]), to a carriage journey with Maria to the station that "takes in part of the auditorium so that the boy running with the wheel 'enchants' itself into the onlookers' minds" (30), to a walk over a bridge ("a plank over two chairs" [74]), to a wild storm ("Weather vanes turning. . . . Great armies of branches waving, creaking and groaning" [94]), to a final dance ambiguously enchanted by giant shadows. These separate spaces, each especially designed with its own economy of hieroglyphs, an alphabet partly manifested in lines, circles, squares, and cross-overs, are all con-tained within the one enveloping space and *idea* of the theatre itself (however its audience/spectacle relationship happens to be articu-lated) within, that is, the ultimate form behind "all the shifting scenes." Such a theatre, with its own memory shadows, its rich and ambiguous metaphorical value, its fusion of sacred and secular "chunks of handy reference," folds the act of watching in to the act of playing. In Reaney's notes, "Colours in the Dark," he writes,

At the very beginning John Hirsch asked me to do what I liked — something free form, personal and using as much material already written as possible. I took out my diaries and notebooks and started not writing, but drawing. Paul Klee's *Magic Squares*, each square either a slight variation on or contrast to its neigh-bouring square, is really the design behind the play. There are forty-two episodes — each a small scene with its own shade and point — forty-two magic squares — sundogs, someone trailing all the string in the world behind him, someone crawling into a hollow log and emerging as a tortoise — or a luna moth. A masked figure fighting with some children over a lightning rod. . . . what were the forty-two episodes and what did they add up to?
One person really. Living, almost dying, then living again.

There are dozens of characters in the play, yet they are all part
of one personality — one personality made up of a man who
has found someone to love. (140)

In *Colours in the Dark*, the theatrical work that was the result of
this primary visual inspiration, space contracts and expands to a
degree greater than in any other work by Reaney, revealing through
the "shade and point" of a series of small scenes what Bachelard
called "intimate immensity." Immensity is within ourselves, he
wrote, "attached to a sort of expansion of being that life curbs and
caution arrests, but which starts again when we are alone. As soon
as we become motionless, we are elsewhere; we are dreaming in a
world that is immense. Indeed, immensity is the movement of
motionless man. It is one of the dynamic characteristics of quiet
daydreaming" (*Poetics of Space* 184). A sick child sitting in the dark
with his Planter's Peanut colouring book initiates an imaginative
re-creation of his own life, his ancestral life, his nation's life, the
world's life. Through the dual paradox of intimate immensity and
motionless movement, Reaney explores the "space you inhabit not
just with your body but with your head" to disclose those hidden,
sometimes "magic" connections between inner and outer worlds —
connections that permeate and enrich the simplest of Klee's multi-
shaded hieroglyphs. Only the complex polylingualism of an "Unbound Theatre," with which Reaney was by this time increasingly
confident, could articulate the multitudinous verbal, physical, and
spiritual designs that erupted from the rummaged-through play box.
    In *Listen to the Wind*, the spatial inscriptions of props and
performing bodies include the alphabet of circles (for games, journeys, whirling weathervanes, tumbling maple keys that "helicopter
down"), squares (for houses, for Owen's bed), and lines (for avenues,
including the auditorium aisles, the railway, various ladder configurations, the ceremonial feast at Caresfoot Court, the stream from
the haunted well). These inscriptions do not draw special attention
to themselves as readable signs, although to a degree they possess
such potential. They do, however, serve concretely, within the purely
theatricalist idiom of the work as a whole, to represent the action of
improvisational *playing* with different inner and outer realities, each
of which generates its own kinetic and spatial values.
    In *Colours in the Dark*, a similarly theatricalist spirit pervades, and
the highly fluid spatial scoring of scenes helps to sustain what Reaney
called the "mosaic-all-things-happening-at-the-same-time-galaxy-

higgledy-piggledy feeling" (*Colours* 5). However, in this play, certain scenic configurations are less obviously improvisational and seem to announce something of their symbolic value as primary forms. The play opens with an arrangement of geometrical forms that will work their way through the subsequent series of scenes. A young man circles around the stage on a bicycle; vaguely echoing Klee's "magic" squares, a square projection screen at the back of the playing space depicts colours; there is a line of six chairs at centre stage. This formal arrangement is scenically related to a variety of more casual visual impressions that the theatre space might produce — including the view of the audience itself — as the auditorium lights remain up and a game of musical chairs is played. This establishes, as the ball-tossing did at the beginning of *Listen to the Wind*, the appropriate image and experience of playing. The musical chairs game, we are told, is a real game, and during the first run "... no one ever knew who was going to win and great rivalry for Mother's prize — a balloon handed up by the pianist — great rivalry grew up between grown-up actors and children" (*Colours* 9). The circling bicycle, its turning wheels inscribing circles within a theatre space considered as a "globe of life," echoes other images of circles within circles in Reaney's work. Describing the use of "rings within rings" as a structuring device in "Mome Fair" from *A Suit of Nettles*, Stingle cites the following from Wendy Doniger O'Flaherty's discussion of myth and theatre: "The locus classicus for this onion-layer technique of story-telling is the play within the play, which often carries with it the implication that the audience witnessing the play, within which there is a play, is itself part of a play — perhaps part of a play within another (metaphysical) play" (43). As Stingle reminds us, the narrator in Reaney's poem asserts that "When you're on it you don't notice this phenomenon but by that time you're a clown enjoying your pastime: right now we are learneds and we are enjoying the puzzle of the ferris wheel" (*Poems* 175). And, of course, as "clowns" we can enjoy the assorted scenic images that open up for us the life of *Colours in the Dark* — appreciating at the same time, perhaps, or later, much more likely as "learneds," the ambiguously shifting memory-shadows some of these images cast.

This circle within circles image is replaced, as the auditorium lights dim, by that of a single circle of children around a blindfolded man who proceeds to read their palms: "An image of upraised hands to a bandaged face" (10). A short time later this becomes an image of upraised hands that hold flowers up to him. The circle image absorbs various associations of intimacy and immensity. It is intimate in its relationship to and expression of the family, to the familiar parlour game, to the man's naming of names within the circle of children (Erasmus William Wrigley, Sarah Elizabeth Brody, Daniel Pickett). It is immense, by way of intimacy, in its symbolic value as the pupil of an eye ("the essential diagram of man's first condition"), paradoxically blindfolded yet able to "see" (thus the fleeting echo, perhaps, of the supplicating chorus encircling the blind Tiresias in Guthrie's production of *Oedipus*). It is also immense in its social reverberations (the man identifies a variety of occupations — postman, rich young lady, dressmaker — that compose, in part, the "environmental circle," which in time will lay claim to all save the boy who will grow up to be a poet or painter, who leaves the circle to sit on one of the chairs used earlier in the game), and in its cosmological, paradisal and ontological implications: "Guess who we are" (10). Visible space contracts towards the close of this sequence as the stage lights gradually diminish, the screen lights up with "all sorts of colours" (12), and the primary field of play reaches inward to encompass the intimate immensity of the Son-Father-Grandfather's experienced and dreamed worlds. Space and time are released from their familiar frames and realigned through the spatial rhythms of a rich theatricalist idiom. Through the language of "scribbling bodies," marionettes, masks, stationary and mobile props, music (which creates its own acoustical space), lighting, colour, the fragmentation of scenic volumes, and the series of particularized and abstract screen images, the inter-locking, "never finished" stories of the Self, the Nation, and the World, are accorded scenic articulation. Within the terms of such an "Unbound Theatre" in which, as Delevoy said of collage, ". . . the parameters of becoming replace the rigid configurations of the perspectival system" (*Dimensions* 116), metaphorical value is given to certain spatial signs. One of these is the circle; another is the triangle/pyramid.

Jay Macpherson says that the starting-point of Reaney's "Existence Poem," which, as he remarks, "ties the whole play together" (*Colours* 20), might be the "Tree-of-Life diagram Yeats learned in his association with the Golden Dawn," which Reaney accounted for in his study of Spenser and Yeats (Macpherson 97). A variation of such an image also informs the family tree pyramid which, within the terms of Reaney's "positive theatricalism," is on four occasions accorded corporeal expression, formed as it is by the cast in a "triangle arrangement" (*Colours* 24). The image does not carry the same weight of complex religious and literary allusion that resonate with a variety of "kernels of vision" ascribed by Macpherson to the form behind the "Existence Poem" (97). As a purely scenic composition, however, it has its own metaphorical value. On one level, the image "subsumes into itself a child's growing knowledge about his birthright, natural phenomena, the episodic, inconsequential grind of daily living and the presence of 1024 great great great great great great great great grandparents in any one child" (Miller 93–94). As such an image, it signifies concretely the continuity of past and present, reaching, on the mythic level, back to the edenic state of the Original Parents (we see on the screen Durer's Adam and Eve) and, on the "documentary," historical level back through those interconnecting planes of ancestral life that the play weaves in and out of the story of one man's existence and growth.

One of the most interesting and scenically complex appearances of this pyramid is at the close of Act I, in the sequence called "The Bridge." To begin with, improvisational "body scribbling" establishes the bridge as a space, beneath which there is a swan ("A girl with long white glove as swan's neck"). The hero is afraid to cross: "I was like one of those people you hear about in mental hospitals who can't go through a doorway" (46). He then recites part of the "Existence Poem" and is chased by the Bear to the middle of the bridge. A brief tug-of-war ensues until he is pulled over. The primarily linear arrangement (the bridge, the tug-of-war shapes) then dissolves, and the family tree pyramid is formed as the stage slowly turns yellow. The pyramid is then inverted so that it becomes an arrow "pointing at a child standing on the trestles. This child turns his face. He is masked and dressed as Adolf Hitler" (47).

The interconnecting movements of plastic forms in space upon which the scenic dynamics of this whole sequence is based, in its linear and pyramidal composition (the latter undergoing an inversion similar to that of the "upside down" church steeple in the "Antichrist as a Child" poem, recited while the Son plays the spokes of his upside down bicycle wheel), is partly reminiscent of the regulated plasticity that informs the theatre of Meyerhold, and, especially, of such painter-designers as L. Moholy-Nagy, Oskar Schlemmer, and Kassimir Malevich, whose designs for *Victory Over the Sun*, for instance (Rischbieter 137), employ a similar geometrical scenic vocabulary. There is also an interesting echo here of the compositional values and dynamics of triangle and arrow of Klee's painting *Eros*. However, in the theatrical presentation of such an underlying design, Reaney eschews all evidence of the compass and the ruler which would create generally tight and sometimes predictable compositions, as they appear to in Malevich and many of his contemporaries, or in some more recent experimenters in the use of scenographic space such as Jacques Polieri in "Systematisation de l'espace scenographique." In other words, the spatial rigidity ascribed to the perspectival system is not abandoned only to be replaced by an equally rigid geometry. However, the geometrical volumes *are* present. We are conscious of lines becoming circles becoming triangles becoming arrows becoming squares; and we are conscious of the juxtaposition of such patterns operating effectively as an alphabet of spatial signs, scenically articulating Reaney's meaning in their own terms. Yet they operate almost entirely within a field of *play,* as they do, for example, in Miró's *The Farm* and in many of Klee's works, fusing their more sophisticated and at times secret symbolic language with the improvisational spirit inspired, in this instance, by thirty-two people at a Listeners' Workshop on a Saturday morning designing "the thousand ancestors behind every human being" (*Colours* 24).

The pyramid next appears in juxtaposition with a wedding arch and a model of the Sharon Temple. Through this arch all the ancestors had in their time passed to create through "acts of love" those who now kiss beneath it and those, the children, who also come through it wearing "large mother and father heads" in anticipation of their procreativity (86). Another group of children pass through the arch wearing Halloween masks and carrying a coffin, signifying the cycle of life and death that the entire ancestral pyramid manifests and preparing for the "Dance of Death at London, Ontario" sequence which follows. The Sharon Temple is the "white temple all made of wood and 12,000 panes of glass," as it was described earlier when a photograph of this early nineteenth-century structure north of Toronto was shown on the screen and into which, we were told, the soul of the hermit Mr. Winemeyer, in the form of a moth, had disappeared (62). For its designer, David Willson, this temple was an attempt to establish through the architectonic values of space, light, line, circle, arch, and square and through various numerical significations a structure that would reflect the sacred order (and sound — as the temple was to become known for its music) of the universe.[2] As such a spatial statement, it corresponds to the ideal of the ontologically revelatory "magical theatre" with its very precise rendering of secular and sacred orders. Its presence as a referentially complex model-image within the context of the pyramid, the wedding arch, and the theatrical *performance* itself (that is within the physical and metaphorical space in which we are ourselves incorporated as spectator/players) serves to reinforce scenically some of the ideational values of space, including performance space, that inform Reaney's "positive theatricalism." The conjunction of universally significant shapes in this whole composition also reflects ironically upon the chaos of the city from which the play's hero is attempting to disentangle himself, a city whose spatial values are most aptly manifested in the "cement tapeworm" of Yonge Street (82). The spiritual and imaginative restoration of the hero is, thus, partly drawn by Reaney in terms of primary geometrical signs.

Throughout *Colours in the Dark*, these signs move in and out of what appear as the more improvisationally "scribbled" and less spatially closed movements of the actors and of their multitudinous props. Many of these movements provide strictly linear accents within what Klee calls the dynamics of "polyphonic simultaneity," in which there is the simultaneous playing of different, thematically independent, but inter-related motifs (*Thinking Eye* 340). Linear structures are to be seen in such scenic compositions as the opening game of musical chairs; the bridge; the tug-of-war contest; the clothesline upon which Granny hangs "all the clothes I wear — have worn, will wear in my life" (18); the blue cheesecloth stretched across the stage to represent the sea upon which sailboats bringing "Ancestors & a Cradle" journeyed (33); the episode with the string that involves the incorporation of the audience space as ". . . they wind back the string — pull the lady and her parcel up out of the audience, down the aisle, onto the stage — but when they wind her back the first time they get a skeleton lady holding the parcel" (45). We are told in the stage directions that the string routine "will go on forever" (46), suggesting a comic realization of Klee's observation "The longer the line, the more of the time element it contains. Distance is time, whereas a surface is apprehended more in terms of the moment. This gives the linear element a mutual relation to imaginary space" (*Thinking Eye* 340). Linear structures are also to be found in the variety of confrontational situations throughout the play. These would include the various school scenes (rows of chairs facing the Schoolmaster/Professor), the battle between the hardwood and the conebearing trees, the double rows formed for the "Fantasia on the Street Names" of Winnipeg.

Reaney's question whether in the Donnelly trilogy "this sense of design I didn't have 11 years ago comes from the intervening workshop experiments" can be answered positively. The workshops and the plays that grew so directly from them were based upon a strong visual and *physical* sense of polyphonically arranged shapes and movements that, in their improvisational and formal spatial statements, embody the dichotomous but interrelated impulses towards playing and symbol-making. In the Donnelly trilogy, this spatial grammar is employed with complete artistic assurance. As Reaney's director Keith Turnbull came to recognize "It's all very intentional,"

> and the structures of stage action are very very intentional. Sometimes you just have to get the right image for yourself. I went in and did a very angular blocking for Part II. And I realized, after two weeks of rehearsal, "My god, I've been doing this ALL WRONG." The play is based on straight lines meeting spinning. And I had based everything on the geometrical patterns, like Part I, on the lines without the spin. Well, the rhythm of the language didn't work properly. The lines are punctuated in a different way and unless you're aware, unless the stage action is moving properly, the actors don't breathe it properly, they don't speak it properly, it doesn't mean what it's written to mean. Things like that are very very conscious. (Turnbull, "Interview" 154)

The trilogy represents Reaney's most successful and complex attempt at story-telling and environmental theatre in which, as Schechner observed, "There is no dead space, nor any end to space" (83). Drawing very broad but, in this instance, useful distinctions, Schechner went on to say,

> Orthodox theater is mimetic: a reflection of prior experiences and an attempt to recreate them or give the illusion of recreating them. Psychodrama is entirely actual: the creation of circumstances in which the participants relive in the present troubling moments from their past. Environmental theater is neither mimetic nor psycho-dramatic. *The fundamental logic of environmental theater is not the logic of the story but the logic of story-telling.* (*Environmental* 83)

The trilogy employs a vast array of documentary material that ideally should envelop the spectators as it does the actors/story-tellers, situating *both* groups within the ontologically creative triad of facts, story, and story-style. The impulse of the three plays to erupt, in the manner of environmental theatre, into the surrounding space was evident in the productions at the Tarragon Theatre in Toronto, but, naturally enough, most evident in the productions they received in the Drama Workshop at the University of Western Ontario at the start of the national tour. Here the *environmentally* identifying documents and artefacts — the land-grant maps, the place names scribbled on the theatre walls along with the multitudinous signs of political, religious, and commercial life (the latter becoming increasingly evident from play to play) — were also, in every respect, *regionally* identifying signs. As such, they give the theatre space itself another dimension, which it possessed in the classical and the Elizabethan theatres, which mirrors the structure of the surrounding spaces of the city and the countryside. At the opening of *The St Nicholas Hotel*, for example, Reaney presents the situation and scene in the following stage direction:

> Passengers for the stages to the north slowly fill the benches at the sides of the room we too are waiting in; we see actors spinning tops (each one seems to have one) and hear them singing songs from the play. Like a cloud shadow the stage picture is slowly invaded now by the story of a road; the actors stop being actors and become fighters for the ownership of that road, a map of which goes all around the walls of the theatre from Crediton to Exeter to Clandeboye down to Lucan to Elginfield to London to St Thomas to Waterford. . . . (17)

In these particular productions, the "room in which the story is presented," as Reaney describes his playing space at the beginning of *Sticks & Stones* (35), was *itself* a product of the interlocking forces that inform at different levels of history and myth the Donnelly story and the story of the road.

Like the playing spaces of *One-Man Masque*, *Listen to the Wind*, and *Colours in the Dark*, that of the trilogy displays, as Reaney states, "all of the objects and properties required — ladders, barrels, sticks, stones, noise-makers, chairs, etc." (*Sticks* 35), and, in the course of the story-telling, many of these objects, along with the "foot and body movements" of the actors, will inscribe a complex series of design images that, like those of *Colours in the Dark* especially, manifest improvisational playing as well as symbolic patterning. The cat's-cradle image, introduced early in *Sticks &*

Stones during the surveying of Biddulph Township, is, in many respects, an apt emblem of the infinite number of shifting geometrical and linear patterns that the plays as a whole present within the squared-off playing space. As such, the image provides an effective diagram of the kinetic and spatial aspects of the *story-style* and, as Reaney reminds students in a Teaching Kit circulated during the tour, of characterization as well. "Since the cat's cradle changes every time the string changes hands," he wrote, "it can be seen as an image of the constantly changing relationships in this play; even the way one actor will change his role from one moment to another" (*NDWT*). The image also represents the *facts* of the Irish land systems, which, as Reaney remarked in *14 Barrels* when he was discovering quite different systems in British Columbia, "show up ever so shadowily in nineteenth century Biddulph" (69). On one occasion, the actors "using ropes and making cats' cradles (Jacob's ladders) out of them with their bodies" are scenically juxtaposed with an early map of Biddulph township, "showing the net of concessions, roads, farms with owners' names on them and a feeling that we have come from Ireland to a closer look at what is happening" (*Sticks* 47). The use of a map here, and elsewhere in the trilogy, recalls Piscator's observation regarding the value of maps in his production of *Russlands Tag* in 1920. The map, he wrote, "showed the geographical location and described the obvious political meaning of the scenes. It was not only an element of the 'decor' but a social, economic, historical and geographical diagram as well. The map was an integral part of the performance . . . intervening at times as the action occurred. It in fact became a dramatic element" (qtd. in Bablet 130). A similar use of a map will be seen later in *Baldoon*. Finally, the cat's-cradles image represents the *story* of "fates with string entangling people's lives" (*Sticks* 47). "The laws of geometry are the laws of geometry," the surveyor in *Sticks & Stones* exclaims, and "people must make do with what right angles and Euclid and we surveyors and measurers provide for them" (47).

These laws of geometry imposing their own conditions and shapes upon personal and social destiny are also depicted through the use of a scenic variation of the cat's-cradle image, the ladder. As the names of the new roads of Biddulph are called out soon after the surveying scene, for instance, ladders are arranged at the back of the stage so that their "shadows and patterns" match those of a "map of Biddulph which is a triangle" (49). Their importance as an image is then verbally reinforced when Mr. Donnelly exclaims,

[MR DONNELLY.] and these roads of Biddulph — you're right
to see them as ladders, yes, ladders that we crawled up and
down on and up other ladders — up to Goderich for justice,
down to London to pay our rent.
  *The ladders have been laid before Mr Donnelly and he uses
  their rungs to illustrate.*
  Why are the roads here rather than here? Why do I live here
rather than here? Wild lands cut by surveyors into people —
with your chain you decided that it would be here, my farm
— that people say I squatted on Concession Six Lot Eighteen
— and you decided —
BOY. So what's his lot, dad?
MR DONNELLY. That's Mulowney's. At his five-acre slashing
  I should kill Farl and there
SURVEYOR. Concession Six Lot Fifteen
MR DONNELLY. I should be caught. Caught in the lines and
  the roads and the farms they made and the quarrels about
  fences and ditches — the Protestant Line, now who settled
  that line. (*Sticks* 49–50)

The actors then form a double line and enact the eviction of the
early Black settlers of Biddulph, complete with the "Burning of house
on barrel routine" (51). The image of the double rows is reiterated
several times throughout the trilogy, and, as Reaney remarks in a
stage direction, it represents "one of the most important design
images of the story, a man caught between the lines of his neighbours,
caught in a ladder, and the big dance at the end of the play will
emphasize this quality of the Donnellys being planted in rows of
people they can't get away from" (53). In a letter to Turnbull, Reaney
explained further,

    The sixteen players are arranged in two rows of eight facing each
    other. . . . One idea behind this is the Irish faction fights where
    Whitefeet would fight Blackfeet, more or less like two street
    gangs.
    The two lines also represent the two sides of the road the
    Donnellys lived on: a constricting gamut. The Donnellys are
    caught in a surveyor's pattern. The Donnelly farm is cut in half;
    so are the Donnellys. Only at the end of the play are we freed
    from the two lines of players. (Letter to Keith Turnbull)

"So the road you lived on could destroy you just like that," says Mr. Donnelly, "and the road you lived on might not turn on you, but decide to have a go at another road. What other road? Why the sixth and seventh concession where I lived. My road" (*Sticks* 52).

In the course of the plays, the linear geometrical configurations — the cat's-cradles, the various ladder formations, the double rows — acquire increasingly recognizable associations and thus contribute to our understanding of the interpenetrating narrative and mythic levels. We are expected to be able to "read" such patterns, for instance, when, at the beginning of Act III of *Sticks & Stones*, Jennie tells her story while "Behind her narration the entire company mime groupings that go through the story backwards and forwards; they make the Roman Line; they do the ladder journey format; they suddenly kneel, cross themselves . . . people caught in the Roman Line" (143). For such reiterative scenic imagery to work effectively, registering and interweaving the appropriate memory-shadows cast, in this instance by the spatial vocabulary of the reels (evoking the other double rows and their meanings), the surveyors' geometry (with its cat's-cradle associations), and the Catholic Mass (kneeling and crossing, the latter sign counterpoised to the cross of Mr. Donnelly's signature "X," the St. Patrick's cross, the crossed arms of Tom Donnelly and Jim Feeney in their pledge of blood brotherhood, and the railway crossings — all such crosses acting as personal, social, commercial, and religious signatures), the patterns and gestures must become, through performance, as established and known as those of a formal dance. But it is a dance in which the whole "story" is known, at any given moment, by both participants and watchers.

Schechner describes what he perceived as such a phenomenon in the dances of Greek drama and suggests how he tried to emulate this in the more profane context of one of his "environments:"

> . . . the Greeks liked watching the dances not as discreet moves but as completed sequences, finished figures — a kind of stepped-out destiny in movement. In some surviving Greek theaters there are pavements of different-colored stones tracing the dance routes: architectural scripts. These pavements help the memories of the dancers and spectators alike. At any given moment the whole dance is known, and the dancers are seen as figures somewhere on the course. We tried for something like this in the *Commune* environment where different maps, figures,

routes, and writing were marked on the floor and other parts of the environment. (*Environmental* 21–22)

The suggestion of such an architectural, certainly of a spatial, script functioning as a scenic reinforcement of Jennie's story (as it does later in *Handcuffs*) in a complex dance sequence that, we're told, "is a reprise that brings together the musical and dance themes of the whole trilogy" (*Handcuffs* 98) is reminiscent of the Elizabethan "memory theatre" examined by Yates. In such a model, she says, an *idea* of the theatre was developed that "adapted the ancient plan to the needs of its own times" (*Theatre* 112). Such conscious spatial scoring also recalls Reaney's experience of a strong "memory shadow" when the trilogy was performed in the "Methodist rounded" Bathurst United Church in Toronto, his recognition of the "architectural organization forcing you to gesture, to kneel, to lift up your head" in the empty Ottawa church, and, of course, the symbolic and phenomenal sense of space that determines much of the "stepped-out destiny in movement" of *One-Man Masque*.

Towards the close of Act I of *Sticks & Stones*, the Roman Line "formation queues up for a drink, then begins to handspike barrels towards stage centre" (81). The Shamrock Concert Company is performing their melodrama, *Black Donnellys*, and the "Farl and Donnelly boxing" scene is enacted within the "circle of watchers" (81). Soon afterwards, a circle is formed as the "actual" fight is staged. The circle here, as elsewhere, is a constricting, intimidating configuration. It appears as such a form later in *Sticks & Stones* when the chorus forms a circle around Mr. Donnelly, pointing at him, as the guilty verdict is read (111); when Maggie, in *The St Nicholas Hotel*, follows the imagined inscription of the Donnelly stage coach around the hotel barroom "in a circular, birdlike, trapped motion" (30); when a "mob circle" is formed, again in *The St Nicholas Hotel*, as Tom Ryan is caught and carried out (141), followed shortly afterwards by Mrs. Donnelly's circular journey around the bare stage ("a 'Listen to the Wind' wheel & horse with Mrs Donnelly running behind") as she encounters various parts of what is becoming for her and her family the crushing "environmental circle" (142); and in *Handcuffs* when a mob circle is again created around Mr. and Mrs. Donnelly depicted as caged birds: "Birds attack the 'different' bird & kill her & him with chirping sounds" (81).

In *The St Nicholas Hotel*, as Turnbull said, there are "straight lines meeting spinning." Many of these spinning inscriptions within the larger, threatening circles formed by the chorus, metaphorically express the wheels within wheels of a social structure and environment that is increasingly machinelike, inexorably enveloping all within the laws of its "mechanical geometry." The spinning tops, the sewing machine, the (human) threshing machine in *Handcuffs*, the danced-out image of trapped birds within the circular cage, these images all spatially inscribe the operation of this machine, intersecting with the various linear patterns that, as we have seen, tell their own story of people caught in rows, lines, and ladders. In *Sticks & Stones*, Mrs. Donnelly verbally evokes such an intersecting of straight and spinning forms, which appear spatially to articulate entrapment. She speaks of her journey to Goderich and back (on a road represented earlier by various ladder formations) and her momentary transfixion — echoed later at the end of Act II when she holds her lamp as the moon does, "a seal in the air" (136), waiting for her husband's release from prison — beyond ordinary time and space. She holds a letter, a single, isolated document, the verbal contents of which can effectively change the whole design, the whole dance with its "stepped-out destiny in movement":

> I walked all the way to Goderich. I met him. I gave him the three petitions and now they've all turned into this letter and I won't open it. It's so hot and bright, the cicadas shrill shrill shrill away. Everything turns into a letter. That letter. It's like the handspike he saw on the ground and he picked it up. I hate the fact that there's moments each like a bridge of dread and why does there have to be an earth that goes round and round. (119)

* * *

The image of a map dominates the setting of *Baldoon*. The map is intended to situate us in the "very southern part of Upper Canada" where the "legends enact themselves in front of us." The map is also a scrim behind which shadowy figures are seen travelling with some difficulty "through a lower band of dark material; the land masses on the map could be made of bulrushes" (1). In front of the map, on a bare stage, there is a stick house, "quite skeletal," which represents Troyer's house. The beams of this house later become, Reaney tells us, "the poltergeist-smashed beams of McTavish's strawshed" (1). Establishing the participatorial values of shared audience and player space, as was accomplished at the beginning of *Listen to the Wind* and *Colours in the Dark*, Reaney's company of actors enter from the back of the auditorium singing Tunkard, Mennonite, and Shaker hymns and carrying a model of Macdonald's house at Baldoon:

> this house is really like a hand puppet stage, can open out to reveal interior rooms and is in effect a magic box wherein witchcraft and poltergeist will be seen at their work perhaps more effectively than if the local magicians had to work in the naked stage area; so, an illusion box. (3)

In addition to the emblematic "illusion box," there are three bird puppets on sticks representing the souls of McTavish (a hawk), Mrs. Pharlan (a black goose), and Troyer (a white lake-gull).

The Killdeer was similarly concerned with the journey of souls towards recognition. There, however, the exploration and the dramatic expression of such a journey was primarily verbal. The souls of Harry and Rebecca were also associated with birds, as was that of Mrs. Donnelly, but the association was evoked through speech in the former and through a simple gesture of arm-raising in the latter. In *Baldoon*, the stricter bifurcation of theatrical signs into verbal and non-verbal elements is much more evident. The heavy reliance upon toy models, stick houses, bird puppets, and the like throughout the play creates the sense of an almost autonomous, self-conscious theatricality very busy on its own terms providing surprises and excitements not always related to the potentially deeper, ontological reaches of the play's action. The interweaving of the discursive and simultaneous modes of articulation, evidenced by the interrelatedness of verbal and visual signs in the plays from *Listen to the Wind* through to the *Donnelly* trilogy, appears in *Baldoon* to have been sacrificed. There is, instead, a less focused, less disciplined theatricalism that is over-crowded with "things."

Compare, for example, the economical and symbolically potent way in which the chorus in the *Donnelly* trilogy would, through the "scribbling" of lines, rows, and ladder-climbing transform the playing space into St. Patrick's church in Biddulph with the following, somewhat uncertain, stage direction from *Baldoon*:

> ... the bell rings for morning service, the mists and dark disperse and the company enters bearing a model church and singing. . . . The church should have on its steeple a hand pointing upward — see Macrae's Hallowed Walls. As the model church is put

behind the scrim curtain, probably a skeletal outline church should be established with a pulpit in front as in the case of Dr Troyer's house. It could be ropes? At any rate we need a place suggested out of which Dr Troyer can lure the congregation when he sets up his rival viewpoint; the procession, psalm &c. as laid out. Troyer & McTavish are watching this from the side and occasionally walking down the river of shadows behind the scrim — maybe they keep circling the stage area as if on their journey. (61)

The layers, here, of language (that of prayer, sermon, commentary, and hymns), sound, and scenic imagery (the mixture of toy models, a procession of actors, the shadowy scrim curtain, the encircling movement of Troyer and McTavish) seem to keep us outside the play rather than "folded in." In an extended footnote to this sequence in the play, Reaney recommends sources for the type of Presbyterian service to be used here:

. . . what we're doing is showing audiences an impression of what a Sabbath church meeting was like; it has to have tension and build as it also tells audiences a mood in contrast to Long Point and a background that explains McTavish's toughness and the hysteria that results from repression. (63)

Such tension, however, that would express and "explain" the contrasting toughness and hysteria is weakened through its theatrical dispersal into too many competing particles.

In his notes to the play Reaney gives an account of the use of puppets and marionettes. The bird representations, he says, are associated with particular characters. Drawing upon workshop experience, he notes that often ". . . an actor, while trying to get a firm grasp on his role will associate his character with a beast. Thus, Falstaff can be seen as a cross between a sloth and a hippopotamus, Lear as a snowy owl with a broken wing. This is the sort of association which is at the heart of the birds in *Baldoon*, and it comes out in the script" (113). And, for the most part, this is true: it does come out in the script — clearly enough to render the puppetry unnecessary. The extra scenic level of articulation, that of puppetry, is too forceful in its own terms, creating the impression of two plays being presented simultaneously: a play of words with "real" characters and a play of puppets that, as Reaney observes, "can say things which a real person cannot, or would not. We can play at being a creator by fabricating them, and once they are given the spark of life through the manipulation, others can enter their world through observation" (113–14). When marionettes were used, sparingly, in the *Donnelly* trilogy to represent the Governor General and Lady Head, the effect was entirely suitable. They were, as Reaney notes, "out of the play, both in fact and effect. Perhaps marionettes. They look down on us — at them — their subjects." The scenic juxtaposition of live and marionette figures in a moment of judicial pleading for the life of Will Donnelly reinforced the encounter between living and abstract forces central to the action of the trilogy. The distance between the world of Mrs. Donnelly carrying a petition naming names from a community and that of Sir Edmund and Lady Head "walking slowly along the railing of his yacht" to a background of "salon music of the 1857 period" is theatrically *clarified* through the marionette dimension (*Sticks* 116). In *Baldoon*, however, the puppetry and the toy model world appear superfluous, embodying a concrete actualization of a spiritual dimension that restricts rather than imaginatively expands the play's expression of "more depths and heights to existence than our present day usually discovers" (*Baldoon* 119).

The theatrical tracings of a possible "secret alphabet" of geometrical forms, of corporeal inscriptions that offer to the actors and the spectators "a physical feeling for the design of the play," appear to be absent in *Baldoon*. In an earlier essay on *Night-Blooming Cereus* and *One-Man Masque*, Reaney commented that in many poetry readings the "great difficulty was the spaces between poems. If there were no spaces at all the listeners tended to suffer from over intake of images" ("Evening with Babble and Doodle" 42). In *Baldoon* such spaces are very few; there is, in both verbal and scenic terms, an "over intake of images." The *poésie de théâtre* that Reaney had developed in his Listener's Workshops loses much of its potential for lyricism and, instead, appears as a theatre of "effects." In an essay on a theatre of "confluence," R. Murray Schafer warns of the dangers in a theatre of mixed means of "sensory overload" ("Theatre" 37). The danger of "uncontrolled synaesthetic exercises," he writes, "is that an overindulgent piling up of resources merely brings about a confusion of the senses rather than an acuity of sensorial experience" ("Theatre" 37). One is reminded, in part, of the case of Jean Cocteau as he moved from stage to film, from *Parade* and *Les Maries de la Tour Eiffel*, towards a film medium the obvious scenic fluidity of which appeared more satisfactorily to sort out the verbal and visual dimensions. The difference between the stage pieces *Parade* and *Les Maries de la Tour Eiffel* and the film *Le sang d'un poète* is in the more convincing *scenic* representation of metamorphoses that the medium of film provides. "Every poem is a coat of arms. It must be deciphered": Cocteau's words, which we see on the screen at the opening of the film, invite us, as did Reaney's essay on the "secret alphabet," to explore the visual dimension not in terms of a succession of "effects," but as signs of another reality. (Cocteau dedicated his "collection of allegories" to a number of painters such as Paolo Uccello and Andrea del Castagno, "painters of coats of arms and enigmas" [*Two Screenplays* 8].) The scenic effects of *Baldoon* (including, ironically, the puppet-theatre dimension itself) seem to be reaching towards a cinematic dimension in which a greater editorial control over the synaesthetic exercises, including the tensions inherent in the word/non-word dialectic, is possible.

If the artistic exploration of experience in Reaney's drama has the sort of relationship to the art of Klee and others that I have indicated, in which the primary forms of geometry are of particular symbolic importance, yet another kind of exploration of experience as endless metamorphoses finds its appropriate form in collage and film. A number of Reaney's plays since the Donnelly trilogy appear, in scenic terms at least, to be increasingly filmic. In his essay " 'Your plays are like movies — cinemascope ones,' " written in 1979, Reaney discusses the influence of films upon his drama and examines aspects of the Donnelly trilogy in terms of film language, a language, he wrote, "whose point is fluidity, juxtaposition and latent design" (33). These values, however, are equally possible in purely theatrical expression, as Reaney's plays from *Listen to the Wind* through to *Handcuffs* show. Although he describes many of the stage designs throughout the trilogy in filmic terms, they are in fact founded in the *poésie de théâtre* with which Reaney had become increasingly confident. In *Baldoon*, however, and in *The Canadian Brothers*, a filmic language appears increasingly detached from the quite different corporeal demands of theatre. In some ways, Reaney has come to see in terms of a medium he is not using.

This is not so entirely the case with *Wacousta!*, generally a more disciplined theatrical work, the scenic dimensions of which are less obtrusively autonomous. The "blazons and enigmas" of the British-Native confrontation in this play are simply represented by an emblematic stage set:

The action takes place in forts Detroit and Michilimackinac in the fall of 1763. A backcloth shows the Detroit River banks as if seen by an English water colourist whose profession is that of a military surveyor. In front of that a raked stage with two pictures painted on its floor: stage right an heraldic lion; stage left a shaman pictograph. Scaffolding up right. A tall flagpole dominates with its imperial symbol. (*Wacousta!* 10)

One is reminded of the mediaeval theatre in which, as Glynne Wickham says, there was "contentment with emblematic comment on the significance of the visual world" as opposed to the "new, scientific questing for the photographic image" (209). There are other theatrical echoes as well: the theatre of W.B. Yeats, particularly his scenic references to the Japanese Noh tradition in, say, *The Only Jealousy of Emer*, the emblematic settings for such plays as Obey's *Noah*, with its central ark, and Cocteau's *Orphée*, with its mirror. Then, of course, there are the clear echoes of Reaney's emblematic sets for *Night-Blooming Cereus*, *Listen to the Wind*, and *Colours in the Dark*. The difference here, however, is that the simple suggestions of place evident in the earlier plays are replaced by symbolically more potent signs of historical and racial stories and values.

These signs would include the painted pictures of the lion and the shaman pictograph, the scenic arrangements implicit in Reaney's use of dance, the geometry of military manoeuvres, and the games played by the Natives and the British. The play begins with the singing and performing of an "Indian Round Dance around a figure wearing deer antlers." Following this, the actors disperse, and a square is formed by four sentinels patrolling the "walls of the fort" (11). These patterns are reminiscent of the different spiritual and material dimensions described by Yates in her discussion of "round art" and "square art" noted in connection with some of the scenic configurations of the Donnelly trilogy. Such a visual dialectic is confirmed in Reaney's account of the workshop activities through which the play assumed its scenic shaping:

As I recall now, we took words and phrases from the novel and used them in choral chants which . . . shaped the sounds till the ear-picture was three dimensional and textured. . . . we built images and shapes of the Fort: a geometric, square shape. Around "dark forest labyrinths," an undulating circular dance developed — Indian, shamanistic, magical.

Sounds become allied to floor patterns as half the group in a square move towards the rest in their circle and blot them out. This was the beginning of the play; on the very last night it was performed in Toronto, in the early spring of 1978, these two shapes were still evident in set design, movement and plot development. (*Wacousta!* 116)

The Pontiac uprising (an attempt, Reaney commented, "by the native people to see that the world of farms and factories would never get started" [*Wacousta!* 7]) observed in the terms of such conscious shaping, has its own "stepped-out destiny in movement."

Other scenic configurations include those of the military manoeuvres, which in their arrangements of lines and squares are similar to the threatening "laws of geometry" associated with the surveyors in *Sticks & Stones*. Reaney hints at such a similarity in the description of the scenic backcloth that shows the Detroit River banks "as if seen by an English water colourist whose profession is that of a military surveyor." Two iconically representative games are played by the warring factions in *Wacousta!*, lacrosse and shuttlecock, and these too are informed by visual patterns that can be "read" as signs of contrasting and interwoven stories. This is seen on several occasions in the play, particularly at the opening of Act II where the two games are scenically juxtaposed through what Reaney calls a "dissolve" (48). The game of shuttlecock between Clara and Madeline is threatened by the less controlled, encircling configurations of lacrosse, a game feared by Clara because in a dream she sees herself as the ball. In the next scene, in conversation with Frederick, "We see a dark figure, Wacousta, throwing the lacrosse ball at her. . . . she is playing catch with someone in the surrounding darkness" (55). In his account of "The Wacousta Process," Reaney observes,

Pontiac sat talking peace with the governor of Fort Detroit while outside his warriors played lacrosse, struck the ball into the fort, and ran in after it hoping to join their leader in surprising Fort Detroit . . . but meeting instead an unpleasant surprise from the governor who had foreknowledge of their plans. The lacrosse seemed like a miniature North American Trojan Horse. (*Wacousta!* 7)

The darkness from which Wacousta throws the ball at Clara, along with the various signs of nature (especially forest and water), are representative of the mysterious, shadowy world of the Natives. The forest and water images are effectively established through the use of green cloth, a ball of green wool "unrolled from actor to actor to create a dense pattern of foliage" (34) and "an actor trailing a long blue cloth on a stick" (24). Accounting for the creation of such images during the workshops, Reaney wrote that

> With eighty people in a circle holding lengths of green yarn across the circle, visually you could create the scene. . . . The result is a textured forest in sound, more like a film or a symphony . . . than your "normal" theatre painted forest backdrop. (*Wacousta!* 111)

Despite the film reference, these images are entirely evocative of a *poésie de théâtre* that is capable of its own kind of scenic fluidity. Reaney's polarizing of "film" and "normal" painted scenery is an unnecessary repudiation of a *theatrical* idiom he has been developing and using with considerable success since the mid-sixties.

One of the most significant and theatrically effective images in *Wacousta!* occurs near the end of the play when Reginald Morton is stripped of his military insignia and branded as an outlaw. The lights dim, and ". . . the company fall into the shape of a giant on the floor with Morton as its head" (94). He changes "from the miniature painter of 1745" to the "hardened, older and taller Wacousta" as he exclaims,

> A price on my head, I stooped to drink one day and saw in the water a form so distorted I could no longer recognize myself. Do you see me there from your neat square fort with your round spyglass de Haldimar. . . .

A light at the base of the giant helps to form a Wacousta shadow that "stands tall as the theatre itself." "Wacousta," chants the chorus as Morton/Wacousta "comes swearing to kill you child by child" (95). This is Reaney's theatrical realization of the "giant dream figure" he discovered in Richardson's novel ("Topless Nightmares" 3). This realization, as well as that of the whole Pontiac uprising and the concomitant bifurcation of shaman and lion blazons, owes much to the inscriptions of spatial signs. These include, significantly, those of the theatre itself invoked here, in the shadow effect, as a phenomenal space enclosing player and watcher.

The Canadian Brothers, which continues the story of Wacousta's revenge, written in 1977 and revised for its first full-scale production in 1983, is less discriminatory in its use of a scenic strategy. The play, somewhat in the manner of *Baldoon*, is presented to us on two levels: that of live actors and that of toy models and puppet-effigies. The result is a diminution of the play's poetic potential as a literal descriptiveness encumbers the scenic space. The creative dialogue between "maker and spectator," in which, as Delevoy asserted, the latter is solicited to complete an image "with his gaze," is frequently interrupted in *The Canadian Brothers* as an assortment of models and complex scenic arrangements usurp such a task; the participatorial values of the act of "playing" are consequently lessened, our imagination unaroused.

The range of scenes and settings in *The Canadian Brothers* is much more extensive than in any other of Reaney's plays, including *Colours in the Dark*. In that play, the multitudinous spaces within which the search for identity occurs are shaped through the centrality of the sick child sitting in the dark "dreaming," as Bachelard said, "in a world that is immense" and through the more carefully inscripted spatial scoring of experience. In the complex sequel to Wacousta's story, Reaney presents scenic images of the battle of Queenston Heights and the death of General Brock; the "verandahed house in Amherstburg" (667), many years before the battle; a Southern Plantation in Frankford, Kentucky; and a number of forts, forests, and rivers. For example,

> HENRY *walks away from the officers hostile to his brother. We should get the sense of a river bank crowded with on-lookers. The boat drama should be played with model boats held by actors: some actors hold the islands and other pieces of scenery required, e.g., Bois Blanc Island, Grosse Island and six other islets. There should be something for the opposite American shore. . . .*
>
> *Crowd reacts as cannons sound, smoke puffs from American shore.* GERALD's *boat comes out of hiding, chases the American boat around, grapples and hauls it ashore where we transfer the focus to a large white sail gliding in.* . . . (686)

At best, such scenic arrangements are unnecessarily cumbersome. At worst, they are reminiscent of Richard Brinsley Sheridan's parody of stage spectacle in *The Critic* when, at the close of the play, Puff's "magnificence — my battle — my noise — and my procession" are introduced: "This is blending a little of the masque with my tragedy," he asserts, as we watch and hear the

> Flourish of drums — trumpets — cannon, etc., etc., Scene changes to the sea — the fleets engage — the music plays . . . Spanish fleet destroyed by fireships, etc. — English fleet advances. . . . The procession of all the English rivers and their tributaries, etc. . . . (377)

A similar accretion of scenic details is required later, when we follow Gerald's journey towards Fort Detroit: "The next sequence has to establish conventions of canoe, night crossing of river, shore-line of Detroit at night, portholes of ships, windows of houses getting closer etc." (697). For the next scene at Fort Detroit, we're told to

> *Stylize — bring out a model of the fort. Americans behind it.* HULL *on stick between model and Americans. Canadians, British and Indians in a big circle shoot off cannon, whoop it up, draw in closer.* BROCK'S EFFIGY *gets closer and closer.* HULL'S EFFIGY *begins to waver, revolves and eventually falls. A white flag appears on top of the Fort Detroit model.*

Once again the stage appears encumbered by things, by a pictorial literalness that, despite its toy dimension and obvious theatricality, impedes rather than enhances the fluidity Reaney intends these sequences to possess. In the Donnelly trilogy, and in *Wacousta!*, a more theatrically effective series of visual formations was created by the "scribbling with . . . body/bodies." The extra scenic dimension of the models and the effigies distracts from the cleaner, more readable lines of such scribbling, drawing attention to what appears as a masque effect which, as Ben Jonson complained in his altercation with Inigo Jones, was mere "Painting and carpentry," devised by Skenopoios, the "maker of properties" (304). The few actors, who scenically establish the square fort in *Wacousta!* or, say, the roads of Biddulph in the Donnelly trilogy, seem to move from the demands of the text and not simply from some need to illustrate the text, as is the case in *The Canadian Brothers* with its *tableau vivant* configurations.

Compare the representation of Mrs. Donnelly's journey in *Sticks*

& Stones, or the way in which she leads James, in *The St Nicholas Hotel*, "backwards and forwards through a life he had forgotten the deeds and maps to" (93) to the journeys and flashbacks in *The Canadian Brothers*. Towards the close of the play, Gerald and Matilda are "sitting on the floor facing out to us — books and papers surround them. Behind them will appear several flashbacks. They have been walking backwards through their lives" (719). In contrast to the scenically focused and lyrical "ritual walking confession" of Mrs. Donnelly, this one is graphically exteriorized, the tableau of effigies, with accompanying sound and music, providing an almost autonomous scenic statement as superfluous as were some of the lengthy verse passages of *The Killdeer*. If there are, on occasion, too many words in Reaney's early play, in *The Canadian Brothers*, there are, on occasion, too many pictures.

Part of this is due, I believe, to Reaney's apparent use of the film as a compositional model. Much of the text of *The Canadian Brothers* reads as a film scenario of cross-fades, dissolves, and multiple-focus effects associated with the split-screen convention. "Movies," said Reaney, "can jump from image to image with the nimbleness of a mad scene in *King Lear*" ("Your Plays" 33). This, of course, is true. But so can plays; so, indeed, did Shakespeare in what Peter Brook called the "pop-collage" scenic strategy of *King Lear* itself. So too did Strindberg, as he helped to formulate a theatre language that would express the kaleidoscopic randomness of dream:

> The scene is changed without lowering the curtain. The stage is darkened and a medley of scenes, representing landscapes, palaces, rooms, is lowered and brought forward; so that the characters and furniture are no longer seen, but the Stranger alone remains visible and seems to be standing stiffly as though unconscious. At last even he disappears, and from the confusion a prison cell emerges. (241)

This sequence from *To Damascus* (which play, like *The Canadian Brothers*, also involves the splitting of characters into other characters) and similar ones in *A Dream Play* and *The Ghost Sonata* (see Parker, "Spectator") typify Strindberg's dramaturgical experiments to incarnate his own experiences of fluidity and design. Strindberg was, to some extent, hampered by the scenic conventions of his day, and such a theatrical incarnation was not always possible. Since then, however, the theatre has devised means of convincingly portraying the interpenetrating inner and outer dimensions of experience. To some extent, these means owe much to technology, which, ironically, Reaney seems to object to — in spite of the prominence given to Skenopoios and the lighting-board operator in *The Canadian Brothers*. In his conversation with Geraldine Anthony, he remarked that his ideal theatre was not to be the "sort of theatre it is now where Technology . . . creates ever more horrifying and sinister spectacles; no, but a place where we ourselves, with just our bodies and the simplest of props" create and perform the play, where, in fact, the play and the act of "playing" are one. As much as the plays from *Listen to the Wind* through to the Donnelly trilogy and *Wacousta!* attempt to embody such an idea of the theatre, so *The Canadian Brothers* seems to disavow it.

In both *The Dismissal* and *King Whistle!*, however, the situation is very different. These plays employ specific and entirely suitable *theatrical* models for their different kinds of visual and kinetic effects. *The Dismissal* is, in fact, a college revue while *King Whistle!* is, as Reaney said, in the form of a "thirties musical comedy" ("Story" 51).

The Dismissal opens with a chorus in an archway and three groups of "church-goers" in the auditorium singing hymns and responding to a cacophonous assortment of sermon-fragments (9). After the old, blind Sir Daniel Wilson taps and fumes his way towards one of his final tantrums against anarchists and Labour Socialists, the chorus forms two groups, one on each side of the stage. During this opening sequence, the entire theatre is used, the audience being, simultaneously, spectators, congregation, and mass meeting. The multi-directional exclamations from stage and auditorium are gradually focused and clarified as the chorus creates a more disciplined scenic arrangement on the stage. This very simple and general pattern of verbal and scenic disorder moving towards order is repeated several times during the play and is central to the play's scenic structure and meaning.

Several sequences are especially exemplary of this general scenic patterning. In the first part of the play, in a manner that clearly recalls the way a variety of straight lines were used in the Donnelly trilogy, the chorus, once assembled into the two groups, becomes a group of travellers at Union Station. This line then becomes a "line of examinees as a small procession hits the stage," which is soon confronted by a "solid phalanx of gowned academics." As the academics shout their questions, the students "eventually form a waiting group outside the gates." The sounding of a bell marks the beginning and the end of this sequence. Then convocation arrives and another procession, "fuller and more colourful than the examination one, sweeps up the aisle" (14). We now have three principal groups: the students, the professors, and the highest University officials who carry photo-placards of themselves. Following convocation the scene is set for the dining-room sequence, which dissolves in a "hubbub of hailings jeers," and a "storm of buns" (16), prefiguring the scene in which King and Tucker are "rained at by a shower of Political Economy books — being thrown at them by lecturers, raining down from above, piling up on the floor around them. Sort of Hrolfsaga where bones are thrown at a court fool until only his hand waves up out of the pile" (26). Then follows the "madcap lecture sequence" (16), which ends, as the examination sequence did earlier, with the students "stunned and gyrated as if by a hose of water" (18). This, in turn, prefigures the hosing down of the students after their Halloween prank of tearing down the old shed. The next ceremony is that of Professor Right, in the Chapel at Lollard College, as he "wrestles at the altar of his God with a great temptation" before a robed and hooded figure "upholding the white whiskers of Jehovah." After Right manipulates the whiskers of Jehovah to "solve" his question of conscience ("is it simply, God, a desire to make more money?" [19]), a new procession of hooded initiators forms, a group of freshmen are intimidated in the coal cellar of University College, and a mock trial of President Fury is held.

In Act II, Reaney features a Lacrosse sequence in which teams of students and professors face each other, and ". . . the tossing of the lacrosse ball alternates with the tossing back and forth of words" (29). This is followed by a hockey sequence played with a decanter sliding over a table in "darkest Rosedale" (30) and then with proper sticks as the students (inspired by Tucker working at his typewriter) confront the faculty. In Act III scenic images, which echo and reinforce the order/disorder and confrontational configurations of these sequences, include that of the students behind the gates that have just been locked ("so that we get the image of hands, arms, feet coming through grille work" [44]) and the trial of Tucker. The latter episode is the most sinister and menacing version of the confrontational sequences in the play and is reminiscent of the surreal inquisitional scenes of Strindberg's *To Damascus* and *A Dream Play*.

The confrontation between what in Dale's journal is called the "integral" and the "fractional life" is accorded scenic articulation on two important occasions in *The Dismissal*. The first is when Dale, at the farm, smashes the ice to provide water for the cattle:

> Down the back line drifted with snow. Sudden precipitous slope to Fish Creek. The ice of the creek is iron thick and I raise the crowbar *smashes the ice* until cold and clear water. *He raises his scarf — we hear cattle lowing.* Behind me the cattle dark brown on the hill running down over the snow on the window I've made with this! (39)

This is unlike the window, with its "mocking white imitation / Of what I wish for, in frost," that helped seal the frustration and discontent of the Speaker at the Winter farm in the 1949 poem "The Canadian" (*Poems* 39). Dale's window is entirely restorative; it is an active symbol of the interpenetration of life and thought, life and labour, reason and imagination, inner and outer experience. Its entirely practical value, accommodating the cattle "thirsting out of their minds" (39), fuses with a metaphorical role as Dale is seen standing with the raised crowbar (labour dignified as in Ford Maddox Brown's painting *Work*) as the chorus, acting as cattle, advances to the stage through the auditorium, reciting passages from Dale's letters and journal. The second important scenic representation of this idea occurs at the end of the play, when the chorus forms a line-up of "farmerish shapes" that slowly fans out, "opening — as if it were a book." Supported by music associated with his home town of St. Mary's, Dale steps forward holding a copy of Livy's history of Rome:

> I survived dismissal. The following summer at Queen's University I met a student whom I later married. We lived with our children on my father's farm where I raised cattle and worked away at my history of Rome. (54)

In each instance, the image of the farm, and of the dignity of manual labour, is inseparable from that of a book — the journal, the histories of Rome by Livy and Dale, the chorus fanning out to become a book.

As this account of the scenic dimension of the play suggests, the primary physical designs are associated with the frenetic energy of a college revue, as scenes flow one into another, the chorus engaged in an unrestrained spatial scoring of undergraduate life. At the same time, the interwoven lines, circles, chaos/order configurations possess an emblematic value. Such physical "scribbling" is also — as in *Colours in the Dark*, throughout the Donnelly trilogy, and in many parts of *Wacousta!* — a spatial grammar that, in this instance, discloses many of the underlying motifs of the play in its representation of confrontational situations, elements of the "integral/fractional" dialectic, and the concluding image of the book/farm. A third scenic dimension is regionally particularized. In its initial staging at the University of Toronto on the occasion of its sesquicentennial celebrations, the play was able to erupt into the surrounding theatre space with its many local "Identifiers." As a result, recalling the Donnelly trilogy in its productions at the University of Western Ontario, some of the particularized past and present environmental images could be "folded in" to the play's scenic structure. Hart House Theatre is itself part of the story of William Dale's rebellion, insofar as this rebellion contributed to the continuing life of the university that Reaney himself attended, and at which, in this same theatre, his early plays were produced. In environmental theatre, Schechner observed, "Two groups of people agree to meet at a certain time and place. One group comes to witness a story, the other to tell a story. The story is important to both groups" (*Environmental* 83).

King Whistle! was, like *The Dismissal*, a commissioned work, and it is similarly located within a specific environmental context, telling a story important to both players and watchers associated, either through the investigatorial process that helped to produce the play, or through the simple fact of their living there, with the space in which the story is being told. The first room in which its story was presented was the auditorium of Reaney's own secondary school, Stratford Central Collegiate. Thus, the multitudinous "concrete localisms" within the play were, on one level at least, given spatial significance within a playing space that was itself a product of the interlocking political, social, and economic powers that are disclosed as elements in Reaney's story of Stratford's strike in 1933. In one sequence of the play, a silhouette of this school is shown while an English teacher is giving a lesson on Keats's "Ode on a Grecian Urn" (18).

In his account of the play, Reaney indicates the form *King Whistle!* was to assume: a thirties musical comedy. During some preparatory workshops, Reaney saw the Busby Berkley film, *Gold Diggers of 1933*:

That film was a turning point for me; it handles grim material both frivolously and deeply; it rings the changes on a collapsing society which nevertheless is still laughing, still clutching each other's knees under tables, still has dreams, still refuses to believe that poverty is the answer. What we were going to do was take the reality of 1933 and, like this film, pour all that sadness and economic puzzle into a form that has tap dances, ballets, songs. . . . ("Story" 51)

The techniques of collage served the purposes of a story that dealt with such a variety of events and shifts of mood. Many of these were shaped by what I referred to earlier as a mixture of messianic and caricatural impulses. Reaney also took delight, he wrote,

> seeing just how much design and surprise you could squeeze out of the Assembly Hall — a vaguely Art Deco place with terrible acoustics, a curtained stage, no rake, splitlevel ceiling. Well, we used the aisle (Al Jolson and Kabuki), we hid things behind the curtain and then whisked it open or we lowered the film screen . . . and then let it float up to reveal people behind it — say R.B. Bennett and Mitch Hepburn holding big photos of themselves over their shoulders on placard sticks. . . . I found myself wishing at this time that people could be more contented with plays that are musical pictures. The final form of *King Whistle!* was to "grow organically out of the collage mud as it were. . . . in a play you obey the anatomy of the play's body, not the anatomical laws of so-called real life." ("Story" 58)

The primary scenic arrangement for *King Whistle!* juxtaposes projected images, often in silhouette, of the town's houses, City Hall, school, and various factories with minimally suggested interior scenes (at work, in the church, and at home). Such a consistently realized visual interweaving of home, church, and work spaces recalls the ideologically polarized emblematic stage images of cottage and factory in such plays as Brecht's adaptation of Maxim Gorki's novel *Mother* (1951) or, earlier, in Caspar Neher's designs for Brecht's *In the Jungle of the Cities* (1923). The scenically established interconnections of where people live and where they work, central, of course, to a play about a strike, provide a series of pictographs, which, independently, comment upon the central actions of the play. Against such a backdrop the many actors in the play create an assortment of physical structures that recall those of *The Dismissal* in their sense of pure play and kinetic fluidity. A particularly effective sequence occurs in Act I as the space is established for "egg grading, chicken plucking and butter wrapping," with the girls working with "identical precise movements," while a foreman speeds them on: "tough, brutal, lording it over 50 girls" (10). This image of mechanization is then transformed into a confrontational situation when lines are formed by workers and management. Ollie rides a bike in circle eights with the factory image as a backdrop: "on stage right — the white collar world with its typewriters, clerks etc. frosted glass: and on stage left, the blue collar world with its huge spindle, its hundreds of belts descending to, from the factory long spindle, the work benches" (12). We then see Ollie Kay at work and the workers lining up to be paid. Alice enters with a baby in a carriage that she wheels down a street where we "spot JESSIE reading a novel to her grandmother on a front porch." The space is then gradually changed to represent a dance hall, and a tap dance sequence is followed by a "realistic dance sequence with its period dance music" (13). In the course of the latter, we hear church bells ringing, and the dancers become church-goers, then members of the Young People's Bible Study Class. The dance configurations are reiterated, and, as ". . . storm sounds and thunder increase, tap dance dwindles as dancers stand at the door of closing hall" exclaiming,

October 1929 — Halloween the dance was over in more ways than one, for Hard Times started — the greatest depression the world had ever known. People started losing their jobs — this man — that girl — this one, that one. It was as if an invisible sharpshooter picked off people at random — you lost your job, you went on relief — you couldn't afford to go to movies or dances — you dropped out of sight — nobody knew what to do.

The sequence concludes with the workers/dancers/church-goers clutching for pay packets that fall through the air; some of them "contain a pink slip & the last pay that worker will see for six years — sometimes a red slip meaning he owes the company money for spoiled materials" (15).

The whole play's scenic structure is evidenced in this last sequence wherein aspects of the town's life in work, home, play, and church are interwoven with confrontational images that point directly to the gulf between the powerful "Uptown Bunch" and the workers. The act concludes with the arrival of tanks and troops, and "We see the largest furniture factory in Canada with the rebellious houses in front of it: In front of these stand the workers" singing their song of revolutionary defiance (28). The final scene of the play reaffirms this factory/house relationship. It occurs in the cottage of Miss Jessie Burke, newly engaged to "that hated class enemy — Lieutenant Adrian McNab at present rolling in his tank back to Snobtown — otherwise known as London, the capital of Western Ontario" (44). The concluding scenic image is that of a reprise:

> More and more people come into the Burke's cottage until it bursts & becomes a series of silhouettes that reprise the story; i.e. City Hall, Swift's &c, but the last silhouette or image behind the cast should be the largest furniture factory in Canada with the five houses in front of it. (46)

As was the case with the concluding image of *The Dismissal* with its reprise of farm and book motifs, that of *King Whistle!* is intended to be a scenically articulated collage reading of the town's economic story and of Reaney's superimposed story of Blake's Spectre of Urthona, "the personification of our will to control the environment." In this "play about contemporary life; about factories, about economic problems, about Marxism and Capitalism," the will is located within the "rebellious houses" that, through the efforts of their striking inhabitants, altered the relationship between home and work, between workers and factory owners.

Gyroscopes, wrote Reaney, "keep their balances under the most adverse circumstances. . . . 'Gyroscope' then seemed an appropriate title for the images, the sketches and the ideas I found in my notebooks of the two years leading up to December, 1979, when, quite quickly, this play started to take final shape" (Introd., *Gyroscope*). The principles of visual thinking that Reaney outlined in "Search for an Undiscovered Alphabet" are still situated at the centre of the creative process: a diagram is sought that both structures and communicates experience. Schechner operates in the same fashion in his environmental projects. "The first thinking I do on a project," he wrote, "is in pictures — drawings I make in my notebook — visual flashes of spaces-in-action. These *actograms* occur at the level where environment, physical action, knowledge of the performers, concept of the play, and my own drives are identical" (*Environmental* 83). As an image, Reaney's gyroscope gives expression to a world in which both personalities and spaces are "spinning out of one phase into another." It is not, however, so completely an *actogram* as were some of the spinning, circular, and linear configurations we have seen in many of Reaney's plays to this point. Despite Reaney's account of the play in terms of its gyroscopic values, its employment of space is relatively uncomplicated, closer in style to such works as *The Sun and the Moon* and *The Easter Egg* than to the more intricate scenic scoring of, say, *Colours in the Dark*, the Donnelly trilogy, or *Wacousta!*. As a sort of chamber play, *Gyroscope* is also, of course, far less scenically demanding than *The Dismissal* and *King Whistle!* with their large casts and communal stories.

The story of *Gyroscope* is interiorized. Consciousness itself is the centre of the play's action. The image of the gyroscope, then, seems conceptually appropriate as expressive of the never-ending metamorphic impulses of the poetic imagination. This conceptual pictograph, however, is not translated into concrete theatrical form in the play. In this respect, there is a "gap between idea and incarnation," which Gilman identified as one of the theatre's problems. What is finally made *visible* in this play is not a gyroscopic scoring of experience (something that might have been accomplished in a film, as Cocteau did in *La sang d'un poète*) but, rather, a space that, with the addition of a few props (tables, beds, telephone, tape-recorder), is able to represent Henry's Restaurant Cafe, Hilda and Greg's apartment, and a cafeteria. Within this space, the five characters of the play move, essentially, from conversation to recitation to conversation. In short, what we *see*, in theatre terms, is restrained despite Reaney's rather elaborate description of a space that "elasticizes" and "balloons" (*Gyroscope* i) as it enters into the gyroscopic tempo of the work. What we *hear*, however, is a very different matter. *Gyroscope* "elasticizes" and "balloons" sonically, if not scenically. What Schafer, in *The Tuning of the World*, calls the "acoustic environment" is what Reaney exploits, appropriately enough, in this work about creative playing with words and sounds.

"THE MAGIC TONGUE"

So in the end the international theatre-group, swooping by jumbo-jet from one cultural function to another all over the world, has ceased to attempt to communicate specific ideas about anything to anybody — a non-verbal compost of currently-received physical images which can mean all things to all men is trundled from stage to stage between Tokyo and Nancy, Zagreb and Singapore. "Controversy," if aroused at all, is set afoot only by such classless generalities as naked bodies, cursorily-motivated violence, and a broad demonstration of "compassion for the human condition." (Arden, "Playwrights" 177)

Faced with the virtual textlessness of what Barthes calls "a whole carnal sterography" (66), the modern playwright — such as John Arden in this particular lamentation against the "jet-set of World-Play" (Blau 65) — has been challenged to refine and to defend perceptions about the "old idea of a play-text consisting of a series of speeches interspersed by a few 'stage-directions.' " If the value of the "regular scripted play" is rejected, Arden continues,

> are we to assume that recent generations of theatre-workers
> have hit on something that remained hidden throughout the ages
> which produced a Shaw, an Ibsen, a Shakespeare? That the body
> of European classical theatre was in fact deficient in a major
> dimension of dramaturgy — that playwrights traditionally con-
> cerned themselves only with verbal statement and neglected all
> those other aspects of their art — such as movement, abstract
> sound, sculptural or painterly values of spectacle? ("Play-
> wrights" 175)

Establishing his terms for a reading of such plays as *Lear* and *Richard III*, Arden reaffirms the familiar perspective regarding the dual structure of dramatic art, wherein the structure "worked out of words, metre, metaphor and the other tools of a poet's skill" and that which is "communally imposed by the company at work in the theatre" are interwoven in a reciprocally advantageous manner. In the resulting aesthetic intertexture, the playwright's awareness of the medium permits him or her to "call upon the devices of the theatre to illuminate his theme as freely and as fruitfully as he called upon the mythology of Ovid or the dogma of the Bible to invigorate his dialogue" (185).

An appreciation of such an intertexture was fundamental to Cocteau's influential preface to *Les Maries de la Tour Eiffel* (1922), where the "delicate" and the "grosse" laces of *la poésie de théâtre* and *la poésie au théâtre* (*Oeuvres complètes* 14) are described, the former in especially commendatory terms as the basis for a new scenic strategy. Reaney recalled this preface when speaking of the early performances at the Stratford Festival Theatre:

> The first years at Stratford Festival showed me the playwright in a more influential way than ever before; I can remember realizing that Cocteau is right when he says that theatrical metaphor is like lace; when the big reading image of Richard III came up — bluebottle, spider in a bottle, or whatever — it just whizzed by in a second, hardly noticed. On the page I used to linger over it. In the Alex Guinness-Tyrone Guthrie production, what one was thrilled by was the larger design around all the scores of metaphors — a malignant shape in the centre of a circle eventually and suddenly banished after bending the circle for a long time in whatever way it pleased. ("James Reaney" 144)

What Reaney observed was the "transference of metaphorical power from words alone to scene and persons" (Peacock 217), involving an intricate relationship between language and the overall dramatic and theatrical structure.

This relationship between verbal and non-verbal structures in theatre performance has been of central concern in the modern theatre for quite some time, and it is not simply a critical preserve of the advocates of some sort of "verse drama," or of those who yearn nostalgically for an enriched, reinvigorated dramatic *literature*. The problem has expanded well beyond the question of one particular kind of verbal structure (verse, say) to the investigation of the very existence, or possibility, of significant verbal drama of any kind. If, as Steiner suggests, the "image of the world is receding from the communicative grasp of the word" (*Language* 25), then the strictly verbal component of drama is endangered by the same pressures that beset contemporary verse and fiction. Among the pressures particularly relevant to dramatic art we find the prestige (at different times, and with varying force, largely depending upon the director — usually upon the director's possible connection with Artaud and his successors[1]) of non-verbal, unscripted, corporeally rooted expression. Another pressure arises from the critique of language itself, the intensification, Kennedy writes, "of doubts about words as a living and workable medium." There is in drama, and *only* in drama, he continues,

a permanent tension between verbal and non-verbal elements . . . this unique interaction between word and non-word — from the single gesture to the whole concert of signals of stage — has itself been put under pressure by the heightened critical questioning of the value of the word in the theatre. In brief, the quickest escape-route from the internal tensions of language . . . is the enlargement of the area of wordless drama: mime and ballet, music and sound effects, the promised freedom of physical expressiveness: the actor's body, the "events" on the stage, the spontaneous instants of performance. The very word language . . . has been extended to include almost anything we might hear about the language of movement, about action-language. This extension is interesting; it is partly metaphorical, partly influenced by the modern structuralist approach which sees every system of signs, from menus and garments to ways of pointing, as a language. (8)

Most serious playwrights during the sixties and seventies, perhaps as self-consciously as ever in dramatic history (although such famous imbroglios as that between Ben Jonson and Inigo Jones should accord us a wider perspective on such matters) saw their work within the complex terms of the tension between word and non-word. Commenting upon the preparatory workshops for the national tour of the Donnelly trilogy, Reaney writes:

Of great interest to an artist (because they were a palette of all the possible body and vocal movements) were the warm-ups in which a different member of the company each day led everybody through their favourites. . . . All the exercises, all the vocal training and drill . . . the dance and movement classes . . . paid off in that you could close your eyes and hear some really sensitive webs of sound and voice-texture; you could hold your ears and open your eyes — liquid stage movement; there being so much sound and so much movement, necessarily rapid, in the trilogy, Keith's mixtures here could be alcoholic. I remember in 1974 coming back from Part One in Toronto and going to a play locally produced; our ears grated — we had been ruined forever so far as bearing with what sometimes passes for meaningful speech on our local stage. By the way, I'm sorry the pavene Kevin taught the company . . . got cut; I can still see the straight line she made her body hold for the Irish dances — how clean after all our contemporary phoney writhing. (*14 Barrels* 21)

The theatrical composition and effectiveness of the interlaced sound, voice, and scenic values that Reaney addresses here are seen as necessarily connected to "the larger design around all the scores of metaphor." The underlying metaphorical energy and design must be heard and felt and seen to inform all of the verbal and non-verbal values of performance. Ronald Peacock's understanding of the idea of the "poetic" in drama provides an apt description of the sort of metaphorical range and patterning Reaney observed in Richard's "malignant shape in the centre of a circle." Peacock accounts for the "principle of metaphor and symbol not only in language and verse but in all the varied imagery of which as an art [drama] makes use" (217). This would include the entire range of sonic and scenic values — including the purely physical scoring of the actors' bodies.

A theatre whose idea of "playing" is restricted to, or excessively given over to "contemporary phoney writhing" or a "non-verbal compost of currently-received physical images," in which words, if not banished, are reduced to a severely limited role, is as objectionable to Reaney as to Arden and for much the same reason. Both playwrights are devoted (sometimes with almost acquisitive zeal) to language: to words. "Before men read," writes Yeats "they loved language, and all literature was then, whether in the mouth of minstrals, players or singers, but the perfection of an art that everybody practiced, a flower out of the stem of life. And language continually renewed itself in that perfection, returning to daily life" (*Explorations* 212). Reaney's "magic tongue / Stuffed with names and numbers" (*Poems* 125) is also valued in similar terms as an *energeia* rather than an *ergon*: a continuing, ever-renewable resource, the most reliable vehicle for discovering and understanding the self and the world. But its value as *ergon*, as a fixed, discoverable entity, is also explored by Reaney. If language can reach through into the essence of "daily life" and find constant renewal there, it can also tend towards a degree of self-sufficiency, at times almost closing itself off from the less predictable pressures of that same life.

It is this latter sense of language that bpNichol discerned in some of Reaney's work:

> Reaney's concern is also with language with the materials of language you can see the jump in consciousness in the differences between 12 letters to a small town 7 emblems in 12 the drawings illustrate the text in EMBLEMS the text & the emblem are inseparable the materials of the poem are no longer external it *is* the object it describes no more duality here reaney comes close to writing writing he has finally done in his poetry what he has done in his plays which is to say he has made them self sufficient they exist as real objects in the real world (5)

Woodman has also described Reaney's language as something of an *established* talisman through which access to another universe is possible. In Reaney's study of Greek, in particular, Woodman writes, ". . . the world within the alphabet began to open up to him. He dimly recognized that words transmuted things into thoughts, that the manipulation of words was in fact the shaping of reality into a human form. Word lists became an inventory of the world, the stuff from which a cosmos is made; declensions were the beginning of a structure which grammar brought to completion" (*Reaney* 13). In the plays, as of course in some of the poems, especially *A Suit of Nettles*, such a view of language gives the word itself, insofar as its self-sufficiency is made apparent to us, the primary role of protagonist. "We are here with a word. That's all. That's particular. Let the word dance" exclaims Serjeant Musgrave in Arden's *Serjeant Musgrave's Dance* (36).

A theatre in which language could so self-assuredly dance was what Reaney (immediately inspired by his first impressions of the Guthrie productions at Stratford) recognized as having existed for the Elizabethans:

> The bare Stratford stage, of course, designed to create an emphasis on speech and actor that helped one think of new

techniques; the fluidity of a bare stage in which this author emphatically does not need to worry about a box set being changed every ten minutes — that impressed. Also here's a writer who was allowed to (and *could*) use rhythm and as many words as he could get in a mouth. The general feeling I've met in our community is that this is all right for the past, but now — why, there are close-ups instead. Alas, one is not a filmmaker although that may be what people say the results of the above thinking may be; when one works with words it is a relief to be asked to use them. In a verismo play the set and the lighting quite frequently are doing what the words used to be able to do, and I object to my soul being squeezed through a fuse box. . . . Imagine being able to write for a living; there's this busy town by a river and it's got several silo-like buildings where people have got used to going to see plays written in verse. The audience loves to hear people talk and talk well in rhythm with lots of imagery. Not only that, but this audience has staying power; a whole afternoon, not just the thin shank of the evening before the baby sitter has to go home and the buses start going slower. Furthermore, they have quick ears and the actors can go quite fast if they like. What a world in which a verbal invention such as blank verse is as profitable and sought after as now a technological device such as 3-D or Technicolour and is a magnet for audiences. As I see Peele's *Old Wives Tale*, or the cliff scene in *Lear* or Ariel and Caliban, I envy them their world where they could get away with it; today, there'd be Jack Shenk in New York and Sam Goldwyn in Hollywood asking what it all means. ("James Reaney" 145)

Reaney's complaint is a common one uttered frequently, in similarly querulous tones, by many poet-playwrights in this century who have looked mournfully at the general meanness of language in the theatre. To many such writers the enriched aural sensitivity of Elizabethan and Jacobean drama remains one of the touchstones against which the less capable, less acoustically sophisticated modern "listener" is measured. But, as Reaney discovered, there *was* an enthusiastic audience for Guthrie's lace at Stratford, and there is still, as Kennedy has observed. A variety of modern playwrights (Jean Cocteau, Christopher Fry, T.S. Eliot, Harold Pinter, John Arden, Edward Bond, John Osborne, Tom Stoppard, David Mamet) have demonstrated that an audience "accepts — or even expects — a dramatic language that 'plays' with itself, cannot be 'fixed' in one setting, cannot be simply paraphrased or 'verified' on one level only. . . . In this way the contemporary equivalents of the Jacobean feeling for words, for complex verbal patterns — in short, for a 'poetic' complexity in language — have been brought into play again." This, Kennedy writes, is true, "even if we remain aware of the risks: mannerism, banality, the cliches of 'non-communication,' the involutions of a language-mirroring language" (236).

The basis of Kennedy's study, and of others since, is that there is a heightened *critical* consciousness regarding language in drama and, among the playwrights, an awareness of the weakening efficacy of language always to deal thoroughly and truthfully with thought, feeling, and action. What has occurred, in large part as a creative response to this situation, is the development of a wide *variety* of theatre languages owing not a little to the vastly increased spectrum of theatrical expression implied in Cocteau's *poésie de théâtre*. This is a spectrum always available to the playwright, but not always so consciously cultivated as in our time. Thus the acceptance of language that is not necessarily "fixed" in one mode; thus the development of a theatricality that, as Kennedy remarks, "extends and externalizes, breeding composite languages out of old ones." These "dramatic collage-languages" contribute to the idea of a theatre where, as in a "living museum of speech," dialogue itself is sometimes a dialogue "between this and that language" (34). In examining Eliot's various experiments with dramatic language in which, to a degree, "every attempt / Is a wholly new start," Kennedy says that for the first time the writer's involvement with language has itself become dramatised. Such an involvement can be seen early in Reaney's career as a poet in *A Suit of Nettles*, where the forms and conventions of poetic discourse are themselves, in part, the subject of the poem, and "country life in Ontario, Canada as an object of conversation and Edmund Spenser's *Shepherd's Calendar*" (*Poems* 145) provide the inspiration for the extraordinary technical range of tone and voice. Reaney's interest in the *forms* of dialogue was, it appears, well marked before he turned increasingly to the drama. When he did turn, from what particular spectrum of voice and form, from what *musée imaginaire* could he draw — especially when drama was "something somebody else wrote thousands of miles away"?

As a modern poet (quite apart from being a modern Canadian poet) Reaney's problem was to some extent analogous to that of

Eliot, when in his persistent search for the appropriate "third voice"
of poetry, "the voice of the poet when he attempts to create a
dramatic character speaking in verse" ("Three Voices" 89), he
justifiably dismissed the exhausted tradition of blank verse in which
so many rejected suitors of the stage from Keats and Shelley down
through Tennyson and Robert Browning to John Masefield and
Stephen Phillips have unprofitably toiled. The obvious absence in
modern England of a living tradition of "poetic" drama, of a
recognizably vital and sustaining tradition of dramatic utterance in
verse or in prose, informed Eliot's dejection when he wrote, "To
have, given into one's hands, a crude form, capable of indefinite
refinement, and to be the person to see the possibilities — Shakespeare was very fortunate. And it is perhaps the craving for some such
donnée which draws us on toward the present mirage of poetic
drama" ("Possibility" 57). The loss of such a tradition meant, for
Eliot, the loss of "our hold on the present" ("Possibility" 62), and it
meant that the whole problem of speech in drama had to be faced as
if there had been no beginning. Eliot was to discover that this
problem of speech was, in the end, inseparable from the whole
question of dramatic *form*. As one of his speakers in "Dialogue on
Dramatic Poetry" observed,

> Let me for a moment transfer the discussion to the question of
> form. A few years ago I ... was delighted by the Russian ballet.
> Here seemed to be everything that we wanted in drama, except
> the poetry. It did not teach any "lesson," but it had form. It
> seemed to revive the more formal element in drama for which
> we craved. ... If there is a future for the drama, and particularly
> for poetic drama, will it not be in the direction indicated by the
> ballet? Is it not a question of form rather than ethics? And is not
> the question of verse drama versus prose drama a question of
> degree of form? (46)

Here, perhaps, are some of the underlying aesthetic conditions for
what Arden came later to fear from those swooping jumbo-jets: a
lingua franca of physical and scenic "signs" that avoided the problem
of speech by pushing the whole idea of dramatic form closer towards
the non-verbal, towards the revitalized vocabularies of the *poésie de
théâtre*. Such a direction for the drama was, of course, evident to
Eliot and to some degree aesthetically exciting; yet it was of the
utmost importance for him to combat the possible tyranny of such

182

a *poésie* with a viable dramatic language drawn from the drama of his own country and from his "own language as it is actually spoken around him" ("Social Function" 22). There was, as Kennedy notes, "no fully universal 'imaginary museum' for language, though there may be one for form" (90).

It was Eliot's intense language-consciousness that led him to explore the vital signs in Christian liturgy, Elizabethan and Jacobean drama, drawing-room comedy, the music hall, Greek tragedy, and mediaeval drama, not simply for models of dramatic and theatrical form, but also for modes of dramatic speech. What was central to this exploration, however, was his acknowledgement, implicit in his rejection of the tradition of Elizabethan blank verse, that some conventions in art, especially language, undergo organic patterns of growth and decline, that verbal conventions in poetry, drama, in speech generally, become in time exhausted. The question of dramatic language, then, becomes, in part, one of asking whether a "new" form of drama could face such a situation of verbal uncertainty and exhaustion directly and incorporate a certain degree of verbal "playing" into the verbal structure of the play. If this were possible, the wide choice of verbal styles stored away in the poet's personal museum need not induce a creative paralysis, but instead be consciously released as a sampling of "voices," some "dead" others "living," intended to arouse as much a spectatorial as a participatory experience in the audience. As we *participate* in the verbal idiom of the play through the recognition of our *own* voice, we are also *spectators* to a drama of human and social relations established "at the level of language itself . . . wherein man's words are held up to us as a spectacle" (Vannier 182). The act of writing the play becomes one of choosing among what Eliot called "possibilities," of sorting out anew each time a collage of verbal textures.

As a poet "of the learned kind," Reaney's own *musée imaginaire* is a crowded, complex world of voices and forms. In many of the plays, disparate verse and prose forms are augmented by the direct use of familiar and unfamiliar songs, ballads, hymns, and the like drawn from a variety of sources. These would include the Glee Club carols in *Three Desks* and *The Dismissal*; hymns, patriotic songs, national anthems, popular songs in *Colours in the Dark*, *Baldoon*, *Wacousta!*, and *King Whistle!*; ballads, Victorian parlour songs, hymns, liturgical chants in the Donnelly trilogy. As I have indicated elsewhere (" 'The key word' "), many of these passages of musical expression perform a "gestic" as well as a purely "atmospheric" function — as do many of the songs in the plays of Brecht, Arden, Luscombe, and John Gray, as they often do in documentary drama generally. Many of them, particularly the most familiar ones, serve as signs of the social, religious, political, and racial life of the different, often disputatious, communities. In the theatre, they are meant to direct the spectator's viewpoint toward some of the under-lying components of individual and social character, action, and belief, and, at times, to encourage a critical attitude toward them.

Reviewing the assortment of verbal styles in Reaney's plays, we can see that the "possibilities" within his imaginary museum include heightened and conversational verse; lyric verse; choric incantation; heightened and conversational prose; documentary language (from contemporary newspapers, legal transcripts, government docu-ments, political speeches, letters, and the like); liturgical and Biblical rhetoric and incantation (Roman Catholic in the Donnelly trilogy, Protestant in *The Sun and the Moon*, *Colours in the Dark*, *Baldoon*), popular nineteenth-century melodrama; modern "concrete" poetry; dialect; various, usually parodic, examples of academic discourse (in the Dr. Button episode of *Colours in the Dark*, for instance, or the lecture sequences in *Three Desks* and *The Dismissal*); popular song lyrics; and a wide variety of voices in nineteenth-century fiction — particularly the Brontës, Rider Haggard, Walter Scott, and John Richardson. As many of these "possibilities" are used at different times in many of the plays, it is impossible to distinguish, except, perhaps, in the plays up to *Listen to the Wind* (excluding *One-Man Masque*), in any one play a dominant verbal tone or voice. In many instances, the purely verbal experience in the theatre is one of constantly often unexpectedly shifting keys and tones, as Reaney juxtaposes verse (of different sorts) and prose; metaphorically enriched passages and flat conversational tones ("the roar of talkersation" as Harry describes a dinner at the Coonses' house in *The Killdeer* [26]); documentary language (a "given" language showing "how people actually phrased things") and ballads, hymns, and songs, some of which express an energetic folk presence and voice.

Francis Fergusson wrote persuasively about the "centerless diver-sity" of the modern theatre, in which the "very *idea* of a theatre, as Hamlet assumed it gets lost; and the art of drama, having no place of its own in contemporary life, is confused with lyric poetry or pure music on one side, or with editorializing and gossip on the other" (15). Assuming the truth of this, and recognizing intense language-consciousness as a fundamental sign of a "centerless" time, then, as Denis Donoghue remarked, there can be no authoritative "tone of the centre" (257). But there is a tone or style for our common verbal *experience*, as there is, to a large extent, for our visual experience: collage. Michael Tait in a study of some of Reaney's earlier plays remarked that in *The Easter Egg* Reaney "seems at a loss to know what language to have them speak. As a consequence the accents of colloquial conversation mingle and collide with more formal verse rhythms" ("Limits" 46). To some degree, Reaney's language in the earlier plays is *dramatically* uncertain as discordant accents do collide. Eliot's language was also, on occasion, disturbingly disincarnated, leaving undisclosed the particularized and experienced sound of human beings. Such a hazard was recognized by Reaney in the course of the Donnelly tour when, in Winnipeg, he met families whose ancestors had lived in Biddulph township:

Only a fellow researcher could understand the excitement I felt at meeting these people; previously they had been just a scrap of paper in the Chancery Court files under B for *Blackwell vs Brown*; now in Row S of the Salle Pauline Boutal the verbal universe dissolves into human figures and faces telling me things that enable me to go back into the patterns I am weaving in the world of words and adjust here, shade more there. (*14 Barrels* 42)

Reaney's dramaturgical experiments led him towards the writing of plays "where it's all rapids," as opposed to the style of *The Sun and the Moon*, *The Killdeer*, and *Easter Egg*, where as on a river in voyageur journals he wrote, "You go smoothly along in an apparent realistic way, and then there is this big leap" ("Ten Years" 59). Dramatic collage, including verbal collage, became the formal *donnée* within which, and with the techniques of which, the array of voices was to be assembled. What Reaney finally sought out were all imaginable forms of personal and public utterance, including the dramatic and non-dramatic literature of the past. His creative response to the sudden "presence" of Biddulph in Winnipeg, then, is registered in his restatement of the central question of language (any language) in drama. The relationship between the verbal universe and the human figures and faces that tell us things is rendered more complex in that this special relationship between voice and face is not the only one being presented in the variety of patterns in the world of words. There are others, and, because they also reveal something of our lives and times, Reaney strives to depict them as well.

As a playwright who, by the time of writing the Donnelly trilogy, was interleaving the documentary with the "poetic" and the "mythic," he recognizes that the Browns and the Blackwells *do* also exist as "scraps of paper." The Donnellys did have an existence as newspaper items and as monstrously simplified figures in popular melodrama. In fact, all of the figures of the plays possess a historically rooted documentary definition as well as a more elusive, ambiguous "real" existence as human figures and faces. Furthermore, as a poet-playwright, he recognizes that their lives, individually and collectively, are also imbued with metaphorical import, that they sometimes stand (like Mrs. Donnelly, lamp in hand, awaiting reunion with her husband) poised at the intersection of myth and history. Reaney's imagination is one that needs both document and myth, wherein, as Cassirer remarked, an acute sense of "primary 'experience' itself is steeped in the imagery of myth and saturated with its atmosphere." Just as complex patterns of scenic imagery can be devised and manipulated in the theatre to address such a vision, so too can verbal imagery, in which metaphor is understood as a transaction between contexts. The increasingly complex *intertextual* nature of Reaney's drama, embracing documentary and metaphorical planes, necessitated the exploitation and "playing" of different languages. The result is a linguistic pastiche in which all voices are accorded theatrical life. These include those arid speech acts that can enclose like armour the speaker's world (his "environmental bubble") and render the vital human figure and face a "scrap of paper."

I I

Some of the initial critical responses to Reaney's early plays reflected the view that this was an example of yet another intrusion into the theatre by someone whose essentially lyrical vision and idiom tended to preclude the wider, more objective human sympathies required by *dramatic* speech and action. Reaney's reputation as a poet was well established by 1960 through the Governor-General Award winning publications *The Red Heart* (1949) and *A Suit of Nettles* (1958). This reputation seemed destined to play a major part in how *The Killdeer,*

The Sun and the Moon, and *The Easter Egg* were to be received. Some critics welcomed this intrusion, taking the opportunity to voice their approval of the recovery of a theatre in which language, capable of daring metaphorical exuberance, was accorded its traditional role in activating the mind, imagination, and aural sensibilities of an audience. (One recalls the critical excitement of some when they greeted the plays of Christopher Fry during the 1950s.) Others were less enthusiastic.

Nathan Cohen wrote of *The Killdeer,*

> The Killdeer is a desperately bad play, which only someone of talent could write. James Reaney's ability as a poet is a fact, and there's no doubt the University Alumnae Club performance of his first play will teach him much about plot construction, relationship of character, artistic unity and theatrical know-how. Whether he has an honest-to-goodness affinity for play-writing, however, or just a dilettante's interest, it is too soon to say. . . . As he handles it, the play is a mass of unsorted ideas, story threads, poetic devices, literary and visual symbols, verse techniques, and emotional climaxes, all flung together in a tentative, disconnected stage patchwork . . . if James Reaney interests you as a poet then 'The Killdeer' will interest you as an example of his first attempt to discover the workings of a wholly unfamiliar medium. (35)

Michael Tait commented in a review of the early plays that the question "surely is why, when Reaney's poetry . . . is so compelling, the verse plays should be so unsatisfactory." *The Killdeer,* he found analogous, in part, to the "macabre violence and intermingled richness and confusion" of Jacobean drama, and the lack of structural and verbal coherence in the play, he thought, undermined and rendered uncertain the different levels the play sought to express. *The Easter Egg* he found "structurally superior" and yet equally problematical in the establishment of a convincing and consistent verbal tone ("Limits" 46). Louis Dudek began his examination of the plays with a comprehensive lament that Reaney was "born in an evil time and in an ill country for dramatic productions or for the creation of a genuine dramatic literature." The plays, he thought, were generally expressive of a complex "poetic subjectivity" similar in broad outline to the private, symbolist world of Yeats and Maeterlinck: "The last ditch stand is that witches' brew, an all-inclusive mythology, all-mythology-at-once as a key to existence" (17). Writing in the same year, Don Rubin commented that "Reaney almost never lets one forget that deep-down he's a literary man rather than a man of the theatre." His plays, Rubin continued,

> for all their obvious expressionistic fascination and symbolic sense, constantly betray a self-consciousness which is often self-defeating in terms of production. His plays on stage seem to work their best when they are at their least pretentious, their least aware of themselves as literature. But when the scripts are given literary full-rein, they often disintegrate into allusion, illusion, and ultimately confusion. However, one cannot deny the originality and fascination of Reaney's mind, and he may yet break from his literary consciousness and create a truly viable work for the stage. (*Creeping* 17)

Other responses to the earlier plays were more favourable. Having a couple of years earlier described something of the nature of Canada's "famous blank face" and the opportunity such a *tabula rasa* could give to the aspiring playwright, Mavor Moore, for example, greeted *The Killdeer* production in 1960 as "likely to become an historic event — and perhaps even the most important one in contemporary Canadian arts and letters." Reaney's accomplishment, Moore wrote, "is that he has succeeded in doing for Canadian character and speech what John Synge did for the Irish. He has taken a regional dialect . . . fed it through his own highly personal imagination, and produced a flexible, full-bodied idiom which no human being ever spoke but which all of us recognize at once" ("This Play" 35). Milton Wilson expressed reservations regarding the occasional polemical tone in the early plays, the underlining of the "cosmic leitmotif with a heavy pencil." However, he acknowledges the unique *poetic* voice of the plays, and, in considering Reaney's *Night-Blooming Cereus*, he concluded that the "qualities of Reaney's recent work come less from the academy and its supposed influences (to which some of his least perceptive critics would attribute them) than from the demands of the workshop" (75). Many years later, Ronald Heubert discussed with Reaney the "creative tension between lyrical and dramatic forms of expression," noting Reaney's response that "I think you've got a thesis set up where I'm supposed to be a lyric poet and I change into a theatre one. Not so." Many of his earlier poems, Reaney goes on to say, were already "quite dramatic," and the transition to the verbal demands of a different medium was not nearly so abrupt. The important change in Reaney's work, for Huebert, came with the Donnelly trilogy. The "distance which separates *The Killdeer* from *The Donnellys*," he wrote, "corresponds to the distance between the medieval *Everyman* and Shakespeare's history plays" (126).

This particular idea of "distance," which in the case of the sixteenth century implied the very gradual *development* of a dramatic language and a corresponding theatre form resulting in something like the *donnée* for which Eliot pined, is misleading in the case of Reaney. It would also be misleading for any modern playwright who recognizes and then creatively accepts the crisis of language as a starting point. This crisis imposes on him the burden, as Kennedy writes, "of re-creating the language for himself, possibly for each new play, and for a splintered audience which has to be *taught*, by the work itself, to respond to the unfamiliar language, as if it were a new code to be deciphered . . ." (3). In this sense, it is perhaps more accurate to suggest that after his earlier plays, Reaney attempted to create a dramatic language that deliberately raided the past. By so doing, he consciously used a variety of possible languages and attempted to integrate, as it were, the disparate idioms of an Everyman and an historical Shakespeare play, as well as a host of other voices, into one theatrical collage, a code containing multitudinous echoes. There is, however, as is generally recognized, a significant enough difference between such plays as *The Sun and the Moon*, *The Killdeer*, and *The Easter Egg* and those beginning with *Listen to the Wind*, which suggests some reordering, on Reaney's part, of the relationship between verbal and scenic expression and between language and the overall dramatic structure and vision. This reordering involved, among other things, a deliberate splintering of characterization, theme, time, action, and above all "story-style." As Reaney increasingly embraced what he called the "multiple focus effect" ("Letter from James Reaney" 2), he became creatively hospitable to nearly every kind of language, shifting, not uneasily, but necessarily, from one to another, producing the "pop collage" Peter Brook described as central to the Shakespearean strategy of images within complex texts which continually "change gears" ("Finding Shakespeare on Film" 118).

Verbal gears do change in these three early plays. Changes that redirect or refocus the spectator's attention do not occur because of some underlying idea of *theatre* form and vision. They occur because of an attempt conceived largely in *poetic* terms to relate primary with symbolic modes of experience and seeing and to discriminate linguistically between them. In short, there is a strong sense that the order and function of language has been, as Arden said, "privately developed by the Playwright in his study" ("Playwrights" 185), and the quite different grappling with the intertexture of verbal and scenic values has not yet been undertaken. The mature dramatic voice, one which is more thoroughly integrated with a more sophisticated sense of the theatre — as "play," collage, circus, symbolic Globe — is yet to appear in Reaney's writing. In these plays, although some scenes possess an effective fusion of theatricality and poetic vision, the tone remains generally uncertain and problematical.

Consider, for example, the opening scene of *The Sun and the Moon*, beginning with the formal exclamation of hatred and evil by the Old Tramp. This figure is partly, as Reaney describes him in his stage-directions, "like a dwarf in a fairy tale," partly a distant echo of the villainous spokesman who might have started off a typical Jacobean revenge play on its path of ruin and confusion, and partly a less distant echo of an evil-doer in Victorian melodrama: "Haha! I've got you." The imagery, diction, and, above all, the phrasing of the speech are awkward, unanswerable to any sense of concrete dramatic character and situation:

> And no doubt writing the smooth lying word
> Which up in the pulpit on Sunday you gab.
> Your sissy son's in there right now practi-
> Sing his piano — annoying poor travellers.
> I can hardly hear myself think, you pup!
> Your big grown-up daughter who's a doctor
> Still asleep and stuck up so high. (93)

Following this, and the first brief speech of Mrs. Fall with its clumsy phrasing — "I shall write down — in this small green book — / This — ear training. This and more of this. / And play me this to finish up the lesson, Andrew" (94) — the scene switches into a generally lively and colloquial prose, heightened occasionally by the more imaginative reach of Ellen.

In one scene, the play's primary level is that of a small town labouring under a familiar load of gossip, youthful alliances distasteful to parents ("Well, you young whippersnapper, we do live in the Middle Ages whatever they are and we're lucky we do. I'll get you locked up next" [100]), church attendance, summer vacation, schooling, music lessons, trips to Toronto, and so on. Then the tone shifts again as the trio of Kingbird, Susan, and Andrew pause to reflect, listening to "the late afternoon sounds — a cow mooing, a crow cawing" (103). With mutual sympathy and imagination, they quietly reflect on things past ("those days when we played down by the river in the swamp and built our hut and watched the herons nesting or looked for a scarlet tanager feather — I wish they'd never have gone" [103–04]), things mysterious and troubling (Andrew's dream of marrying Ralph: "I was being given a wedding bouquet — and there was a donkey in the churchyard cropping the grass"), things lost (Ralph's ring), and things threatening (the Old Tramp "shouting at us as he walked by" [104]). The several strands of thought, imagery, and feeling are then realigned as Susan introduces the central motif in the play, the conjunction in the evening sky of the sun and the moon, an event of both scientific and metaphorical import:

SUSAN. Tonight as the sun sets — large and red in the north-west, in the east a full golden orange moon will rise and look across at the sun.
Both children draw very close to their father.
KINGBIRD. Here's to finding your lost ring, Susan.
SUSAN. How do things get lost, Father?
ANDREW. Here's to the lost three children playing in the green shadows.
KINGBIRD. They are not really lost, darling. Your ring is somewhere between the Sun and the Moon.
SUSAN. Oh. Here's to the Sun and the Moon then.
They all raise their glasses. As the scene fades out ANDREW *goes over to the piano and begins to play.*

The verbal economy and emotional intensity of this final passage of the scene, reinforced by the late afternoon sounds and the music, effectively transfers the play's verbal tone from one level, that of Edna's persistent giddiness and provinciality, to another, one of metaphorical richness and ambiguity that, for the moment at least, holds in abeyance the sense of loss, of time passing. In the image of a unique summer solstice, light and darkness, victory and defeat, real and borrowed light coexist in a fundamentally Manichean dualism. This condition prevails at the close of the play when the destructive world of the Tramp, Mrs. Shade, and Stephen and the creative world of Kingbird, Andrew, and Susan go their different directions, each with full consciousness of the other's "country" (170).

There is a sense in this scene, as there is elsewhere, that one kind of speech of surface and appearance is meant to act as a foreground to more important speech in which metaphor is the primary agent of understanding and vision, the means through which the conjunction of the sun and the moon is seen as more than simply a unique astronomical event. Kingbird's admonition to Stephen revolves around the image of spiritual parentage:

> You may be my son! Stay with us wherever
> We go. Leave that lady of Death who sits
> There — grinning like a full spiderweb.
> Come to me. You are not my son in the flesh
> But you are — you may be in the spirit.
> All our life we seek our real parents
> Those who can beget and bear our souls. (163)

Stephen's response is equally rich in metaphor:

> Leave me alone. I am her son!
> Not in the flesh but in the spirit.
> I feel the pus that she calls blood
> Jellying in every creek and inlet
> Of my body. The stinking freemartin
> That cavorts in the stable of her mind
> Stables in mine too. My own breath
> Is her breath, my hands and eyes hers.
> I am her! (163–64)

The vehemence and imagery of Stephen's speech echoes that of his earlier confrontation with Mrs. Shade, when he still held open the possibility of crossing over to Susan's kingdom with the "music and love and laughing and games and brother and sister" of her house (144). In the earlier outburst, however, Reaney uses a rich, metaphorically dense prose voice in which the *dramatic* sense of character, feeling, situation, and, most importantly, of recognizable *speech* is more directly perceived at the same time as it reaches outwardly, as a single moment in the play, to participate in the overall design of the play. This design is intended to portray the interpenetration of fact and metaphor, body and spirit, village and cosmos, good and evil. "You have all this power," he shouts at Mrs. Shade,

> And you're the god of a hell of people but you have no joy. The poor English orphan bitch that was tossed out into the colonies and climbed and climbed up, every step someone's crotch or face. Climbed not to be rich or have children or music. Climbed because her grave was at the top of the ladder. And the top was the bottom — where it might be all over. Whenever I've had enough courage to look into your eyes I've seen the bottom there — of all things.
>
> You know once in a tavern I went out into its yard — it actually had a yard — to vomit. When I finished vomiting a friend of mine who'd come out to laugh at me flicked on his lighter and we saw — I'd vomited over the face of a tramp who was lying there *dead*. He ran back, got his camera and we took a picture of it. That's the bottom. That's there in your eyes. And it's what you want. The final stink. And I'm free of you. (145)

Whether in such dramatic prose (a foreshadowing of some of the effectively *dramatic* prose in the Donnelly trilogy and *Baldoon*), or in the verse-passages of the play, the most significant departures, for good or for evil, from the stifling, petty provinciality of Edna's village are related to language and the imagination. Kingbird, Stephen, and Mrs. Shade, in their respective kingdoms in the Manichean duality, are gifted with language. The characters on both sides use words in a special way. The form of the play incorporates such an understanding of language by means of the sudden shifts of verbal gears. This was the technique commonly used by Eliot, Fry, Yeats, Claudel, and by most practitioners of verse-drama in the twentieth century who, to a large degree, provided the only contemporary models to a poet starting to write for the theatre. The verbal dualism within certain scenes of Eliot's *The Cocktail Party*, or Fry's *Venice Observed*, for instance, wherein a more-or-less conversational idiom (mostly less in the case of Fry) is suddenly enriched by a shift in diction and imagery, acts as a sign that the realms of the ordinary and the mythical are separated linguistically. We are left with the impression that those with words (including the playwright who has chosen among the "possibilities" of form one in which language is central) can travel further into the mythical realm.

The village surface, against which the metaphorical import of such language is seen in relief, is represented by Edna and the ladies of the Millbank Women's Institute. They gladly welcome the false voice of Mrs. Shade as their guest speaker and listen avidly to her discourse of "Social Purity" in the province (109). In addition to her obvious rhetorical skills, Mrs. Shade has "studied acting," and has remarkable histrionic techniques designed for "getting the gospel across" (112). She mimes drunkenness and "writhes on the floor" (122). During her speech to the Institute she "makes great theatrical use of her chair" (123), mimes the assembly line when recounting her story of working at the china factory, greets Stephen's outburst — ". . . you're the god of a hell of people" — with "Bravo! Wow! Build my little boy a theatre" (145). When she is finally unmasked she exclaims, "The show is over" (165). In drawing attention to Mrs. Shade as actor, Reaney introduces a motif that will become increasingly more central in the plays starting with *Listen to the Wind*: the actor's world as both "play" (or "show") and as revelation. In the later plays, however, every element (plot, character, language, setting) is informed and shaped by such self-conscious theatricality. In *The Sun and the Moon*, it is simply the dominant attribute of one character — just as acting, stage-managing, and directing were the principal attributes of one of Mrs. Shade's mischief-making ancestors, Jonson's Mosca. The overall traditional linearity of this play's form, its mimesis of an action (personal, social, and universal) rather than more self-referential mimesis, precludes the degree of theatrical self-consciousness that, in the later plays, accords to language, as well as character, an entirely different role in performance. Language is not yet "playing with itself," deliberately allowed to change gears within the dynamics of collage. Thus in *The Sun and the Moon*, as in *The Killdeer* and *The Easter Egg*, words draw attention to themselves for different reasons and sometimes appear to fall short of the dramatic as opposed to the poetic demands. Mrs. Shade's different ways with words, the silliness of the eagerly attentive ladies who rush to telephone with their "tribal signals" the "lovely lovely news" of Kingbird's earlier indiscretion (128), and the empty-headed machinations of Edna provide the play with a strong comic-satiric energy. In the face of this, those few scenes intended to serve a "higher" purpose appear somewhat artificial, employing language that, to a degree, is *imposed* upon the situation and speaker rather than rooted in them. Significantly, the major exception to this is the quiet scene in which the image of the sun and the moon is first presented, a scene written in prose and very simply reinforced, in the theatre, with the subtle auditory score of late afternoon sounds and piano music.

In one of these important scenes, that which begins with Mrs. Shade's fabricated "death" and "resurrection" of Andrew in Act III, in which nearly all of the figures of the play participate, a verse-form is employed that, as dramatic *speech*, is fairly neutral. There appears to be little reason for many of the speeches here to be *written* as verse, since, in the theatre, their linguistic value as speech is dependent upon an underlying rhythm, intonation, and cadence indistinguishable from prose. What distinguishes the various scenes is a much more complex range of elements, not entirely dependent upon language alone. As Ronald Peacock explains,

> The customary opposition between prose and "poetry" is really inept when applied to drama. The reason . . . should be clear enough. The language of a play is one element in an intertexture of imagery, including stage decor and acting, so that the substitution of verse for prose, although of far-reaching effect, does not imply the same degree of acute contrast as it does, for instance, in narrative, a form for reading only. Moreover the language, whether prose or verse, is dialogue; it is speech. This is also an assimilating factor, since the language in both cases serves the same — a dramatic — purpose, in which the dissimilar functions of prose and verse in other literary forms and usages are no longer of importance. (216)

The characteristic intertexture of imagery in this play is drawn from the range of characters and the simple spatial relationships and evocations of the set that establish a "poetic" aura in the deliberate avoidance of realism, as well as from an action both real — involving young love, the process of growing up, concealed pasts, family identity, revenge, church meetings, cooking, and the like — and suggestively allegorical, involving the interpenetration of the ordinary and the mythic.

Unlike the verbal and scenic techniques devised for telling the story in the later plays, techniques that start from the central assumption that any story can be told simultaneously in a number of ways, those in the early plays show Reaney attempting, as Eliot, Fry, and others did, to tell the story in one way, using a language that is at times satirically flat, conversationally neutral, or metaphorical, depending upon the needs of the scene and the design of the poet-playwright.

As a result, the characters do not always sound like themselves and convince us of their essential autonomy as dramatic characters. Sometimes the characters sound more like verbal constructions that draw attention to the fact that they are speaking poetry. Such a deliberate privileging of language can succeed when all the other facets of the play (lighting, sound, gesture, movement, setting) are accordingly arranged and rearranged to accommodate the shifting verbal gear — as they are in *Colours in the Dark* and most assuredly in the Donnelly trilogy. In the plays up to *Listen to the Wind*, however, such self-conscious verbal playing is not theatricalized in the same way, for the same purposes, and, when the shifts come, they too often draw attention to purely poetic as opposed to dramatic ends.

The burden of narrative, sometimes presented in lengthy expository passages, sometimes in awkwardly self-conscious dialogue, is what strikes one upon first reading or seeing the 1960 version of *The Killdeer*. Nearly one-fourth of the text is given over to such material, and its frequently impeding presence suggests that Reaney has yet to discover a story-telling style. Clearly, Reaney's handling of exposition and verbal discriminations between the ordinary and the mythic, is, in this play as in *The Sun and the Moon*, formally in accord with the versions of a verse drama evident in the mid-century British theatre. Unlike *The Sun and the Moon*, however, nearly all of both versions of *The Killdeer* is printed as verse. Only very occasionally, and inexplicably, does Reaney use prose in the first version; in the second, more is used in the second act, which is the rewritten portion, written, Reaney tells us, "after I had been composing more whirling and fluid plays, influenced by continuous contact with workshop situation" ("Author's Note" 199). The revised second act incorporates a greater repertoire of conscious theatricality. The first version of the play, generally a richer metaphorical and symbolic composition, permits us a good picture of Reaney's dramatic interlacing of possible verbal strategies before the workshop experiences made more accessible to him the expressive opportunities of spatial and physical languages of the theatre and of deliberate linguistic collage.

The Killdeer is quintessentially Reaneyesque in its blend of a closely perceived and recorded social, historical "reality" and idiomatic fascinations that nourish the melodramatic and symbolic underpinning of the story. Jacques Ehrmann, in an examination of the "tragic" and "utopian" readings of history, observed that tragedy "begins at the moment when the tragic voyager sets out *en route* to his destiny. His story, his history consists of this progression toward the tragic place, this elsewhere to which he turns his back at the same time that he draws near to it, which finally surrounds him . . . it is precisely at the moment when he finds himself in the centre of this place that he finds himself expelled from it" (19). The overall shaping of this play's many and interconnected actions is within the formal boundaries of a romantic comedy from which particular consolatory values can be drawn. Yet the main "voyage," to use Ehrmann's image, is directed towards a central place and a central act that ultimately define, but, unlike a tragic recognition, do not inexorably "fix" the seeking figures. The "expulsion" in this case implies a movement towards continuing growth and maturity which fully contain the place and the act, and not the alienation and death towards which the tragic figure assumes his solitary way. The play's dark insistence upon the disclosure of secret places and acts — an "elsewhere" to which much is owed and from which much is still to be gained — provides it with the sort of thematic focus that other ancient and modern explorations of remorse possess. Three modern, dramatic, treatments that similarly blend the historical and the mythical readings of such experiences, are Ibsen's *Rosmersholm*, Yeats's *Purgatory*, and Eliot's *The Family Reunion*. In each of these plays, as in *The Killdeer*, the central characters must relive events of the past, must return to the "tragic place" — the mill-race in *Rosmersholm*, the ruined house in *Purgatory*, Wishwood in *The Family Reunion*. With a fuller understanding of the sexual, social, and religious sources of their beings and actions, they must attempt to reach through the remorse that imprisons and consumes them, just as the "abominable smell" of a "rotting thing" permeates and imprisons the interior and exterior atmosphere within which Madam Fay, Rebecca, Eli, and Harry conduct their respective voyages (59).

The voyage towards success in *The Killdeer* is conducted on different levels. As Reaney expressed in a letter to Stingle, this play was intended to contain "Lots of symbolism & poetry with an exciting story — so it moves on all the old levels — like Satan in chaos" (qtd. in Stingle 32). When Harry says,

I must find my source soon or fall.
I circle and circle in the dark and cannot sense
The nest below where I must be born. (38)

he is seeking release *from* the unaccommodating, domineering worlds of his mother and his new wife, Vernelle, as much as he is desiring active and positive disclosure of sexual, social, and spiritual identity. Consequently, Reaney turns his attention, especially in Act I, to the depiction of a rural and small-town world from which the autocratic values of his mother and wife are derived and within which their power is firmly rooted. The generally lighter, often satiric tone of much of Act I signifies that, although the stifling settled surface of Mrs. Gardner's world can endanger the urge towards sexual and moral growth, it is more readily overcome, then finally *accepted* into and by the "play" of the mature imagination, because it is but surface. In the effective and quiet reiteration of images that concludes the play, Harry recalls "a small front room crowded with a million things." Dr. Ballad does not say "change that," as he did when Eli recalled the "bearded man waiting for me" and Rebecca recalled "a floor of blood" (88). The mother's room, once such an embarrassment to him ("It's where I've spent most of my life and it's not / Real pretty" [12]), is now seen differently and reclaimed as an integral part of "The nest below where I must be born." As Victor-Emile Michelet once observed, in connection with the world of Villiers de l'Isle-Adam, "Alas! we have to grow old to conquer youth, to free it from its fetters and live according to its original impulse" (qtd. in Bachelard, *Poetics of Space* 33). Just as Harry is freed from the fetters of his mother's front parlour and from all that contributed to its authority — the "church-going biddies" (8), clocks, "Mother with her white apron" (11), Saturday night baths, the bank, the self-congratulatory endorsement of loveless, socially advantageous marriages ("My son of humble birth to marry the daughter / Of the Royal Bank of Canada's this branch's / Manager" [13]) — so too is the parlour freed from the negative consequences of disavowal. Through being reimagined, it is forgiven. Such forgiveness and understanding are reached by way of the more important dramas of the play, of which the strictly social drama of Act I is but a mask.

Our first glimpse of a social order as just such a mask is provided through Madam Fay's lively encounter with Mrs. Gardner as she tries to "Sell Beauty" (5) — an endless range of cosmetics designed to sustain and to flatter the duplicitous surface of things. Madam Fay's language, here as elsewhere in the play, is effectively driven by a bold, natural syntax, enlivened by an assortment of colloquial "Yeahs," "Y'knows," "Whaddya means" (7); it is a version of what in the August Eclogue of *A Suit of Nettles* was called the "language of the common sparrow" (*Poems* 167). After relating her version of her violent story to Mrs. Gardner, and dismissing all thoughts of "forgiveness," she directly challenges Mrs. Gardner and her society on the question of belief, giving expression to some of the play's central issues: the relationship between belief and action, between an entropic moral code and genuine spiritual illumination, and between a surface of calm and order and an insatiable appetite for accounts of disorder and violence. "Whaddys mean you can't believe it," Madam Fay exclaims,

> You're dying to believe it. You believed it
> Even before my mouth ever opened. You bought
> That pot of vanishing cream and those toenail scissors
> So you could hear me and then say, 'I can't believe it'!
> What in Hell's name is it you don't believe?
> . . . .
> And you like hearing it, don't you. That's my pitch
> With you church-going biddies. You'd buy
> The rouge pot Jezebel used the day she was tossed
> Off her balcony to the dogs just to see
> The woman that caused four deaths and one
> Of the spatteriest nervous breakdowns I ever saw
> And one blighted boy — my son — and one blighted girl —
> My sister's daughter. (7–8)

Further expressions of Mrs. Gardner's closed world become clear in the next scene with Harry. In this scene, Reaney's language reflects something of the impoverished surface of ordinary speech and a mildly parodic value, reminiscent of Eliot's conscious parody of such speech in *Sweeney Agonistes* and *The Cocktail Party* and Pinter's theatrical exploitation of verbal desolation and the discomforting spaces between words. In the attempt to dramatically portray such a language, Reaney allows the words, phrases, clichés, and, in production, the sound and rhythm, to become to some degree spectatorial: he allows the exercise in colloquial cross-talk to draw attention to *itself* as language, as well as to the imaginatively barren roots of such language in the front parlours of Mrs. Gardner's world. The "magic tongue" is not, here, "stuffed with names and numbers," but, rather, with profane repetitions of clichés that, in tonelessly rhythmic utterance, become almost incantatory: a tribal dialect as effective in its masking of the creative self and source of being as were the things in Madame Fay's cosmetic case.

> MRS GARDNER. Harry, I wish you'd come in the back door with your Bicycle. If a piece of mud dropped off it onto this Floor I'd skin you.
> HARRY. Yes, Mother.
> MRS GARDNER. Did anything interesting happen to you today?
> HARRY. No, nothing happened at the Bank, Mother.
> MRS GARDNER. Anything new on the way home?
> . . . .
> Here's your tea. Have it like a good boy. I'm just on the verge of fixing you your supper.
> HARRY. That's just it, Mother. I won't be home for supper. I can't stay home for supper if it's all right with you, Mother, that is.
> MRS GARDNER. Where are you going for supper, Son?
> HARRY. No sugar, please, Mother.
> MRS GARDNER. And what is wrong with my sugar, pray?
> HARRY. It's — it's what was causing my acne, Mother! I went to a doctor. Doctor Smith. He said —
> MRS GARDNER. And you never told me. Went to a doctor!
> HARRY. Why should I. Doctor Smith says, 'Harry, What are you eating?' So I told him.
> MRS GARDNER. My home cooking. (9–10)

The unnerving tone of such verbal repetition is briefly echoed later when Harry is attempting to describe the dinner-party at the Coonses:

> HARRY. So we sat down to dinner.
> MRS GARDNER. You sat down to dinner.
> HARRY. We sat down to dinner.
> MRS GARDNER. You sat down to dinner, and —
> HARRY. A roar of talk —
>   Talk, talk, talk, talk, talk, talk — (25–26)

Harry's account of the ensuing "talkersation" at the Coonses disclosed further aspects of the unambiguous world to which his mother owes her allegiance and into which she is attempting to place her son. Mr. Coons argued, we're told, that ". . . all schools and colleges, conservatories / Should be closed because they breed — communists!" Harry "smashed his arguments. I was stunning!" His success in this exchange, we gather, is crucial in that for the first time in the play he sees something of himself in his language: "It's *me* talk. Me talk now" (26). Much later, in *The Dismissal*, Professor Dale urges the discovery of the soul through language. Although only briefly hinted at in this early act of verbal self-assertion on the part of Harry, and not so thoroughly worked into the fuller intertexture of the play as it is in *The Dismissal* and in other plays (including *The Easter Egg*), the discovery of the self through a language that effectively invades the calcified, but authoritative, verbal gestures of such figures as Mr. Coons, is an important idea in *The Killdeer*. Interestingly enough, Harry answers his mother's predictable query "You can't go back to the bank after this, / What else could you do?" with

> ... I'd like to be a tramp
> Or work on a farm or maybe both and read
> Difficult books on easy haystacks (27)

This image foreshadows that of Dale, after his dismissal from the University of Toronto, returning to his father's farm to write a history of Rome.

In the next scene, between Mrs. Gardner and Mrs. Budge, Reaney's verse loses some of its lively colloquial tone and the self-consciousness of verbal parody, as central images are introduced that, in the course of the play, assist in relating the social surface of the small town to other patterns of thought and feeling. During the gossiping between Mrs. Gardner and Mrs. Budge, we hear the cry of the killdeer over the town, and Mrs. Budge offers this description of their talk:

> Do you know what we are like? Two old crows
> Gliding over the spring fields trying to pry out
> Where that delicious decaying smell is from.
> Is it a dead horse? My dear! By the willows!
> . . . .
>   And still
> The delicious unsavoury rotting stink
> Drives me on with my old black wings. (17)

Upon the entrance of Rebecca, the scene is lifted further from the level of the ordinary by means of scenic and verbal imagery. The first is granted comic treatment as cut-out brown paper outlines of the two men in Rebecca's life — Eli and Clifford — are displayed ("They laid themselves down after their bath last night / On big sheets of brown paper and chalked out / Each other's outline" [20]). These are held up and danced with by Mrs. Budge and Mrs. Gardner after Rebecca leaves, releasing some erotic fantasies as Mrs. Gardner exclaims, "This little runt's mine then. Whoop de do! / Stark naked!" (22). Rebecca interjects the important verbal imagery in the course of her account of preparing to marry Eli:

> It's love's solution to the puzzle of hatred.
> Eli and I will untie the evil knot.
> Mr. Hopkins will help us both. Thank you.
> I feel very happy. I shall drive
> The old blind horse out of town down the road
> Into the country until the marsh gets closer and
> Closer. I can feel its damp sweet darkness
> Brooding with frogs singing against my face.
> The road goes down across it — dark, dark, dark. (21–22)

Harry's search for sources places us firmly within the familial and social context of his mother's front parlour and all that it represents. Rebecca's takes us further, as it will soon take Harry further, into a moral and mythical sphere wherein the gruesome murder story and a higher action of love and understanding will interact making much more complex the relatively unambiguous (and essentially comic) action of youth versus age. Rebecca's voyage is towards a world in which good and evil remain inseparable. It is towards the Manichean dualism wherein the light and the dark are to be taken together, each defined and enhanced by the presence of the other. As Madam Fay exclaims much later in the play, "How can you grab hold of light with arms of dark! / No, the light must give us a stair of darkness first" (59).

The swamp drawing Rebecca's old blind horse towards its "damp sweet darkness" is the swamp from which her rescue finally comes. Old Dr. Ballad lives, he tells us, "in a small house in a secret place, / In the depths of the marsh" (83). From this marsh comes the interleaving of crime and nature, life and death: "flowers and butterflies, grass / Growing from the dead horse's body in the ditch" (84). In this first brief scene with Rebecca, Reaney's verse is considerably heightened with the central images of moonlight ("Have you watched the moonlight outside?" she asks upon entering, foreshadowing the prison scene when she awaits Harry watching the moonlight [18]), salvation (Rebecca is raising hens and sitting up all night to "see that the weasel didn't get them" — reinforcing her association with the killdeer as a bird sacrificing itself to save its young, an association made clearer when she leaves Harry a letter containing a killdeer's feather [19]), love as the "solution to the puzzle of hatred" (21), and the swamp as the "secret place," an "elsewhere" towards which several interrelated voyages are directed.

On the verbal level Reaney is shifting gears in order to redirect our theatre experience towards something more significant than the surface drama of a small town with its gossip, its discontented youth, its provinciality. Beginning with Mrs. Budge's image of their gossiping as "Two old crows / Gliding over the spring fields" (17) the language becomes more consciously "poetic," indicating to us an important verbal distinction between the ordinary and the extraordinary experience. We become increasingly aware of the central images of light and dark, of good and evil, salvation and damnation, crime and punishment.

Such a consciously "poetic" tone is struck in the opening speech of Mrs. Budge in Act II:

> Oh the river of time, the river of time.
> The clouds of moments, the clouds of moments,
> Clouds of escaping birds from the dark barn:
> I grab here, I grab there, birds you escape me.
> The wind of the hours, the wind of the hours,
> The snow of the minutes, the snow of the minutes,
> It all falls into the river of time and is swept away. (30)

This sympathetic apprehension of time passing and of the desperate and futile human attempt to resist the corrosive effects of a world measured as temporal intimidation — "Beastly watches and clocks / Growing you up," as Eli later remarks (69) — extends the prominence of the play's store of natural imagery, of birds and darkness. In its heightened, stylized cadence, it also reiterates the choric role Mrs. Budge had assumed in the earlier gossip sequence with Mrs. Gardner. In the ensuing dialogue with Mrs. Delta, however, as the two scrubwomen clean the courtroom (with light but noticeable gestures towards the symbolic structure of events: "I could plant it with seeds," Mrs. Budge observes of the judge's desk [30]), plainer expository demands are met with a plainer conversational verse that

reverts, on occasion, to the parodic tone of some of Act I. Many years
have passed, and much has happened: Mrs. Gardner has died
("When Harry left she cooked herself to death"); Harry has gradu-
ated from Osgoode Law School and has married "well — / Into
money" (31); Mrs. Frank's son Frank, acting in a conventional
saving role as an overseas' missionary, thus in contrast to the more
central acts of mission associated with Rebecca and Harry, has been
eaten by a "wicked little cannibal fish" in the Amazon (32); Rebecca
has married Eli Fay and is now scheduled to be hanged for the murder
of the hired man Hopkins who was, "My friends all said: / Homosexual if you know the word at all, Mrs. Budge." Rebecca confessed
it all:

> Confessed she'd done it. Said so herself!
> But she might have got off with life if only
> She hadn't carved him up so. His ears!
> Several fingers and ripped his belly open.
> A regular fury. (32–33)

The scene concludes with a repetition of the "River of time" refrain
(34), thus providing a very deliberate verbal framework to the
sequence.

A similarly distinctive verbal structuring of dramatic moments is
seen later in three important episodes in Act II. The first is the
exchange between Harry and Mrs. Soper, where the sparse, repeti-
tious dialogue echoes that of Harry and his mother earlier. It is meant
to signify here, as it did then, the closeness of two minds, each reading
the thoughts and feelings of the other. In this case, however, the
verbal treatment is not intended to be parodic. In this case, Harry's
mind is no longer the empty shell into which his mother could reach
and find only herself. In a sense, Harry's position has altered so that
he is now able to do the reaching into someone else's mind:

MRS SOPER. Mr. Gardner. Why did you want to see me?
HARRY. I want to see you about a very important thing.
MRS SOPER. Is the important thing my prisoner?
HARRY. Your prisoner, your prisoner, your prisoner since your
husband's away.
MRS SOPER. My prisoner since my husband is away.
HARRY. Your prisoner. Your prisoner Rebecca Fay who has
been

MRS SOPER. Sentenced on a Friday, to be hanged in September.
HARRY. But she's not the important thing, no.
MRS SOPER. It should be. She's my only prisoner. It weighs
HARRY. Down upon you because you think she's innocent.
MRS SOPER. You know what I am thinking. How?
HARRY. It's the important thing. You — the jailer's wife.
MRS SOPER. The jailer's wife is the jailer when the jailer's away.
HARRY. The important thing is what are you like?
MRS SOPER. The jailer's wife is like this. Wife to a bunch of keys.

. . . .

HARRY. Still — what *is* the jailer's wife like?
MRS SOPER. She hates the bunch of keys. Hates shutting up people.
HARRY. Hates the bunch of keys. Hates shutting up people.
MRS SOPER. Hates the lust that locks a soul in a jail of mud.
HARRY. Hates the key that locks us in a life. (38–39)

Once again the verse is quietly incantatory in effect and, incidentally, not unlike the final, mutually hypnotic exchange between Rebecca and Rosmer in Ibsen's *Rosmersholm*, a sign of a symbolic-psychological relationship, an intensely psychic exchange between two people coming closer to the secret place, the "jail of mud," from which release is sought. The quiet, insistently regular cadence of the passage is in sharp contrast to the previous scene's disputatious tone (between Harry and his wife) and the next scene in which the verbally gifted Mr. Manatee is introduced, and the play assumes an even more determined allegorical shape as creative and destructive powers are locked in a familiar struggle.

With Mr. Manatee's entrance, the verse becomes more expansive, denser in an imagery that reaffirms the importance to the play's symbolic structure of the courtroom as a place where strictly legal intentions, like Manatee's steel tape-measure, can twist and diminish the human face and heart; of birds (the shrike, great blue heron, the song sparrow, the carrion crow); of the dead horse rotting in the swamp; of the farm rendered sterile by the powerful and morally corrosive consequences of hatred:

MR MANATEE. Sir, I decided long ago that I wanted to be a carrion crow.

Pick out all the nice eyes.
When I was a boy, a boy on the farm
I used to watch the crows and the dead horses.
HARRY.   You still have a farmer's hands.
MR MANATEE.   Still.
My farm was in the County of Night and grew nothing
But fields of nightshade and bladder campion.
Gardens of burdocks. Mandrakes in the haymows.
I fed my cattle on such fare as made their udders
Run black blood and their wombs bear freemartens.
I raised weasels in my hen houses and I
Set traps for barley but bred rats who
Ate the little pigs as they lay sucking the sow.
One day the only man who could have hanged me
Died and ever since I have been designing
Swings, devising trapdoors and tying knots.

.   .   .   .

I'm the doctor who delivers your immortal soul.
Like a greasy burlap moth it flutters out.

.   .   .   .

I am allowed to kill an innocent young girl.
My secret wish has always been to be — a murderer.
The luxury of annihilating life, turning out the
Light. She'll hang! (41–42)

In these speeches, the immediate emotional and intellectual qualities of a unique dramatic character, whose grounding in the ordinary
and familiar affairs of the world (the farm, growing up, observing
and using the natural phenomena about him, learning to hate) are as
dramatically articulated as are the symbolic dimensions of his character within the play's overriding *psychomachia*. In the degree to
which such language, cadence, and imagery respond to these separate demands of the different levels of action, the writing in this part
of the play is reminiscent of some of Yeats's most successful dramatic
verse in *Purgatory*, in which isolated and unique passion is expressed
as itself and as connected to a wider human feeling. In this scene,
Reaney achieves something of the artistically problematical and
elusive "third voice."
The threatening, dark sardonic loquacity of Manatee, with his
tape-measure and his piercing flashlight, dissolves into the ensuing
storm sounds. In the act's final scene in the prison cell, Rebecca is

looking at the moon as Harry enters:

> I knew you'd come, Harry. All day I've watched
> The light. Daylight, lightning, a candle,
> And now this moonlight. And then I heard
> The light walking toward me. (44)

The interconnected images of waiting, light, and possible salvation in this quiet passage, verbally distinguishable, as the entire scene proves to be, from the expansive sound of Manatee's hatred, is echoed later by Reaney in *Sticks & Stones* when Mrs. Donnelly stands by the gate with her lamp waiting for her husband's return from prison:

> I'll stand out here with my lamp. You will come tonight.
> I know you will. I'll hold this lamp until either its
> oil runs dry or you're home. Moon, you hold your lamp,
> stars; I hold mine. (136)

Harry carries the killdeer feather Rebecca had left for him years earlier, and their identification with its symbolic value is reaffirmed. Then their intense psychic closeness is established when they play a game of Chinese pictures, each guessing what is in the other's mind. There is an echo here of the Harry-Mrs. Soper scene earlier, and a foreshadowing of the ontologically motivated games in *The Easter Egg*, *Listen to the Wind*, *Colours in the Dark*, *Wacousta!*, and *Gyroscope*. Harry has Rebecca guess, by way of images of a lilac flower, a peacock, and Singapore, his mother's "fantastic front parlour with all the things" that are firmly rooted, without agitation now, in Harry's sense of his sources (48). Harry, in his turn, guesses, by means of burdock, a vulture, and the deadly upas tree, the murder of Clifford Hopkins.

As their talk now turns to the crime, to Eli, Hopkins, and Rebecca's life with them, the verse begins to reiterate the disturbing, confusing images that inform Rebecca's life and present predicament. The speeches become longer, the imagery more complex, dense with strong, ambiguous, almost surreal visual values. They speak of the deadly upas tree that leaves everything dead for twelve miles around; Clifford always there, in the house, "Sulking and smirking, grinning and sulking" (49); the doll that Rebecca had as a child and from whose body a big black beetle wriggled out; the "place in the swamp"; the sense of impending disaster, which "whirled and whirled like a big red top / Closer and closer"; the death scene itself:

> It was death. It is death.
> You come in from outside — the floors are red,
> Cardinals fly out of the veins of brothers,
> A great scarlet tanager pecks at my mother's heart —
> Some day I'll know where the red bird comes from. (50–51)

Like the imprisoned souls in the Chamber plays of Strindberg, especially *A Dream Play* and *The Ghost Sonata*, Rebecca's innocence and goodness are threatened by and partly defined in terms of a world of violence and moral obtuseness. And, as in Strindberg's plays, the way through such a world for Harry and Rebecca, as it was for the Student and the Girl in *The Ghost Sonata*, and for the Daughter, Agnes, in *A Dream Play*, is the action of self-sacrifice, symbolized here by the Killdeer. This sacrificial myth has Christian and Brahmanic roots. As one of Strindberg's philosophical influences, Eduard von Hartmann, writes,

> in order to be freed from the earthly element, the descendants of Brahma sought renunciation and suffering . . . And so you have pain as the deliverer . . . But this yearning for pain comes in conflict with the longing for joy and love . . . now you understand what love is: the highest joy in the greatest suffering, the most beautiful in the most bitter. (qtd. in Vallency 328)

In his examination of Strindberg, Maurice Vallency remarks that the "sacrificial act by which God gives birth to the world, and by which men in turn reintegrate themselves into God, involves the giving up of the individual life" (330), an action that has sexual ramifications. In *A Dream Play*, this is symbolized by the Growing Castle. In *The Killdeer*, it is evident in the phallic imagery and the sexual action of Harry and Rebecca. In Act III, Harry confronts Eli with the essence of the latter's fear of sex in imagery that recalls that of Strindberg's Growing Castle, which springs from the manure and straw of stables and culminates in a blossom:

> You Eli,
> Are the hawk — a falcon — afraid to build
> The tower of air and cast the field of fear.

Afraid as you were afraid to build
The tower of blood that could have made my child
Yours. But first the tower of air. Your falconer
Am I! I pluck off the hood of Mother and night.
You see the light. You must fly up to it.
I let you go.

. . . .
Turn upside down and find your proper ground
Which is the sky, your drink the wind, your farm
The clouds. (66–67)

As is frequently the case in what Frye called Strindberg's "archetypal masques," the way up is also the way down. Rebecca's journey towards the "damp sweet darkness" of the swamp, Madam Fay's "stair of darkness," Harry's "field of fear," and Manatee's "County of Night" must all be experienced and understood within the ambiguous enclosure of a blessed and a cursed world. In the final scene of the play, the blessings of procreation, of the "delighted senses" — "tracks in the snow," sedges, grasses, flowers, clouds, and butterflies — are "interleaved" (83) with the cursed world of crimes, "robberies, incests, rapes, murders." As Dr. Ballad observes, we find "flowers and butterflies, grass / Growing from the dead horse's body in the ditch" (84).

The inner strength for the journey towards such a place — this "elsewhere" — is, of course, derived in part from the individual's power of imagination: the power (and will) to exert upon experience other ways of seeing and, thus, of shaping the world. The prison scene concludes with one of the play's most dramatically effective expressions of this power: Rebecca's dream.

Be still.
Watch the moonlight.
Do you know, Harry. I once had a very happy dream.
When I was a little girl I had some pet chickens,
Bantams, and my special favourite was a rooster,
Red and green with Scarlet Comb and yellow beak.
One night I dreamt — it was the depth of winter —
I dreamt that I was standing in the snow in the yard,
The moon like a beautiful pale white egg.
I heard the tinkle of a small bell. Where?
Then up through the snow he came — my pet rooster

Pulling behind him a golden sleigh. He stopped for me.
He had a golden bell — small — about his neck.
My he was grown very big. Up to my waist.
I knelt down on the sleigh. He ran along and flap!
We were on top of the elm tree. Another tug
And we were sleighing on the snowy moon. (53)

The quiet, even cadence of the speech returns us to the tone struck
at the beginning of the scene, as well as to the interwoven imagery
of the moon, the egg, the seasons, the farm, nature, and the action
of deliverance. In addition, the dream's hold upon Rebecca, and its
essentially positive value as a reading of inner and outer, real and
"dreamed" experience, signifies the restorative function of Rebecca's
imaginative power. A winter scene is transformed into one of both
real (her union with Harry) and mythological (the moon as an egg)
procreation, and the whiteness of the snow and the moon is infused
with the bright colour of the rooster pulling the golden sleigh. As
Bachelard has observed, "*cogito* is assured in the soul of the dreamer
who lives at the centre of a radiating image." A dreamer such as
Rebecca becomes a "world dreamer," one who can see and understand the world well because she also dreams what she has seen
(*Poetics of Reverie* 153).

Madam Fay's story dominates the first part of Act III as the focus
shifts to glimpses of her "secret heart" (57). Some of the complicated
exposition from Act I is repeated, but in a verse that eludes entirely
the lighter, satirical tone accorded it then. Madam Fay's language is
also stripped of its "yeahs" and other sparrow utterances and
rendered more poetically self-conscious in its expression of the evil,
guilt, rage, and hatred that inform her character. This scene with
Mrs. Budge concludes with an extravagant outburst in which a
verbal "memory shadow" is cast that momentarily associates
Madam Fay with a host of Jacobean villains whose entire beings were
consumed by passions and insatiable appetites for violence and crime
— such figures as Reaney was encountering around this time in his
adaptation of John Tourneur's *The Revenger's Tragedy*.[2]

Oh, but I will let her go. I'm going to
Let her hang! I'm going to hit her one!
Oh Rebecca if I kill your daughter will you
Send me your hatred soon. Send me Hell
To consume me. To eat the wounded bird.

I don't want my wing to be fixed. I want
You to take a stick of wood and beat me to death!
Rebecca! Rebecca!

This passion, linked as it is to her story, to a specific context of action
and behaviour, is sharply juxtaposed with a more ambiguous expression of malignity. She *"writhes on the floor and screams, terrifying*
MRS BUDGE. *Then she gets up and laughs"*:

Look at her! She wants to have a run. With what she
Knows. Now there's nothing I like better if it's not
Smashing up birds with broken wings and letting
Innocent young ladies get hanged than chasing
Old ladies down wet slippery dark streets. Yahoo!
I'll give you a head start to the poorhouse.
And when you get there — right at the gate — I'll
Leap out at you. (61)

In her next scene with Eli, she reinforces this malignity in a passage
verbally and rhythmically constituted further to remove her character and action from the prosaic level of small town iniquity. As she
will "leap out" at Mrs. Budge, so too will she encase Eli even more
irrevocably within dread:

You'll have to sleep in a room somewhere alone
Maybe out at the farm.
I'll be the orange devil waiting in the stove
I'll be the chimney trumpeting the night
Sucking in the cloud with the lightning eels.
I'll be the wind moaning in the old pantry
Whistling for some stale pie.
I'll be the back door tapping like a blind man
I'll be the cistern dripping like an idiot's mouth
I'll be the ratcoach rattling down the wainscot road
I'll be the lock and keyhole mouth.
Crying like an iron baby crouching with the north
Wind wailing through its keyhole mouth.
I'll be the clock striking — half-past twelve, one
O'clock or is it half past one? I'll be the bannister
In the velvet hand of darkness.
I'll be your eye like the twisting white doorknob
I'll be — Eli! You'll be me. You'll be mine. (63)

This passage is strikingly similar to some of the repetitive, intensified choric utterances of Eliot's *Murder in the Cathedral* and *The Family Reunion*. The repetition, syntax, incantatorial tone — all recall the expressions of the empty dread and fear experienced by the Women of Canterbury and by the more urbane inhabitants of England's north country. And, as in *The Family Reunion*, the shift in dramatic tone and focus from the ordinary to the extraordinary is accomplished verbally. Suddenly one level of language is superseded by another, one dramatic mode of speaking by another. Here, as elsewhere in *The Killdeer*, Reaney's dualistic approach to dramatic speech, shared by Eliot in his plays following *Murder in the Cathedral*, infuses character and immediate event with a more "poetic," abstract quality. As a result, the uniquely vivacious Madam Fay of Act I, selling Beauty and feeding the town's appetite for gossip, is transformed. She becomes a voice meant to function on a higher level of symbolic import, just as, in *The Family Reunion*, Gerald, Charles, Violet, and Ivy suddenly evoke a different order of experience, blending their voices and personalities:

> Why do we all behave as if the door might suddenly
>   open, the curtains be drawn,
> The cellar make some dreadful disclosure, the roof disappear,
> And we should cease to be sure of what is real or unreal?
> Hold tight, hold tight, we must insist that the world
>   is what we have always taken it to be. (*Complete* 243)

Throughout the last act of *The Killdeer*, especially, Reaney's verse seems abstract in this way, directed more towards the expression of the play's overriding concerns with symbolic patterns of thought, feeling, and experience. Except on rare occasions, the livelier colloquial tones of dramatic utterance (sometimes verbally intensified, but fundamentally present to reinforce the sense of actual people engaged, on one level at least, in actual events) are replaced by more purposeful words and images. These are intended to direct our attention to the level of argument, statement, and counterstatement altogether too neatly synthesized by Dr. Ballad's interleaving of his and the judge's journals. Reaney's "third voice" is sacrificed, as it so frequently was by Eliot in *The Family Reunion*, to the verbal requisites of argument.

* * *

At the bottom of each word
I'm a spectator at my birth.

Bachelard includes these lines from Alain Bosquet's "Premier poeme" as an epitaph to his examination of the oneric functions and properties of words: "Reveries on Reverie: The Word Dreamer" (*Poetics of Reverie* 27). They are an equally suitable epitaph for Reaney's next play, *The Easter Egg*. Just as Rebecca and Harry play a word game in order to initiate a reaching through to their hidden selves, so, too, in *The Easter Egg*, do Polly and Kenneth play word games that function as mid-wives for Kenneth's "birth," of which he becomes both an astonished spectator and narrator.

The struggle for Kenneth's soul is largely played out on a field of language. For Bethel, the word is something to be manipulated, twisted through complex legalisms until it rests, often tyrannically, in an arid document. The word as such a "thing," for instance, could with the connivance of Ira, be used to commit Kenneth "to the mental place" (10). Bethel also uses language — as Madam Fay and Mrs. Shade do — to control and intimidate others. She gives lectures ("travel talks to college girls" [13]), and, acting somewhat as a remote descendant of implacable matriarchal power in English Restoration comedy, she uses her considerable wit to keep her family, her home, and her social ambitions within strictest measure and design. Bethel's comic loquacity at the opening of the play is directed effectively at the nearly silent Kenneth with complete assurance. For Polly, on the other hand, the word is taken to be the supreme catalyst for the changing of humanity and reality, for the releasing and realization of the Self:

Where is the attic? (*He points.*) And where is the cellar? (*He points.*) Where is the threshold? (*He is undecided.*)
Show it to me, Kenneth. Show me the threshold! (*He stamps his foot and shakes his head.*) I see. You did say the word, but you won't use it. Oh my dear. If only you'd use the new words I give you, why, you'd be free. But if you only use the old words you knew before it happened you'll always be back before it happened. (23–24)

In André Breton's theory of dramatic art such a process is called *l'alchimie du verbe* — the alchemy of the word through which the central and essential action of internal and external *change* (implying the growth and strengthening of imaginative and creative power) is achieved. In Henri Pichette's *Les Epiphanies* (1947), for instance, the Word acts as a talisman, a sacred sign of the unknown, of the interacting visible and invisible universes. Possessing and being possessed by the Word, the Poet re-creates reality; the alchemical magic of language releases the self from ordinary time and space (as Kenneth is released from the attic and from Bethel's despotically insistent clock). "The word slides," the Poet exclaims, "has no more landing place, it explodes, and I possess, unknowingly, prairies, road, steamships, quarries, veritable sliced cakes in space in all directions and not disturbing each other" (qtd. in Orenstein 37). Likewise, in Aime Cesaire's *La tragedie du Roi Christophe* (1963), Christophe uses words to transform the nature of things: "Power to speak, to make, to construct, to build, to be, to name, to bind, to remake" (qtd. in Orenstein 51). In another of his plays, *Et les chiens se taisaient*, the word is the most potent agent of revolutionary change: "I only have for my defence my word," the Rebel-Poet says,

> My word, power of fire
> My word, breaking up the mud
> of the tombs, of the ashes of the lanterns
> My word that no chemistry could
> tame nor gird, hands of milk
> without words. (qtd. in Orenstein 41)

Cassirer's enthusiastic endorsement of language as the "gateway to a new world," of the child's initiation into the symbolism of speech as a "real revolution" (131), is echoed throughout these plays and is similarly embraced by Reaney. Word games, lists (of names, places, things), hallucinatory chants, monologues, choric speech — all possible ways of exhibiting the creative and redemptive energies of language are exploited by the theatre of surrealism. In this theatre, an almost doctrinaire faith in the word refashions reality and enhances the participatorial as well as the spectatorial roles of language in performance.

Standing in opposition to such an understanding and evaluation of the word as such is Artaud's advocation of *l'alchimie du corps* — the alchemy of the body wherein the desired transformation is accomplished through non-verbal, corporeally experienced *events*. In Reaney's later theatre, the implicit dialectic and synthesis between these two processes is expressed in theatrical terms, the verbal and the non-verbal components situated formally in a complex reciprocal relationship. In *The Easter Egg*, although there are suggestions of such a theatrical, that is, a *performed* dialectic, its presence is more abstract, more a matter of the play's argument than its form. The "event" in Kenneth's life that arrested his verbal and emotional growth at the age of six, and what would undoubtedly be the central experience in a rendering of the story in terms of *l'alchimie du corps*, was when his "father took a gun and blew the top off his head in front of him." After that Bethel tells us, ". . . he hasn't been able to tell a man from a woman, a garden from a lawn, a tree from a cloud" (20). A degree of re-enactment, or of restored corporeal sensation, for Kenneth, is suggested towards the close of the play when the blood-soaked rocking chair in which the child-Kenneth was forced to sit during the "event" is brought on stage, and its direct relation-ship to Kenneth's imprisonment is established by Bethel:

> Do you see here on the cushion. And on one of the arms, not where your hand was clenched so tightly we had to pry it off, but on either side soaked deep because I took the goddam filthy spattered thing and threw it as far back in the attic as I could (*Red light;* KENNETH *stumbles into the silver glitter of the cutlery and begins to collapse.*) Say it, Kenny. Don't be afraid. 'Pretty knives, forks and spoons.' My dear one. I've been a harsh mother but am I not gentleness itself compared with what she has given you this afternoon? I locked you in a room whose walls were covered with just the words you knew. Your words. Polly lets you into a room whose walls are covered with so many fierce bad words you can never understand. Like 'His father hated them both. The cruelest thing that man ever did was to leave the boy alive. It would have been a kindness to take the boy with him and he knew it.' (89)

This traumatic episode from his childhood is Kenneth's "elsewhere"; he must be taken back to this time and place just as Rebecca, Eli, and Harry had their respective, compulsory voyages to their "sources." In both plays, the action is comic: the tragic place, the scene of violent death, is arrived at, then assimilated into a continuing action of life. Instead of expulsion, there is reconciliation and acceptance. Bethel's dinner party, meant to celebrate her social advancement and acceptance, becomes Kenneth's "birthday" party, celebrating his release from the attic, from Bethel's witchlike spell. For his birthday, Kenneth dresses himself with words, clothing (including Polly's Girl Guide tie and his father's cuff links), and knowledge (about his mother and father). But he also remains consciously bare-footed, thus partly still the "child" who so impressed Ira many years earlier:

> I looked up to see what my brother saw:
> It was you. At five years old. Stark naked.
> Out of a silk scarf of your mother's you'd
> Made a turban. That was all your dress.
> While your parents had their afternoon nap
> You escaped from this house, ran naked,
> Through the sleeping village, the meadow,
> Naked through the forest — just for fun.
> You saw us. You stopped. A naked child
> With all green light and sun streams about you.
> You turned and vanished. I'll take that.
> So far as I see that's what it all means.
> And that naked innocent who gave me God
> Is still lost in the forest and I shall bring him
> Back to powerful friends who love him. (16)

Kenneth carried into his "birth" both this green and sunlit innocence and the darkness of the blood-stained rocking-chair. What makes this double burden possible to bear is language — the sense of language given him by Polly. This is not the relentless verbal tyranny of Bethel, which established the tone and rhythm of the opening scene of the play with its cruel and cold command of witty metaphor, assaulting the uncomprehending Kenneth as mere sound. It is, instead, the richly communicative language of art — literary, visual, and musical — that connects the solitary and the social, surface reality and moral structure, document and myth.

Such a use of language is implicit in the story of Anna Karenina told and dramatized (with props, music, and doll-actors) by Polly at the close of Act I. Transfixed like a child in a toy theatre, watching the train bear down upon the despairing, paralysed Anna-doll, Kenneth "leaps forward and stops the train with his arms. He gets the doll away." He has understood the story. In fact, he has creatively and actively intervened in the story, changing it, wanting it changed:

Oh, Kenneth, Kenneth. You do understand. You do understand the story. You don't want Anna to die. And she won't die. There,

there. I'll change the story. It's wonderful you understand, Kenneth. There, there — I'll change the story, Kenneth. (29)

Polly also replaces Bethel's "slave bell" with a "simple uprushing series of chords on the piano" as a means of signalling that she "needs" Kenneth (30). In this way, both the speech (as word-noise) and the sound (as thinglike) with which Bethel ruled over Kenneth are replaced by the metaphorically enriched speech and sound of literature and music. Kenneth's release from the attic is *aesthetically* inspired. The process of coming to understand a story, or a sound, is identified with the process of coming to understand one's self. Art-play games with words, dramatized scenes, musical signals provide Kenneth with the means of escape and self-realization. By changing Anna Karenina's story, he is changing his own. He is becoming increasingly conscious that he has a story, a structure upon which to arrange separate experiences and pieces of information: his few words and objects, the vision of the girl tied to the picket, the garden with its flowers and butterfly, Polly's cutlery, bits of clothing, his father's last words "abyssal nothingness" (83), the musical rocking-chair, his white kitten, the glass Easter Egg. As Frye observed, every "creative person has an interconnected body of images and ideas underneath his consciousness which it is his creative work to fish up in bits and pieces" (*Spiritus* 11). As Kenneth fishes these up, and makes the connections apparent, he becomes himself a story-teller, a sign to us of his imaginative and creative restoration and of his recognition of a Self, having up to this point been "told" by others.

In an episode that foreshadows the narrative techniques of later plays, Kenneth arranges the linguistic and experiential fragments in such a manner that he can begin to narrate himself. He places the glass egg on a chair and directly addresses the audience as story-teller and dresses for Bethel's party as he recalls having dressed for another party:

I remember then I wanted to say that between her and me there had also once been more than just a white kitten and a glass egg. There had also been my father. *(He starts removing his shirt and using the place behind the couch from which he sprang out at* GEORGE *he slowly changes into clothes for the party.* IRA *and* POLLY *help him).* How was I to know you aren't supposed to change your clothes in front of everybody in the parlour? I can still hear her shrieking and saying

BETHEL. Ira! Ira, it's a new floorshow. A strip-tease. A male one. (81–82)

Walking about with the glass egg above his head, he engages himself and us in the split time-levels, acting and narrating the procreative essence of the egg as a unifying symbol:

> I had to have something if I was going to keep my head above water. No father, there was the kitten; no kitten there was this. No this, there was immediately a skin over everything. Bethel's skin. When Polly gave me back this, this *(He walks about holding the egg above his head).* it was being circumcised of a tight fold of skin that held you back from ever quite touching anything or being a father or seeing — oh God, it hurt when she gave it to me, more than when I saw the window and the pigeons came flocking at me as I threw myself out — it hurt like a rabbi with a sharp bright silver knife, it cut away Bethel's skin over my eyes and I saw. (82)

In his preface to *The Masks of Childhood*, which contains the first published version of *The Easter Egg*, Reaney describes the origin of the play in a "collection of glass Easter eggs I made from 1945 to 1955." Such glass, he says, "cannot fail to set the story-telling instinct free. So a godmother gives a boy a glass Easter egg; he is drowning in an evil world and the present could float him to a shore. Someone steals the egg and the boy goes under a wave of wordblindness and dumbness. Fourteen years later the Easter egg is found again and . . ." (v). Another impulse behind the play, he continues, was to "write for Pamela Terry a neat, tidy play, concentrated in time and place, with few characters" (vi). Such a work, he thought, might present fewer directorial and production problems than had the more expansive, complex *The Killdeer*. *The Easter Egg* is, in fact, more of a chamber play than any other of Reaney's works, with the exception of *Gyroscope* with its five characters, and single, multi-levelled "poetic" set.

Although a complex family story lies behind the central action of the rescue and rebirth of Kenneth and although the play's imagery evokes other levels of social and moral action, the language of the play is relatively unadorned. It is much less given to the "poetic" aspirations observed in *The Killdeer* and *The Sun and the Moon*. In the first place, most of the play is written in prose, and those passages that are in verse (the first two scenes) do not possess a diction, cadence, or tone that would, in the theatre as dramatic *speech*, render them distinguishable from the prose. The result is a greater verbal consistency than in the two earlier plays, suitable for what Reaney wanted to be a "neat, tidy play." For the most part, Reaney's language throughout *The Easter Egg* adequately suits the educated talk of a college environment, a small group of people whose reading, we assume, has included Wordsworth, Chaucer, Catullus, Blake, Austen, Stein, and Tolstoy — the authors directly mentioned in the text. Although we're told that Bethel is capable of "slangy" talk (a remark occasioned by a relatively mild exclamation: "My mother used to knock the stuffing out of me" [39]), her roots "up over the mountain" (33) cannot be detected in her language — as, say, Madam Fay's origins are more directly noted in her's. Bethel has diligently and purposefully climbed up through cunning, marriage, and what the play defines as an ecclesiastically regulated social ladder. As Polly says to Bethel,

. . . you allowed yourself to be converted and soon you and father were both paddling around in the baptismal font. Why I'm your godmother! You knew he liked his Anglicanism high off the incense stick so you put on a regular circus for him. You memorized all the saints' days, your accent changed. . . . (37)

Bethel, herself, offers a frank and full account:

The whole village and the college knows, the very grass knows, I was born in a hovel and my mother is an old hag who runs a blind pig and that I ran away — down the mountain into this valley I could see every morning with the beautiful college buildings and the chimneys here sticking up through the elms. I came down and I climbed. I'm mistress of the largest and oldest houses in the village. I married a professor, I married a bishop. And it hasn't just been going to bed either. I'm really smart. (39)

She is also really witty and, to an audience, attractively so. Although her role in the play's overriding *psychomachia* is clearly established as that of a repressive, sterile, life-denying power, capable right through to the end of considerable evil disruption (like Madam Fay and Mrs. Shade she remains herself and is not reformed or altered), she is also the most lively and articulate embodiment and spokesperson of the play's satirical thrust. This is seen especially in the play's opening scene and in the scene of her sexual and verbal assault on George, culminating in the promise of marriage because he killed the bat. Her role as satirical spokesperson is also evident in the closing scene of the play, in one part of which we jump suddenly from the mental and spiritual voyage of Kenneth back to the 8:30 dinner party with the telephone message that the Principal is coming and will expect to be fed:

> Ada, stop blubbering and put all the extra leaves in the dining room table. I should have served whale rather than turbot there's that many coming. Yes, a great big whale. Leviathan himself. And a side order of frozen hairy mammoth. (79)

The other characters, with the obvious exception of Kenneth, are not verbally distinguishable one from the other. Their dialogue is rendered throughout in a dramatically conversational idiom, only rarely enhanced with imagery that, as it did much more prominently in the earlier plays, functions to connect the surface with the symbolic levels of action. One of these more "poetic" passages has already been cited — Ira's account of the vision of the five-year-old naked Kenneth with "all green light and sun streams" (16). Another is Ira's description of Kenneth as

> . . . a carp down in the village pond
> That comes up to the surface and then as you
> Throw him a piece of bread he sinks down
> Because the piece of bread casts a shadow. (15)

The pond image is used again, this time as a restorative, baptismal place, when Kenneth, having broken through both the "word barrier" and, in response to Bethel's musical signal, a window, articulates his mental-physical-verbal victory in a speech that suggests dawning poetic power:

> I heard you play the third time, so I ran at the window! Don't whip me, Bethy, and I fell — I rolled down the woodshed roof onto the hot-bed windows — mossy soft on the woodshed roof and my pet pigeons all flew up but crack, tinkle bang bang in the hot-beds. . . . I fell kersplack into the wet pond lilies. (68)

Later, when he recalls the lost white kitten, he effortlessly uses a metaphorical speech:

> Cocoanut is my White Persian cat I have. He is half as old as I am and his hair is like shredded cocoanut you know and when he is scared — by a dog or a ghost — it was the most beautiful sight in the world. Like a huge icy white teazle or porcupine or thistle but all silver glitters sticking out. (76)

Finally, during the "flashfront" episode (81), Kenneth is appropriately the one to express the significance of the play's central symbol, the glass Easter Egg, in the passage already cited. Here the window glass, like the pond's surface, is broken through and connected, in Kenneth's mind, with the physically and symbolically initiative action of circumcision. In the fullest possible sense, Kenneth is the "spectator" to his birth and to his voyage from childhood to manhood.

In Reaney's stage directions, he tells us that the sound made by the breaking of the window should be a "formidable, magic sound that should fill the whole theatre" (67). In *The Easter Egg*, a variety of objects and sounds function as important extensions of Reaney's theatrical vocabulary. As a consequence, the non-verbal visual and auditory values of performance attract greater attention to themselves as significant vehicles of play-experience and meaning. Suggestions of Reaney's attentiveness to the theatrical values of sound are evident in all of his earlier plays. In *The Killdeer*, for instance, the mortal world is present in the ticking and striking of the clock, as well as in the sound of Madam Fay's car. The natural rural soundscape is evoked through the sounds of rain, thunder, wind, frogs singing, and the cry of the killdeer over the town, for which, in his notes for the 1968 version of the play, Reaney suggests that the Roy Petterson recording of the bird's sound be used (*Masks* 199). There is also a brief moment in the play when the theatrical expressiveness of sound is more surrealistically manifested and suggestive of the sort of effect that Reaney will strive for in his later plays. This moment occurs at the close of Act II when the sound of a triangle reinforces Rebecca's account of her dream of the pet rooster with a "golden bell — small — about his neck" pulling the golden sleigh on the "snowy moon" (53). Here the sound assists in the evocation of a world beyond that of the clock and the natural environment, and it contains an immediate theatrical value similar to that achieved by the violin and triangle sounds at certain still moments of the Donnelly trilogy. In *The Sun and the Moon*, the piano seems to sound out the soul and the imagination of Andrew. As a melodic sound, the piano is countered by that of the clock ticking (which, as Murray Schafer remarks, reaches "into the recesses of night to remind man of his mortality" [*Tuning* 56]) and, of course, that of the telephone with its "tribal sounds" (128). Sounds that are more agreeable and thus allied with the piano are those of the natural world, which we hear, especially in Acts I and III, as "later afternoon sounds — a cow mooing, a crow cawing" (103), and then, at the close of the play, we hear the birds singing along with the church bell, the hymn verse, and Andrew on the piano. In *One-Man Masque* and *Night-Blooming Cereus*, there are many examples of Reaney's exploitation of the sonic environment. The collage arrangement of *One-Man Masque* utilizes in primary and secondary roles the many sounds that the masquer makes with a variety of instruments and props at hand, as he invites the "listener and looker, through the worlds of life, of life and death." This sonic environment is created, for instance, by the "ancient barrel" within which the speaker's voice "changes into something wet and hollow and deeper" (176), the rattle, which makes the telephone sound, the empty pop-bottles thrown into the carriage, the megaphone through which the speaker addresses the audience and makes the wind sounds, and, most importantly, the several voices of the speaker — as normal, as "wet and hollow and deeper," as a baby, as a child whose voice "slowly changes from four years old to twelve years old" (178), as "an older voice" on the telephone (183), and the "various old voices indicated" (185) in the sequence of Granny Crack, the Scavenger, Death's World, the Ghost, Doomsday, the Dwarf, and the Lost Child. Through these various voices, with, ideally, their rich auditory tonal and rhythmic variations and values incorporating at times the quality of chant, the purely verbal medium of Reaney's essentially non-dramatic poetry assumes a concrete theatrical shaping. Among other things, the voice's own potential as a *sound instrument* in the theatre was beginning to be realized by Reaney.

Sounds were also of importance in *The Three Desks* in which the different worlds of the students, the professors, and the college space itself were sonically identifiable through the assortment of "clouds of foot shuffling (stratus), cumulus clouds of student muttering" (95), Glee Club songs, a bell that "rings continually and continuously night or day, full or empty, vacation or term . . . [which] causes people to hold their ears: the Glee Club songs are sometimes snarled up by it, at other times — the competition between the human voice and a mechanism" (95–96). The central divisions in the play are also, as they were in *The Easter Egg*, related, in part, to language. The conflict between Max Niles, Jacob Waterman, and Edward Durelle is based upon competing ideas of education. For Niles, the "important thing about a college isn't the course work at all — but the students' social contacts, and in a large part their talk among themselves." For Waterman and Durelle, knowledge of the subject is paramount: ". . . what would they have to talk about among themselves? Get some ideas first and then talk" (130). As Brian Parker has observed in "Reaney and the Mask of Childhood," Niles's "easy sensationalism" is in opposition to an "integrity" that Waterman and Durelle share with Old Strictus in *A Suit of Nettles* (279) who taught his students "to know the most wonderful list of things" (*Poems* 166). When Niles teaches a poem, as he does in a scene of considerable parodic value with Flossy who can't understand Waterman, he insists upon "getting down to a direct sensuous appreciation" of the poem itself (*Three Desks* 158), in opposition to Waterman's approach, which starts with knowing words and meanings. Such words and meanings derive from wide reading and a literary experience that includes Old English and Greek. *The Three Desks* makes its case for a "classic literacy."

The play is written entirely in a conversational idiom, interspersed with Glee Club songs. The Glee Club is, Reaney remarked in the preface to *Masks of Childhood*, "in and out very quickly, barely there at times, could be just a bunch of chairs. Their carols combined with all the languages (Greek, Old English &c) in the play should give a feeling of what a college could be like" (viii). A similar interplay of college languages and sounds is seen later in *The Dismissal*, although in a very different, more deliberately theatricalized idiom. *The Three Desks*, along with *The Easter Egg*, was written, Reaney tells us, "before my experiments with Listeners' Workshop and its Saturday morning group improvisations" (*Masks* viii). Nonetheless, we do find in these two plays a further development of an aesthetic in which the idea of the "poetic" is broadened, as it had been in the work of Cocteau, in the expressionist and surrealist theatres, and elsewhere, to include the synaesthetic values of the visual and the auditory in performance. In *The Easter Egg* and *The Three Desks*, our attention is drawn to some of the non-verbal resonances of certain sounds and objects that seem to gain in theatrical importance as the verbal language becomes somewhat flatter, more conversational. The poetic imagery is, to some extent, transferred to some of the special visual and auditory effects, which, like verbal imagery, can press the surface of ordinary reality and disclose, in their own terms, ambiguous, often symbolic relationships and patterns. These disclosures are increasingly dependent not only upon how we use and respond to words but also upon how we look and listen.

Exercises in looking and listening preoccupied Reaney in the Listeners' Workshops from which his next play, *Listen to the Wind*, evolved. What Reaney, along with others during the sixties, was creating, through an understanding of the idiom of a radical theatricalism itself, was a highly complex, multi-levelled form. In this form, personal, subjective materials of experience (including those of memory, reverie, and chance associations) could be interlaced with more objective and shared experiences (especially those derived from the social or "public" realm, thus verifiable through various documentary means) and freed from the conventions and restrictions of a linear framework. Some of the possible shared experiences might also be derived from *reading*. This is one reason why Reaney's workshops, as well as his various published pronouncements on theatre and drama include references to, and strong recommendations to read, a wide range of books and articles. Some of these are popular, thus presumably shared by author, performer, and spectator, some entirely within the public domain (such as newspapers and various sorts of archival material), and some are relatively obscure, remote from a *common*, not to mention a *classic*, literacy.

To some extent, such literary references can provide touchstones of recognizable, familiar imagery or dramatic tones and themes that can enhance a scene or a character — as, for instance, literary references do in *The Easter Egg* and *The Three Desks*. In *Listen to the Wind*, however, yet another dimension of such literary reference is explored resulting in a significant change in the way Reaney uses language. The more or less conventional tones and techniques of modern dramatic verse are largely absent in *Listen to the Wind* and in the plays that follow. In *Listen to the Wind*, there is the juxtaposition of distinctly different *kinds* of language, not in order to provide periodically a degree of "poetic" heightening of a basically conversational idiom as in *The Sun and the Moon, The Killdeer*, and *The Easter Egg*, but, rather, to create a theatrically and verbally self-conscious *collage* of linguistic modes that draws attention to speech itself and, at times, to the *literary* sources of that speech. In a completely new way the different kinds of speech become themselves a central part of the action of the play, and the tensions between "real" or "ordinary" speech, and "literary" or "theatrical" speech become a focal point of the play's form and meaning. The synaesthetic values of theatre performance, then, which inform the non-verbal structures and signs of *Listen to the Wind*, are reinforced with a verbal structure completely unlike that of Reaney's earlier plays. Just as objects, sounds, gestures, movement, colours, and the like are *assembled* in a variety of ways in order to depict and evoke different "messages" and "different parts of the soul" so too are different languages assembled in order to depict and evoke the variety of worlds that can be constructed with words.

Three very distinct verbal worlds inform the shifting narrative and theatrical planes of *Listen to the Wind*. First of all, on the primary level, there is the world of the four children playing together in Owen's West Room. Their voices, the first we hear in the play, are presented very simply with "flat" conversational values. When they decide to try to lure Owen's mother back by putting on a play, a second verbal world begins to intrude, and the conversational idiom is self-consciously heightened by some of the hyperbolic rhetoric of childhood reading and imagining:

What'll we put on? We could put on Tarzan of the Apes.
  Tarzan jad guru! Hotan woten madzewk! It's a special language he learns in this lost country. There's a glossary in the back.
  . . . .
  You could be Mad Bertha, the German missionary lady who's really a German general in disguise trying to blow up our ammo dump in Dar es Salaam.
  . . . .
Tarzan leaps upon the stunned wildebeest, tears at the creature's jugular vein, then utters the wild ape's victory cry. (15)

They decide to stage the "terribly melodramatic" *Saga of Caresfoot Court* (15) from which text violent and lurid scenes have already shaped corners of their imagination: "That dreadful part where the dog gets him by the throat by the well. And they can't get the dog's jaws loose so they bury them together. . . . And that awful part where she thinks she's poisoning herself but actually she only gets paralyzed from the waist down" (16). This second verbal level of the "terribly melodramatic" is drawn from specific sources — Brontë's *Wuthering Heights*, Rider Haggard's *Dawn* (James S. Reaney 72–87; Lee 148–54), and from an even more popular storehouse of tones, gestures, imagery, and language associated with the instinctual, "unspoiled" melodramatic sensibility of children, who, as Reaney remarked in his first *Halloween* letter, understand the "script thoroughly even when it involves the most esoteric and ancient matter of Light's yearly fight with Darkness" ("Letter from James Reaney" 2). A third level upon which words create an interconnecting but at the same time verbally autonomous world is present in the choric renderings of poems by Emily Brontë — especially parts of her epic *Gondal Chronicle*. Reaney initially planned to "tell the Brontë biography and the Gondal saga . . . and some of the Angria epic . . . at the same time," in order to depict the "real" and the "imaginary" lives of the Brontë children. In the revised play, the children became Reaney and his own cousins with whom he used to put on plays in a room called the West Room, and parts of the Gondal Saga relegated to a completely different role as a formal choric voice. The chorus of a "dozen young people like the orchestra of the Peking Opera" (13) reinforce the verbally incantatorial values of the poems with a strictly theatricalist idiom of sonic and scenic effects (a whirling weather-vane, branches, window panes, "Bird sounds and cockcrow outside, branches against reddening sky" [146]) transforming, to a certain degree, *poésie au théâtre* into a *poésie de théâtre*.

These three verbal worlds of childhood, melodrama, and the chorically rendered *Gondal Chronicle* remain linguistically separated throughout the play (despite the complex interleaving of tones and styles as the planes of the play's focus shift through "real" and imaginary time and space), each with its own particular range of experience and evocation. Language itself becomes one way of theatrically manipulating an audience's "fix" on the multi-level narrative through its increased "spectatorial" as well as participatorial value. To a degree, as Kennedy observed of Eliot's later plays when he returned to use some conventions of speech he had once rejected (including some from melodrama itself), it is as if the playwright's involvement with forms of language has itself been dramatized, "a conflict enacted in public" (97).

The first of the three voices, a sort of "realistic," conversational norm against which the others are seen in relief, is prominent in about one-third of the play. The choric voice (when parts of the Brontë poems are actually recited and not the "voice" of various

sound effects) is heard on thirteen occasions, some extended, others
very brief. The bulk of the play is verbally evocative of the generally
inflated tones and values of melodrama. Melodrama strives to say
everything and to *appear* to be saying everything. The sententious
rhetoric, with its matching gestural reinforcement, is meant to
articulate without embarrassment a degree of instinctual imma-
culacy wherein the strongest emotions are, in a sense, released from
the repressive and agonizing layers of psychological complexity and
ambiguity. Its hyperbolic quality, like the outward signs of costume
in, say, mediaeval drama, in Japanese Kabuki theatre, in Brecht, is a
direct, unobstructed conduit for something morally absolute and
lucid. When the children re-enact the strong narrative and character
features of the *Saga of Caresfoot Court*, then, they employ a language
of immense participatorial and spectatorial benefit. On one level —
the participatorial — it releases and clarifies their repressed feelings
(separated cauldrons of fear, love, hate, anxiety). On another level
— the spectatorial — it notifies the audience through its repertory of
unmistakable verbal signs, that the Manichean dialectic is still,
despite the debilitating one-dimensionality of the "environmental
bubble," a motivating idea. Looked at in this light, such melodramatic language maintains something of a *magic* property through
which, as Cassirer observed of its use by the "primitive" and the
"child," the "consanguinity of all forms of life" is recognized (110).
The metaphorical texture of Rider Haggard's prose, on its own as
read or spoken aloud, is, to a modern reader, awkward and inflated.
When its *magic* life, however, is recovered through the play of
children, then what on the surface appears to be of primarily parodic
value is significantly modified and the out-moded speech revived
within a theatricalist idiom.

When Ann suggests that they play in "Something where we can
dress up in old clothes from the attic . . . Six people die in bed . . .
from broken hearts . . . or poison . . . or get betrayed . . . That sort
of thing" (15), various conventions of melodramatic action, characterization, and language are put in place within the play as a whole.
These are invoked and assembled (as one element in the theatrical
collage) as they are appropriate to the children's inter-connecting
needs for emotional release, moral clarity, and imaginative play.
Melodramatic conventions, in this instance, carry within their clear
lines, which are their fundamentally unambiguous verbal and character signs, the stimulus and art-boundaries for that ontological
creativity with which Reaney frees the "child" from the hazy and

baffling equivocations of the adult world. Once accepted as such, these conventions can proceed to provide the appropriate aesthetic for the rhetorical and metaphorical excesses of the language that permeates much of *Listen to the Wind*. Various "primitive immensities" (Bachelard, *Poetics of Space* 102) are unquestioningly evoked as the children and, ideally, their spatially and imaginatively "infolded" audience *play* through the "old" words, phrases, cadences, and metaphors:

> You prefer to stick to that slut you've doubtless got up in town, eh? I give you a choice, Piers. Keep your woman whoever she is and lose the land or marry Miss Lawry and keep your birthright. Oh God, all my plans come to this end. The only power left me is the power of vengeance . . . Vengeance on my own son. (40–41)

> I . . . Pity her? I hate her. Look you, I suffer. She shall suffer more. Her love will be fouled and her life made a shambles. Such a shambles that she will cease to believe there is a God. In return I shall give her . . . *You*. (70)

> Because I reflect that Douglas Caresfoot had made up his mind to marry you and I have made up mine to help him to do so and that your will, strong as it certainly is, is as compared with our united wills what a dead leaf is to this strong East Wind. Angela, the leaf cannot travel against the wind. It *must* go with it and you *must* marry Douglas Caresfoot. You will as certainly come to the altar rails with him as you will to your deathbed. It is written in your face. Goodbye, Angela. (78)

> As to her person, Angela Caresfoot is one of the most beautiful women I have ever seen. As to her character, she is deep as the haunted well at her father's house and is as filled with strange springy fantasies and musings combined with a simple forgiving innocence. A woman, I might add, immeasurably above the man on whom she has set her affections. (81)

> Piers Caresfoot, you have broken the vow you made to me to look after our child. You have sold her for money like an animal! Hear my revenge! My teeth are sharpened with the North Wind of Hunger. My tongue is parched and famished with the East

Wind of Hate. I shall slake my hunger and thirst upon you until people will ask where you were and find only the palms of your hands. (105)

The several voices are verbally indistinguishable (Devil Caresfoot, Piers, Geraldine, Lady Eldred, and Claudia are represented in these selections). The problematical "third voice" is disregarded as the playwright deliberately raids the "museum of speech" and employs for his own purposes a "ready-made" rhetoric — just as Curnoe had raided his environment for old verandah posts and the "sign right off the Spittal Straw Hat Warehouse."

"The introduction of the chorus," Nietzsche wrote, "is the decisive step whereby we declare war, openly and honestly, on all Naturalism in art" (qtd. in Kennedy 98). The anti-naturalistic choric voice of *Listen to the Wind* is created verbally, by means of Reaney's "raid" on the poems of Emily Brontë, and theatrically, by means of some sonic techniques derived in part from the Peking National Opera, bpNichol (some of whose concrete poems Reaney had published in an issue of *Alphabet*), Carl Orff (whose influence upon the choric dimensions of Guthrie's production of *Oedipus* at Stratford Reaney had observed), and a variety of sound-making experiments in the Listeners' Workshops. As in the productions of the Peking National Opera, Reaney was seeking to achieve in theatrical terms the desired unity of visual and auditory structures, wherein both the actor and the props are made to occupy and to suggest an aural as well as a visual space. Thus the continual, almost frenetic activity of the actors throughout *Listen to the Wind* as they perform as "characters," as members of the chorus, and as sound-makers, using props at hand (the sticks, stones, pieces of metal, coconut shells, combs, chains, whips, bells) and their voices (barking, whistling, murmuring, humming). On one level, this activity is aurally representational, designed to evoke the various sounds of the wind, the sea, birds, dogs, crickets, wheels, hoofbeats, hammering, wagons, and trains. On another level, these separated and combined sounds become essentially non-representational and operate in conjunction with the visual elements to create a "concrete" experience of the theatre as John Cage described it: "There are things to hear and things to see, and that's what theater is" (qtd. in Kostelanetz 51).

The Brontë poems supply an immediate verbal heightening as they provide much of the imagery of the winds, the various settings of the Caresfoot Saga ("the drear moor stretches far away" [17]; "woods

... dark with the new green leaves" [76]; "here / Beneath these sullen skies" [50]; "tropic prairies bright with flowers / And rivers wandering free"[80]; "Over the hills and under the sky" [95]) and as they reinforce and aesthetically shape the various moods of the children playing and telling the story. For the "educated" listener (a "person only a little familiar with the lives of the Brontës," as James S. Reaney suggests [77]), there is another level of "richness" to be worked out that involves an appreciation of a timeless world of the imagination and of ontological creativity, shared by the four Brontës in Haworth parsonage and the four children in Perth County. This literary-biographical dimension, like that of melodrama, is evoked by means of a ready-made language that signals both the similarities in the familial, environmental, and creative situations of the two groups of children-artists and what James S. Reaney called "the land that the Brontës created in their childhood, stretching from the bleak north-land heights to the south Pacific and vibrant with love, hate, confusion, death, new life emotion" (77). On the verbal level, then, the choric voice of *Listen to the Wind* is centrifugally expansive, moving from its immediate *theatrical* role of reinforcing the action of playing (with words, sounds, and bodies) towards a primarily "literary" role that provides a recognizably analogous exercise in the creation of a "world of words" with which the inarticulate "dull township" is reshaped and ultimately transcended.

Such a direction towards the use of a language that is not fixed in one mode, but permitted freely to signify different worlds and meanings (both "literary" and "theatrical") through the juxtaposition implicit in collage, is even more evident in *Colours in the Dark*. Among the ready-made literary worlds prominently evoked through the language of this play is that of Reaney's own achievement as a non-dramatic poet. Raiding his very personal poetic museum, as he had already for dramatic purposes in *One-Man Masque*, Reaney assimilates into the play a wide variety of poems familiar to his readers in such works as *The Red Heart*, *Twelve Letters to a Small Town*, and *The Dance of Death at London, Ontario*. To a much greater degree than is evident in any of the earlier plays, the sense of place, of region, is particularized in *Colours in the Dark*. Yet this particularization is not achieved through language. There is hardly evident anywhere throughout the verbal level of the play a recognizably colloquial or regional voice that corresponds to the distinctively regional vision and subject matter assembled for us in the assortment of documentary and scenic materials and techniques. The languages of this play appear to possess an even greater spectatorial value and function as they project a variety of verbal worlds implicit in Reaney's own poems, in ballads, hymns, popular songs, and the like. The verbal effect is not unlike that achieved in W.H. Auden and Christopher Isherwood's *Dog Beneath the Skin*, John Arden's radio play *Life of Man*, or, to a degree, Edith Sitwell's *Facade*, in all of which works languages, as languages, are engaged in a sort of dialogue. (Plays by other poet-dramatists such as Bertolt Brecht, T.S. Eliot, e.e. cummings, and Edward Bond in which previously published non-dramatic poems are incorporated into the dramatic context also come to mind.) Auden's program note for *The Dance of Death* (1933) addresses the sort of communal experience, and suggests formal models, that Reaney was also seeking in his workshops and plays following *The Easter Egg*:

> Drama began as the act of a whole community. Ideally there would be no spectators. In practice every member of the audience should feel like an understudy.
> Drama is essentially an art of the body. The basis of acting is acrobats, dancing, and all forms of physical skill. The music hall, the Christmas pantomime, and the country house charade are the most living drama of today. (qtd. in Spears 92)

Shortly after *Colours in the Dark* was produced at Stratford under Hirsch's direction, Reaney writes,

> One name for this is *collage* and I had already written for the composer John Beckwith several scripts which, with his fragments of music and sound, gave collage views of Stratford, Ontario (*Twelve Letters to a Small Town*) and Winnipeg (*Message to Winnipeg*). Another possible name is *The Christmas Concert* — an evening of recitations, drills, playlets, choruses and Santa Claus appearances that used to be produced in public schools. There was even that rarity the Halloween Concert which with some of its macabre detail *Colours in the Dark* is actually very much like. ("Colours" essay 142)

Earlier, in "Afternoon Moon," Reaney had described the Christmas Concert with its "jabbering recitations about Sonambulists, My Christmas Stocking and Pa Shaving," the monologues of

distressed Irish ladies with seven children, an absent husband
and taking in washing besides; the dialogues between negroes
whose necks were lily-white and whose faces were licorice-
black; the Japanese umbrella drills, the Crow-drill that never
failed to send all the babies in the audience into screaming
convulsions, the silly old plays containing a stage Swede, a stage
absent-minded professor, a stage clergyman, a stage Irishman;
the pantomime where a great deal of enthusiastic slapping went
on. . . . (44)

Such models do not require, indeed they deliberately eschew, a verbal
consistency. In their collage-as-play structures, language itself
becomes like the "wonderful list of things" taught by Old Strictus in
the July Eclogue of *A Suit of Nettles*, "a marvellous deck of cards in
your head that you could shuffle through and turn over into various
combinations with endless delight" (*Poems* 166).
      One important aspect of the verbal collage central to *Colours in
the Dark* is composed of the juxtaposition of Reaney's "private"
poetic voice in, say, the "Existence Poem," "The Sundogs," or
"Antichrist as a Child," with the highly familiar and popular, thus
more "public" and communal, voices of hymns and songs. Throughout the play, these hymns and songs ("Shall We Gather at the River,"
"Big Rock Candy Mountain," and many others) possess, first of all,
a musically atmospheric value that, along with their leavening value
in the summoning of childhood memories, effortlessly engages the
audience as, in Auden's expression, understudies. As such, they also
signify a settled and comfortably "known" religious and communal
context against which the metaphorically rich and much more
ambiguous poems stand in stark contrast. If there is in the poems, as
James S. Reaney observes, a "profusion of reference and experience"
(51), some of which retains a highly personal, more lyrical (as
opposed to dramatic) impulse, then their linguistic-poetic separate-
ness from the immediately accessible communal poetry of hymns and
songs is all the more apparent. The "situation" of the poet within
such a world is itself dramatized as we witness, or, rather, *listen* to
the play of his language against that of the community whose
appetite for and expectations of poetic utterance are happily, and
effortlessly, satisfied by the hymnbook, the songbook, and
everychild's recitation on "Pa Shaving."
      The multitudinous references and experiences of the poems help to
provide the play's primary events — birth, childhood, education,

marriage, parenthood, death — with some of the glamour and atmosphere associated with the "mythical form of conception." As many writers have pointed out in their readings of *Colours in the Dark* (Dudek, Woodman, Germaine Warkentin, James S. Reaney), Reaney's regionalist vision, in which the particularities of time, place, and event are directly manifest, is the principal vehicle for his poetic-symbolist vision wherein these are re-imagined and re-shaped as an "alphabet or iconography or language of symbols and myths." Thus, for example, the recitation of "The Sundogs" reinforces the initiatorial-inquisitorial sequence of the Father confronted by the Grandmother and the Son:

> I saw the sundogs barking
> On either side of the Sun
> As he was making his usual will
> And last testament
> In a glorious vestment. (*Colours* 14)

The scenic arrangement for this sequence is a simple one that has the Father standing with "a figure on either side of him" confronting the Grandmother, "who keeps cracking a slapstick and asking partly embarrassing, partly footling questions," and the Son, who "appears with a megaphone and accuses, questions in a very judgelike tone" (13). The poem itself does not have a strictly dramatic origin. It does not *necessarily* arise from this particular arrangement (many other poems, or none at all might have been just as appropriate), nor from the particular participants in the drama of the Father's inquisition. It doesn't "arise" at all, in fact. It rather "arrives," fully completed, ready-made as a previously published poetic "document" (just as the Brontë poems do in *Listen to the Wind*) to shift momentarily the verbal gears and the imagery of the play from one level to another. The particular situation of the Father is now imbued, by means of the juxtaposed poem, with the imagery, rhythm, and cadence of the sundogs who cry out their subversionary tactics:

> We shall drown the crickets,
> Set the killdeer birds crying,
> Send shingles flying,
> And pick all the apples
> Ripe or not.
> Our barking shall overturn

Hencoops and rabbit-hutches,
Shall topple over privies
With people inside them,
And burn with invisible,
Oh, very invisible!

Flames   (*Colours* 14)

The immediate scope of this inquisitorial activity broadens to encompass a much more comprehensive inversion of personal, social, and natural order, a broadening further augmented by the Grandmother's claim that the Father "must be taught pain and joy, good and evil, life and death" (15), and by the slide depicting the "Bosch demons attacking St. Anthony." The collage assemblage of "things to hear" during this entire sequence includes a cracking slapstick, a megaphone voice, the recited poem, hoof sounds (to reinforce the question of the number of horses in the county in 1871 and at present), dog sounds as "all the kids come yapping across the stage" (17), and thunder. "Things to see" include the "dim-coloured shapes" (13), the two figures on either side of the Father, the Grandfather with a bear mask, projected images of a "sensual looking gentleman" (15), the "80's floozies in tights" (16), the Bosch demons, and the bright light that fills the stage at the close of the sequence. Not only is the poem, as a poem, expressive of an essentially solitary, lyrical experience, verbally and metaphorically remote from the communally expressive hymns and songs, but, to a degree, it is also theatrically inundated by the dynamics of the sonic and scenic arrangements. Its unique language as a poem, together with its imagery of disorder, is placed into a sort of theatricalist dialogue with the *equally* authoritative languages of all the things we hear and see.

One important element of this dialogue is that which, in a sense, is occurring between Reaney the poet who *made* a poem, a fixed verbal arrangement that exists, now, as *ergon*, and Reaney the *developing* dramatist who has but recently acquired a new "magic tongue" stuffed, not with "names and numbers," but with a miscellany of things to hear and see. With the explosive *energeia* of such a tongue, he is *making* a scene, a "mosaic-all-things-happening-at-the-same-time-galaxy." And not only is he making the scene, but, as we observed earlier in connection with the ontologically creative aesthetic of collage, the spectator-auditor is invited to participate in this art-act. In this way, the "situation" of the artist in his immediate society is again addressed, and the theatre's (at least *this* theatre's) own formal affinity with, say, the Christmas Concert, actively elicits creatively "aroused" companionship for one whose earlier poetry so often spoke of loneliness and estrangement. The private poem is incorporated into communal "play."

The various dialogues between word and non-word and between language as *ergon* and language as *energeia* that are implicit in this scene are equally apparent as Reaney incorporates into the theatricalist collage such poems as "A Fantasia on the Street Names of Winnipeg," "The Existence Poem," "Antichrist as a Child," "Yonge Street," and "The Dance of Death in London, Ontario." In some instances, the verses are divided for different voices and accorded choric presentation, which, in the case of, say, "The Existence Poem" and "A Fantasia on the Street Names of Winnipeg," realizes their incantatorial values and thus augments the purely sonic dimension of the play. In all instances, they are theatrically situated within varied scenic arrangements that, like the engravings of Blake, both reinforce the verbal meanings and, simultaneously and autonomously, offer their own, distinct, pictorial meaning. Since these poems are very different in tone, structure, diction, syntax, and imagery from one another, there appears to be no strictly formal constrictions placed upon the choice of poems to be included. As long as they are relatively short, can be recited singly or divided into choric sections, and as long as they are thematically pertinent to their situation in the play's underlying narrative structure, then practically *any* verbal form will serve. The entire poetic-drama aesthetic that informed the earlier plays is thus abandoned, and the problem of speech, inasmuch as it was concerned with discovering and establishing an authoritative and recognizable "tone of the centre," the "third voice," or the playwright's "own language as it is actually spoken around him," is resolved, essentially, by being ignored.

As the play traces the growth of an individual, related on several levels to the story of a region, a country, and "the world's story" (21), we see language itself, as was the case in *The Easter Egg* and *Listen to the Wind*, becoming a principal means by which interior and exterior experience is transformed and shaped. The discovery of language, then, and the recognition of its magical powers is a central issue in the play and the most important means by which the various elements of play's collage aesthetic, with its serialization and separation of verbal, aural, and visual experience, are integrated. The "tone" of this play's centre is that which arises from metaphor, and a poet-playwright who has discovered and mobilized its magical power is, in the course of the play, reliving its discovery and urging his actors and his audience to be drawn, as co-creators, into the all-important ontological art-acts that it makes possible. Thus the play that displays all the things one can do with words and metaphors (compose poems, compile lists, engage in word-games of all sorts) and pedagogically suggests how to acquire a battery of words and a sensitivity towards metaphor (through games, books, and a particular kind of education). The numerous question and answer sequences (interrogation of some form is the basis of most of the play's "dialogue"), Bible Sal's copying of the whole Bible, the recurring "Existence Poem," the early School Sequence, the choric chanting of the names of the "Sailboats that Brought Ancestors & a Cradle," the various poetry recitations, the university sequence, "University College: the Lecture of Dr. Button," "A Fantasia on the Street Names of Winnipeg," the "Writing Class," all have to do with hearing, reading, learning, and using words as a means of constructing patterns and meanings, and, most importantly, as a means of playing. It is in the episode of Dr. Button's lecture that the significance of metaphor is established in a Manichean confrontation of the dark and the light, of Dr. Button's

> Oachghwkwk! A flower is not like a star! Nothing is like anyone else. Anything else. You've got to get over thinking things are like other things

and the Son's

> Then if a flower is not like a star, and nothing is like anything else then — all the spring goes out of me. I used to take such pleasure in little things — images, stones, pebbles, leaves, grasses, sedges — the grass is like a pen, its nib filled with seed — but it all seems — lies. I can't go on. There seems no reason to go on living or thinking. (67)

The sequence concludes with Button's defeat and the triumph of Bible Sal's love of words. (Much later, Reaney was to describe "the Bible I was canoeing down — exhausting, lumbering, gorgeous, authorized by a dead king, lousy with strange words and names" ["Digesting" 69].) The Son renews and strengthens his faith in metaphor: "Try this. A flower is a star" (70). Something not unlike

the Baudelairian "l'analogie universelle," with its complex assembly
of "correspondences," lies at the centre of the world of metaphor
celebrated here. Following through with such an aesthetic, transpos-
ing its values on to the different theatricalist keys of verbal, pictorial,
and aural expression, Reaney re-creates his own submission to
metaphor as an act of faith ("Try this"). Relying upon what Frye
called the "naivete of the participating response," he attempts to
"transfer to others the imaginative habit and energy of his mind"
(*Stubborn* 161).

What was it that quite changed the scene
So desert faded into meadow green?
The answer is that he met a Tiger
The answer is that he met a Balloon

Who was the Tiger? Christ.
Who was the Balloon? Buddha.
Emily Brontë and the Emperor Solomon.
Who sang of his foot in the doorway.
All these met him. They were hopeful and faithful. (82)

In the Donnelly trilogy, all of the synchronous "possibilities"
within Reaney's verbal world are present to one degree or another:
lyric verse, various kinds of choric incantation, conversational and
heightened prose, documentary language, liturgical and biblical
rhetoric, popular nineteenth-century melodramatic speech, modern
"concrete" poetry, dialect, the popular ballad. There is no other play
by Reaney, and very few in the whole of modern and contemporary
drama, that are as semantically complicated as these plays. Obvious
risks of a confusing semantic richness, which might derive from an
overindulgent verbal collage, are, however, inhibited by the functioning in the trilogy of three major modes of discourse. The first of
these is what Kennedy refers to as a "speech-of-appearance" (31), a
colloquially inspired speech through which most of the characters
engage themselves in what are taken to be ordinary events and
situations. For the most part, this speech represents a conversational
idiom, relatively flat and unembellished for some, and metaphorically and rhythmically (at times melodramatically) heightened for
others, especially the Donnellys, in whose speech Reaney has placed
the cadences, rhythms, and diction of a version of Irish dialect.
(Reaney recognized that this speech evoked but did not entirely

recreate a strict dialect: "In the Donnelly plays there has been a big problem with the creation of a language for the actors that isn't Irish dialect and isn't the way we talk now; I've been told that Mrs. Donnelly should say begorra more" ["James Reaney" 153].) As we might expect, their speech dominates the trilogy, calling to mind other plays (by Synge, Eugene O'Neill, Arden, Bond) in which a particular dialect operates as a central and vigourous vehicle for the intertwining dramatic claims of character, action, and *specific* time and place. Yeats spoke of the need to recover a dramatic language that realized the "passionate personality," a speech of "personal utterance," and not that "poetry of abstract personality" often exhibited in a persiflage that exists "not in the midst but on the edge of life" ("The Theatre" 30). To a greater degree than is evident in any other of Reaney's plays, the speech of the Donnellys represents such a recovery and suggests a considerable advance in the confident handling of a lively *dramatic* speech from the self-conscious "poetic" abstraction of large parts of *The Killdeer*.

The second mode is also a kind of "speech-of-appearance" that, however, moves in a formidably abstract direction. As the community of the Donnellys becomes increasingly regularized through its laws, politics, religion, economics, and "communications," then the "environmental bubble" assumes a readily identifiable *verbal* shape. This shape is derived from what Reaney called the "printed rhetoric . . . beginning to wrap itself around Canadian life." At its best, such a rhetoric helps to define and clarify the boundaries of legislation and the polarities of political discourse. However, the interaction of politics, religion, and law with language also produces what Steiner calls "speech-acts":

> The imperatives of articulation, unfolding out of an internalized logic of extremity, make plurality, compromise, reconciliation impossible. Human speech, which ought to be the most supple and provisional of media, stiffens to monism. It closes the speaker's world, as in armour . . . in the dramatic presentment of the process whereby the political word comes to dominate the speaker and agent, coercing him, by its own unleashed dynamics, to propositions, to gestures, from which there is no return. (Rev. of *Pierre Corneille* 1259–60)

Such speech-acts in the Donnelly trilogy spring from within the increasingly managerial and authoritative impulses of evolving and interlocking commercial, political, and religious powers. Their presence is felt in the plays' strictly documentary dimension, in some of the fixed modes of speech represented by such figures as the Bishop in Act III of *Handcuffs* and in the various forms of printed rhetoric that Reaney derived directly from the public record — including, most importantly, the newspapers of the period. On occasion, the calculated inflationary nature of this rhetoric comically reinforces the melodramatic impulses of the trilogy ("RURAL ROUGHS ON RAMPAGE," "THE MIDDLE AGES REVIVED," "DISGRACEFUL CONDUCT OF LOVE SICK SWAIN" [*St Nicholas Hotel* 56]). More often, however, this rhetoric not only stifles the imaginative and spiritual energies of the "folk," but contributes to, and finally defines, a sub-literacy in which live meaning attains a verbal calcification fully concomitant with the more menacing dimensions of hatred, bigotry, and know-nothingism, and, we can add, with the ideals of a "technological 'go-aheadism' that is," as Reaney remarked, "eventually destructive of not only man, but of the newspaper itself" ("Myths" 257).

The third mode of discourse is consciously and variously "poetic." This includes a wide range of traditional, "popular," and essentially experimental verbal and aural forms evident in the Roman Catholic liturgy, ballads, lyrically heightened passages, and concrete poetry. This metaphorically enriched level of discourse, evoking, alternately, both the privately lyrical and the more objectively referential choric dimensions of character and event, remains throughout the trilogy in sharp contrast to the less malleable speech-acts of strictly institutionalized existence.

The intricate intermingling of these three verbal styles within the dynamics of Reaney's collage form is evident throughout the trilogy and is firmly established in the opening scene of *Sticks & Stones*. The play begins with the off-stage singing of the "Barley Corn Ballad," heard again at the end of each act, thus reinforcing, on one level, a ballad-world framework for the play. In *The St Nicholas Hotel*, a similarly popular and "folk" framework is provided by such songs as "Buffalo Gals," "Hector O'Hara's Jubilee Song," and "St. Patrick." In *Handcuffs*, such a world is evoked by means of a selection of popular Victorian parlour songs — as it had been in *Colours in the Dark* — such as "When You & I Were Young, Maggie" and "Grandfather's Clock." As Reaney observed, "The John Barleycorn song . . . ties the whole play together" (Letter to Keith Turnbull), a point reiterated by James S. Reaney when he wrote that the ballad "fades into the body of the play" and that the identification of the

Donnelly narrative with that of John Barleycorn, in terms of seasonal death and rebirth patterns, is made "explicit in several scenes" (63). To a degree, Reaney is using this ballad much as Arden uses "Johnie Armstrong" in *Armstrong's Last Goodnight* and O'Neill uses "Shenandoah" in *Mourning Becomes Electra* to evoke a world, as Yeats described it, "below the newspapers, politics, science" ("Contemporary" 42), in which a naturally passionate and vital expression seems possible and, at the same time, a more sophisticated, symbolic world wherein a "dance with metaphor" links the minute particulars with a larger design. As the singing fades, members of the chorus, employing the sound-making techniques developed in the workshops and previously incorporated into *Listen to the Wind*, imitate the "whistle of a deep forest bird — the peewee" (36). Upon entering a space rendered "natural" in terms of the purely theatricalist idiom of sound, Mrs. Donnelly and her son Will engage in the established questions and answers of the Catechism. This introduces a mode of discourse and a structural pattern drawn from liturgical sources that will also inform, like the ballad and popular song worlds, the various personal and social narratives of the trilogy:

> MRS DONNELLY. Which are the sacraments that can be received only once?
> WILL. The sacraments that can be received only once are Baptism, Confirmation, and Holy Orders.
> MRS DONNELLY. Now Will, why can Baptism, Confirmation, and Holy Orders be received only once?
> WILL. Baptism, Confirmation, and Holy Orders can be received only once because they imprint on the soul — a spiritual mark, called a character, which lasts forever. (*Sticks* 36–37)

As a refrain from the ballad is heard softly in the background, Mrs. Donnelly then brings into play the "speech-of-appearance" that, as dialect, is to become the dominant speech of the trilogy. This malleable dialect is confidently employed by Reaney as the medium of conversation, the voice of story-telling, and as the verbal embodiment of a generally lively, unrestrained metaphorical energy, capable, on occasion, of sliding into a more consciously "poetic" mode. It is also the voice of a geographical and historical elsewhere that speaks of an Ireland whose "last hill" was once crossed by the Donnellys with their firstborn, as they "saw the sea" and freedom (*St Nicholas*

Hotel 152). In the location and recreation of this speech of the place, Reaney was guided by his archival muse:

> Propelled by the magnetic names "Donnelly" and "Biddulph" I read all the Huron District and County archives from the beginning to 1863 when Biddulph Township leaves Huron County; I knew that I wanted to write a play about these people, but I wanted to get *inside* their world first and these hundreds of boxes filled with blue paper — it gets white about 1870 — were the keys to the state. Whoever filed away things in the Huron County Courthouse filed away everything, and I am eternally grateful to him since it enabled me to see not only the big stories and people . . . but also the little things that are really much more of what sometimes drives us mad or sane; the conditions of the privies in the various inns along the road that is now known as Highway Four — the way people phrased things: "Not a mit nor a whip has ever been lost at my tavern . . . ," the names of horses and dogs, the way people in North Easthope call a stallion a stud, but those in Biddulph call him an incomplete horse! My favourite Chattel Mortgage has to be that of the Buffalo, Brantford, and Goderich Railway which lists the names of its ten locomotives — Growler, Sparker, Temperst! Do you know that I could read Chancery records forever. . . . here you quite often get pictures of whole families talking at each other in a way that no history book ever thinks of showing you: one of my favourite lines from the trilogy — "It's not enough that we must starve, but we must freeze to death as well" — comes right out of a Chancery document. ("Souwesto Theatre" 15)

As a purely dramatic speech, Reaney's recreation of the "way people phrased things" is linked to the diction and rhythm of the ballads and is, perhaps, the nearest in Reaney's work to what he considered to be the Elizabethan ideal of talking "well in rhythm with lots of imagery" ("James Reaney" 145):

MRS DONNELLY.   Oh indeed it was justice and the Whitefeet rode around at night dressed up like ladies, mind you, so they couldn't be recognized. They made it hot for landlords and bailiffs. The trouble was they made it hot for everybody. Will, there was one family — the Sheas — they lived twenty miles off, they said no to the Whitefoot Society, no they wouldn't

give up the farm they'd just rented, and a good farm it was in
those hard times, just because the Whitefeet wanted nobody
ever to rent that farm at all to spite the landlord. So, no, says
the Sheas. Well, what the Whitefeet did to the Sheas one night
is so terrible I'm going to whisper it to you and don't ever talk
about it again. (*Sticks* 39)

.   .   .   .

MR DONNELLY. It was love at first sight. Shure Johnson's
stallion was mounting my one mare before I could stop him.
Would you have me break up a pair of true lovers? Would
you? And I had my back turned for the merest minute getting
the other mare's tail out of a thornbush. (41)

.   .   .   .

MRS DONNELLY. Uh, it's his tattletale mother is a fat woman
has to be raised in and out and onto her bed with a pulley. No
feet at all should be her name and his — the nofeet with all
the belly. She's got wind of something and the child has
overheard. Will, after this harvest, I'm telling you your father
will own this very ground we're standing on and shortly after
that we'll own to another heir, not our fifth boy, pray, but our
first girl may it please Heaven and when he owns the very
ground we stand on and the fields he has made, you'll see
they'll never drive us off. We won't be druv! (45)

The interconnecting images of defiance, land, harvest, nature, law,
economics, and oppressive confrontational tactics in these passages,
as elsewhere, testify to Patricia Ludwig's account of the dense text of
the trilogy in which "each phrase interconnects on many levels. We
have to learn to race with it, catch a breath with each comma, sing
with it, soar. . . . We have to open our ears; each word, each bell,
each throwing of a stone is a carefully placed effect in a collage of
created sound" (133).

As our ears are opened and we become accustomed to the rhythmic,
metaphorical, and sonic values of this speech, we readily recognize
the competing, generally less acceptable values of those speech-acts
that, in large measure, define the world within which the affairs of
commerce, law, politics, and institutionalized religion are conducted.
This world first enters the collage of sound through the Surveyor and
the Census Taker in this first scene of *Sticks & Stones*. As soon as we
hear the precise, dry utterance "Concession Six Lot Eighteen" (46),
we recognize the voice of a "printed rhetoric" — the other speech-

of-appearance Reaney uncovered in the "hundreds of boxes filled with blue paper." The physical action of "wild lands" being "cut into concessions," scenically represented through the Jacob's Ladders configurations, is reinforced by a verbal shift towards a less supple speech that closes the speaker's world ("The laws of geometry are the laws of geometry" [47]) and that of the world to which it is addressed. The established questions of the catechism are coldly parodied by those relating to the census and property:

Situation — lot?   Eighteen
Concession?   Six
Religion?   Church of Rome
Natives of Ireland in each family?   Three
Total number of persons resident in
the house when the Census is taken?   Four
Lands — Number of acres held by each
family?   One hundred
Uncultivated, of wood in wild land?   One hundred
Neat cattle   None
Horses   None
Hogs   Three
Proprietor or Non-Proprietor?   Non-Proprietor
Landlord   John Grace, carpenter, London Township
. . . .
MR DONNELLY. and it's my duty to Name the roads of
Biddulph!
Front Road Coursey Line Gulley Road Sauble Line
Revere Road Granton Line Swamp Road Roman Line
. . . .
Why are the roads here rather than here? Why do I live here
rather than here? Wild lands cut by surveyors into people —
with your chain you decided that it would be here, my farm
— that people say I squatted on Concession Six Lot Eighteen
(48)

At the beginning of Act III of *Sticks & Stones*, the connection between the two catechisms is made by Jennie:

No, I did not know it at the time but in those few months and years after my father returned from seven years in prison, we — the entire Donnelly family — mother, father, seven sons and one daughter — were up for confirmation in a church called the Roman Line. No, it was a bigger church than that for it involved Protestants too. We were going to be tested for confirmation in a church called — Biddulph. Most of the people liked us at the time. That doesn't matter though. Those with power did not. Our confirmation came up and although we had known our catechism well, we failed. (143)

Susanne Langer has described a process whereby one kind of language is superseded by another. Such a process is implied here in the Donnelly trilogy, as it had been earlier in some of the pedagogical sequences of *Colours in the Dark*. A conception of nature founded upon what Cassirer calls the symbolic forms informing mythic consciousness is weakened and re-articulated through the evolution of "discursive form." As "mythic thinking," she writes,

> determines the form of the language and then is supported and furthered by language, so the progressive articulation and sharpening of that supreme instrument ultimately breaks the mythic mold; the gradual perfection of *discursive form*, which is inherent in the syntax of language as metaphor is inherent in its vocabulary, slowly begets a new mode of thought, the "scientific consciousness," which supersedes the mythic, to greater or lesser extent, in the "common sense" of different persons and groups of persons. The shift is probably never complete, but to the degree that it is effected, metaphor is replaced by literal statement, and mythology gives way to science. (*Feeling* 189)

It is to just such a "discursive form" that Reaney's "printed rhetoric" belongs, and its introduction to the trilogy at this point signals the clash of scientific and mythic forms of consciousness, each with its way of "phrasing things," which, on one important level at least, informs the Donnelly story.

After the "Burning of house on barrel routine," the language of litigation is heard — Reaney's "shaky fading paper rope" leading us towards the apparent verbal intractability of the law's "environmental bubble" into which the Donnellys and their neighbours increasingly sink:

MALE VOICE. Whereas about midnight of Thursday the 19th day of October now last past, certain Barns the properties of

William Bell, Ephraim Taylor, and the Reverend Daniel A. Turner, Coloured Inhabitants of the Township of Biddulph in our Province of Canada were destroyed by fire.

STUB ET AL. And whereas there is reason to believe that the said fire was not caused by accident, but was the act of Incendiaries at present unknown. Now Know Ye, that a Reward of

MALE VOICE. 50 pounds will be paid to any person

FEMALE VOICE. Witness. Our right trusty and right well beloved Cousin Earl of Elgin and Kincardine and Governor General of British North America

A true copy. (51)

The full imprisoning power of this rhetoric is verbally and scenically established in the "Return of Conviction" sequence when the actors arrange themselves in three files to "say and illustrate the three columns" of Sticks, Stones, and Others. The company, Reaney says, should look "like an old document which suddenly bristles with stones that hurt as they come zinging through the air" (55). Verbally, the sequence moves towards a crescendo of slogans; scenically, the movement is towards a configuration that depicts a Protestant line facing a Roman line. The immediate theatrical effect is not unlike that of the game of politics played out by the inhabitants of Pat's lodging-house in Brendan Behan's *The Hostage*, which concludes with the sinister surrounding of Leslie by the various slogan-intoxicated Free-Staters, Republicans, English, and the like: "The train stops and the dancers are left in the position of forming a ring around Leslie which resembles a prison cage" (77). In the "Return of Convictions" sequence, however, the documentary world is not simply echoed in the verbal duel between the two sides, it is scenically represented, and as the sequence evolves the "old document" both inspires and *is* itself the riot.

Another world constructed of words, reinforced by a complex web of gestural and musical notation, is introduced in the Angelus sequence. The language here reiterates that of the opening Catechism and of the Confessional sequence between Cassleigh and the friar:

FRIAR. Angelus Domini nuntiavit Mariae
POPULUS. Et concepit de Spiritu Sancto. Ave Maria
FRIAR. Ecce ancilla Domini
POPULUS. Fiat mihi secundum verbum tuum. Ava Maria

FRIAR. And the word was made flesh.
POPULUS. And dwelt among us. Hail Mary.
FRIAR. Ora pro nobis, sancta Dei Genitrix. (*Sticks* 64)

In a letter to Turnbull, Reaney gave an account of the role of the Mass in the organization and verbal/gestural rhythms of *Sticks & Stones*:

> ... the play is about a man who refused to kneel. ... I suggest, too, that since the whole play is patterned on the Masses — the Mass for the Uninitiated being Act One, the Mass of the Faithful being Act Two that the liturgical gestures of the Mass should be put in wherever smooth and possible. Kissing the altar can become Jenny kissing her parent's coffin; the smoking and drinking at a wake — incensing and communion. The bowing, joining of hands is already in the play, as is the ringing thrice of a bell. You may want to indicate very clearly to the audience the divisions of the Mass even more than I've indicated. Kneeling and standing are the very theme of the play, of course. ... As I read through the play again I get three or four basic feelings. The Ceremony of the Mass enfolds almost all the time; we are constantly preparing a sacrifice — not Christ, but the Donnellys. The wretched half naked Jim Feeheley is 'elevated' to the sound of a cowbell rung by the Fat Woman.
>
> The First Act is also a Wake and one feels that the people there are praying that the dead people safely cross some land of the dead with bridges, groves, mountains. Then if Jennie can stay awake she can pray her mother and father into Heaven.
>
> The Second Act is almost filled with the Mass of the Initiated; it takes place in a Church. Act one took place in a house. At the end we are in a wheat field.

The Latin/English liturgical language is heard on many more occasions throughout the trilogy, usually as part of a collage of other dramatic languages and sounds. For example, in Act II of *Sticks & Stones*, we hear such refrains during the Christening scene for Jane Donnelly (121) and again during the Mass in Biddulph where "everyone is kneeling but it would be hard to tell when we saw Mrs. Donnelly kneeling" (131). In *The St Nicholas Hotel*, as Maggie is "remembering a world of power and love that might have been hers forever," we hear a Vespers service in the background (39), and in Act II we hear fragments of liturgical chanting as part of the speech/sound collage that reinforces the "photograph scene" where the Donnelly boys are seen within red glares suggestive of "Hell with a mob of farmers in front of them with sharp hayrakes" (88). A short time later, when William Donnelly and Norah Macdonald are married, we see and hear the "rite of our holy Mother the Church" (96), which is sharply juxtaposed with the refrains from "Boney over the Alps" as Will is taken off to jail and arranging to meet with Norah in ten days at Fitzhenry's Tavern (*St Nicholas* 97).

The liturgical dimension is especially important throughout *Handcuffs* as the action moves forward and backward through the multitudinous dreams and stories of living and dying in Biddulph. As a component of the verbal/sonic structure of *Handcuffs*, the Mass speaks of a sacrificial action through which a passage into paradise is made possible:

> May the angels take you into paradise
> in tuo adventu suscipiant te Martyres
> And lead you into the holy city of Jerusalem
> Chorus angelorum te suscipiat (157)

This redemptive action is reinforced by the following images of seasonally rooted restorative and procreative values as the chorus speaks of the growth, from March to August, of a "green field . . . ready for harvest" (157).

The liturgical dimension, however, also speaks of the far less procreative alliance of politics, commerce, and religion. In *Handcuffs*, this is accorded concrete theatricalization in the scenic/verbal/sonic image of the threshing machine, a purely technological image through which the metaphorical and mythic propensities of liturgical language are superseded, in Langer's terms, by scientific ones. The threshing machine sequence begins in St. Patrick's church where O'Halloran complains about his dealings with the Donnellys:

> O'HALLORAN. At night — someone takes out my horses —
> after we've gone to bed, father, and after we are sound asleep,
> and they ride those horses from one toll gate to another all
> night. But in the morning I find my horses back in my stables
> again — out of breath and nigh death.
> CHORUS. Domine, non sum dignus/ut intres sub tectume
> meum: / sed tantum dic verbo/ et sanabitur anima mea
>
> . . . .

O'HALLORAN. Father Connolly, this summer my big field of wheat ripened and was cut and bound and we stooked it and it stands there and it stands there yes because of the quarrel between us and two of the Donnelly family, the brothers John and Tom. Father Connolly, they have sworn that I will not thresh that grain. Must my grain rot in the field and must my granaries cobweb because so says Donnelly?

CHORUS. In thine infinite goodness, we beseech Thee, O Lord, to watch over Thy household, that even as it relies solely upon the hope of Thy heavenly grace, so it may ever be defended by Thy protection. Through our Lord. In nomine Patris et Filii, et Spiritus Sancti. Amen. Visited Donnelly (50–51)

A little later, following a quiet scene with the Donnellys ("How quiet it is on the line tonight, Mr. Donnelly. I can hear Bridget ironing handkerchiefs and you mending harness and Tom polishing it, but there's nothing else to hear"), the machine-liturgical alliance is reinforced:

Threshing machine slowly approaches with Priest intoning the following litany as the machine is elaborately cranked & set going by Curtin. This human threshing machine should behave with busybody solemnity led in by the cleric chanting from a small black book:
Holy Mary, *pray for us.*
Holy Mother of God,
Holy Virgin of virgins,
St. Michael,
Fades into O'Halloran's speech & under the noise of the machine
St. Gabriel,
O'HALLORAN. St. Raphael, We got it nearly all threshed. Well All ye holy Angels & Archangels, more than half way. And they stood All ye holy order of blessed on the road looking over at us with Spirit, broad grins. I guess they knew what St. John Baptist, was going to happen. One of the St. Joseph sheaves I was pitching in felt a bit All ye holy Patriarchs & Prophets heavy. By the name of God they had &c. hidden horseshoes and iron pins in the sheaves by the road and small stones that —
pray for us

.   .   .   .

*As the machine breaks down, Fr Connolly's face is blackened
by an inner explosion*
PRIEST. *pulpit* Things will be better in Biddulph. *Congregation kneels in front of him.* I do not care if I get a bullet through
my head, but they will get better. I propose to form a Peace
Society. I have stated the purpose here at the head of this
paper. . . . All those who do not sign I shall consider backslid-
ers, blacklegs and sympathizers with this gang of evildoers
and ruffians in our midst. Any of you who do not sign if they
take sick they may send for William Donnelly. Do not send
for Father John Connolly. As an indication of who is with me
and who is against me will those that intend signing — kneel.
*This leaves the Donnellys standing. They leave the church and
the paper is signed as in Part I with congregation intoning the
Roman Line names.* (60–62)

This image of the church as an important part of the social, political,
and economic machine bearing down upon a family "who refused
to kneel" deprives the liturgical speech of its mythic, restorative, and
reconciliatory values. It also reinforces the sense of a verbally sustained "environmental bubble" requiring of its inhabitants speech-
acts that coerce them, as Steiner remarked, to those propositions and
gestures "from which there is no return."

Reaney's "magic tongue," the alchemical magic of metaphorically
enriched speech, which, as we saw in *The Easter Egg, The Three
Desks, Listen to the Wind,* and *Colours in the Dark,* can release the
self from ordinary time and space and, we might add, from the
deadening constrictions of a "dull township," is, in the Donnelly
trilogy, *tragically* separated and expelled from the authoritative
"church called — Biddulph." The comedic structures of the earlier
plays, to which the power of ontologically creative art-acts (including certain kinds of speech-acts) is central, are replaced here by a
tragic one in which various kinds of printed rhetoric assert their
dominance as the authoritative speech of the place, isolating within
the Donnellys — and their poet story-teller — the mythic consciousness. Reaney's consciously "poetic" voice is heard throughout the
trilogy as an essential value located primarily within the life and
meaning of the Donnelly family. On one level, such a voice is itself
the protagonist, as it had been in *Colours in the Dark,* locked in fatal
conflict with other languages within the complex verbal collage. The

spectatorial interplay of "dramatic collage-languages," which Kennedy identifies as displacing the traditional notion of relatively "fixed" dramatic discourse (whether in prose or verse) is, in the Donnelly trilogy, more than a central structural feature. It becomes itself part of the central drama in which the "way people phrased things" or, in this instance, the mode of discourse that Reaney *chooses* to use for certain moments in the lives of the Donnellys is a direct measure of how some things are ultimately to be seen.

Some things — the working of the land, the sacrificial actions, the seasonal patterns, the family, the sense of home, the spiritual dimension of character — are to be seen through the eyes of a mythic consciousness expressed in a language that separates itself from that of the speech-of-appearance. The first indication of such a vision and speech in *Sticks & Stones* is in a brief reiteration of the catechism motif:

> *A priest interrupts the Donnellys.*
> PRIEST.   Who are punished in purgatory?
> MR & MRS DONNELLY.   Those are punished for a time in purgatory who die in state of grace but are guilty of venial sin or have not fully satisfied for the temporal punishment due to their sins.
> PRIEST.   Who are punished in Hell?
> MR DONNELLY.   Not I. No, not James Donnelly. I'm not in Hell though my friends in Biddulph thought to send me there, but after thirty-five years in Biddulph who would find Hell any bigger a fire than that fire I died in. I'm not in Hell for I'm in a play. (*Sticks* 49)

This sense of being in a play, that is, in part, the sense of existing somewhere (like the Deirdres of both Yeats and Synge) at the intersection of history and myth, caught in the double activity of living and telling one's story, is repeated in two important later scenes in *Sticks & Stones*. In the first, Mr. Donnelly establishes his relationship to the land:

> Because I loved my land so and stuck to it
> I killed and in turn you broke my bones, burnt my home
> Harvested me and my sons like sheaves and stood
> Us to die upon our ground
> Where now nothing will ever grow.

And this earth in my hand, the earth of my farm
That I fought for and was smashed and burnt for

CHORUS
kneeling
Confiteor Deo omnipotenti . . . beato Michaeli Archangelo.
Aufer a nobis quaesumus, Domine, iniquitates nostras.

MR DONNELLY
but kneeling on only one knee
Now my body belongs to its dust
Which dust once belonged to me.
As it is blown away, I forget
Concession Six Lot Eighteen
South Half or North Half which was mine?
    We are blown away and both lost *prayer stops*
        — — — — — Like actor's words. (71–72)

In the second, Mrs. Donnelly stands by the roadway, lamp in hand,
awaiting reunion with her husband, the completion of her story, and
the assimilation into myth:

Now I'll wait for him here by the gate with this lamp. Bring
sheaves with you when you've finished the field. Your father will
want to see what his farm's been doing, right away. I'll stand out
here with my lamp. You will come tonight. I know you will. I'll
hold this lamp until either its oil runs dry or you're home. I'll
stand here years after tonight — a seal in the air — long after
my house and my gate and my curtilage have become dust. A
lamp hanging in the air, held by a ghost lady. (136)

Earlier, a suggestion of Mrs. Donnelly's mythic dimension was given
in the sequence depicting her journey from Biddulph to Goderich:

MRS DONNELLY. At Irishtown the grain wagons were all
    going south
CHORUS. North she was going, north through their dust.
MRS DONNELLY. There at St. Peter's is he buried whom my
    husband killed.
CHORUS. His cold hands across reached the road and held
    back her feet.

MRS DONNELLY.   I dare not enter there to pray for his soul
CHORUS.   The chapel has no shadow. It is noon.
.   .   .   .
MRS DONNELLY.   Oak tree with your shadow Indian dark
CHORUS.   Lie and rest beneath my speaking saying leaves
MRS DONNELLY.   The whip of that carter touched my cheek
   I look like a beggar woman tramping the roads
CHORUS.   Clean white tower clouds walk in the sky
.   .   .   .
MRS DONNELLY.   Falling down down as I sleep till the earth
   wheels
CHORUS.   Down to the dawn whose tollgate opens to all
MRS DONNELLY.   I'll pray for the dawn with these winter stars
CHORUS.   In the chill dark starting out before there were
   proper shadows. (113–14)

The even and quiet antiphonal rhythms of this passage, and the
consciously poetic diction and imagery of all three selections, suggest
Reaney's deliberate choosing of an identifiable voice linguistically
separated from the others. This voice, throughout the trilogy, is one
that summons us, again and again, through our ears and through a
sense of the reverberations of significant poetic images (shadows, the
sky, the earth wheeling, winter stars, the lamp of the moon, bones,
the earth, dust, the dawn) to what is, ultimately, the imaginative and
mythic location of the Donnelly story. Such a mythic location, for
Reaney, means freedom. The final assimilation into myth is the only
way, as Mrs. Donnelly describes it, "straight ahead past this stupid
life and death" (*St Nicholas* 152). In Act III of *Handcuffs*, images of
this freedom are expressed as the ghosts of Mr. and Mrs. Donnelly
encounter a Youth, one of the "toughs from Grand Bend" living
nearly a century after the massacre, in our time, indifferent to the
intricate structures of myth and meaning contained within the
Donnelly story:

YOUTH.   Let me go, please let me go. Take the handcuffs off
   me.
MR DONNELLY.   Make up your mind what you want then, soft
   tough, is it too much when the curtain between you and us,
   between your life and our life, between life and death starts
   wavering and swaying and
MRS DONNELLY.   drawing back like a foreskin from the thigh

of demon lover Christ himself.

MR DONNELLY.   like the mighty eyelid of God the Father's eye,

MRS DONNELLY.   like the wind from the mouth of the Holy
Ghost that flutters her veil as she speaks

BOTH.   undo the handcuffs, Indeed! First unlock the handcuffs
in your mind that make you see us as

MR DONNELLY.   that fierce harridan

MRS DONNELLY.   that old barnburner!

BOTH.   We weren't like that/this! I take you my the hair down
into our grave and beyond where

MRS DONNELLY.   you'll be our son Tom

MR DONNELLY.   you'll see that

BOTH.   I was a child once, a spring
I became a river when my body united with his/hers
From that river came seven sons and one daughter
We were all right, they said, if you left us alone
But there was something about us that made people
Never able to leave us alone and we fought them
Until the river fell into the sea of Death and the Sun of Hell
Changed us into the fog outside this winter night
With our handcuffed boy —

& TOM
look we are everywhere
In the clouds, in the treebranch, in the puddle,
There. Here. In your fork. In your minds.
Your lungs are filled with us, we are the air you breathe.
(132–33)

The handcuffs are removed once the full story, inscribed in the
region's clouds, tree branches, air, roads, place-names, institutions,
is seen and understood. The Donnelly story, for Reaney, serves the
same symbolic function as the image of the swamp did in *The
Killdeer*, expected to draw the life of a community into the fearful
"damp sweet darkness" — the elsewhere — through the labyrinthine
structure that makes release possible (22).

The three principal modes of discourse in the trilogy — the
"speech-of-appearance" mainly rooted in dialect, the speech-acts
rooted in the verbal machinery of commerce, religion, and politics,
the poetic rooted in the variety of lyrical, choric, liturgical, and
popular ballad forms — are interleaved, as Ludwig commented, in
a complex "collage of created sound." The eclectic resources of

Reaney's dramaturgical and poetic *musée imaginaire* provide in these three plays an array of verbal and non-verbal arrangements, chords and single notes. The theatrical exploitation of a variety of such distinct languages, seen in Reaney's work from *Listen to the Wind* on, an exploitation that permits seemingly limitless permutations in different verbal keys, is a feature of much important modern and contemporary drama. Reaney's "magic tongue" was replenished by its various encounters with the "magnanimous milieu" of modernism and its distinctively confident functioning throughout the Donnelly trilogy testifies to a rare and mature knowledge of "how to play."

* * *

One late September night when windfalls were thudding sullenly down from the trees he'd brought across Lake Erie the century before, two thieves came with spades to rob his grave. No sooner had they touched the lid of Dr. Troyer's coffin when a great white bird swept down on them from the sky and drove them out of the orchard forever. The thieves were a man and a woman. After the white bird had finished its work, she perched on the topmost branch of the tallest apple tree and closed her eyes as also did a hawk who had watched from another tree in the nearby bush and a wild goose with certain black feathers nesting in the rushes at the edge of the flats. In the story of these two sleeping birds' lives, the white bird in another form had once taken the part, had once acted the role we have this night shown you. (*Baldoon* 104)

At the close of *Baldoon*, a choric-narrator situates the death of the inimitable "wizard-looking" Dr. Troyer within the context of the play's binding metaphor, ". . . ain't we all birds in our soulshapes?" In his final speech, before his voice fades into a scenic and sonic montage reprise of images — the church, mist, the river "flowing on bulrushes, treeloads, marsh sounds. A faraway bell" — Dr. Troyer explains,

Before we are born we fly about a sky and with their marriages their giving and taking in marriage they shoot us down beneath our ground which is their sky into cradle punts, into the marshes

of life ei ti ti, what a chob it has been this day, where we are each
a rush, some of us light up, some of us don't, and Death the
Huntsman lies waiting in his crib-flatboat, waiting to shoot us,
birds flying in his sky which is beneath the ground we walk on
and. . . . (103)

Baldoon explores the enriched spiritual, folkloric energy of Dr.
Troyer's life and vision in terms of its mysterious and joyful interleaving of life and death, spirit and matter, marshes and sky, and in
relationship to the inhibited, joyless, ultimately imprisoning world
of a narrow Presbyterianism weighted with the accumulated guilt of
undisclosed personal stories and a God who "abhors you" (72). In
this respect, the play is most reminiscent of *The Killdeer* with its
representations of various journeys through a defiled world of
violence and moral obtuseness. And, as in the earlier play, the bird
imagery is the most obvious conduit to an understanding of the way
through such a world — as it was, on occasion, in the Donnelly
trilogy — and Dr. Troyer, like his counterpart Dr. Ballad in *The
Killdeer*, is its prime explicator, the one who knows all the stories
and sees "the order of their tanglings" (*Killdeer* 84):

Ei yi yi. . . . What troubles them is chust what really troubles us
all — I explain and explain. What have I already become, some
sort of authority, people are calling me a witchfinder. . . . I see
the white bird I mustn' shoot till just before I die, and the brown
bird who is coming to see me yet, and the black bird I will go
back with them to see, and the two travellers some miles away
yet walking through he forest, but if I solve their problems, ach,
I'll chust be faced with the same problems the next week already.
The same thing. Chust the same thing all over again. (5)

The scenic reinforcement of this imagery unnecessarily encumbers
Reaney's play with an assortment of bird puppet figures. *Baldoon* is
a play in which Reaney's language-consciousness is much in evidence, and the superimposed scenic dimension diminishes some of
its effectiveness. The problems of an overindulged literary as well as
theatrical consciousness in *Baldoon* result in the play's formal
indeterminacy as the spectator's looking and listening is too indis-
criminately exercised.

In *Baldoon* Reaney examines aspects of the marshes of the Long
Point region of Lake St. Clair in terms of a number of entangled

stories that get told in an assortment of languages. As was the case in the Donnelly trilogy, the several dramatic voices are intended to disclose both the speech of the place and the speech of a "folklore phenomenon of both oral and literary dimensions" ("Topless Nightmares" 4). The primary voices of the plays derive largely from the re-creation of Pennsylvania Dutch represented by Dr. Troyer and the Scottish dialect represented by John McTavish. Through these, simply on the level of sound, something of the shaping of the area's linguistic heritage is suggested. These dialects are placed alongside the middle-American/Southwestern Ontario accents of most others in the large cast — the accents, for instance, of Jane McTavish when she relates her story of living with the Macphersons or of Mary Troyer, Mrs. Pharlan, or of the Chorus when it frequently shifts the verbal gear to a more obviously poetic level and recites, among other refrains, a version of Dr. Troyer's "What troubles them is chust what really troubles us all":

> What troubles them
> troubles us all
> It is something about
> the way we fall.
> It is something that
> we always knew
> Something that draws out
> those evils in you

This choric speech is presented at the very opening of *Baldoon* as we see Dr. Troyer playing marbles with his two grandchildren while the hawk puppet attacks the goose puppet's eggs: "hawk screams and goose hissings supplied by company who sit around the stage each with a bulrush in his/her hand" (3). In its first statement, the Chorus introduces the motif of hidden lives and evils that must be uncovered as the confrontation between Dr. Troyer and John McTavish begins to evolve, the witchcraft of the area casting its spell on McTavish and the Reverend McDorman travelling to meet Troyer:

> What troubles their journey
> troubles us all
> It is perhaps those demons
> towering so tall! (12)

Soon afterwards, the Chorus reiterates the religious level of the action (first established in the singing of Tunkard, Mennonite, and Shaker hymns when the Company entered the playing space) through an exchange with Dr. Troyer who answers his grandson's question "There's writing on the muslin bag, Groszdoddy."

> "INRI. What does that mean?"
> CHORUS. Jesus of Nazareth.
> DR TROYER. Take the bag already down to the lake and you
> will find inside an amulet.
> CHORUS. King of the Jews. . . . (13–14)

As the two men near the Troyer house, the Chorus reinforces the anticipatorial tension of the encounter:

> CHORUS. One step for two men.
> DR TROYER. *hammering the horseshoe* From the creek once
> to this door
> CHORUS. two steps for two men,
> DR TROYER. is twenty-one steps, but the last two rods to the
> house where
> CHORUS. three steps for two men
> DR TROYER. you will be safe from witches following you is a
> flint mount-
> CHORUS. four steps for two men
> DR TROYER. tain pecked at once a year by a white bird. Ei yi
> yi the flint (15)

At times the choric role is to serve as witness to the strange events leading McTavish and McDorman into the Tunkard Mennonite world of Dr. Troyer. On other occasions, it asserts both a spiritual dimension within which the exploration of mysteries and lives ultimately occurs and, more particularly, verbally and musically establishes the historically documented voices of competing religious sects in nineteenth-century Ontario. For instance, the hymns sung at the very opening of the play, as the "skeletal" representation of Dr. Troyer's house is scenically established, are to suggest "a great feeling of bells, wind instruments — joy in God, the easy attainment of His light, joy in His creation" (3). This, we're told, is to be in "contrast with the more austere, bleak music of the Presbyterian Psalm book which we'll use at the beginning of Act Two" (1).

In Act II, one of the most important sequences is that of a "Sabbath Church Meeting," for which Reaney supplies textual notes indicating sources in Ralph Connor's *Man from Glengarry* (61). Here the choric voice is that of a congregation reciting parts of Psalms and the commandments as Reverend McGillicuddy delivers a "far more private prayer" (65). The cacophonous intermingling of the different tones and voices, the juxtaposition of communal and private worlds, and the intrusion during the service of the bird puppets that fly about attacking the congregation create a theatrical impression of disarray. This is a community fractured by fear and uncertainty as it cowers under the threatening admonitions of McGillicuddy's repressive religiosity: "The God that holds you over the pit of hell, much as one holds a spider or some loathsome insect over the fire, abhors you" (72). In opposition to this, Dr. Troyer laughingly asserts,

> Yes, God does hold you over a pit — a valley, an abyss of happiness filled with frankincense and citrons and dancing and music and love — he hangs you by the slenderest chust thinnest filmiest flimsiest cobweb thread ever seen yet and — you spiders — you won't let go, you won't let go. (73)

What "troubles us" is, indeed, "something about the way we fall," poised, as we are, either above a "pit of hell," or an "abyss of happiness."

Throughout such passages, there are numerous indicators of Reaney's archival muse delivering over to him the languages, prayers, sermons, exhortations, hymns, and songs with which to differentiate linguistically between these two ways of falling. In their own way, such differentiated languages, like, for instance, the scenic devices and the different dances used in *Wacousta!*, function as blazons through which the Manichean structure of Reaney's vision is represented. Once again, as we have seen in the plays since *Listen to the Wind*, Reaney chooses from an assortment of ready-made, archivally available languages those that can best embody different worlds, which are, on one important level, worlds "constructed out of words."

"Although the exact religion practiced by Dr. Troyer is unknown," writes Reaney,

> It is clear that he was attached to one of the left-wing offshoots of the Puritan movement — the Quakers, Shakers and Tunkards

— whose followers escaped religious persecution in Europe by settling in the New World. The focus in these sects is on the simplicity, virtue and peace which can, does and should exist in this world. Their adherents are filled with joy by their relation to the benevolent God, and they are happy in the fellowship of mankind. . . . There is evil in this world but one must not be led into so strong a preoccupation with it that one is blind to the presence of good. (*Baldoon* 115)

"How can you grab hold of light with arms of dark!" (59). Madam Fay's admonition towards the close of *The Killdeer* remains of central importance in Reaney's exploration of early nineteenth-century Ontario religious life. The imagery and the "lilting tones" (*Baldoon* 114) of Troyer, then, are intended to assert the presence of joy, of possibility in the world. Into this strange figure, with his appetite for love and change (Reaney's affinity with the "left-wing" aspect of Protestantism is clearly part of his sympathetic portrayal of Troyer) and his metaphorically charged speech, Reaney places those values he expressed earlier in such figures as Dr. Ballad, whose confrontation with Manatee is also, like that between Troyer and the Reverend McGillicuddy, concerned with "the way we fall."

Troyer's speech is intended to reflect this spirit. Jesus, he explains, was not

ashamed to be seen a naked wretch upon the cross. . . . No, like a young warrior, he stripped to climb the seige ladder his Father and He placed against the walls of the Heart of Man, the proud secret Heart of Stone in which the great white bird of all our souls lies trapped forever and forever until this Young Man dared not be ashamed of His being called naked — wretch — blasphemer — fool — (58)

McTavish is exhorted to "come clean," failing which, ". . . no matter where you trek with your flocks and herds, the strange bird with the black feathers will always show up yet in your yard. John, face to face. Chump into the river you've walked along the wrong bank all your life. Chump!" (93). Sacramental imagery is woven into the story of Baldoon earlier in the play. During McIntosh's first encounter with Troyer, a foot-washing ceremony occurs as the Chorus exclaims,

Our Lord when He was here below
washed His disciples feet we know,

and then in language clear & meet
bades us to wash each other's feet. (21)

"Every thing can be with gude common sense explained," asserts
McIntosh. "I know my catechism and my purse is fu' o' siller."
However, Reverend McDorman warns McIntosh to

tell all to Dr. Troyer and his daughter. You know when we've
prayed together in the forest, how slow your words come and
how unwilling you are to admit anything wrong about yourself.
(24)

McIntosh's world here, as well as that represented later by the
Reverend McGillicuddy, is verbally inflexible. Just as the words and
images of Troyer's living faith open his world to endless delight and
provide the restorative values that result from the falling into the
"abyss of happiness," those of McGillicuddy's set prayers and
Readings of the Word claim the world for a "righteous sentence of
condemnation and death" (69).

"Since we were adapting a novel," Reaney writes, "everyone had
to own a copy and read it over and over again; had to underline the
parts that seemed live and dramatic. These underlinings of dialogue,
character and scene description were the basis of a script"
(*Wacousta!* 111). In *Wacousta!* and *The Canadian Brothers*, Reaney
again uses language to differentiate between kinds of worlds, scenically represented, in part, by the pictographs of the lion and the
shaman. Another level of linguistic differentiation, however, results
from the conscious raiding of the language of the novels by John
Richardson during the "basic adaptive sculpturing process"
(*Wacousta!* 112). Such an adaptive process, to some extent first seen
in Reaney's use of Emily Brontë's *Gondal Chronicle* and Rider
Haggard's *Dawn* in *Listen to the Wind*, brings the novels into service
as palimpsests on the level of language as well as on the obvious levels
of theme and narrative.

In *Listen to the Wind*, the heightened rhetoric of the melodramatic
play within the play demanded of the actors, during the actual
performance of the work, a deliberate shifting of the verbal gears
intended, on one level, to simulate the action of children putting on
plays and, on another level, to effect a linguistic differentiation
between "ordinary" and imaginative experience. In *Wacousta!* and
The Canadian Brothers, however, as Reaney's comments on the

preparatory exercises make clear, the creative process of immersion in another language, another world of words, is undertaken *outside* of the actual play during the workshop/rehearsal period. The workshop space itself becomes, for the actors reading Richardson, learning and then playing with his language, analogous to the imagining and creating space of Owen's West Room in *Listen to the Wind* where the four children, having, presumably, already learned the language of the melodramatic *Saga of Caresfoot Court*, decide to draw Owen's mother home by putting on a play. In *Listen to the Wind*, we are witnesses to the actual sculpturing process as the children verbally create the melodramatic dimension. In *Wacousta!* and *The Canadian Brothers*, the sculpturing must already have occurred; it is not itself a significant feature of the play's representational idiom. It is, instead, completely subsumed in the playwriting process. As a result, we respond somewhat differently to the melodramatic dimension, particularly to its language. In *Listen to the Wind*, Reaney's enthusiasm for, and his ontological expectations of the extravagance of melodramatic utterance, are themselves dramatized; obvious verbal self-consciousness is made to be part of the play through the verbal playing of the four children as they interleave the melodramatic story with their own. In the latter plays, however, such a degree of verbal consciousness has been worked through during the workshop sessions, and the actors are ready with a language rather than "playing" with different languages before us. What they are ready with is, as Reaney observed, a partly adapted language traceable, from the perspective of the audience, not to the act of verbal playing, but, rather, to those who already know this, or, more likely, are told in the programme notes, to Richardson's prose and to the literary tradition to which it belongs. Without this knowledge, there is the danger that the stilted and dramatically awkward language of much of the plays will be traced simply to bad writing, the audience remaining largely unaware of Reaney's more sophisticated adaptive intentions.

However, as Reaney observed in his *Halloween* letter that discussed adapting Richardson, "We can't have a theatre with any depth to it until we get some sort of literary and historical programme going" ("Topless Nightmares" 8). Therefore, the workshops that culminated in the production of *Wacousta!* in 1978 included as much reading as they did playing. A potential audience was also prepared through direct instruction. While teaching *Wacousta!* at the University of Western Ontario, Reaney had his students perform parts of a nineteenth-century melodrama based upon the events of Richardson's novels, called *Wacousta the Renegade; or the Siege of Detroit*, which had been produced in London in 1856. "If it had been done here once," Reaney observed, "it could be done again and I promised myself the pleasure of tracking down this dramatic adaptation some day to see how on earth anybody had been able to pour what I remembered as a huge panoramic Gothic romance into just one evening at the Theatre Royal on our Market Square here in London, Ontario" (*Wacousta!* 7). The text was tracked down and published in *Black Moss*, a John Richardson Conference was held at Western featuring papers on a variety of editorial and other issues (Ross), and, with a series of workshops that involved the students, some of Reaney's colleagues, and members of the general community, a "huge, modern, crazy adaptation of the book" was "hammered out" (*Wacousta!* 8). The danger of an audience missing something of the complicated adaptive process was at least minimized in London: "When, eventually in 1978, the final professional version of *Wacousta!* arrived in London, Ontario, it played to a packed and knowledgeable house" (*Wacousta!* 8).

Observing this phenomenon from a slightly different perspective, we can recall Eliot attempting, self-consciously, to write and to legitimize critically dramatic verse in the absence of a living tradition of plays in verse. One has the impression, as Kennedy observed with reference to Eliot and Arden, of the dramatist being "outside" rather than within his verbal medium, "reframing this or that language, a subtle practitioner of parody and pastiche, a linguistically conscious ventriloquist" (3). Reaney's use of melodramatic utterance, in this respect, is analogous to Eliot's "reframing" of liturgical speech in *Murder in the Cathedral*. The ostensibly "knowledgeable" houses for both playwrights, one presumes, would not anticipate a dramatic representation of their own language "as it is actually spoken" (Eliot, "Social Function" 22), but are, instead, prepared to hear and accept the heightened cadences, imagery, and hyperbolic features of either liturgy or melodrama. And, just as a study of Eliot's dramatic verse would disclose further classical, mediaeval, and Elizabethan literary and dramatic sources, so would the study of Richardson's novels remind the reader that much of his language is itself a complex set of verbal refractions of the prose and verse of such writers as James Fenimore Cooper, Milton, Shakespeare, Scott, and Edward Young, whose popular play *The Revenge* provided Richardson with images of the "fix'd and noble mind" that makes "vengeance of calamity," along with images of racial conflict.[3] That Reaney discovered such a "fix'd and noble mind" in the "giant dream figure" ("Topless Nightmares" 3) of Wacousta is made clear again and again in his comments on Richardson's work. He also makes clear his liking for melodramatic structures with their

> extremes and blacks and whites . . . fiction . . . that is more like a myth than it is like villains and fair damsels. E.A. Poe goes in for the same kind of polarized visions — a guitarist-poet who has buried his twin sister alive, a beautiful woman destroyed by the ghost of another, a treasure reached through a skull, and there seems to be something about the Industrial Revolution that breeds these Gothic this/that stories: all the rationality of progress only expels Orc, desire, fancy, love to have it come back one foot higher and ravening for your bank account guts. ("Topless Nightmares" 7)

Much of the language of Reaney's dramatic adaptation, is designed to embody such a world of extremes. The surface of experience is pressed to disclose something of the unequivocal polarities of a "this/that" dimension with its melodramatically encoded and, for the audience, largely spectatorial speech-acts.

Such a note is struck at the beginning of *Wacousta!* as de Haldimar emerges from the shadows wherein Wacousta's first act of sabotage occurred exclaiming,

> Treason! Which way did he go? . . . there are traitors in the fort — an intruder. There he is! Bring him here! . . . . Have you escaped all of us then, dissolving now into the bush and night from which you came? How, since last I saw you, how giant and distorted you have grown. (11)

When a scene is established for the court martial of Frank Halloway who had been in charge of the gate, his wife Ellen exclaims, in the cadences last heard in the melodramatic sequences of *Listen to the Wind* and the medicine show *Black Donnellys* in *Sticks & Stones*:

> Cruel man, governor of our lives and deaths, for once be merciful. Since the siege began one hundred days ago I've watched you shoot a man a week because he couldn't obey all of your innumerable regulations. You shoot them to encourage

the others, don't you? By Heaven and earth, if you have a heart and not a grindstone, believe what my husband says. If not — shoot him — and then I shall curse you. (14)

After Halloway's execution, Ellen's cry evokes the rhetorical extravagance of an all-encompassing obsession with revenge, an obsession which, as in many of the works in the long tradition of revenge drama and literature to which such a rhetoric belongs, embodies apocalyptic impulses:

> Inhuman murderer! If there be a God of justice — avenge . . . .
> "One day, gentlemen," you over there said, "because my gates were sealed shut with the blood of traitors, this fort will grow into a great city." May it do so and — as I have seen perish before my eyes all that I loved on earth with no mercy, no hope. Yes! Your children's blood shall wash away the blood of my husband and your city shall fall into ruins, trees grow again where I am standing, trees through your eyes — through your children's ribcages! (47)

Wacousta's revenge is clothed/"armoured" with the same melodramatic verbal values:

> You loiter too long outside your father's gate, Frederick de Haldimar — whistling that, of all tunes, grates most damnably on my ears. Do you wonder now whose large hands look up your mouth? Tell your mother's ghost it was the hands of Wacousta whose revenge tears off this trophy *scalps him with one slice of his hunting knife* Keys. Why I shall visit your father with double proof that half way across the world my hatred pursues him like his shadow. (33)

> But have you been able to destroy these places? Use my hatred for them. Fallen suddenly from the sky, Pontiac, I am like a sharp flint star in your path. If you can, hurl me against them. (40)

Throughout the play, such verbal explicitness defines and regulates the structures of thought and feeling. This is a language that has been grafted onto the company of actors before us with their bloody tale of betrayal and revenge. This is the language with which the actors, following the lengthy workshop/rehearsal process, are ready. Language is, in this respect, quite deliberately, *ergon* rather than *energeia*. Its potential as *energeia*, however, is sometimes realized when phrases from the novel are directly incorporated into a complex *poésie de théâtre*, as Reaney explains in an account of one of the workshops:

> . . . you want to show the scene where Oucanasta leads Frederick through the forest to the hollow tree at Pontiac's encampment. With eighty people in a circle holding lengths of green yarn across the circle, visually you could create the scene. Now add forty people murmuring Cree words to do with forests and forty people in a prearranged pattern murmuring the phrases below taken from the novel:
>
> 1. closely matted branches
> 2. down, down, down,
> 3. a narrow stream, a single bound
> 4. narrow winding path
> 5. dim and lurid atmosphere
>
> These forty people are broken up into five groups. Each group receives a card as part of a list at the opening of the workshop, which can be shaded and nuanced by animators in their midst. The result is a textured forest in sound. . . . (111)

When such phrases are subsumed in this way into the accompanying intertextuality of scenic and sonic images, then the words lose much of their explicitly descriptive and narrative value, not to mention their almost indelible literary aura, and become increasingly incantatorial — just as words were often pressed to become in the theory and theatre of Artaud, in Eliot's choric exercise *The Rock*, and in many of the choric evocations of Brontë's *Gondal Chronicle* in Reaney's *Listen to the Wind*. An example of this can be found in a scene recalled by Ellen involving Clara and Wacousta/Morton:

ELLEN.
Morton lowers Clara slowly in a rope net So you tried to bring her into our world. For the last time the silver bugle was blown and for the last time — the silver bell rung. . . . but the child of nature had now irrevocably entered the world — our world — shadows, choices —

this way,
that way.
My husband alive, my husband dead.
CHORAL VOICES.
    Bold and precipitous crags. Chasms.
    Lowering fathom after fathom of rope
    Hung over the . . .
ALL.
    The abyss.
CHORAL VOICES.
    The ridge sharp as a knife
    nothing
    Glens and rocks (85)

As Reaney observed in his account of the workshop sculpturing of a "textured forest in sound," the native world of the Cree is evoked through language as well (there are a few passages written in Cree). This world of words and of sounds (those of drums and of the forest) stands in opposition to the language and music of the British. There are numerous verbal and sonic counterparts to the scenically emblazoned pictographs of the lion and the shaman. In a scene between Charlotte and Le Subtil, "the afternoon of a day when we told each other our entire lives' mornings" (21), the two pictographs signifying the different worlds to which different languages belong are explained. Having, in Montreal, "learnt bells and prayers, nouns and adjectives, and a new French name," Le Subtil is now instructed in English as Charlotte identifies for him the dandelion as the "dent-du-lion" and names the various parts of the heraldic lion: "The back, the side, the neck, the rose, the belly. . . ." Ellen, who is recalling this scene, continues the recitation,

the nut, the strings. Then you asked him to teach you his language, for you were heartsick of the language we speak in our civil society. The so-called wise prefer gazing at the cruel stars that teach them to invent new machines of destruction and at the same time trample tiny flowers whose fragrance might teach you the way back to Eden. (22)

Charlotte then learns the Cree words for "the chequered shade" ("agoowastew"), "tree bole" ("mistik"), "a birch tree" ("waskuay"), "the earth" ("uskes"), and "radiance, light"

266

("wasteo") (22). Words function here as they did for Kenneth in *The Easter Egg* when he was instructed by Polly and led towards his "birth." They possess the potential, like the fragrance of the flowers, to lead "the way back to Eden." Words are still, as they generally were for Reaney's maturing children in the earlier plays, a major part of the "gateway to a new world" (Cassirer 132), a "magic tongue" with talismanic properties.

A number of the workshops having to do with the Native material were conducted by Tomson Highway. For several hours, participants reported, the workshops were given over to trying to "adapt Cree words to a kind of 'lacrosse night in Canada' usage" (*Wacousta!* 141). Into a variety of choric sequences, Cree words fused with forest sounds express the sympathetic instincts of Reaney. He clearly sides with those who were ultimately dispossessed, those led by the vengeful Wacousta seeking justice they believe denied them by the British. Pontiac reiterates the association between the natural world and the Natives that is firmly established in the imagery of the play as he prophesizes to de Haldimar the ultimate victory for his commonwealth following the battle at Michilimackinac:

... within this many moons ... the deer will once more browse where this council room now stands and men will ask which side of the river your castle stood. The grass, the deer, the river are my brothers and sisters and they will rejoice with me when the heartless strangers with their clumsy shoes no longer stumble through their delicate feelings.

Pontiac, however, is betrayed, and the edenic verbal imagery of this speech is ironically undercut through juxtaposition with a scenic image of toy friction cars swarming over the stage, and a "giant Pontiac stands exactly where the Renaissance Building stands now in Detroit with modern traffic swirling about his feet" (*Wacousta!* 61). In performance, however, the moment seems trivialized by Reaney's toy dimension; the theatrical collage of language, sound, and picture in this instance is cluttered, the perfectly obvious irony informing Pontiac's prophecy heavy-handedly signalled.

Wacousta!, then, is a play in which one language is chiefly regulated by that of the novel, its phrases, imagery, melodramatic exuberance, its fundamentally literary values, setting the dominant mode of speech for most of the characters. Reaney made a deliberate creative choice to have Richardson's novel serve and be recognized as serving, in this manner, as a palimpsest for Reaney's own verbal and theatricalist inscriptions. The obvious stilted quality of so much of the dialogue is meant to encode what Reaney considers, still, to be genuinely vital properties of melodramatic utterance. We are, presumably, intended not to be concerned sometimes, perhaps painfully, that this or that passage is over-written, or emotionally unconvincing. Nor are we expected to assume a questioning and critical posture towards such utterance, recognizing a possible parodic intention, as, for instance, we are often expected to in Reaney's use of some documentary material in *Colours in the Dark*, the Donnelly trilogy, and *Baldoon*. Instead, we should be sufficiently language conscious, having, ideally, profited from "some sort of literary and historical programme," to appreciate the conventions of a melodramatic verbal underpinning as, in their own way, "paper ropes," or in part, perhaps, "sound ropes" to our past. The past in this instance is the historical past of the Native/British and the British/American conflicts that were, for Reaney, so lucidly "this/that" in their arrangements of racial, social, and political experience (especially in Southern Ontario) and a past that saw the creative reframing of such experience in the fiction of one of Reaney's important signifiers. A major part of what Richardson's work signified, for Reaney, was the role of a "tyrannical" imagination, "the feelings for the terrible and the sublime" in "conjunction with tenderness, woman, Beulah, beauty" ("Topless Nightmares" 6). The language of such an imagination is, perhaps inevitably, given what Reaney so often perceives as a spiritually cheapened and artificial industrial environment, essentially spectatorial and not participatorial. Therefore, like Reaney himself, we remain, in Kennedy's term, "outside" of the verbal medium (3), especially a verbal medium so insistently unlike that of our impoverished, technologically homogenized speech, the language, as Ellen said, ". . . we speak in our civil society."

Such a situation for the poet-dramatist was not so evident in the writing of the Donnelly trilogy where the interrelatedness of history, story, and story-style was founded upon the existence of real models that embodied in a variety of ways the speech of the place. Reaney, we recall, met families in Winnipeg whose ancestors had come from Biddulph Township and relished the creative opportunity this gave him as ". . . the verbal universe dissolves into human figures and faces telling me things that enable me to go back into the patterns I am weaving in the world of words and adjust here, shade more there" (*14 Barrels* 42). Adjusting and shading of this nature enhances the impressions of a felt life, informing language, character, and action. In the case of *Wacousta!*, on the other hand, such experiential referentiality is impossible. The novel is the primary "verbal universe" to which Reaney and his actors have chosen to have recourse. What are, in effect, verbal constructs or speech-acts called Wacousta, Pontiac, Ellen, and de Haldimar never dissolve into human figures and faces. Nor, given the particular sculpturing process recommended by Reaney to begin with, one that demanded reading the novel "over and over again," were they ever really intended to. Following the workshops, productions, and the touring of *Wacousta!*, Reaney's director Keith Turnbull remarked that he

would like to take on something like *Canadian Brothers*, and maybe as a community event where you stage it at Niagara-on-the-Lake and *use* the fort that's there and the army, I mean actually do *that* size of production. ("Interview" 159)

Such an ambitious scheme did not materialize, and the quiet of Niagara-on-the-Lake was not churned up in any such way. (It is interesting to speculate, however, given the uncertain, excessively complicated narrative, scenic, and verbal currents that criss-cross, what such a community event, with echoes, perhaps, of the environmental productions of the Indian Forest Theatre at Oshweken, would have been like. A similar scheme was, in fact, followed through a few years later at the 1989 Chichester Festival, where Patrick Garland produced an adaptation of Thomas Hardy's *The Dynasts* with the people of Wessex in a variety of indoor and outdoor acting spaces, including the streets.)

The informing emblematic spirit of *The Canadian Brothers*, expressed through an assortment of scenic devices and arrangements including toys, effigies, and shadowy apparitions intended to signify this or that historical or imaginative character, place, and dimension, results in an even greater diminution of a felt life and, in its place, a perplexing, unrelenting assault of the "whole carnal sterography." To a greater degree than in *Wacousta!*, language appears to be an essentially non-mimetic vehicle for the provision of awkward expositorial captions for scenic tableaus, audience-directed narrative, and what is for the most part a "costume speech" (Kennedy 32) for characters *speaking* and posturing their way through a multi-layered labyrinth of history/story/myth. In *The Canadian Brothers*, to a large extent, the explicitly heightened *visual* vocabulary of nineteenth-century melodrama, film, and what Reaney considers to be salient scenic features of Japanese Kabuki theatre are the "basis of a script" around which events in the War of 1812 and the bizarre entanglements fifty years after Wacousta's prophecy are arranged and to which language is subservient. There are stylistic tensions between word and non-word in this work, which remain unresolved, and Reaney's language generally lacks the extraordinarily supple values it had in the Donnelly trilogy where words gave expression to so many of the informing layers of fact and myth. Nor does the "old language" of the novel as adapted in *The Canadian Brothers* seem to carry the potentially interesting stylistic referentiality that deliberately evokes the melodramatic dimension to which Reaney has insistently attached his muse. One senses very few of the verbal reverberations that, on occasion, accorded *Wacousta!* such a level of meaning.

In *The Canadian Brothers*, the descendants of Wacousta and Ellen (Jeremiah Desborough, his son Phil, and daughter Matilda) and Colonel de Haldimar (Isabella Grantham and her two sons Gerald and Henry) are haunted and entrapped by a curse, by the conflict between a king and an emperor, by geography ("a border river in the centre of a continent"), and, as Henry exclaims, "a paper sky above" through the ink of which the author is momentarily "glimpsed" (679). In a sense, this paper sky suggests the "idea of pure story" to which Reaney once attributed the shamanistic power of a "Mask that controls all other masks" ("Letter from James Reaney" 5). Thus, when Henry and Gerald, conscious of their entrapment, chorically shout "Change the story" (679), they are appealing directly to the mask behind the other masks "whose subject was itself" ("Letter from James Reaney" 5). The story of *The Canadian Brothers* is an uneasy fusion of historical, fictional, and mythical events and structures. It is also, even more uneasily so, a fusion of Richardson's and Reaney's readings of these events and structures that are cast in a variety of verbal and scenic possibilities. As Hayden White observes, historical narratives point "in two directions simultaneously: toward the events described in the narrative and toward the story type or mythos which the historian has chosen to serve as the icon of the structure of the events." There is, then, a creative mediation necessary between the events themselves and "pregeneric plot structures conventionally used in our culture to endow unfamiliar events and situations with meanings . . ." (287). The fact that there are various possible ways of telling the story, of taking the listener/watcher through the multidimensional patterns of event and meaning resulting from the reframing of the novel, seems more apparent in this play than in *Wacousta!*. The uncertain theatrical exploitation of these *formal* possibilities leads to an aesthetic incoherence characterized in part by the indiscriminate recycling of, by now, familiar Reaney *trucs*. In other words, the mediation between event and mythos, attempting to follow too many different routes, is unsuccessfully realized in theatrical, including verbal, terms.

The language of *The Canadian Brothers* does not resonate with the nuances of the "meeting of human experience with . . . myth, ritual and ceremony" (*14 Barrels* 160). The primary experience in this play is literary. It is also self-consciously and affectedly mythopoeic. Aldous Huxley once remarked that ". . . a talent for manipulating symbols tempts its possessors into habitual symbol manipulation, and habitual symbol manipulation is an obstacle in the way of concrete experiencing" (216). The manipulation of word and non-word to express the complications of the stories of Gerald, Henry, Matilda, and others (including, of course, some of the major military and political figures of the War of 1812) in terms of possible symbolic referents is too transparently contrived. This results in an ordering of words and scenes that is imposed from outside by an author, really, of course, by two authors, whose paper skies lie, at times conspicuously, beneath yet another paper sky inscribed by Homer, Shakespeare, and Milton.

I wouldn't have bothered behaving like Satan jogging across Chaos — O'er bog or steep, through strait, rough, dense, or rare, With head, hands, wings, or feet pursues his way, And swims, or sinks, or wades, or creeps, or flies. . . . (682)

Deuced sorry, Grantham — I was all set to apologize and call off the duel when — rather like the harpies in Aeneid Book One. (692)

What a strange seal to use — Achilles dragging the corpse of Hector around the battlements of Troy at the tail of his chariot. Around and around and around. (700)

GERALD.   Which way I fly is Matilda; myself am Matilda
And in the lowest deep a lower deep

       Still threatening to devour me opens wide.
       To which the Matilda I suffer seems a heav'n
MATILDA. Or then at last relent: is there no place
       Left for Repentance, none for Pardon left?
Gerald, I know John Milton's *Paradise Lost* in more correct
edition than you do. For the speaker continues:
       None left but by submission; and that word
       Disdain forbids me. (718)

These and other such verbal evocations of the learned kind do not
spring from character or situation. They can only serve to suggest
poetic analogues in which language, character, and action are much
more evidently in harmony than they are here, other examples of
successful mediations between event and mythos. Yet there is no sign
that Reaney is invoking such echoes with ironic or parodic intent —
although Matilda's pedantic display comes close. One is reminded
of some of the inflated rhetoric and imagery of Eugene O'Neill when
he sought various kinds of classical reinforcement for his explorations of American life. One is reminded of the disjunction between
word and character/action that characterizes so many eighteenth-
and nineteenth-century tragedies where a language of heightened
intensity is imposed, as a sort of verbal adornment, upon the
essentially domestic and ordinary.

The Dismissal is, in large part, a play about the emancipating and
clarifying properties of language and metaphor. Professor William
Dale's protest against a cultural rape by "teachers who couldn't get
a job in Britain or the States" takes the final form of a plea on behalf
of "ink, pen words" (38). What matters most to Dale is language.
His language, however, is one in which the imagination has cut
through the seemingly impenetrable shield of "things." It is a language in which metaphor is perceived, as it was in *The Easter Egg*
and *Colours in the Dark*, as a power capable of releasing the Self
from a sullied, "fractional" existence: through reading Virgil, Dale
observes, "I finally understand my father and his life" (19).

From the play's concluding scenic arrangement, Dale emerges
holding a copy of Livy's *History of Rome*, and Tucker comes forward
reciting a poem he had written from "exile" in California in which
but "one white December blast" of a Canadian winter possesses a
greater claim on his heart than "all these valleys, verdant, vast" of
Santa Clara Valley under its "languid sky." After a glee club rendition
of the "Envoy" (selected from the University of Toronto *Songbook*),

"Books fly joyfully up in the air and are caught and cradled to be thrown up once more" (55).

The political and "moral" machinations of the young William Lyon Mackenzie King constitute a major part of *The Dismissal*, and, with these, we come to associate the crippling effects of the "fractional" and the manipulation of language as a means of acquiring power. King's Diary entry for 16 February 1895 reads:

> At 12 Max brought the news that Professor Dale has been dismissed & Hellems resigned. I was that excited that I could not keep still, my blood fairly boiled. I scarcely ate any lunch, hurried up to the college, called on Professor Dale, DeLury & others, went to see Tucker. At 3 was held the largest mass meeting I have ever seen, in Wardell's hall, Spadina Ave. I moved the resolution "to strike" until we were granted an investigation. Carried unanimously (except 4). The meeting was very enthusiastic. (qtd. in Dawson 34)

Another resolution passed at this meeting stated that the strike would continue until there was a reconsideration of Dale's dismissal or until a thorough investigation was made. Such a motion was considered to be a compromise manufactured by King: "Jim, I wonder if we shouldn't check over your motion. *Tucker gives him a paper.* I wonder if. . . . *He has a pen*" (*Dismissal* 42). During one of the play's inquisitorial sequences, King's mouth is tied shut with a blindfold, "for already his slippery persuasive tongue is notorious in our infernal halls" (21).

The Willie King of this play is equivocating and manipulative from the very beginning when, with James Tucker, he arrived in Toronto. The King-Tucker relationship is important in many respects. Through it, we observe yet another version of Reaney's educational *psychomachia* in which opposing ideas assert their respective claims on the reason and imagination of the child. The success with which the child thwarts the dangerous oppressiveness of the inhuman, of the literal, of "things," signifies the degree to which authentic maturity is possible. In *The Dismissal*, Tucker with his clamshell from Georgian Bay and King with his *Chalmers Presbyterian Hymnbook* undergo a series of tests from which they emerge at variance. The clamshell is suggestive of the imagination, of the home county ("When I'm homesick, I always put this to my ear" [23]) and of the pilgrim, as St. James and the shrine at Compostella remind us. The hymnbook, on the other hand, is suggestive in this play of a heady pietism relatively untouched by tested virtue. Leaving his mother and Berlin, Ontario, for the University of Toronto, King says, "Mother, I only count five undershirts, and where's my hymn book" (13). The hymnbook is also suggestive of what Dale calls the "upas tree of Christianity — the repetition of stale formulae" (10) — a version of Christianity we last saw in *Baldoon*.

Later in the play, in a relatively quiet moment, King and Tucker reflect upon the images of the clamshell and the hymnbook, which latter holds some photographs of some "young trollops" they met when they arrived in Toronto:

> KING. Do you remember those girls who gave me their photos the moment I arrived in Toronto. *takes photos out of hymn book, Tucker eventually picks them up.* Something McQuaild said yesterday has changed me — what I want to do now, Jim, is make a careful study of the poorer classes — even the very worst of social evils — and that science of poverty, Jim, will give me power and with that power I'll be able some day to do more than just hold their hands while they die.
> TUCKER. It's power over words I want, Willie, I'd like to get good enough at words to do one big thing before I die. A book. (23)

It is evident throughout their university careers that King and Tucker differ as students, just as McQuaild and Dale do as teachers, and that this division focuses upon words and things.

> DALE. Now look — I think I know what I mean by culture.
> MCQUAILD. Do you now Dale what?
> DALE. The study of words.
> MCQUAILD. Wrong there, you see, culture is the study of things.
> DALE. Look if you insist that our young people study only things
> MCQUAILD. *interrupting* And I do, you see — I would eliminate literature from university education entirely.
> DALE. You insist on something they've been saturated with since childhood. What they need is words — French, Greek, German, Latin words, words to cut through the jungle of things — outside that window. (19)

In the final stage of Tucker's personal inquisition, reminiscent of the nightmarish utilitarian pedantry exhibited in Charles Dickens's *Hard Times*, the full destructive energy of McQuaild's world is felt:

BLAKE. Surely you must remember them? Facts not impressions, please.

Things not words. Facts.

Logical proof not emotional subjectivism. Facts.

Reality not illusion. Facts Facts *repeated until it fades away in Tucker's dying mind*

CHORUS *of faculty opposed to Tucker, saying "Facts" in unison with Blake*
1. Facts
2. Surely you must remember them?

1.   Facts
2. Surely you must remember them?

1.   Facts
2. Surely you must remember them?

Facts
Facts . . .

Tucker faints: his clamshell falls to the ground.

BLAKE.   Ill mentally or physically? *picks up the shell* Look at this. A shell. Of interest to an alienist I should say and perhaps the explanation of the whole trouble. You have been led by a madman.

Dale comes down and takes Tucker out.

DALE.   I think, Mr. Blake, that in seeking to break him down with your insane repetitions of the last two days, you have merely engraved forever on our minds the picture of what can only happen to perfect vision and sanity in an insane world. (51–52)

The guardian at the gates of this "insane world" is the Beadle of University College, McKim, who immediately locks the doors behind the departing Dale and Tucker. Like the strange, menacing figure of the Bargee in Arden's *Serjeant Musgrave's Dance*, who discloses much of the savage irony of that insane world, Reaney's McKim presides over the doors and gates of the examination and lecture halls. As Reaney says of him in the opening scene,

A clatter of keys. The Beadle, McKim, a grotesque old army man, with sack slung over one shoulder, a bunch of large keys at his side, and trash sticker in hand, lights candles on a piano to one side of the stage: janitor, spy, constable, general register of festivity, he will thread his way through the whole play rather like a gargoyle come to life. (9)

The Dismissal marks a return on Reaney's part to the verbal collage structure of such a play as *Colours in the Dark*. In both works, a variety of songs, hymns, poems, and documents with their own verbal styles combine with a generally colloquial "speech-of-appearance." Reaney's deliberate adaptation of the college-revue format obviates the need for a central or even dominant voice. He is no longer constrained, as he and his actors were in the adaptations of Richardson, by a specifically "literary" program that demanded a particular kind of verbal sculpturing of the characters. Once again, Reaney avails himself of the freedom to use, as one obviously does in a revue, whatever verbal material is available to him. The "voice of the place," in this instance, arises from variety, from the theatrically explicit juxtaposition of languages and sounds that are directly reinforced by the kinetic energy of a largely choric representation of undergraduate existence.

In his next work, *King Whistle!*, a similarly eclectic verbal format provides us with the voice of another specific place and time — that of his native Stratford in the thirties. The format is that of a thirties musical comedy onto which Reaney grafts the rhetoric and the ideological perspective of agit-prop theatre:

Already paving the way for this dramatic alchemy in which you cut across the grain of the material was the fact that the Marxist agitators had used agit-prop techniques in getting their message across to Stratford's oppressed. If they could dress kids up in rags and tire-chains, put them in trucks and label them with signs saying: "We are the children of Capitalist Oppression" then we could stylize reality as well.

A specific agit-prop work was uncovered by Reaney that, in one scene, he uses to "stylize" the confrontational situation in Stratford. In October 1933, the Progressive Theatre Club of Toronto presented a choral reading of *Lynchuk! or Murder in This Free Land Called Canada.* "An evil landlord," Reaney explains, "had persuaded the police in Montreal to shoot Mr Zynchuk, but did the Marxist dramatist choose to show this realistically? No, he or she did it chorically, a technique I have always found to be the most stylized imaginable" ("Story" 51). Adapting the melodramatic reification of economic experience implicit in such a model, Reaney's players act out their own situation, as the children did in *Listen to the Wind* when they appropriated the language and perspective of *Saga of Caresfoot Court* in order to explore and, possibly, change their own world. They become ERS and EES in *King Whistle!*:

LESLIE.   The "ers" are the employers — the uptown bunch, the factory owners and they stand on Stage Right. The "ees" are the employees and stand on Stage Left — *laughing.*

LINTON.   See here, Comrade Scarlett, since I'm not an "er" in real life — as a matter of fact I got so mad at the bosses I won't work for them at all — how can I play my class enemy — I'm not like that.

LESLIE.   Oh Comrade Linton — you heard of acting? The kind of role playing where you pretend to be the enemy is extremely useful in educating the workers for —

CHORUS.   Negotiations — during six weeks in September, October, November — 1933. (34)

The languages of *King Whistle!* are imbued with the categorical impulses of melodramatic utterance, of overstatement, usually apparent in agit-prop theatre. Nearly all of the characters of the play are intended to represent a variety of established economic, political, religious, and social roles within the terms of an ideological representation of a strike in small-town Ontario. As a result, the language of "appearance," as well as that of the chorus in its many songs and of the political meetings and debates that punctuate the play's narrative surface, is largely inflexible, intended verbally to embody not "life," but, in fact, the absence of life in a world dominated by factories, economic problems, Marxism, and capitalism. This is not to deny *King Whistle!* a *theatrical* liveliness, an *energeia* of sounds, music, multitudinous overlapping events and stage pictures with which the work reverberates. It is, however, generally the case that the words and gestures eschew the provisional, the emotionally exploratory and stiffen, as Steiner observed, into a monism wherein language encloses the speaker's world, rather than providing release and emancipation, as was the ideal, at least, informing *The Dismissal*. The "magic tongue" is merely evoked, momentarily, in *King Whistle!* as a girl is heard reading Keats's "Ode on a Grecian Urn." This brief episode is scenically and sonically juxtaposed with the factory world, which effectively drowns out her reading of " 'Bold Lover, never, never canst thou kiss' " (19). Such a juxtaposition is reiterated later when the police turn Michael Benson upside down and recover a copy of Keats's poems and an introduction to Karl Marx. The suggestion of a connection between literature and "revolutionary" activity is also signalled to us when Reaney describes *"the hero of the play,"* Kay, as representing *"farm, church, books"* (7). The connection, however, is strictly attitudinal rather than experiential. The play does not, in its verbal arrangements, explore such a connection. The liberating and profoundly ontological power of the "magic tongue" is but a fleeting possibility, a proposition among other propositions.

But Reaney was, as he put it, obsessed with the telling of the story of this strike in Stratford in 1933. He has chosen a voice that appears entirely appropriate in its relatively depersonalized diction and cadence. This is, after all, a play about workers, bosses, and prevaricating politicians. The gradations of linguistic differentiation that informed such plays as *The Killdeer, The Easter Egg, Colours in the Dark*, and, especially, and most effectively, the Donnelly trilogy would not appear to be as essential a part of a work such as this in which the main function of the words — in the dialogue, songs, choric sequences, and political speeches — is to represent the various sides of the central confrontation.

Early in the play, Kay confronts the bank manager Mallion with the question of the bank's apparent intervention in private life:

KAY. What's the matter with you Mallion?
MALLION. The matter is that this bank has a rule, sir, that only Grade A bank clerks can get married. Do you earn 400$ a year, no — what do you earn?
KAY. Peanuts — 300$.
MALLION. Why did you marry then — two months ago, why?
KAY. Because you and your bank and your money have no right to set up the rules of my private life.
MALLION. Kay, why do you think Head Office established the law in the first place?

KAY. To make their employees as miserable as they had already
made them by paying them next to nothing.
MALLION. To remove financial temptation — always a danger
when one is married —
KAY. Why not remove it then by giving us living wage? (8)

Such a confrontational spirit informs the various factory, street,
and domestic scenes of the work, wherein language, stripped of
metaphorical embellishment, is similarly pressed to serve the ideological underpinnings of all of the play's central events and characters:

No, you big stuffed shirt — he does not mean just a raise in
remuneration — he means a change in all our conditions of work
and pay — starting with the fact that all the white collar world
— *we hear its sounds and see its decorous textures like one half
of butterfly* paid salary, but that could be less than what this
world paid you. (12)

Who in hell do you think you are that you can be so tight-fisted
with your fellow human beings who've lost everything. Yesterday they owned a six room house which they lost with four
thousand dollars of their equity — after all the taxes they've paid
they've got a right to a lousy bottle of milk, now give them it or
I'll give notice of motion in council — (16–17)

Brother Kay, what you don't realize is that *this* is the worst
financial depression the world has ever seen — there is nothing
you can do about — *song hummed* that or it or anything or —
this! (21)

Well I think the situation demands two hundred soldiers, some
tanks and some machine guns. If we don't watch out we're in
danger of turning into a soviet commune. (26)

Language shouts at us, sustaining, as do the sonic and scenic
arrangements that establish for us factory, home, church, street, the
this/that terms of the play's life wherein, as Brecht observed, ". . .
people adopt attitudes of such a sort that the social laws under which
they are acting spring into sight" (86).
These social laws are particularly articulated in the play's many
songs that, as in Brecht and most agit-prop theatre, possess *gestic*

importance. Money's opening song, "Bank Clerks! My name's Money! / Why should you have any? / Of what turns the universe!" (7) and the first choric song, the "whistle song" which is, in effect *"the industrial history of Stratford,"* establish the nature of the play's personal, social, and political worlds as these are informed by economic structures:

> The bankers lent our masters money
> Six million built these factories
> In which there hums the god machine
> Fed by Niagara's electric stream.
>
> Yes, one by one the factories came —
> Each with its whistle, each with its hum,
> They earn twelve million, three million for us,
> But the exact clear profit's kept mysterious! (9)

In such a song as "The Girls at Swift," the *gestic* dimension is expanded to express the highly profitable gender distinctions of modern factory life:

> 1 Six o'clock
>   Morning fog
>   Women walk
>   To their job
>   . . . . . .
> 2 Thirty girls
>   Caught in a trap
>   Chickens pick
>   And butter wrap

As they sing this, the *"girls mime egg grading, chicken plucking and butter wrapping. All fifty of them do everything at the same time with identical precise movements"* (10).

The scene is an effectively parodic representation of modern factory conditions wherein the lives and performances of the workers are frozen and depersonalized, appropriated by the quantifying imperatives of capitalism, creating another version of what in *The Dismissal* was called the "jungle of things" (19). Later, a worker from the furniture factory exclaims to Moorehead, President of the Canadian Trades and Labour Congress,

This piece and that piece and this piece and that,
Why is it then that I feel like a tree,
Caught in a cage called a factory plant.
That chair you sit on is made out of me! (21)

Such an experience is obviously a far cry from the totemic relationship with the land asserted in *The Killdeer*, by Kenneth in *The Easter
Egg*, by the Donnellys, by Wacousta and his followers, by the early
inhabitants of Wallaceburg in *Baldoon* represented by Dr. Troyer, or
by Dale out on the farm in *The Dismissal*. And the language of such
an experience is appropriately sparser, unembellished by the ontologically creative "mental dance with metaphors" that informs the
"magic tongue." In *King Whistle!*, the resolution of the strike and
the ultimate assertion of the workers of "the right ourselves to be. /
Men and Women" (28) is brought about by the transformation of
economic passivity into an active, critical consciousness that insists
that the outer world can be changed. This consciousness is partly
shaped through language, through the melodramatic this/that rhetoric of Christian and Marxist social analysis that informs the
speeches of Kay, Alice, the chorus of workers, and of Jessie, whose
song and recitative explaining how she met her husband is prologue
to the play's concluding sequence in the Burke cottage:

If they should ask how it was I met with him,
I should reply that it was by a stratagem.
I chose a job where they paid not the minimum.
Miles away he chose to be a millionaire's son.
He was rich I was poor living down in a slum.
If they should ask how it was that he met with me
He might reply that it was quite historically/strange.

Jessie is to marry the "hated class enemy" Lieutenant Adrian
McNab, whose father died "a general in the army" while her father
"had his legs blown off at Vimy."

If you should ask how this might just be possible,
I should reply that my job got so horrible,
My temper snapped and I caused an industrial
Dispute that upset those with a lot they could lose.

.   .   .   .

You men don't understand how dull you've made life
Which produces the long lines of dumb patient girls
Grading eggs, sewing carpets and cushions with identical curls.
There's a sign up there — says NO TALKING, to Hell
With your No, Yeah — you've put a volcano in Jail. (45)

After Kay's election as Mayor of Stratford, backed by a Labour
Council, the play's reprise of scenic and sonic images includes the
choric reiteration of the will to change and the "dream turning into
truth":

In this our last act we have shown
The story of a force that's grown
Is growing and will grow some more
Till Peace has slain his brother War.
. . . .
For we must keep in our control
Our individual selves & souls;
Our wills to work, what to obey;
We have the right ourselves to be.
Liberty

THE BUILDING OF THE TRUE COMMONWEALTH
Then we say, Yes! (46)

The "true commonwealth" in *Gyroscope* reflects the ideal of a
poetic imagination fully awakened to the ontological and alchemical
powers of words. The social, economic, and political spheres so
central to the story of a strike are, in the story of the making of poetry,
relegated to the fringes of consciousness as, in Graff's phrase,
"malleable raw material" (14). The affirmative exclamation "Yes!"
in *Gyroscope* is to the restorative, liberating impulses and properties
of language. The shamanist ideal is applicable. The shaman, Schechner writes, is a kind of "stage magician." He is the "transformer =
the one who is transformed = the surrogate = the link = the one who
connects different realms of reality = the one who facilitates change
by embodying change = the one who by changing himself helps
others change. The shaman is a professional transformer, and very
much like the theater performer" (*Environmental* 180). The *poet*,
then, is the revolutionary.

Dale and Kay acted against particular political and economic situations on behalf of their respective claims for justice. To a degree, in both *The Dismissal* and *King Whistle!*, language is used to articulate the will to change; language is the protagonist and speech itself a kind of action. In *Gyroscope*, however, language is not so much attuned to, or reflective of, the rigid this/that monism of agit-prop rhetoric. Its allegiance is, rather, to the "magic tongue," or to an *idea* of the "magic tongue," "The string of song / The waker from fallen slumbers" (*Poems* 125), which, in its assault upon the tyranny of ordinary linear temporality, leads towards what the surrealists called *le merveilleux quotidien*, the marvellous of daily reality (Orenstein 33), what Hilda calls the "xylophone of possibilities" (*Gyroscope* 48). And, in *Gyroscope*, language includes, most importantly, sound. Listening to a performance of the concrete poetry group the Four Horsemen of the Apocalypse, Reaney writes,

... you may come away with the idea that the sounds they make come out of a circle, as spinning circle of sounds held in their lips, teeth, palates, voice boxes and midriffs. We use a very small area of this circle in our daily speech. So, in their big improvised arias which climax the play, the actors playing Hilda and Gregory La Selva were encouraged to use every sound in their repertoire. And this "using of every sound in their repertoire" from the big circle of sound meant that they had revolutionized themselves in other ways as well. (Introd., *Gyroscope*)

Gyroscope, as much as any of Reaney's plays since *The Killdeer*, is encoded with symbolic structures drawn from the various orders of poetry, myth, and critical thought. Stingle, in his account of the play and of the relationship between Reaney and Frye, shows how totally infused the story of Greg and Hilda is with classical allusion, with for instance "the ritual mystery cult of the androgynous Dionysus" displaced into the contemporary shapes of a poet and her husband engaged in sexual vocational and verbal combat (50). This idea of displacement is described by Nicholas and Mattie to Greg while they prepare him for the play's concluding poetry contest as "The graded adaptation of the unbelieveable to the almost believeable to the all-too-believeable, to the believeable again" (60). As Greg grows physically weaker from not having eaten, Mattie exclaims that "imaginatively" he is "cleaning the windows" of his mind:

NICHOLAS. Most "moderns" go about with a thousand Macdonald's hamburgers over their heads weighing in the trap door above them that if opened leads to the Roof Garden and to Vision and to —

MATTIE. Eden Regained. *They pass food to each other overhead.* Displacement skills — Ariadne and the Minotaur. What would the maze be?

GREG. *with great vigour* The parking lot at Simpson's — Level A-B-C-D — where did I leave my car, said she.

NICHOLAS. Car?

GREG. Chariot?

MATTIE. No, Nicholas — he's got it right — you always displace to the modern, so chariot equals car, pentacostal flame equals cigarette lighter, the Tomb of Tutankhamen equals the Tomb of Timothy Eaton. And the minotaur?

GREG. Would be a retarded youth of nineteen. Ariadne forgot to lock the door of her car and he's hiding in his back seat, her back seat, ready to pounce. (60–61)

Through such playing with the *merveilleux quotidien,* traces of Eden are regained, including, most importantly, a sense of wholeness wherein ". . . nothing has difference, therefore nothing is the same; / All things twin, all things opposed vanish in my doubt's marshflame" (*Poems* 155). The vanishing of "all things opposed" in *Gyroscope* is accomplished in large part through the dreams of Hilda and Greg. The subconscious, wrote Bachelard,

is ceaselessly murmuring, and it is by listening to these murmurs that one hears its truth. Sometimes desires carry on a dialogue within us — desires? memories perhaps or reminiscences made out of unfinished dreams? — a man and a woman are speaking in the solitude of our being. . . . If this intimate man and woman preserve a trace of rivalry, it is because we are dreaming badly, because we are putting everyday names on the creatures of reverie which are outside of time. . . . The subconscious, then, maintains within us forces of androgyneity. Whoever speaks of androgyneity is brushing the depths of his own subconscious with a double antenna. (*Poetics of Reverie* 59)

Hilda awakens early trying to capture her dream: "Like trying to catch fish when you're lying at the bottom of the creek holding your breath . . ." (6). She has had a "Gorgeous dream in colour about a

... a piano? No ... a piece of string. The string dream — I've had it, pieces of it before" (7). She decides to try to steal a dream from her sleeping "husband of the Wood with hardly anything on save your Wild Man of the Wood costume." His dream is also about a piano, a cleared field with a two-mile long piano across it.

> I had an uneasy feeling that if I did strike the lowest note on the longest piano the world has ever seen, the lowest note — the earth herself would uncurl and reply with the voice of an old woman tall as the stars with hair on her chest, a beard yea long and a mouth like the grave. (8)

In Breton's "Manifesto of Surrealism" (1924) he describes a form of surrealist dialogue in which both speakers pursue inner soliloquies that intertwine as the questions of one begin to generate, and then direct, the responses of the other. This leads to a psychic automatism that releases language from its ordinary bearings. Through the interwoven monologues, a new reality is glimpsed, one that obliterates oppositions (32–34). In this respect, the dialogue here between Greg and Hilda resembles that between Harry and Rebecca in *The Killdeer* when they played a game of Chinese Pictures, each guessing what was in the other's mind, establishing a sur-reality of immense ontological significance. As Hilda and Greg pursue the images of androgyneity, of the two-mile long piano, the string, the monster with belly buttons for eyes and as Harry and Rebecca pursue the images of a lilac flower, burdock, and the upas tree their dialogue reflects directly what Milton Wilson describes as the usual pattern of a Reaney comedy: ". . . an action of images moves forward by discovering images, its characters find themselves by the recognition and development of images, and it achieves its resolution by reaching a final pattern of images" (74).

When Greg is initiated into the rites of the society of women poets, the "forces of androgyneity" are further discovered. Hilda, Stingle writes, "performs as one of Euripides' Bacchantes . . . and leads Greg down into the symbolic underworld of Brazil and back up to Toronto. As an aspirant to the role of the poet, Greg is also a male initiate into the mystery ritual of the woman." Stingle cites Erich Neumann regarding the Demeter myth that also informs the "double antenna" of such an exploration of the subconscious, as ". . . the male initiate . . . sought to identify himself with Demeter, i.e. with his own feminine aspect." As a result, Neumann writes, ". . . the male shaman or seer is in high degree 'feminine,' since he is dependent on his anima aspect. And for this reason he often appears in woman's dress" (qtd. in Stingle 50). The shaman, then, as, in Schechner's terms, the "professional transformer," the stage magician, "facilitates change by embodying change," and significant change demands that, at the deepest level of being, "all things opposed vanish." The gyroscope that Hilda gives to Greg at the close of the play is, as he remarks, "a symbol of it all" (65), a symbol of the final recognition, a resolution of the play's intricate pattern of images wherein, as Reaney commented, personalities, sexual differences, and various worlds of words spin about into and through their opposites, "sometimes as the only way of preserving their own freshness, their own individuality" (Introd., *Gyroscope*).

For the most part, *Gyroscope*, although about the making of "worlds out of words," is written in a prose of relatively unadorned, although sometimes affected, colloquial energy. In some ways, the tone and tempo of the dialogue (especially in the scenes with Nicholas, Professor Puzzle, Mattie, and Agnes) is reminiscent of that of *The Easter Egg*, particularly in its representation of a verbal wit, which often seems to self-consciously preen. In other words, the shamanist impulses that appear to inform all the "symbolic structures which operate on several levels simultaneously" (Stingle 32) in *Gyroscope* are not always, themselves, evident in the dominant dramatic speech of the play. The disjuncture between the "idea" and its theatrical incarnation, the gap, for instance, between the *idea* of the "magic tongue" and its concrete actualization in the speech of Hilda, Greg, and the others, or even in the *poésie de théâtre* of the play in performance, results in another level of "displacement" that is entirely verbal: chariots do indeed become simply cars, and, unless we are *told*, as in fact we are, we do not necessarily think these cars might be anything else but cars. Such a problem is, in part, as Gilman observed, perennial to the theatre and obsessively tackled by numerous playwrights, especially poet-playwrights, in our century. A version of such a problem of voice was recognized by Reaney when, in Vancouver during the tour of the Donnelly trilogy, a new president of the Poetry League was elected. "I had forgotten," he writes, "being so much with actors lately, how different poets can be from actors: the lyric ones, and the league contains mostly lyric ones, are churning inside with their private oracle cauldrons and lonely triumphs; by the way of contrast, actors are always trying out new persona masks . . ." (*14 Barrels* 60). Hilda and Greg, and the members of the Poetry

Guild in *Gyroscope*, are themselves privately enraptured, one part of their being *linguistically* differentiated from the world about them. Individually, they are divided by the contradictory impulses of the private and lonely lyric voice and of the more public personae with its obligations towards "things," towards others in society, or, simply, the "other" in the marriage. On the play's more parodic level, the public personae has obligations towards the critical other order of words, a "mandarin madness of secondary discourse" (Steiner *Real Presences* 26), represented by the dissertation-writing Mattie who, from her multitudinous tapes and notes, produces a "three-foot pillar of paper" (66).

In their accounts of their dreams, Reaney employs a degree of linguistic differentiation, according the prose a metaphorical embellishment, a lyricism that suggests the private and lonely realms, distinguishing such speech from the "normal." In the dream-passage cited above, for instance, as in the dream-passages of *The Killdeer* and in the more consciously "poetic" passages of *The Easter Egg* and the Donnelly trilogy, diction and cadence are intended to suggest quite another, less immediately accessible, level of words. But, in the stage between sleeping and waking, Greg's language reaches in two directions: towards the intensity of dream where ". . . you're joining with yourself" — where the subconscious is "ceaselessly murmuring" and a kind of psychic automatism releases the images of androgyneity, the piano, the string — and towards the known, "real," and tyrannical world of time, the world suggested by the barely heard plane to Cleveland that, as a sound, is prologue to an awakening to the lab-world where Greg will "put on [his] whites and . . . suck diseases for a living" (8). As Greg is drawn closer to such an awakening by Hilda, his language draws closer to the colloquial, more self-consciously witty repartee that she establishes from the beginning of this scene:

GREG. Well, we're men. And we'd just come home from a very inflammatory stag party.

HILDA. I suppose. Now, at the beer place you went to the men's washroom.

GREG. Sure, that's why you drink beer. So you can go to the latrine and read the writing on the walls. Methinks I see the puissant body of our nation like a huge latrine scribbled with the wisdom of aroused saints.

.   .   .   .

HILDA. Yes, yes. Now what had some anonymous gentleman written on the walls of the men's washroom just above the toilet paper holder at the Embassy Hotel this time?
GREG. "My mother" — ballpoint pen — "My mother made me a homosexual."
The alarm goes off. HILDA *pretends to slumber.* (9)

As long as the two of them are awake, talking with one another or with the others in the play, the "speech-of-appearance" is entirely colloquial and intended verbally to establish a "real" world of London, Ontario, where people work in labs, eat in cafeterias, write dissertations, love, quarrel, dissemble, compose poems, and join poetry clubs.

That Hilda is a poet, and Greg invading and mastering the poet's world of words, means that the verbal gears of *Gyroscope* shift from the colloquial to the poetic, or at least the metaphorically embellished speech of dream and of the recited poems. These poems, however, are not assimilated into a purely *theatricalist* dialogue wherein the many things we hear and see provide a complex inter-textuality of word and non-word, as is the case with the recited poems in *One-Man Masque* and *Colours in the Dark.* Through the theatricalist idiom of the latter, the poems are incorporated into an idea of communal "play" presided over by Reaney, the shaman "stage magician." In *Gyroscope*, they are simply the result of what some people in society do — write poems and read them aloud to others. In general, the realistic language of this play dominates the theatrical experience, the things we hear. The poems, the sound effects (drums, Henry's "repertoire of subverbal hummings," alarm bells, the "shot of crowd sound" for the cafeteria, the tape-recorder speech, the typewriter, the Paraguayan music), and the verbal autom-atism of the dreams, evoking, as they do, the supposed *l'alchimie du verbe*, are, in the end, trivialized by, rather than assimilated into the real. This "real," as well as the caricatural and parodic levels of the play, insofar as these are verbally distinguishable, have the same effect upon the *idea* of the "magic tongue" as the scenically intrusive toy dimension in *Baldoon, Wacousta!* and *The Canadian Brothers* did upon the ideas of folkloric and mythical action. The dominant language of the play does not successfully mediate between person and archetype, event and myth. The countless mythic allusions and symbolic accretions that presumably informed "the sketches and the ideas" that Reaney tells us he found in his notebooks (Introd.,

Gyroscope) end up by stifling the impression of a felt life, of actual experience. In so many of the earlier works, the "magic tongue," with all of its alchemical powers, was situated within characters whose lives were shaped and expressed through the theatricalist instincts of Reaney the professional transformer. The disjunction, in this play, between such an *idea* of language and its scenic and verbal *incarnation* in what we actually, *in the theatre*, see and hear Hilda, Greg, Nicholas, Mattie, and Agnes doing and saying, obscures, rather than illuminates the "confrontations that living with other people mysteriously and troublingly involves" (Introd., *Gyroscope*).

Perhaps only once does the play successfully escape the tone and theatrical parameters imposed by its self-consciously colloquial verbal style and make some sort of *direct* claim upon the sensibilities of the audience. This is late in the play when the Poetry Guild holds its Ceremony of Exclusion, and Hilda and Greg must "make up a poem on the spot without words, just sounds." They are expected, *in performance*, to actually sculpture sound. They are to "storm the audience with a bravura aria that explores not only familiar sounds, but also sound potentialities our language avoids. The possibilities are endless and the results should be that we finally know HILDA and GREG right down to their navels and past" (63). This is the closest the work comes to a concrete actualization of an art-act. If, as Cassirer wrote, men dream of a *lingua Adamica* (130), then such a dream takes us necessarily to the sounds and cries that precede the actual activity of naming and speaking with which we "mark the desire for the detection and conquest of an objective world" (132–33), for, as Professor Dale observes, ". . . words to cut through the jungle of things" (19). Before the "magic tongue" can awaken us from "fallen slumbers," we must first utter sounds. It is ironic, in this play so self-consciously about worlds being made out of words, that the theatrical *event* is most compelling when the actors momentarily abandon their identities as characters in the play and, more importantly, the play-script itself. We do not really, as Reaney suggests, get to "finally know HILDA and GREG right down to their navels and past" (63). We do, however, get to "know" something about the actors before us and the "Me talk" of pure sound. In the most direct way possible, Reaney's actors are here engaged in the ontologically informed act of *playing*.

POSTSCRIPT

This is the meaning of Eurydice. Because the realness of his inward being lies at his back, the man of words, the singer, will turn back to the place of necessary beloved shadows. (Steiner, *Bluebeard's Castle* 102)

For Paul Klee, the Eurydician gesture was towards Genesis, the "one essential image of creation itself," which he saw as an "act of world creation stretching from the past to the future. Genesis eternal!" In Klee's art, the fundamental pictorial elements of line, colour, and plane were imbued with the values of signs, of a visual alphabet through the reading and understanding of which the spectator joined the artist in the process of creation.

Reaney seeks a similar admission of the listener/looker into the creative process of playing. And, as in the work of Klee, the polemical and pedagogical dimensions of such an idea of creativity are unmistakable. We *must* learn "how to play" if we hope, ever, to realize ourselves as individuals and as members of a *particular* society — as Reaney's "nativist kick" and regionalist bias remind us. Implicit in the theory and art of Klee and Reaney is the recognition of a *lingua Adamica*, the discovery of which is promoted through the participatorial dimensions of art-acts. Furthermore, the idea of Genesis reminds us that these art-acts can be conduits to a recognition that, as Klee went on to observe, "in its present shape [this] is not the only possible world."

The *lingua Adamica* towards which Reaney's own Eurydician glance increasingly gravitated is situated in the interconnecting languages of theatre. The "secret place where primeval power nurtures all evolution" (Klee, "On Modern Art" 53) is the art-act itself which, in the theatre, is necessarily polylingual, as performers and listeners/ lookers are mutually engaged in the intertextual play of scenic, sonic, and verbal interpretations and shapings of experience.

It is, in part, within such a context that this study has situated the scenic and verbal elements of Reaney's theatre and Reaney's *idea* of the theatre as an ontologically significant force. As a poet-play-wright, Reaney gives primacy to the various worlds of words. Words in the theatre, however, occupy physical and acoustical space. Beginning with *Listen to the Wind* in 1966, Reaney's theatre tends towards a clearer understanding and utilization of the inherent polylingual features of the art-act, including, most importantly, the concept of phenomenal space that informs the verbal, corporeal, and aural dimensions of the theatrical *event*. The principles of looking, listening, and "making up patterns (scribbling with your body/bodies)" as these were shaped in the workshops of those early years, have remained fundamental to his theatre ever since. On the evening of 11 May 1989, Reaney and John Beckwith, nearly thirty years after the first production of *Night-Blooming Cereus*, appeared together on the stage at the Guelph Spring Festival following the premiere of their most recent collaborative work, the opera *Crazy to Kill: A Detective Opera*. This was a work musically scored for "Percussion (one player): washboard, cabaza, wood block, sleighbells, two cowbells (high, low), suspended cymbal, Chinese opera gong, medium tam-tam, three drums (high, medium, low), marimba, vibraphone, chain/metal bucket" (*Crazy* 3) and scenically scored for live and doll/puppet performers, projection screens, a complex arrangement of stage levels and curtained alcoves, and intricate lighting patterns that, on one occasion at least, flash "from modality to modality as the visual symbols of . . . mental states come thunderously on" (*Crazy* 44).

This work was a very recent reminder that Reaney's is a fundamentally celebratory aesthetic. It is celebratory in its inherent vitalism, its "delight of listening to words" and "making up patterns of movement of fun and in play." It is also celebratory, and, for the most part, perhaps, unfashionably so, in its assumption that the art-act possesses a conciliatory dimension that can, in fact, change the world we live in. The art-act for Reaney, unlike that for, say, Vladimir and Estragon "doing the tree" or imitating Pozzo and Lucky or insulting one another in *Waiting for Godot*, is not a meaningless action between those alarming recognitions of cosmic indifference and silence, one among many possible actions that simply reinforce the "assumption that alienation is the normal and unalterable condition of human beings" (Graff 60).

The formal and substantive consequences of such a vitalist aesthetic are of considerable importance in accounting for and evaluating our responses to Reaney's work. There are inevitable perils in trying to ride the Heraclitian horse at such a pace as Reaney sometimes insists we should. George Bowering points to one of the features of such a ride when he speaks of the "density, thickness, depth . . . of Reaney's verse and drama, a density not only in the denominative, but in the symbol, irony, rime." The works become "for the reader or audience an environment. . . . Thus the 'everything' effect in the Donnelly trilogy, whose hyperactivity was inspired by the three-ring circus and the medicine-show-*cum*-county-fair, the collage in motion" (8). His adoption of the principles of collage, with their inherent cubist dynamic of simultaneity, can sometimes anatomize his sense of the art-act, and of playing, into such a dense web of what, in *Colours in the Dark*, he described as the "mosaic-all-things-happening-at-the-same-time-galaxy," that the theatrical event within which we are to be enfolded is simply too over-loaded, creating an environment that seems to point, finally, to nothing but itself. The act of playing, in such a case, is informed by an underlying indeterminacy; it verges on the gratuitous and is not itself, as Reaney would ideally have it, a medium of willed change. As Thomas Mann observed of Wagner's theories of the *Gesamtkunstwerk*, "We should be children and barbarians to suppose that the influence of art upon us is profounder or loftier by reason of the heaped-up volume of its assault upon our senses" (207). In other words, the potentially hedonist dimension of such a celebratory aesthetic can impede, rather than release, the ontological powers of word and non-word in the theatre event through their dissipation into an overabundance of associations. Such an over-loading of word and non-word, for example, we can see in such works as *Baldoon* and *The Canadian Brothers*, perhaps the least aesthetically disciplined of Reaney's plays. But the dangers of an over-saturated *Gesamtkunstwerk* are nearly always there.

Reaney's "beloved shadows" towards which he turns as "the man of words" (to use, again, Steiner's reading of the Eurydician situation) are themselves imbued with a complex interleaving of visual, aural, and verbal material drawn from a rich store of looking, listening, and reading. A classic literacy, as we have observed in a number of plays and in Reaney's advocacy of particular "identifying" works in the *Halloween* letters, *Alphabet*, and *14 Barrels* (among them the writings of Blake, Yeats, and the critical structuralism of Frye) informs the *musée imaginaire* of collage-languages wherein different orders of words address us, as well as, on occasion, one another. In addition, Reaney's shadows reverberate with countless sounds (for the making of which Beckwith's eclectic "orchestra" in *Crazy to Kill* is but another version of Reaney's prop table in *Listen to the Wind*) and with an alphabet of visual signs that suggests a degree of "visual thinking" connecting Reaney's "scribbling" with various tendencies in modern painting, scenography, and theatre architecture. In the most successful of Reaney's works — certainly in *Listen to the Wind*, *Colours in the Dark*, the Donnelly trilogy, *The Dismissal* — the action of playing/creating with such an array of verbal and non-verbal "possibilities" does not simply absorb the performers/watchers into the circus-like rhythms of a theatre event, although, of course, as Bowering observed, something of this sort does occur. In these plays, the several languages are also informed with those countless "concrete localisms," with the images and languages of particular place and time, including many from purely documentary sources, that give the self-absorbing, hedonist vitality of the theatre-as-environment historical, social, religious, and political reference. As a result, the theatre becomes an Identifier, a complex art-act intended to be as revelatory of the "native land business" as it can also be of Genesis eternal. Indeed, the "native land business" *is*, it would appear, Genesis eternal.

In Reaney's earlier plays, those before *Listen to the Wind*, the concept of the theatre-as-identifier is evident in the settings, the characters, the structures of the stories wherein the personalities of, say, Andrew Kingbird in *The Sun and the Moon*, Harry and Rebecca in *The Killdeer*, Kenneth in *The Easter Egg* are realized. However, the ontological dimensions of such explorations of place and self remain largely discursive rather than experiential, a matter of theme and argument rather than, as Bachelard observed of the participatorial dimensions of the art-act, expressions of our *own* creativity, "expressing us by making us what it expresses." The recognition of the purely phenomenological dimension of the theatre-event after the writing of *The Easter Egg* resulted in a different *idea* of the theatre and a series of plays far more expressive of Reaney's coming to see, as Frye put it, "more intensely by means of his medium." In short, Reaney discovered "The Theatre Unbound," with its unrestrained urge to try to express everything:

Everything — Egyptian hieroglyphs and crystallography,
Diary of shadows,

Vast God and the interiors of tree trunks, snowflakes
All spin like a fiery corkscrew into his psychology.

(*One-Man Masque* 187)

Each language, Steiner observes, "speaks the world in its own way,"
and each "edifies worlds and counter-worlds in its own mode. The
polyglot is a freer man" (*Real Presences* 57). Reaney's theatre is a
record of numerous attempts to master and exploit the polylingualism of the medium itself as a means of achieving freedom, both for
himself, and for the participating listeners/lookers who, like him, are
learning how to play.

NOTES

Introduction

1 See also L. Moholy-Nagy.
2 See also Strindberg's "The New Arts."
3 See Gerald D. Parker, "The Modern Theatre as Autonomous Vehicle."
4 See also Reaney's satirical poem *Imprecations: The Art of Swearing*.

Chapter 1: "this native land business"

1 See, for example, Bessai, "Documentary Theatre in Canada"; Conolly; Jeanes; Kesten; Leggatt; Reaney's "James Reaney"; Rubin, *Creeping Towards a Culture*; Stuart; Tepper; and Wallace.
2 A year later, Hendry reported on the Canadian Theatre Centre's Committee for the Formation of the Canadian Playwright in *Stage in Canada* 1.11 (1966):1. A decade later, the Guild of Canadian Playwrights had been formed, the first chairman being Mavor Moore. See "Guilding the Writers."
3 See *Theatre Quarterly* [British Playwriting in the Seventies].
4 A similar impression of cultural mismatching is given in Reaney's account of "what Toronto college theatre was like when I first arrived there: Don Harron in *Riders to the Sea* wrapped up in a white sheet with Lawrence Park Collegiate types attempting to keen when all they'd ever known how to do at a death was funeral parlour" (*14 Barrels* 90).
5 As Hilton Kramer remarked in *The Age of the Avant-Garde: An Art Chronicle of 1956–1972*, "Klee made no attempt to keep his art separate from his teaching methods" (127).
6 In Reaney's PhD dissertation, we find another application of the tree image when he records that Yeats liked Burke's notion of "society as representing a tree with its roots deep in time" ("The Influence of Spenser on Yeats" 80).
7 Yeats's own theatre essays are an apt analogy to Reaney's. Indeed, Reaney compared the occasional magazine in which such essays would appear to Yeats's *Samhain* (*14 Barrels* 61).

[8] See Krieg. Some photo-documentation of *The Life of Pauline Johnson* was also included with Krieg's prospectus.

[9] See "Letter from James Reaney": ". . . doesn't Shaw, who by the bye is a playwright interested in *ideas*, say in *Back to Methuselah's* Preface that what his plays are all about is 'the iconography of creative evolution'? If so, why not use some panels of thoughtful iconographies . . . as the core for your festival; the plays are not just Edwardian hits, but are supposed to change your life and your mental habits" (7).

[10] There is an echo here of Jacques Copeau's idea of ten modern *personae*. See Brown 229.

[11] Bethel's account, however, of running away from home "down the mountain into this valley I could see every morning with the beautiful college buildings and the chimneys here sticking up through the elms," is strongly reminiscent of Acadia University in Wolfville, Nova Scotia, where Reaney taught the summer of 1959 (*The Easter Egg* 39).

Chapter 2: "making up patterns (scribbling with your body/bodies)"

[1] See also Reaney's "The Influence of Spenser on Yeats." Yeats and Spenser believed, he wrote, "in a much more energetic assault on the problem of man's recovering 'control of event and circumstance' than is implied in the conservative tradition's programme in which you wait for the world to come to your wells of undefiled language and you wait for the rise of social institutions that will force it to come" (240).

[2] See Reaney's article on David Willson and Thomas Gerry's dissertation.

Chapter 3: "the magic tongue"

[1] As Jacques Derrida says, "all theatrical audacity declares its fidelity to Artaud" (233).

[2] *The Revenger's Tragedy* was adapted for the CBC *Wednesday Night* in 1961 but was not produced and broadcast.

[3] For an account of the sources and the theatre history of Young's *The Revenge* see G.D. Parker, "The Moor's Progress."

WORKS CITED

Primary Sources

Reaney, James. "An ABC to Ontario Literature and Culture." *Black Moss* 2nd ser. 3 (1970): 2.

"Afternoon Moon." *Here and Now* 1 (1948): 38–46.

———. *Alphabet: A Semiannual Devoted to the Iconography of the Imagination* (1960–71).

———. "Author's Note" to *The Killdeer*. B. Parker, *Masks* 199–200.

———. "Broughdale Only." *20 Cents Magazine* 1.1 (1966): 1.

———. *The Canadian Brothers*. *Major Plays of the Canadian Theatre 1934–1984*. Ed. Richard Perkyns. Toronto: Irwin, 1984.

———. "The Canadian Poet's Predicament." *University of Toronto Quarterly* 26 (1957): 284–95.

———. "Coathanger Theatre." *Scene Changes* 9 (1981): 17.

———. "Colours in the Dark" (essay). *Stratford Scene: 1958–1968*. Ed. Peter Raby. Toronto: Clarke, 1968.

———. *Colours in the Dark*. Vancouver: Talonbooks, 1969.

———. *Crazy to Kill: A Detective Opera*. Guelph: Guelph Spring Festival, 1989.

———. "Cycle." *Canadian Drama/l'art dramatique canadien* 2 (1976): 73–77.

———. "David Willson." *Dictionary of Canadian Biography/Dictionnaire Biographique de Canada*. Vol. 2. 1976. 12 vols.

———. "Digesting the Bible." *Saturday Night* Mar. 1983: 69.

———. *The Dismissal: or Twisted Beards & Tangled Whiskers*. Erin ON: Porcépic, 1978.

———. *The Easter Egg*. B. Parker, *Masks* 3–91.

———. Editorial. *Alphabet: A Semiannual Devoted to the Iconography of the Imagination* 1 (1960): 3–4.

———. Editorial. *Alphabet: A Semiannual Devoted to the Iconography of the Imagination* 4 (1962): 3.

_____. Editorial. *Alphabet: A Semiannual Devoted to the Iconography of the Imagination* 8 (1964): 5.

_____. Editorial. *Alphabet: A Semiannual Devoted to the Iconography of the Imagination* 9 (1964): 3.

_____. Editorial. *Alphabet: A Semiannual Devoted to the Iconography of the Imagination* 13 (1976): 2.

_____. "An Evening with Babble and Doodle: Presentations of Poetry." *Canadian Literature* 12 (1962): 37–43.

_____. "A Farewell Portrait of Selwyn Dewdney." *Artscanada* 26 (1979–80): 80.

_____. *14 Barrels from Sea to Sea.* Erin ON: Porcépic, 1977.

_____. *Gyroscope.* Toronto: Playwrights Canada, 1980.

_____. *Handcuffs: The Donnellys, Part III.* Erin ON: Porcépic, 1977.

_____. "The Identifier Effect." *The CEA Critic* 42 (1980): 26–31.

_____. *Imprecations: The Art of Swearing.* Windsor: Black Moss, 1984.

_____. "The Influence of Spenser on Yeats." Diss. U of Toronto, 1958.

_____. Interview with James Reaney. *Globe and Mail* 5 Nov. 1977: 35.

_____. "Interview with James Reaney." By Jean McKay. Dragland 138–50.

_____. "James Reaney." Interview. By Geraldine Anthony. *Stage Voices: Twelve Canadian Playwrights.* Ed. Geraldine Anthony. Toronto: Doubleday, 1978. 140–64.

_____. "Kids and Crossovers." *Canadian Theatre Review* 10 (1976): 28–31.

_____. *The Killdeer.* Reaney, *The Killdeer and Other Plays* 1–89.

_____. *The Killdeer and Other Plays.* Toronto: Macmillan, 1962.

_____. *King Whistle! Brick* 8 (1980): 5–46.

_____. "A Letter from James Reaney." *Black Moss* 2nd ser. 1 (1976): 2–10.

_____. Letter to Keith Turnbull n.d. [in possession of Keith Turnbull].

_____. *Listen to the Wind.* Vancouver: Talonbooks, 1972.

_____. "Manitoba as a Writer's Environment." *Mosaic* 3 (1970): 95–97.

_____. *Masks of Childhood.* Ed. Brian Parker. Toronto: New, 1974.

_____. "Myths in Some Nineteenth-Century Ontario Newspapers." *Aspects of Nineteenth-Century Ontario.* Ed. F.H. Armstrong. Toronto: U of Toronto P, 1974. 253–66.

_____. *NDWT Co. Teaching Kit for the Donnelly Trilogy.* N.p.: n.d.

_____. *Night-Blooming Cereus.* B. Parker, *Masks* 195–224.

_____. *One-Man Masque.* Reaney, *The Killdeer and Other Plays* 173–93.

_____. *Poems: James Reaney.* Ed. Germaine Warkentin. Toronto: New, 1972.

_____. "The Plays at Stratford." *Canadian Forum* 33 (1953): 134–35.

_____. *The St Nicholas Hotel: The Donnellys, Part II.* Erin ON: Porcépic, 1976.

———. "The Search for an Undiscovered Alphabet." *Canadian Art* 22 (1965): 38–41.

———. "Sizing Up 'Applebert.'" *Western News* [U of Western Ontario] 2 Dec. 1982: 7.

———. "Some Critics Are Music Teachers." *Centre and Labyrinth: Essays in Honour of Northrop Frye.* Ed. Eleanor Cook et al. Toronto: U of Toronto P, 1983. 298–308.

———. "Souwesto Theatre: A Beginning." *Alumni Gazette* [U of Western Ontario] 1976: 14–15.

———. *Sticks & Stones: The Donnellys, Part I.* Erin ON: Porcépic, 1976.

———. "The Story Behind *King Whistle!*" *Brick* 8 (1980): 49–55, 57–58, 60–61, 63.

———. "The Stratford Festival." *Canadian Forum* 33 (1953): 112–13.

———. *The Sun and the Moon.* Reaney, *The Killdeer and Other Plays* 93–171.

———. "Ten Years at Play." *Canadian Literature* 41 (1969): 53–61.

———. *Three Desks.* B. Parker, *Masks* 92–194.

———. "Topless Nightmares, Being a Dialogue with Himself by James Reaney." *Black Moss* 2nd ser. 1 (1976): n. pag.

———. "Reaney Replies." *20 Cents Magazine* 1.2 (1966): n. pag.

———. *Wacousta!* Toronto: Porcépic, 1979.

———. "Writing." *Journal of the Royal Architectural Institute of Canada* 37 (1960): 136.

———. "'Your plays are like movies — cinemascope ones.'" *Canadian Drama/l'art dramatique canadien* 5 (1979): 32–40.

———, and Marty Gervais. *Baldoon.* Erin ON: Porcupine's Quill, 1977.

Secondary Sources

Adamson, Arthur. "Identity Through Metaphor: An Approach to the Question of Regionalism in Canadian Literature." *Studies in Canadian Literature* 5 (1980): 83–99.

Apollinaire, Guillaume. Prologue. *The Breasts of Tiresias. Modern French Theatre.* Ed. Michael Benedict and George E. Wellworth. New York: Dutton, 1966. 66.

———. *Zone.* Trans. Samuel Beckett. Dublin: Dolmen, 1972.

Arden, John. "Playwrights and Play-Writers." *To Present the Pretense: Essays on the Theatre and Its Public.* London: Methuen, 1977. 173–212.

_____. *Serjeant Musgrave's Dance*. London: Methuen, 1960.

Arnheim, Rudolf. *Visual Thinking*. Berkeley: U of California P, 1969.

Aronson, Arnold. *History and Theory of Environmental Scenography*. Ann Arbor: UMI, 1981.

Artaud, Antonin. *The Theatre and Its Double*. Trans. Mary Caroline Richards. New York: Grove, 1958.

Atwood, Margaret. "Eleven Years of Alphabet." *Canadian Literature* 49 (1971): 60–64.

_____. *Survival: A Thematic Guide to Canadian Literature*. Toronto: Anansi, 1972.

Auden, W.H. "New Year Letter." *Collected Poems*. Ed. Edward Mendelson. New York: Random, 1976. 159–93.

Bablet, Denis. *The Revolution of Stage Design in the Twentieth Century*. New York: Amiel, 1977.

Bachelard, Gaston. *The Poetics of Reverie*. Trans. Daniel Russell. Boston: Beacon, 1969.

_____. *The Poetics of Space*. Trans. Maria Jolas. Boston: Beacon, 1969.

Bakshy, Alexander. *The Theatre Unbound*. London: Cecil Palmer, 1923.

Barthes, Roland. *The Pleasure of the Text*. Trans. Richard Miller. London: Cape, 1976.

Barzun, Jacques. *Use and Abuse of Art*. Princeton: Princeton UP, 1974.

Beckett, Samuel. *Dante . . . Bruno. Vico..Joyce. I can't go on, I'll go on: a Selection from Samuel Beckett's Work*. Ed. Richard W. Seaver. New York: Grove, 1976.

_____. *Waiting for Godot*. New York: Grove, 1954.

Behan, Brendan. *The Hostage*. London: Methuen, 1958.

Bentley, Eric. *The Life of the Drama*. New York: Atheneum, 1964.

Bessai, Diane. "Documentary Drama: Reaney's Donnelly Trilogy." Dragland 186–208.

_____. "Documentary Theatre in Canada: An Investigation into Questions and Backgrounds." *Canadian Drama/l'art dramatique canadien* 6 (1980): 9–21.

Blau, Herbert. *Blooded Thought: Occasions of Theatre*. New York: Performing Arts Journal, 1982.

Bowering, George. "Reaney's Region." Dragland 1–14.

Brecht, Bertolt. "On the Use of Music in Epic Theatre." *Brecht on Theatre*. Trans. John Willett. New York: Hill, 1957. 84–90.

Breton, André. "Manifesto of Surrealism." *Manifestoes of Surrealism*. Trans. Richard Seaver and Helen R. Lane. Ann Arbor: U of Michigan P, 1969. 3–47.

_____. *Second Manifesto of Surrealism*. Trans. Richard Seaver and Helen R. Lane. Ann Arbor: U of Michigan P, 1977.

Brook, Peter. *The Empty Space*. London: MacGibbon, 1968.

_____. "Finding Shakespeare on Film." *Tulane Drama Review* 11 (1966): 117–21.

_____. Introduction. *Marat/Sade*. By Peter Weiss. London: Calder, 1964.

Brooks, Peter. *The Melodramatic Imagination: Balzac, Henry James, Melodrama and the Mode of Excess*. New Haven: Yale UP, 1976.

Brown, Frederick. *An Impersonation of Angels: A Biography of Jean Cocteau*. New York: Viking, 1968.

_____. *Theatre and Revolution: The Culture of the French Stage*. New York: Viking, 1980.

Cassirir, Ernst. *An Essay on Man*. New Haven: Yale UP, 1962.

Cheney, Sheldon. *The New Movement in the Theatre*. New York: Kennerley, 1914.

_____. *The Open-Air Theatre*. New York: Kennerley, 1918.

Cocteau, Jean. Preface. *Les Maries de la Tour Eiffel*. Vol. 7 of *Oeuvres complètes de Jean Cocteau*. Paris: Marguerat, 1946–50: 11–18. 10 vols.

_____. *Two Screenplays: The Blood of a Poet, The Testament of Orpheus*. Trans. Carol Martin-Sperry. London: Calder, 1970.

Cohen, Nathan. "Mr. Reaney Writes a Play." *Toronto Daily Star* 14 Jan. 1960: 35.

Conolly, L.W. Ed. *Canadian Drama and the Critics*. Vancouver: Talonbooks, 1987.

Curnoe, Greg. Letter. *20 Cents Magazine* 1.3 (1966): n. pag.

Davies, Robertson. "A Dialogue: The State of Theatre in Canada." 1951. *Canadian Theatre Review* 5 (1975): 16–36.

Dawson, R. MacGregor. *William Lyon Mackenzie King: 1874–1923*. Toronto: U of Toronto P, 1959.

Delevoy, Robert L. *Dimensions of the Twentieth Century: 1900–1945*. Trans. Stuart Gilbert. Geneva: Skira, 1966.

_____. *Symbolists and Symbolism*. Trans. Barbara Bray, Elizabeth Wrightson, and Bernard C. Swift. New York: Skira, 1978.

Denison, Merrill. "Nationalism and Drama." 1928. *Canadian Theatre Review* 8 (1975): 72–78.

Derrida, Jacques. *Writing and Difference*. Trans. Alan Bass. Chicago: U of Chicago P, 1978.

Donoghue, Denis. *The Third Voice: Modern British and American Verse Drama*. Princeton: Princeton UP, 1959.

Dragland, Stan, ed. *Approaches to the Work of James Reaney*. Toronto: ECW, 1983.

Driver, Tom. *Romantic Quest and Modern Query: A History of the Modern Theatre*. New York: Delacourt, 1970.

Dudek, Louis. "A Problem of Meaning." *Canadian Literature* 59 (1974): 16–29.

Ehrmann, Jacques. "The Tragic/Utopian Meaning of History." *Yale French Studies* 58 (1979): 15–43.

Eisenstein, Sergei. *The Film Sense.* Trans. Jay Leyda. London: Faber, 1968.

Eliot, T.S. *Complete Poems and Plays.* New York: Harcourt, 1958.

_____. "Dialogue on Dramatic Poetry." *Selected Essays.* London: Faber, 1951. 43–58.

_____. "The Possibility of a Poetic Drama." *The Sacred Wood.* London: Methuen, 1920.

_____. "The Social Function of Poetry." *On Poetry and Poets.* London: Faber, 1957. 15–25.

_____. "The Three Voices of Poetry." *On Poetry and Poets.* London: Faber, 1957. 89–102.

Evans, Chad. "Herman Voaden and the Symphonic Theatre." *Canadian Theatre Review* 5 (1975): 37–43.

Fergusson, Francis. *The Idea of a Theatre.* New York: Doubleday, 1953.

Forsyth, James. *Tyrone Guthrie.* London: Hamilton, 1976.

Free, William, and Charles Lower. *History into Drama: A Source Book on Symphonic Drama.* New York: Odyssey, 1963.

Frye, Northrop. *Anatomy of Criticism: Four Essays.* New York: Atheneum, 1969.

_____. *The Bush Garden: Essays on the Canadian Imagination.* Toronto: Anansi, 1971.

_____. *Creation and Recreation.* Toronto: U of Toronto P, 1980.

_____. *Educated Imagination.* Bloomington: Indiana UP, 1964.

_____. *The Modern Century.* Toronto: Oxford UP, 1967.

_____. "The Narrative Tradition in Canadian Poetry." *Canadian Anthology.* Ed. Carl F. Klinck and Reginald E. Watters. Toronto: Gage, 1966. 523–28.

_____. "The Royal Bank Address." *CEA Critic* 42 (1980): 2–9.

_____. *Spiritus Mundi: Essays on Literature, Myth, and Society.* New York: Fitzhenry, 1976.

_____. *The Stubborn Structure.* London: Methuen, 1970.

Fuerst, Walter Rene, and Samuel J. Hume. *Twentieth-Century Stage Production.* New York: Dover, 1967.

Gerry, Thomas. "David Willson: Canadian Visionary Writer and Hymnodist." Diss. U. of Western Ontario, 1983.

Ghéon, Henri. *The Art of the Theatre.* Trans. Adele M. Fiske. New York: Hill, 1961.

Gilman, Richard. *The Making of Modern Drama.* New York: Da Capo, 1987.

Glassco, Bill. *Performing Arts in Canada* 18 (1981): 23.

Gordon, Mel. "Meyerhold's Biomechanics." *Drama Review* 18 (1974): 73–88.

Graff, Gerald. *Literature Against Itself: Literary Ideas in Modern Society.* Chicago: U of Chicago P, 1979.

"Guilding the Writers." *Canadian Theatre Review* 17 (1978): 94–98.

Hamand, C. Carol. "El Lissitzky's Theoretical Writings." *Arts Magazine* 56 (1982): 102–06.

Hauser, Arnold. "The Origins of Domestic Drama." *The Theory of the Modern Stage.* Ed. Eric Bentley. London: Penguin, 1968. 403–24.

Heilman, R.B. *Tragedy and Melodrama.* Seattle: U of Washington P, 1968.

Hendry, Tom. Editorial. *Stage in Canada* 1 (1965): 1.

Heubert, Ronald. "James Reaney: Poet and Dramatist." *Canadian Theatre Review* 13 (1977): 125–28.

Hirsch, John. "My Life in Canadian Art." *Canadian Theatre Review* 34 (1982): 39–45.

Hughes, Robert. *The Shock of the New: Art and the Century of Change.* London: BBC, 1980.

Huxley, Aldous. *The Island.* New York: Harper, 1962.

Jeanes, Rosemary. "Equity Showcase Workshops: Revitalizing the Actor." *Canadian Theatre Review* 28 (1980): 44–49.

Jonson, Ben. "An Expostulation with Indigo Jones." *Poems of Ben Jonson.* Ed. George Burke Johnston. London: Routledge, 1954. 304.

Kaplan, Donald M. "Theatre Architecture: A Derivation of the Primal Cavity." *Tulane Drama Review* 12 (1968): 105–16.

Kennedy, Andrew K. *Six Dramatists in Search of a Language.* London: Cambridge UP, 1975.

Kesten, Myles. "The NAC and the National Mandate." *Canadian Theatre Review* 28 (1980): 34–44.

Klee, Paul. "On Modern Art." Trans. Paul Findlay. *Modern Artists on Art.* Ed. Robert L. Herbert. Englewood Cliffs NJ: Prentice, 1964. 74–91.

_____ . *The Thinking Eye.* Trans. Ralph Manheim. Ed. Jurg Spiller. New York: Wittenbann, 1961.

Kostelanetz, Richard. *The Theatre of Mixed Means.* New York: New Dial, 1968.

Kramer, Hilton. *The Age of the Avant-Garde: An Art Chronicle of 1956–1972.* New York: Farrar, 1973.

_____ . "Some Reflections on Art and Nationalism: Roots of the New York School, 1930–1950." *Artscanada* 36 (1979): 19–22.

Krieg, Robert E. "A Study of Forest Theatre." Diss. U of Western Ontario, 1978.

_____ . "Prospectus." *Black Moss* 2nd ser. 1 (1966): 29–32.

Langer, Susanne. *Feeling and Form.* New York: Scribner's, 1953.

_____ . *Philosophy in a New Key.* Cambridge MA: Harvard UP, 1951.

Lee, Alvin. *James Reaney*. Twayne's World Authors Ser. 49. New York: Twayne, 1968.

Leggatt, Alexander M. "Playwrights in a Landscape: The Changing Image of Rural Ontario." *Theatre History in Canada* 1 (1980): 135–48.

Lentricchia, Frank. *After the New Criticism*. Chicago: U of Chicago P, 1980.

Ley-Piscator, Maria. *The Piscator Experiment: The Political Theatre*. New York: Heineman, 1967.

Ludwick, Patricia. "One Actor's Journey with James Reaney." Dragland 131–37.

Mann, Thomas. *Essays by Thomas Mann*. Trans. H.T. Lowe-Porter. New York: Viking, 1957.

Macgowan, Kenneth. *Continental Stagecraft*. New York: Harcourt, 1922.

_____. *The Theatre of Tomorrow*. New York: Boni, 1921.

Macpherson, Jay. "Educated Doodle: Some Notes on *One-Man Masque*." Dragland 65–99.

Miller, Mary Jane. "Colours in the Dark." *Canadian Drama/l'art dramatique canadien* 2 (1976): 90–97.

Mitchell, W.J.T. *Blake's Composite Art*. Princeton: Princeton UP, 1978.

Moholy-Nagy, L. "Theatre, Circus and Variety." *The Theatre of the Bauhaus*. Ed. Walter Gropius. Middleton CT: Wesleyan UP, 1961: 49–72.

Moore, Mavor. "A Theatre for Canada." *University of Toronto Quarterly* 4 (1957): 1–16.

_____. "This Play May Become Part of Our History." *Toronto Telegram* 27 Jan. 1960: 35.

Moussinac, Leon. *The New Movement in the Theatre*. 1932. New York: Benjamin Blom, 1967.

New, William H, ed. *Dramatists in Canada: Selected Essays*. Vancouver: U of British Columbia P, 1972.

Nichol, bp. "Letter re James Reaney." *Open Letter* 2nd ser. 6 (1973) 5–7.

O'Driscoll, Robert, ed. *Yeats and the Theatre*. Toronto: Macmillan, 1975.

Orenstein, Gloria. *The Theater of the Marvelous: Surrealism and the Contemporary Stage*. New York: New York UP, 1975.

Parker, Brian, ed. *Masks of Childhood*. Toronto: New, 1972.

_____. "Reaney and the Mask of Childhood." B. Parker, *Masks* 279–89.

Parker, Gerald D. "History, Story and Story-Style: James Reaney's The Donnellys." *Canadian Drama/l'art dramatique canadien* 4 (1978): 150–59.

_____. " 'The Integral versus the Fractional': Reaney's *The Dismissal*." *Canadian Drama/l'art dramatique canadien* 6 (1980): 213–25.

_____. " 'The key word . . . is listen': James Reaney's 'sonic environment.' " *Mosaic* 14 (1981): 1–14.

_____. "The Modern Theatre as Autonomous Vehicle." *Modern Drama* 16 (1973): 373–91.

_____. "The Moor's Progress: A Study of Edward Young's Tragedy *The Revenge.*" *Theatre Research International* 6 (1981): 172–95.

_____. "The Spectator Seized by the Theatre: Strindberg's *The Ghost Sonata.*" *Modern Drama* 14 (1972): 373–86.

Peacock, Ronald. *The Art of the Drama.* New York: Harcourt, 1957.

Peterson, Len. "Playwright's Notebook." *Stage in Canada* 3 (1967): 17–19.

Poggioli, Renato. *The Theory of the Avant-Garde.* Trans. Gerald Fitzgerald. Cambridge MA: Harvard UP, 1968.

Polieri, Jacques. "Systematisation de l'espace scenographique." *Scenographi Semiographie.* Paris: Donoël, 1971. 99–108.

Rans, Geoffrey. "For the Record: A Reply to Reaney." *20 Cents Magazine* 1.3 (1966): n. pag.

Razgaitis, Peter. "Synopsis of Events Surrounding the Student Strike of 1895." Reaney, *The Dismissal* 56-57.

Reaney, James Sewart. *James Reaney.* Toronto: Gage, 1977.

Rewald, John. *Post-Impressionism from Van Gogh to Gaugin.* New York: Museum of Modern Art, 1978.

Rischbieter, Henning, ed. *Art and the Stage in the Twentieth Century.* Greenwich CT: N.Y. Graphic Society, 1968.

Roose-Evans, James. *Experimental Theatre.* London: Studio, 1970.

Rosenberg, Harold. *Art and the Actor.* Chicago: U of Chicago P, 1970.

_____. *Artworks and Packages.* New York: Horizon, 1969.

_____. *Discovering the Present: Three Decades in Art, Culture and Politics.* Chicago: U of Chicago P, 1973.

_____. *The Tradition of the New.* New York: Horizon, 1959.

Ross, Catherine Sheldrick, ed. *Recovering Canada's First Novelist. Proceedings from the John Richardson Conference.* Erin ON: Porcupine's Quill, 1984.

Rubin, Don. "Aside: Looking Back and Ahead." *Canadian Theatre Review* 5 (1975): 4–5.

_____. "Celebrating the Nation." *Canadian Theatre Review* 34 (1982): 12–22.

_____. *Creeping Towards a Culture: The Theatre in English Canada since 1945.* Guelph: Alive, 1974.

Ryga, George. "Theatre in Canada: A Viewpoint on Its Development and Future." *Canadian Theatre Review* 1 (1974): 28–32.

Schafer, R. Murray. "The Theatre of Confluence (Notes in Advance of Action)." *Canada Music Book* 5 (1974): 33–52.

_____. *The Tuning of the World.* Toronto: U of Toronto P, 1977.

Schechner, Richard. *Environmental Theatre.* New York: Hawthorne, 1973.

_____. "6 Axioms for Environmental Theatre." *Tulane Drama Review* 12 (1968): 41–64.

Sheridan, Richard Brinsley. *The Critic: The Plays of Richard Brinsley Sheridan*. London: Oxford UP, 1960.

Sherrill, Grace. "A Northern Quality: Herman Voaden's Canadian Expressionism." *Canadian Drama/l'art dramatique canadien* 8 (1982): 1–14.

Simonson, Lee. *The Stage Is Set*. New York: Harcourt, 1932.

Spears, Monroe K. *The Poetry of W.H. Auden: The Disenchanted Island*. Oxford: Oxford UP, 1968.

Spender, Stephen. *The Struggle of the Modern*. London: Hamilton, 1963.

Steegmuller, Francis. *Cocteau: A Biography*. Boston: Little, 1970.

Stein, Gertrude. *Wars I Have Seen*. New York: Random, 1954.

Steiner, George. *In Bluebeard's Castle*. London: Faber, 1971.

_____. *Language and Silence*. New York: Atheneum, 1967.

_____. *Real Presences*. Chicago: U of Chicago P, 1989.

_____. Rev. of *Pierre Corneille. Oeuvres completes*, ed. George Couton. *Times Literary Supplement* 19 Nov. 1982: 1259–60.

Stevens, Wallace. "Noble Rider and the Sound of Words." *The Necessary Angel*. London: Faber, 1951. 1–36.

_____. "Of Modern Poetry." *Collected Poems of Wallace Stevens*. New York: Knopf, 1954. 239–40.

Stingle, Richard. "'all the old levels': Reaney and Frye." *Dragland* 32–64.

Strindberg, August. "The New Arts, or the Role of Chance in Artistic Creation." *Inferno, Alone and Other Writings*. Ed. Evert Sprinchorn. New York: Doubleday, 1968. 99–103.

_____. *The Son of a Servant*. Trans. Evert Sprinchorn. New York: Doubleday, 1966.

_____. *To Damascus: Eight Expressionist Plays by August Strindberg*. Trans. Arvid Paulson. New York: Bantam, 1963.

Stuart, Ross. "Theatre in Canada: An Historical Perspective." *Canadian Theatre Review* 5 (1975): 6–15.

Sypher, Wylie. "The Aesthetics of Revolution: The Marxist Melodrama." *The Kenyon Review* 9 (1948): 431–44.

Tait, Michael. "Everything Is Something: James Reaney's *Colours in the Dark*." *Dramatists in Canada*. Ed. William New. Vancouver: U of British Columbia P, 1972. 140–44.

_____. "The Limits of Freedom: James Reaney's Theatre." *Canadian Literature* 19 (1964): 43–48.

Tepper, Bill. "The Forties and Beyond: The New Play Society." *Canadian Theatre Review* 28 (1980): 18–33.

Theatre Quarterly [British Playwriting in the Seventies] 6.24 (1976).

Thomas, Clara. "Towards Freedom: The Work of Northrop Frye." *CEA Critic* 42 (1979): 7–11.

Turnbull, Keith. "Interview with Keith Turnbull." By Jean McKay. Dragland 151–64.

––––––. "Report on Summer Theatre." *20 Cents Magazine* 1 (1966): 1.

Vallency, Maurice. *The Flower and the Castle*. New York: Crosset, 1966.

Vannier, Jean. "A Theatre of Language." *Tulane Drama Review* 7 (1963): 180–86.

Wagner, Richard. *Wagner on Music and Drama*. Ed. Albert Goldman and Evert Sprinchorn. New York: Dutton, 1964.

Waldman, Diane. *Mark Rothko: 1903–1970. A Retrospective*. New York: Abrams, 1978.

Wallace, Robert. "Growing Pains: Toronto Theatre in the 70s." *Canadian Literature* 85 (1980): 71–86.

Weill, Kurt. "Gestus in Music." *Tulane Drama Review* 6 (1961): 28–32.

Weiss, Peter. "Three Materials and the Models: Notes Towards a Definition of Documentary Theatre." *Theatre Quarterly* 1 (1971): 41–46.

White, Hayden. "The Historical Text as Literary Artifact." *Clio* 3 (1974): 277–303.

Wickham, Glynne. *Early English Stage*. London: Routledge, 1963. 2 vols.

Williams, Raymond. *Modern Tragedy*. London: Chatto, 1966.

Wilson, Milton. "On Reviewing Reaney." *The Tamarack Review* 26 (1963): 71–77.

Woodcock, George. "There Are No Universal Landscapes." *Artscanada* 24 (1978): 37–42.

Woodman, Ross. *James Reaney*. Toronto: McClelland, 1971.

––––––. "London (Ont.): A New Regionalism." *Artscanada* 24 (1967): insert Ag-S.

Yates, Frances. *The Art of Memory*. Harmondsworth: Penguin, 1969.

––––––. *Theatre of the World*. Chicago: U of Chicago P, 1969.

Yeats, W.B. "Contemporary Irish Theatre." *Yeats and the Theatre*. Ed. Robert O'Driscoll. Toronto: Macmillan, 1975. 41–59.

––––––. *Essays and Introductions*. London: Macmillan, 1969.

––––––. *Explorations*. London: Macmillan, 1962.

––––––. *Selected Plays*. Ed. A. Norman Jeffares. London: Macmillan, 1964.

––––––. "The Theatre." *Yeats and the Theatre*. Ed. Robert O'Driscoll. Toronto: Macmillan, 1965. 16–25.

INDEX

Wordsworth, William 40
Woyzeck (Büchner) 86

Yates, Frances 50, 112–14, 117–18,
    128, 155, 161
Yeats, W.B. 10, 12, 15–18, 46, 48,
    64–65, 95, 113, 116, 118, 120,
    137, 146, 161, 178, 187, 193,
    197, 206, 238, 292
Young, Edward 262–63

Zone (Apollinaire) 38